Dying, Death, and Bereavement

Dying, Death, and Bereavement

Lewis R. Aiken
Pepperdine University

ALLYN AND BACON, INC.

BOSTON • LONDON • SYDNEY • TORONTO

Production Coordinator: Helyn Pultz

Production Services: Comprehensive Graphics

Series Editor: Bill Barke

Note on the cover illustration:

The mourning tree depicted on the cover was derived
from 19th Century mourning pictures, which were
created by young ladies in memory of deceased family
members. Usually painted in watercolor on silk or
paper, these pictures are an important form of folk art
for that period.

**Copyright © 1985 by Allyn and Bacon, Inc.,
7 Wells Avenue, Newton, Massachusetts 02159.**

All rights reserved. No part of the material protected by this
copyright notice may be reproduced or utilized in any form or
by any means, electronic or mechanical, including photocopying,
recording, or by any information storage and retrieval system,
without written permission from the copyright owner.

Library of Congress Cataloging in Publication Data

Aiken, Lewis R., 1931–
    Dying, death, and bereavement.

    Bibliography: p.
    Includes index.
    1. Death. 2. Bereavement. I. Title.
HQ1073.A47   1984   306'.9   84-14649
ISBN 0-205-08251-3

Printed in the United States of America

10 9 8 7 6 5 4 3 2 1   89 88 87 86 85 84

To Bill,
who loved life
but was not afraid of death

The great tragedy of life is not death, but what dies inside of us while we live.

NORMAN COUSINS

Contents

Contents

Preface

Thanatology, the study of dying and death, has made important strides since the 1950s. Prior to that time, death and dying were viewed primarily as the concerns of poets, clergymen, and mystics, to be avoided as much as possible by physicians, and somewhat taboo topics even for social scientists. The research and writings of Herman Feifel, Geoffrey Gorer, Elisabeth Kübler-Ross, Robert Kastenbaum, Edwin Shneidman, Richard Kalish, and others, however, now have made thanatology a legitimate topic of scientific research and theory. The growing elderly population and the popularization of the topics of dying and death by the media also have contributed to an interest in empirical studies in this area.

During the past two decades, hundreds of articles and books dealing with the results of medical, psychological, anthropological, and sociological studies of dying and death have been published. A number of bibliographies and abstracts of such source materials have been compiled (e.g., Fulton, 1981; Guthmann & Womack, 1978; *Thanatology Abstracts,* 1978). Responding to this growing volume of literature, the periodical *Omega: The Journal of Death and Dying* began publication in the early 1970s. In addition to reports of empirical investigations, theoretical and other speculative writings concerning death have increased; creative works of literature and art pertaining to the topic also abound. Media reports and features on dying and death, including many excellent television documentaries and films, are now almost commonplace.

In response to the increased interest in death and dying, courses devoted exclusively to the topic have become more popular. In fact, outlines for such courses have been published (e.g., Cherico et al., 1976, 1978; Margolis et al., 1978). Despite the many courses concerned with the topic, relatively few comprehensive textbooks on dying and death are written from an interdisciplinary perspective. However, many excellent books of readings can be used as supplemental material for an introductory survey text such as this one. Among the most well-known books of readings are Larry Bugen's *Death and Dying* (1979), Herman Feifel's *New*

Meanings of Death (1977), Elisabeth Kübler-Ross's *Death: The Final Stage of Growth* (1975), Edwin Shneidman's *Death: Current Perspectives* (1984), Robert Weir's *Death in Literature* (1980), and Sandra Wilcox and Marilyn Sutton's *Understanding Death and Dying* (1982). In addition, there are books on more specialized topics such as children and death, suicide, the funeral industry, hospices, life after death, and bereavement and widowhood.

Dying, Death, and Bereavement is designed to fill what the author perceives as a need for a truly interdisciplinary, compact but comprehensive survey of death and dying. This book is sufficiently complete to serve as the primary text in a semester course on dying and death, but short enough to be used as a supplementary text in many other courses. The focus of the book is holistic or eclectic, considering medical, psychological, religious, philosophical, artistic, and demographic matters pertaining to dying, death, and bereavement. Because the author is a psychologist, psychological factors in death and dying are emphasized. However, the book is not a narrowly focused treatise on the psychology of dying and death. A variety of viewpoints and research findings on the topic receive thorough consideration in individual chapters devoted to special areas.

Although an effort has been made to write the book in an informative, factually correct style, including a wide range of empirical findings and theoretical viewpoints on dying and death, it has been designed with the emotional needs of students in mind. Motives for taking the kinds of courses for which this book is designed vary from person to person, but not the least of these are to achieve some understanding of the death of a close relative or friend and to come to grips with the inevitability of one's own death. Additional insights can be obtained from the individual and group activities and projects described throughout the text and especially in Appendix C.

This textbook has been written specifically for college and professional school (medicine, nursing, psychology, social work, law, sociology, etc.) courses on death and dying, but it should be comprehensible to the layperson as well. Every chapter has been read and critiqued by at least one expert in the discipline(s) associated with the chapter. Among my colleagues at Pepperdine University who deserve a heartfelt word of thanks for this are Ola Barnett, Nancy Magnusson-Fagan, Ronald Fagan, David Gibson, Clarence Hibbs, and Charles Nelson. I also am grateful to Senior Editor Bill Barke of Allyn and Bacon, Inc. and the following thorough reviewers whose talents he engaged: Burt Hayslip—North Texas State University; Dee Shepard-Look—California State University—Northridge; Marguerite Kermis—Canisius College; Gary Lee—Washington State University; Larry Ewing—University of Oregon; and Vivien Feyer—Alameda, GA.

L. R. A.

PART
I

Characteristics
and Causes of Death

1 Mortality and Thanatology

Questions answered in this chapter:

- How does modern man feel about death?
- How is death defined and determined?
- What are the causes of death, and how common are they?
- What is the death rate in a population, and what factors are related to it?
- Why has public and professional interest in death and dying increased during the past two decades?
- What professions are concerned with death and dying, and in what activities are they engaged?

*D*eath eventually comes to everyone—poet and peasant, saint and sinner, wise man and fool. It is a fate human beings share not only with each other but with all living things. The inevitability of death and the shortness of life have been expressed frequently in literature and art, from the time of Cicero's statement that "no man can be ignorant that he must die, nor be sure that he may not this very day," to Longfellow's

> Art is long, and Time is fleeting,
> And our hearts, though stout and brave,
> Still, like muffled drums, are beating
> Funeral marches to the grave.[1]

---

1. Canby, H. S. (Intro.) (1947). *Favorite poems of Henry Wadsworth Longfellow* (p. 302). Garden City, N.Y.: Doubleday.

and Millay's

> Death devours all lovely things:
> Lesbia with her sparrow
> Shares the darkness, —presently
> Every bed is narrow.[2]

Macabre though these sentiments may seem, they underscore the certainty of death and the importance of not wasting the time one has. Sooner or later, each person must face his or her own vulnerability and the inevitability of his or her death. Distraction and denial may postpone the realization and acceptance of the inevitable, but they can not eliminate it.

Denial versus Acceptance of Death

Humans are presumably the only creatures who know they are going to die, but how do they cope with this knowledge? How does it shape their attitudes, beliefs, and actions?

Human attitudes toward death generally are not polarized; instead they form a continuum. At one end of the attitude-toward-death continuum, death is viewed as mankind's mortal enemy, the fearsome Grim Reaper equipped with scythe for cutting down human lives. According to this viewpoint, death must be actively combatted with whatever heroic measures are necessary. Both medical science and religion have promoted the idea of death as an enemy. At the other end of the continuum is the acceptance and even welcoming of death as a passage to a more blissful state of being. Somewhere near the center of the attitude-toward-death continuum, and perhaps most typical of people's perceptions, is a feeling of mystery or bewilderment about death, the will-puzzling "undiscovered country from whose borne no traveler returns."

Familiarity with Death

To a great extent, fear and acceptance of death vary with its familiarity. Dying and death were more visible in the Middle Ages and Renaissance Europe than they are today. Publicly viewed executions, mortal skirmishes involving ordinary people, and mass epidemics that claimed the lives of thousands of people were common before the nineteenth century. For example, the Black Plague killed approximately 25 percent of the entire

---

2. From COLLECTED POEMS, Harper & Row. Copyright 1921, 1948, by Edna St Vincent Millay.

population of Europe in the fourteenth century. Travelers to London in the sixteenth century likely viewed the severed heads of the king's enemies spiked on London Bridge.

Before the nineteenth century, a dying person frequently organized a ritual in his or her own bedroom. This deathbed ritual was largely replaced by a postmortem ritual during the nineteenth century, and by the middle of the twentieth century even these postmortem activities had been minimized (Aries, 1974). A typical funeral in the United States in the 1980s is a rather cut-and-dried affair, often noted more for its efficiency than for its ritualism and expression of grief for the departed. In addition, because 80 percent of dying is now done in institutions rather than at home or in public, personally witnessed death has become a rare event for most individuals in Western countries today.

Denial of Death

The decline of public dying and death rituals reflects and promotes the denial of death in contemporary society. This denial is not completely successful, however. Modern humans are aware of death, or at least become aware of it from pictures and reports of violence, disease, and deterioration vividly displayed and portrayed by newspapers, television, and other media. Many of the deaths during this century have been caused by war, often considered a ''noble and romantic'' human enterprise in previous times. But two world wars, the Korean War, and the Vietnam War have reduced the seeming nobility of armed conflict for many people in the United States. Television and motion pictures, with their graphic depictions of violent death, have horrified some but anesthetized many more to the reality of dying. Death in the media and movies is usually impersonal. If it does become upsetting, the spectator can simply turn off the TV set, throw away the paper or magazine, or walk out of the theatre. Consequently, without thinking about it too much, one can maintain the illusion of personal invulnerability and even exemption from death for some time. Freud's statement that no one is truly capable of imagining one's own death is not even an issue for such a person; he or she simply never tries.

Understanding death, and especially one's own death, is especially difficult for young children. Adolescents comprehend it better, but to a typical teenager death is a distant and perhaps even romantic event. The reality and imminence of death become clearer as one ages and experiences the demise of his or her contemporaries. Then the illusion of personal invulnerability in the face of death becomes harder to maintain.

The tendency to deny or overlook death obviously does not keep it from occurring. Estimates indicate that over 110 million ''unnatural'' or ''human-caused'' deaths have occurred in the twentieth century alone. Approximately fifty million of these deaths resulted from violence, and sixty million from starvation and deprivation. Furthermore, approximately fifty million people worldwide die from all causes every year. One million people in the United States alone are in the process of dying at any given moment (Simpson, 1979).

Definitions and Determination of Death

Dying is a process, but *death* is an event. The death of an individual, however, does not take place at a single moment in time. Furthermore, there are many definitions of the event. The dictionary defines death as "the end of life; the cessation of all the vital functions of an animal or plant." These definitions are closest in meaning to *biological death* (somatic death), the irreversible breakdown of respiration and consequent loss of oxygen utilization by an organism. Biological death is indicated by the cessation of vital functions such as respiration and heartbeat. When the respiratory center in the brainstem fails, oxygen is no longer inhaled and diffused by the lungs into the blood, and when the heart fails the oxygenated blood is not pumped through the blood vessels. But the deaths of body cells come progressively later. Different cells die at different rates: higher brain cells die first, five to eight minutes after respiration ceases; lower brain cells die next; then kidney cells after one hour; striated muscle cells after several hours; and epithelial cells (hair and nails) after several days.

Multiple Meanings of Death

Biological death is not the only kind of death. One is said to be *psychologically dead* when his or her mind (seat of conscious experiencing and knowing) ceases to function, and *socially dead* when other people act toward the person as if he or she were dead. The usefulness of these distinctions is seen, for example, in conditions such as catatonic stupor, an extreme form of withdrawal in which a person becomes immobile and unresponsive. Such a person is biologically and perhaps psychologically alive but is treated by others as not present or dead (socially dead). An individual may also be biologically dead and yet be talked about and related to as if he or she were socially alive, as in the motion picture *Psycho*.

Another concept is that of *legal death,* in which case a person is adjudged dead by a legal authority and his or her possessions are distributed accordingly. In such instances, the individual may or may not be biologically dead, as when a person who is missing in action or otherwise cannot be found is declared legally dead. A related term, *civil death,* is no longer used, but in old English common law it referred to a person who had lost his or her civil rights but was not naturally dead. An individual who entered a religious order, was convicted of a serious crime, or was banished from the state or nation could be declared legally dead (Kalven, 1974).

Determination of Death

The definition and determination of death are not exclusively medical matters; ethical, legal, and economic considerations are also important. For example, in certain legal cases it is necessary to set an exact moment of death, difficult though it may be. Both ethical (moral) and economic factors are involved in deciding if and when to "pull the plug" on a seriously brain-damaged patient who is in an irreversible coma, or to attempt a costly heart transplant that may prolong a life only for less than a year. Biological scientists and medical specialists are, understandably, more concerned with the medical aspects of death, but these individuals also need to be aware of the legal, ethical, and economic ramifications of their activities.

Traditional Indicators of Death

Among the traditional clinical indicators of death are cessation of heartbeat (and peripheral pulse) and respiration; unresponsiveness of the eyes to light and of other sense organs to sound, touch, and pain; and bluing of the extremities (mouth and lips). Signs of further progression in death include purplish-red discoloration of the skin (*livor mortis*), stiffening of the muscles (*rigor mortis*), and gradual decline in body temperature to that of the external environment (*algor mortis*).

The methods employed in previous times to determine death (no fogging of a mirror when placed near the mouth, no response to a feather about the nose, no constriction of the pupils to light, no reaction to a pinprick, etc.) were imperfect indicators and, on occasion, led to premature burial. Premature burials were more likely to occur during epidemics or wartime, when death determination was often slipshod and there was a greater urgency to bury the dead. As a result, many tales from the nineteenth century describe the fear and potential danger of being buried alive, one of the most famous being Edgar Allen Poe's fictional account "The Premature Burial" (see Report 1-1). The practice arose of not burying the body of a deceased person until it began to putrify, which was accepted during the last century as the only sure indicator of death.

7

REPORT 1-1

Premature Burial

The wife of one of the most respectable citizens—a lawyer of eminence and a member of Congress—was seized with a sudden and unaccountable illness, which completely baffled the skill of her physicians. After much suffering she died, or was supposed to die. No one suspected, indeed, or had reason to suspect, that she was not actually dead. She presented all the ordinary appearances of death. The face assumed the usual pinched and sunken outline. The lips were of the usual marble pallor. The eyes were lustreless. There was no warmth. Pulsation had ceased. For three days the body was preserved unburied, during which it had acquired a stony rigidity. The funeral, in short, was hastened, on account of the rapid advance of what was supposed to be decomposition.

The lady was deposited in her family vault, which, for three subsequent years, was undisturbed. At the expiration of this term it was opened for the reception of a sarcophagus;—but, alas! how fearful a shock awaited the husband, who, personally, threw open the door! As its portals swung outwardly back, some white-apparelled object fell rattling within his arms. It was the skeleton of his wife in her yet unmoulded shroud.

A careful investigation rendered it evident that she had revived within two days after her entombment; that her struggles within the coffin had caused it to fall from a ledge, or shelf to the floor, where it was so broken as to permit her escape. A lamp which had been accidentally left, full of oil, within the tomb, was found empty; it might have been exhausted, however, by evaporation. On the uttermost of the steps which led down into the dread chamber was a large fragment of the coffin, with which, it seemed, that she had endeavored to arrest attention by striking the iron door. While thus occupied, she probably swooned, or possibly died, through sheer terror; and, in falling, her shroud became entangled in some iron-work which projected interiorly. Thus she remained, and thus she rotted, erect.

From Quinn, A. H., & O'Neill, E. H. (1976). *The complete poems and stories of Edgar Allan Poe*, Vol. 1, (p. 532). New York: Alfred A. Knopf, Inc.

Contemporary Indicators of Death

Until fairly recently, loss of heartbeat and respiration were the principal medically accepted signs of death. But cessation of heartbeat and respiratory movements are no longer interpreted as sufficient for a clinical diagnosis of death. Emergency measures such as cardiopulmonary resuscitation (CPR) and countershock are frequently successful in restoring these functions, while artificial pacemakers, mechanical respirators, and heart-lung machines sustain them.

The concept of "brain death" has gained credence during the past fifteen years or so, and irreversible cessation of all functions of the entire brain, including the brainstem, has now joined loss of circulation, breathing, and responsiveness to external stimuli as criteria for determining death. Although about half the states have passed legislation linking legal death to brain death, the usual definition of death centers on the loss of *all* vital functions. The importance of indicators other than brain function vary from state to state.

The following four clinical indicators are widely accepted by the medical profession throughout the world to determine death or irreversible coma.

1. Unreceptivity or unresponsivity to touch, sound, light, and even the most painful stimuli that it is ethical to apply.
2. Absence of movements, notably those of spontaneous respiration, for at least one hour. Patients on respirators must not breathe by themselves for at least three minutes when the respirator is turned off.
3. Absence of reflexes, namely, no pupillary constriction to light; no blinking; no eye movements when ice water is poured into the ears; no muscular contractions when the biceps, triceps, or quadriceps tendons are tapped; no yawning or vocalizing.
4. A flat electroencephalogram (EEG) for at least 10 minutes.

Several commissions established to study and make recommendations concerning the determination of death have pointed out, however, that these four signs are not always foolproof. For example, in patients with severe barbiturate overdoses or marked hypothermia (body temperature below 90° F), depression of brain waves and respiration can occur. Consequently, it is recommended that the four clinical indicators previously listed should be present for twenty-four hours before a final diagnosis is made (Ad Hoc Committee . . . , 1968). Furthermore, because of the necessity of making certain that death is irreversible, it has been recommended that the determination be made by two physicians. In this era when heart, liver, and kidney transplants are commonplace, it is important that neither physician be a member of a transplant team that considers the deceased as a potential organ donor. One obvious reason for this caution is the remote possibility that a physician may be so eager to obtain a viable transplant organ that the donor is declared dead, literally murdered, by oversight or even by intention.

Many hospitals now equate irreversible coma in a patient with death and can legally suspend the application of heroic, life-saving measures in such cases. Irreversible coma is indicated by lack of responsiveness to external stimuli and a loss of normal reflexes controlled by the spinal cord and brainstem.

Death Rates and Demographic Characteristics

One of the most important items on a death certificate is the cause of death. Many causes of death involve gradual intrinsic deterioration of cells and tissues. The effects of other more extrinsic causes such as severe accidents, murder, and suicide are more rapid. In certain cases the cause of death is fairly clear, but in many instances there are either multiple causative factors or the cause is unknown. The latter is more likely to be true in the deaths of very old people, for whom it is often difficult to identify a single, specific cause of death. In any event, the causes of death vary with age, sex, nationality, socioeconomic status, and other demographic variables.

Demography

Before discussing the various causes of death in detail, specifically in Chapters 2 and 3, it will be helpful to have some knowledge of the terminology and methods of *demography*. This science, which began with the work of John Graunt in the mid-seventeenth century, is concerned with examining both the structural (distributions by age, sex, marital status, etc.) and dynamic (births, deaths, migratory patterns, etc.) factors of human populations. The *mortality table* (life table), a listing of the number of deaths occurring between successive birthdays in a group of people born in the same year, was introduced by Graunt. Other scientists in the eighteenth and nineteenth centuries made further contributions to the study of demography. Sir Edmund Halley, a famous eighteenth century British astronomer, was the first person to conduct scientific analyses of life expectancy. And in the nineteenth century the Belgian scientist Adolphe Quetelet conducted statistical studies of death rates and suicides and their relationships to chronological age. The efforts of these men and others led gradually to the establishment of civil registries of births, deaths, marriages, and other demographic events. The availability of this information, especially mortality tables, was important to the growth of life insurance companies during the nineteenth century.

Civil Registries. Until the early nineteenth century ("Demography," 1983), local church registries recorded births, deaths, and marriages; no central governmental registries existed. Establishment of accurate, centralized registration of these vital statistics occurred much earlier in France, Britain, and other European countries than in the United States, which was a rapidly changing nation with many sectional and religious differences. A "Death Registration Area" comprising ten states, the District of Columbia, and a few cities, was constituted in 1900, but it did not include the entire nation until 1933 ("Vital Statistics," 1981). Such registration has provided invaluable information to governmental leaders and other interested parties about population trends, and has helped guide national policy on public health and other civil matters.

Crude Rate.   Demographic analysis, as it is practiced today, is concerned with the quantitative analysis of vital statistics and census information. Birth, death, marriage, and divorce rates are determined on the basis of certificates prepared locally and submitted to state and federal governments. An important unit in demographic analysis is the *crude rate*, defined as the number of events occurring in a given year, divided by the total population size. The crude rate of an event typically is stated in terms of so many events per 1,000 or 100,000 population; it is a figure that disregards sex, age, ethnicity, and other demographic characteristics of the population. For example, the crude death rate in the United States in 1982 was 857.6, which means that, on the average, 857.6 persons died per 100,000 population in that year. Yearly death rates in the United States are not calculated on the entire population. A 10 percent systematic sample of death certificates received each month in the fifty states, the District of Columbia, and New York City is selected, and death rates for the entire nation are estimated from this sample (National Center for Health Statistics, 1983).

Age-Specific and Age-Adjusted Rates.   Overall crude death rate is not the only way to describe the rate of occurrence of death in a specified population during a given year. *Age-specific death rates* are crude rates computed separately for each of several designated chronological age groups, and depict how death rate varies with the age of a population. The computation of *age-adjusted death rates* that take into account the dependency of death rate on chronological age is more complex than the computation of crude rates. Age-adjusted rates, however, are considered more useful than crude rates in analyzing the rate of change in a dynamic characteristic of a population from one year to the next.

Life Expectancy.   Another important demographic index is *life expectancy*, the average life span in years of people who were born in the same calendar year (members of the same "cohort"). Life expectancy may be computed at birth, at age 65, or at any other age. Life expectancy at birth, for example, is the average number of years that a group of infants can be expected to live, assuming that they are subjected to the age-specific death rates existing in the year of their birth. This assumption is obviously risky, but life expectancy projections are usually fairly accurate over a span of a few years. They become more tentative as the time period over which they are projected increases.

11

Death Rate and Life Expectancy in the Late Twentieth Century

The estimated crude death rate in the United States in 1982 was 857.6, a decrease from the rate of 866.4 in 1981. The estimated life expectancy of a person born in 1982 was 74.5 years, up from 74.1 in 1981. The life expectancy figure of 74.5 years represented a new high for this country (National Center for Health Statistics, 1983). Even this figure is low when compared with the projected life expectancy in the year 2000 of 74.3 years for men and 86.2 years for women ("Big Rise in Life Expectancy," 1983).

As indicated in Table 1-1, an estimated total of 1,986,000 people died in this country in 1982. The most common cause of death was heart disease, followed in frequency by cancer and stroke. Note that the death rates given in Table 1-1 are crude rates. Because over two-thirds of the total number of people who died in that year were over age 65, the relative ranking of causes in this table is more applicable to the elderly than to younger people.

TABLE 1-1
Number of Deaths and Crude Death Rate for Fifteen Leading Causes
of Death in the United States in 1982

Cause of Death	Number of Deaths	Death Rate[a]	Percent of All Deaths
Diseases of the heart	759,050	327.8	38.2
Malignant neoplasms (cancer)	435,550	188.1	21.9
Cerebrovascular diseases (stroke)	159,630	68.9	8.0
Accidents and adverse effects	95,680	41.3	4.8
Motor vehicle accidents	46,630	20.1	2.3
All other accidents and adverse effects	49,050	21.2	2.5
Chronic obstructive pulmonary diseases and allied conditions	59,980	25.9	3.0
Pneumonia and influenza	50,460	21.8	2.5
Diabetes mellitus	33,220	14.3	1.7
Chronic liver diseases and cirrhosis	27,250	11.8	1.4
Atherosclerosis	26,550	11.5	1.3
Suicide	27,860	12.0	1.4
Homicide and legal intervention	22,320	9.6	1.1
Certain conditions originating in the perinatal period	20,760	9.0	1.0
Nephritis, nephrotic syndrome, and nephrosis (kidney diseases)	18,390	7.9	.9
Congenital anomalies	13,110	5.7	.7
Septicemia (blood poisoning)	11,340	4.9	.6
All causes	1,986,000	857.6	100.0

Source: National Center for Health Statistics. (1983). *Monthly Vital Statistics Report, 31* (13). Washington, D.C.: U.S. Dept. of Health and Human Services.
a. Per 100,000 population.

Age, Death Rate, and Cause of Death

Both the rate and causes of death vary with chronological age. The crude death rate per 100,000 in 1982 declined from 1143.7 in infancy to less than 100 in early and middle childhood. It rose gradually from late adolescence to the beginning of middle age, subsequently accelerating to over 10,000 in old age (see Table 1-2).

The age distribution of deaths has changed dramatically since the founding of the United States, when the majority of deaths occurred in children under age 15. An estimated 20 percent of newborns in 1776 survived to old age; 80 percent of those born 200 years later could expect to reach age 65. With improved obstetrical care and breakthroughs in combatting infectious diseases, the infant death rate per 1,000 live births has continued to decline since the mid-twentieth century, from 29.2 in 1950 to 26 in 1960, 20 in 1970, and 11.2 in 1982. The decline in infant mortality has been accompanied by a lowering of the maternal death rate per 1,000 live births from .83 in 1950 to .09 in 1982. Despite these impressive declines, life expectancy is higher and infant death rate lower in many European countries than in the United States.

Because of the decline in infant mortality and infectious diseases during childhood, dying in the United States now is more characteristic of the very old than the young and middle-aged. The major killers of yesteryear—infectious diseases such as influenza, pneumonia, and tuberculosis—struck all age groups, but especially children. These infectious

TABLE 1-2
Age-Specific Death Rates by Sex and Race in the United States in 1982

| Age (years) | Sex | | | | Overall Rate |
| | Male | | Female | | |
	White	Nonwhite	White	Nonwhite	
Under 1	1129.2	1823.8	906.2	1440.4	1143.7
1–4	55.5	95.0	44.3	62.9	55.2
5–14	32.1	45.4	20.2	23.7	27.8
15–24	148.2	186.8	52.3	60.9	104.7
25–34	156.7	334.9	62.8	126.2	126.9
35–44	237.7	510.5	129.7	248.0	207.9
45–54	671.0	1179.5	357.6	630.0	556.4
55–59	1304.1	2000.0	679.3	1102.4	1033.5
60–64	2028.3	2955.9	1053.3	1553.7	1574.6
65–69	3230.9	4045.2	1639.7	2148.8	2411.7
70–74	4770.8	5558.9	2489.2	3156.1	3516.7
75–79	7232.4	7225.1	3991.9	4528.0	5270.7
80–84	10809.8	9782.2	6750.8	6511.9	8107.1
85 & up	18333.3	15507.7	14278.0	11204.5	15228.6
All ages	957.6	876.2	802.3	610.1	857.6

Source: National Center for Health Statistics. (1983). *Monthly Vital Statistics Report, 31* (13). Washington, D.C.: U.S. Dept. of Health and Human Services.

diseases have given way to chronic conditions such as heart disease, cancer, and stroke as the major killers (see Table 1-3). Due to advancements in the treatment of the last three disorders that attack older people more often than the young, smaller percentages of older people are dying of heart disease, cancer, and stroke than ever before. Nevertheless, these diseases remain the leading causes of death in the elderly. Teenagers and young adults, on the other hand, are now more likely to die from accidents, especially accidents involving motor vehicles. Suicide and homicide, although infrequent, are also significant causes of death in young people.

The following list summarizes the leading causes of death by age in the United States during the early 1980s.

- *Infancy* (0–1 years)—low birth weight and birth complications, for example, anoxia and congenital malformations.
- *Childhood* (1–14 years)—accidents and congenital malformations.
- *Adolescence and early adulthood* (15–24 years)—accidents, homicide, and suicide.
- *Adulthood* (25–64 years)—accidents, heart disease, cancer, suicide, and cirrhosis of the liver.
- *Old age* (65 years and over)—heart disease, cancer, stroke, influenza, and pneumonia.

Time of Death

The decline in infectious diseases in this century had led to a steady reduction in the death rate and an increase in life expectancy. Life expectancy for an average American increased from approximately 47 years for a person born in 1900 to 75 years for one born in 1982. Going even further back in time, life expectancy is estimated to have been about 22 years in the Roman Empire two thousand years ago, 33 years in England during the Middle Ages, and only 36 in the 13 colonies at the time of the American Revolution (Smith, Bierman, & Robinson, 1978). The sharp rise in life expectancy during the nineteenth and twentieth centuries is attributable not only to the conquest of infectious diseases, but also to significant improvements in food supply and shelter, and to a less hazardous lifestyle in general.

Advances in technology and improvements in production, distribution, and transportation are major reasons why our lives are longer and safer than those of our forefathers. Unfortunately, modern technology has liabilities as well as benefits. The effects of air, water, and ground pollution on the environment and health of human beings are a heavy price to pay for a more comfortable, predictable existence. It might be concluded that modern man has traded early death from infectious diseases for later death

TABLE 1-3
Ten Leading Causes of Death in the United States in 1900, 1940, and 1982

Rank	1900	1940	1982
1	Influenza and pneumonia	Heart diseases	Heart diseases
2	Tuberculosis	Cancer	Cancer
3	Gastroenteritis	Stroke	Stroke
4	Heart diseases	Accidents	Accidents
5	Stroke	Kidney diseases	Chronic pulmonary diseases
6	Kidney diseases	Influenza and pneumonia	Influenza and pneumonia
7	Accidents	Tuberculosis	Diabetes
8	Cancer	Diabetes	Suicide
9	Early infancy diseases	Atherosclerosis	Liver diseases
10	Diphtheria	Syphilis	Atherosclerosis

Sources: Population Reference Bureau. (n.d.). *Major Causes of Death in the United States, 1900–1975.* Washington, D.C.: U.S. Dept. of Health and Human Services. National Center for Health Statistics. (1983). *Monthly Vital Statistics Report, 31* (13). Washington, D.C.: U.S. Dept. of Health and Human Services.

from cancer! But it is doubtful if anyone who suffered through the epidemics of bubonic plague, cholera, influenza, poliomyelitis, and mass starvation of former times would view the trade as an unfavorable one for contemporary man.

Monthly Mortality. Time in a more restricted sense is also related to mortality. As shown in Figure 1-1, the 1982 death rate in the United States was higher during the cooler months of winter and early spring than during the warmer months of summer and early fall. One reason for the monthly variation in death rate is the greater incidence of influenza and other cold-weather diseases during cooler periods.

Ceremonial Occasions. There is some evidence that time of death is related to important events (birthday, holidays, etc.) in the dying person's life. For example, Phillips and Feldman (1973) reported evidence of fewer deaths than expected before three ceremonial occasions—presidential elections, the Jewish Day of Atonement, and an individual's birthday. These researchers suggested that some people literally postpone dying until after occasions of great personal significance to them.[3] The reasons for these findings are far from clear, however, and they have been criticized on methodological grounds (Schultz & Bazerman, 1980). A patient's attitude or state of mind unquestionably is an important factor in the prognosis of an illness, but whether or not dying persons can actually delay

---

3. It is noteworthy that both Thomas Jefferson and John Adams died on the fourth of July.

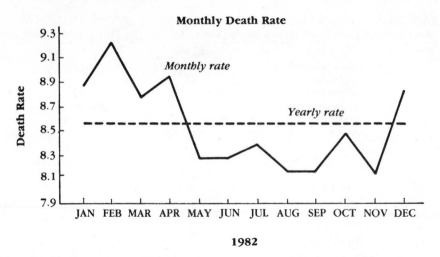

FIGURE 1-1
Monthly death rate in the United States in 1982. (Data from National Center for Health Statistics. (1983). *Monthly Vital Statistics Report, 31* (13). Washington, D.C.: U.S. Dept. of Health and Human Services.)

their day of death by attitude or will power has not been conclusively demonstrated.

Place of Death

Life expectancy and death rate also vary according to geographical location. Recent estimates of crude death rate, infant mortality rate, and life expectancy in various world regions are given in Table 1-4. Note that all three of these indices are related; more often than not, a higher death rate is accompanied by a higher infant mortality rate and a shorter life expectancy. Higher death rates are more characteristic of less-developed nations such as those in Africa and middle South Asia, and less characteristic of the more highly developed, technologically based nations of Europe and North America.

Variations in death rate among different areas or sections of a particular country are perhaps less impressive but still are interesting. The 1982 U.S. death rate varied from a low of 4.0 for Alaska to a high of 13.4 for the District of Columbia (see Table 1-5). The reasons for these differences in death rate are complex, involving interactions among cultural, climatic, and other demographic and situational variables.

Place of death can be narrowed down further to where the people within a particular locality die. In the early years of the current century, most people in the United States died at home. But the number of home deaths had fallen to 50 percent by 1949, to 40 percent by 1958, and to less than 25 percent by 1980 (Lerner, 1980; Veatch & Tai, 1980). Today, most people die in hospitals, nursing homes, or other institutions, and the percentage of institutional deaths continues to rise.

Sex, Race, and Marital Status

Death rate has declined and life expectancy has increased steadily for both sexes during this century, but the changes have been more pronounced for women than for men. The age-adjusted death rate per 100,000 U.S. population in 1982 was 395.1 for white females and 570.9 for black females. The rate was 709.7 for white males and 1045.5 for all other males.

TABLE 1-4
Mortality Statistics for the World Population

Region or Country	Crude Death Rate[a]	Infant Mortality Rate[b]	Life Expectancy at Birth (years)[c]
Africa	17	121	49
Northern Africa	13	110	54
Western Africa	19	140	47
Eastern Africa	18	112	47
Middle Africa	20	122	45
Southern Africa	12	98	59
Asia	11	91	58
Southwest Asia	12	102	58
Middle South Asia	16	125	49
Southeast Asia	12	86	53
East Asia	7	41	66
North America	9	12	74
Latin America	8	67	63
Middle America	7	60	64
Caribbean	7	62	66
Tropical South America	9	74	62
Temperate South America	8	40	68
Europe	10	16	72
Northern Europe	11	11	73
Western Europe	11	11	73
Eastern Europe	11	21	71
Southern Europe	9	19	72
USSR	10	36	69
Oceania	9	42	69
Entire World	11	85	60

Source: Population Reference Bureau. (April 1982). *1982 world population data sheet* (prepared by Carl Haub, demographer). Washington, D.C.: U.S. Dept. of Health and Human Services.
a. Annual number of deaths per 1,000 population.
b. Annual deaths of infants under one year of age per 1,000 live births in a given year.
c. Average number of years an infant can be expected to live under current mortality conditions.

TABLE 1-5
Death Rates by State in the United States in 1982

State	Rate[a]	State	Rate
Alabama	8.9	Missouri	9.9
Alaska	4.0	Montana	8.2
Arizona	7.9	Nebraska	9.3
Arkansas	9.6	Nevada	5.8
California	7.8	New Hampshire	7.8
Colorado	6.6	New Jersey	8.9
Connecticut	8.1	New Mexico	6.1
Delaware	8.5	New York	9.4
District of Columbia	13.4	North Carolina	8.1
Florida	10.5	North Dakota	8.5
Georgia	7.9	Ohio	8.7
Hawaii	5.5	Oklahoma	9.0
Idaho	6.9	Oregon	8.2
Illinois	8.5	Pennsylvania	10.1
Indiana	8.6	Rhode Island	9.5
Iowa	9.2	South Carolina	7.6
Kansas	8.8	South Dakota	9.4
Kentucky	8.9	Tennessee	9.3
Louisiana	8.3	Texas	7.6
Maine	8.9	Utah	5.6
Maryland	7.8	Vermont	8.7
Massachusetts	9.8	Virginia	7.5
Michigan	8.2	Washington	7.9
Minnesota	8.1	West Virginia	9.8
Mississippi	9.0	Wisconsin	8.8
		Wyoming	6.0

Source: National Center for Health Statistics. (1983). *Monthly Vital Statistics Report, 31* (13). Washington, D.C.: U.S. Dept. of Health and Human Services.
a. Per 1,000 population.

In every age group, for both whites and nonwhites, the death rate was higher for males than females (see Table 1-2). On the other hand, the death rate was higher for nonwhites than whites at every age below the 75–79 age bracket for males and the 80–84 age bracket for females. Similarly, life expectancy at birth in 1982 was greater for females than males and greater for whites than nonwhites: it was 78.7 years for white females, 75.2 years for nonwhite females, 71.4 years for white males, and 66.5 years for nonwhite males (National Center for Health Statistics, 1983).

Sex Differences in Mortality.   At the turn of the century, there were more males than females in the United States, but now there are more females than males. This is especially true of the 65-and-over age bracket, in which women outnumber men three to two (U.S. Bureau of the Census, 1981). There has been a great deal of speculation and some research on why females have a lower death rate and a longer life expectancy than males. Certainly fewer women are dying in childbirth than ever before, but this fact alone does not explain the magnitude of the sex difference in mortality. It is true that women usually have a greater resistance to infectious diseases and degenerative conditions such as atherosclerosis, but why? Retherford (1977) maintained that the female hormone estrogen provides women with some protection against hardening of the arteries in old age. But the sex difference in mortality is present even in infancy and before birth; more male than female fetuses die before term, and more boys than girls die during the first year of life.

Biological differences are, of course, not the only possible explanation for female superiority in health and longevity. Men presumably have more stressful lifestyles than women and are less likely to seek medical assistance for pain or illness (Lewis & Lewis, 1977). They also smoke and drink more, factors that may account for a sizable percentage of the gender gap in longevity. For example, in a statistical study of residents of Erie County, Pennsylvania, Miller and Gerstein (1983) found that, after eliminating those who died because of accident, suicide, or homicide, the life expectancy figures for nonsmoking men and women were almost identical.

Marital Status. Also of interest in regard to sex differences in mortality and longevity are the effects of marital status. In general, women live longer than men, and married people live longer than unmarrieds. There is, however, an interaction between sex and marriage: the difference in longevity between married and unmarried men is much greater than the difference between married and unmarried women. Men who are living with their wives live longer than widowers, but the difference in longevity between married women and widows is insignificant. A number of explanations of why marriage appears to protect men have been offered. For example, older married men are more likely to have adequate nutrition and much-needed emotional support than widowers and other unmarried older men. Since these factors have positive effects on physical health, married men tend to recover from illness more quickly than single men and widowers (Atchley, 1977). Furthermore, Kobrin and Hendershot (1977) point out that unmarried men usually have fewer social ties and a lower social status than married men. Widows, divorcees, and single women, on the other hand, have as many interpersonal ties as married women. Unattached single women may possess even higher social status since they are not subjected to the physical and psychological demands of married life.

19

Socioeconomic Status

White U.S. males live five years longer than black U.S. males on the average, and white females live nearly five years longer than black females. A similar picture of greater longevity for whites is seen in comparisons with other minority groups in the United States. That these differences are due primarily to environmental factors is seen in the relationships of improved nutrition and medical care to greater gains in life expectancy for nonwhites than whites in the United States. Poverty, poor education, poor housing and unsanitary living conditions, malnutrition, inadequate health care, and hazardous working conditions are all more common among nonwhites. As the socioeconomic status of minorities rises, more nourishing food, better housing, better medical care, and a higher educational level result, which leads to a narrowing of the longevity gap.

Socioeconomic status is significantly related to life expectancy and death rate in all ethnic groups (Kitagawa & Hauser, 1973). Sometimes the reason for the relationship is patently obvious, as when the supposedly unsinkable steamship *Titanic* struck an iceberg on the night of April 14–15, 1912. Only 705 of the 2,200 persons on board survived, and most of these were women and children.

> The official casualty lists showed that only four first class female passengers (three voluntarily chose to stay on the ship) of a total of 143 were lost. Among the second class passengers, 15 of 93 females drowned. And among the third class, 81 of 179 female passengers went down with the ship. (Lord, 1955, p. 107)

As in wartime, it was the less affluent who bore the brunt of the *Titanic* disaster.

Although mass food production, modern technology, and modern medicine have done much to reduce social class differences in mortality, differences still exist.[4] These differences are greater when mortality rates are high, as in underdeveloped countries. Social class differences in mortality tend to rise until the middle years, reaching a peak from ages 30–44 and declining after then. Infant, child, and young adult death rates are all higher in lower-class groups. This is because death due to infections, influenza, pneumonia, and other disorders of childhood are more common in poor people. For example, poor mothers have smaller babies, and smaller babies are more likely to die during infancy. The infant death rate in the United States for 1980 was 12.3 for whites and 21.7 for blacks (Erickson & Bjerkedel, 1982). On the other hand, heart disease, cancer, stroke, and other "affluent, white-collar" diseases are more common among the middle-class and during middle and late life.

---

4. It has been said that "if the rich could pay people to do their dying for them, the poor could make a living" (Simpson, 1979, p. 7).

Not only are lower-class people more likely than middle-class people to develop serious illnesses, but they are even treated differently by medical personnel. In a study of efforts made to resuscitate victims of cardiac arrest, Simpson (1976) found that the lower the apparent social class of the victim, the less energetic were the efforts at resuscitation made by medical personnel. Other factors, such as the perceived moral character and age of the victim also appear to affect the extensiveness of efforts to revive him or her. Therefore, Simpson (1979) recommended that if persons with catastrophic illnesses wish to improve their chances of being rescued, they should look as young as possible, dress well and conservatively, disguise personal deviances, and have clean, fresh breath!

Public and Professional Interest in Thanatology

Current research activity on demographic variables related to death and dying is only one indicator of the "Death Awareness Movement," as it has been termed by Robert Kastenbaum. During the past two decades, what was formerly something of a taboo topic has become the subject of extensive study and debate. Death is now a popular topic of discussion, not only among physicians, clergymen, and psychologists, but among specialists in many other disciplines, popular writers, and laypeople. Spurred by the media and by popular and professional discussions about death and dying, interest in the topic has grown. Hundreds of articles and books dealing with the results of medical, psychological, anthropological, and sociological studies of death and dying have been published. Responding to this growing volume of literature, the periodical *Omega: The Journal of Death and Dying*, which is devoted exclusively to the topic, began publication in the early 1970s.

In addition to reports of empirical investigations, there has been an increase in theoretical and other speculative writings on death, dying, and survival. Creative works of literature and art pertaining to the topic have also become rather common. The demand for academic courses and course units devoted exclusively to the topic at the college level and also in elementary and secondary schools has grown. In fact, some universities report that courses on death and dying are almost as popular as those on human sexuality. In courses on death and dying, students read and talk about death, listen to recordings made by dying people, view films about death and dying, draw pictures or write poems illustrating their ideas about death, plan their own funerals, and write their own obituaries and epitaphs. In addition to providing information, these activities help people become more aware and accepting of their own mortality and more sensitive to the needs of the dying.

Events Promoting Interest in Thanatology

What factors are responsible for all this interest and activity in a seemingly rather deadly topic? To begin with, it should be pointed out that *thanatology*, the study of death and dying, is an interdisciplinary field. It involves the biological sciences (biology, medicine, biochemistry), the social sciences (psychology, sociology, anthropology), the humanities (history, philosophy, literature, art), theology, politics and law, and even business. The contributions of each of these disciplines to an understanding of death are dealt with in various chapters of this book.

The impetus for the Death Awareness Movement has come from cooperative efforts and interchanges among specialists in many disciplines. Especially noteworthy in medicine and psychology are the research and writings of Elisabeth Kübler-Ross. Kübler-Ross's 1969 book, *On Death and Dying*, which introduced her conception of psychological stages in the dying process, has sold well over a million copies. However, the very fact that Kübler-Ross's work has been so popular in both professional and lay circles suggests something about the U.S. social climate of the late 1960s and early 1970s. As the reader may recall, this was a time of nightly news broadcasts depicting the gore of war and describing it in terms of "body counts" of people who were "wasted." It was a time when students were interested in subjectivism, Eastern religions, and holocaust (genocide) studies. There was wider public acceptance of freedom of individual expression in behavior and alternative lifestyles than before. The elderly population was expanding, the average age of the population was increasing, and scientists were beginning to understand the biology of aging and dying. It was also a time when Karen Ann Quinlan and other irreversible coma victims prompted the medical profession to reexamine its definition of death. All these events, collectively and interactively, have contributed to an increased interest in death, dying, and survival.

Organizations Concerned with Death, Dying, and Survival

Numerous professional, governmental, and lay organizations are concerned in part or exclusively with death, dying, and/or surviving. The names and addresses of many of these organizations are listed in Appendix B of this book. Most of the organizations publish some kind of newsletter or professional journal, and a number of them hold annual meetings or conventions.

Certain professional and lay organizations focus on a specific concern or interest, such as cancer, capital punishment, euthanasia, hospice care, near-death experiences, pain control, suicide, or widowhood. A number of national organizations have local chapters, and there are also many independent local societies. For example, locally run *cryonics* societies (Bay Area Cryonics Society, Cryonics Society of San Diego, ALCOR Society for Solid State Hypothermia, etc.) preserve deceased persons by freezing them to the temperature of solid carbon dioxide. It is possible, but rather unlikely, that the frozen corpse will be thawed and restored to life sometime in the future when a cure for the terminal illness of which the person died has been discovered.

There are also organizations concerned with the commercial and political aspects of death and dying. Innumerable associations of nursing homes, funeral homes, and other primarily business establishments are connected with death and dying. Almost every American town has at least one funeral home, and there are over 25,000 nursing homes in the United States. Consequently, national organizations of these businesses can be quite powerful and influential in affecting legislation pertaining to their affairs.

Much of the research and training associated with death and dying is conducted at university-based centers such as the Center for Death Education and Research at the University of Minnesota. These activities are financed by private foundations and by state and federal government agencies. The research and educational activities of publicly and privately financed organizations concerned with death, dying, and survival are considered in greater detail in appropriate chapters of this book. In fact, much of the scientific information presented in this book was obtained from reports of the findings of research that was either conducted or supported by governmental and private foundations and agencies.

SUMMARY

Human beings realize the inevitability of death, but they often have difficulty applying it to themselves. Death has become less visible today than it was in former times, and this very fact supports avoidance or denial of its imminence. Direct experiences with death are unusual for most people, although vicarious exposure through news stories and motion pictures is frequent.

The term *death* has multiple meanings—biological, psychological, social, legal, and theological. Reference to the death of a human being, however, usually implies biological (somatic or natural) death, the irreversible breakdown of respiration and consequent loss of the body's ability to utilize oxygen. The medical determination of death has become more complex in recent years and now includes such traditional indicators as unresponsiveness to sensory stimuli, absence of respiration, and absence of reflexes, in addition to the more recently adopted indicator, a flat electroencephalogram (a sign of brain death). These signs must be verified twice by two physicians before the determination of death is made. In cases of deep coma the signs may be present for a time, but the patient may eventually revive. Consequently, the presence of these four indicators of death must be redetermined after twenty-four hours in order to make a certain death pronouncement.

The computation of death rates (crude, age-specific, and age-adjusted), life expectancies, and similar vital statistics is the business of demographers. The crude death rate in a population is the average number of deaths per 1,000 or 100,000 people during a given year. Life expectancy is the average life span in years of people who were born in the same year. The overall crude death rate for the United States in 1981 was 866.4 per 100,000 people, and life expectancy was 74.1.

Both the rate and causes of death vary with historical period and chronological age. Current death rates in the United States drop from 1,000 or more per 100,000 in infancy to less than 100 in middle and early childhood, and rise to well over 10,000 in old age. Nearly 70 percent of the residents of the United States who die in a given year are over age 65, whereas only 20 percent of people born 200 years ago could expect to reach that age. The major killers of yesteryear were infectious diseases such as influenza, pneumonia, and tuberculosis; the greatest percentage of deaths today are due to heart disease, cancer, stroke, and other chronic disorders.

Death rate varies from year to year as well as monthly. The rate is higher during the colder months of winter and early spring than at other times of the year. There is also some evidence that people are less likely to die on days of special significance to them, but the methodology of this research has been criticized.

Death rates are higher in less-developed regions of the world (e.g., Africa and middle South Asia) and lower in the more highly developed nations of Europe and North America. The death rate also varies from state to state within the United States. The majority of deaths no longer occur in private homes; over three-fourths of U.S. deaths occur in institutions such as hospitals and nursing homes.

Women in the United States, both white and nonwhite, live longer on the average than men, and married people live longer than nonmarrieds. Death rate is higher and life expectancy lower among U.S. nonwhites, but the mortality gap between whites and nonwhites has narrowed substantially during the past 50 years. Differences in death rate and life expectancy among ethnic groups are related to social class. People of higher social class live longer than people of lower social class. Social class differences in death rate are greater during infancy, childhood, and young adulthood than in middle and late adulthood.

Interest in death and dying has increased during the past two decades, despite the fact that it was formerly somewhat taboo as a topic of discussion in Western nations. Academic courses, books, media stories, and research investigations concerned with the topic increased during the late 1960s and 1970s, a trend that continues in the 1980s.

Thanatology, the study of death and dying, is an interdisciplinary field. Specialists in a variety of natural and social science disciplines, theologians, lawyers, and historians are interested in the problems of death, dying, and survival. The interdisciplinary focus of thanatology is reflected in the content of this book, which deals with biological, psychological, sociological, philosophical, theological, legal, and even commercial matters related to death and dying.

Many research and educational projects concerned with death, dying, and survival are supported by private foundations and governmental agencies. These foundations, agencies, and other organizations composed of professional people, public officials, and laypeople usually focus on one or more specific issues related to death and dying. Among these matters are methods of treating and curing cancer, heart disorders, and other serious diseases, the pros and cons of capital punishment, legal and ethical aspects of euthanasia, the advantages of hospice care over other methods of caring for terminally ill patients, the meaning of near-death and out-of-body experiences, cryonics, the use of addictive drugs for controlling pain in terminal patients, the prevention of and intervention in suicide, and the problems of bereavement and widowhood.

SUGGESTED READINGS

Agich, G. J. (1976). The concepts of death and embodiment. *Ethics in Science and Medicine, 3,* 95–105.

Aiken, L. R. (1982). *Later life* (Chap. 1). New York: Holt, Rinehart & Winston.

Devins, G. M., & Diamond, R. T. (1977). Determination of death. *Omega 7,* 277–296.

Goldscheider, C. (1984). The social inequality of death. In E. S. Shneidman (Ed.), *Death: Current perspectives* (3rd ed.). (pp. 34–39) Palo Alto, Calif.: Mayfield.

Rupert, M. K. (1976). Death and its definitions: Medical, legal, and theological. *Michigan Academician, 8*(3), 235–247.

Schultz, R., & Bazerman, M. (1980). Ceremonial occasions and mortality: A second look. *American Psychologist, 35,* 253–261.

Thomlinson, R. (1976). *Population dynamics: Causes and consequences of world demographic change* (2nd ed.). New York: Random House.

Vovell, M. (1980). Rediscovery of death since 1960. *Annals of the American Academy of Political and Social Science, 447,* 88–99.

Williamson, J. B.; Evans, L.; & Munley, A. (1980). *Aging and society* (Appendix B). New York: Holt, Rinehart & Winston.

2 Aging, Disease, and Accidents

Questions answered in this chapter:

- What structural and functional changes in the human body occur with aging?
- How and why does the rate of aging vary with the individual, and what environmental and behavioral factors affect it?
- What processes cause aging, according to the various theories of aging?
- What are the most fatal diseases, what are their dynamics, and how do they vary with time and place?
- What lifestyle variables and psychological factors are related to fatal diseases?
- How serious are accidents as a cause of death, and what are the death rates for different types of accidents?
- How, where, when, and to whom do accidents occur?

*A*s any health professional should know, a majority of the five thousand or more people in the United States who die on a given day are over age 65. But they do not die of old age per se; that is, no genetically programmed clock within them automatically stops because their allotted time on earth has been used up. Rather than dying of "old age," approximately three-fourths of those who die do so because of heart disease, cancer, or stroke—the three leading causes of death in the elderly. Others die accidentally, but the great majority die of one or more diseases.

Although death in highly industrialized countries is more common in old age, it is no stranger to youth and middle age. Even in the United States, approximately one-third of those who died in 1982 were under age 65. In fact, despite a decline from 1960 to 1982 in the overall death rate, the rate actually rose in the 15–24 year age group. Disease was not the culprit in this case, however. The rise in the death rate for adolescents and young adults during those two decades was due to an increase in the number of fatal accidents, homicides, and suicides. While accidents ranked only fourth in the list of causes of death in the general population in 1982, they ranked first among teenagers and young adults.

This chapter focuses on aging and disease, so-called natural or intrinsic causes of death, and accidents, unnatural or extrinsic causes. Two other unnatural causes of death, homicide and suicide, will be considered in Chapter 3. Although the natural causes of death—aging and disease—would seem to be purely physical in nature, like accidents, homicide, and suicide they also have psychological components. As Kastenbaum and Costa (1977) pointed out, there is no such thing as a "purely physical" or "purely psychological" death. The dying process is influenced by biological, psychological, and social factors interacting in a complex way. Therefore, both this chapter and the next one are concerned with the influences of all three sets of factors on human mortality.

Aging and Longevity

Only a handful of individuals live to what scientists consider the maximum life span for human beings (110–120 years), so people do not ordinarily die of old age as such (see Fries & Crapo, 1981). Everyone ages, and physical deterioration in all body systems occurs as a result of aging. But this gradual deterioration, referred to as *senescence*, is accelerated by disease processes, physical trauma, inactivity, psychological stress, and other conditions. Although many individuals appear to die of old age, their demise is typically the result of an interaction between the natural process of aging, which increases vulnerability to disease and accident, and the more direct effects of illness and/or trauma. Aging is particularly accelerated by lethal diseases such as cardiovascular disorders and cancer.

Whether a specific physical disorder is considered to be a disease or a natural result of aging often depends on one's point of view. For example, *atherosclerosis*, a type of arteriosclerosis (hardening of the arteries) produced by accumulations of fatty material on the walls of arteries, results in clogged arterial channels and eventual heart failure. Atherosclerosis may be viewed either as a disease or as a natural degenerative process associated with aging (Timiras, 1972). In actuality, all people who live long enough develop a variety of "old age" disorders and probably die of heart failure. Heart failure is usually the consequence of a disease process, but in certain instances it appears to be a normal result of aging.[1]

Despite the difficulty of separating the specific effects of aging from those of disease, gerontologists make a distinction between primary aging and secondary aging (Busse, 1969). *Primary aging* (natural aging) consists of a genetically regulated set of biological processes that occur over time and result in the gradual deterioration of the organism. *Secondary aging*, on the other hand, consists of decrements in structure and function produced by disease, trauma, and other environmental events that are independent of heredity.

Age-Related Changes

As a person ages, declines in body structure and function occur at many different levels. Age-related decrements can be observed in the functioning of cells, systems, and combinations of systems. For example, there are decreases in the number of neurons and neural cell dendrites in the brain, as well as a slowing of the neural transmission rate. The little tubules and filaments of neural tissue in the brain also become entangled, giving it a spaghetti-like appearance (Terry & Wisniewski, 1975). There is an increase in *lipofuscin* (the tiny yellow-pigmented granules in neurons), an accumulation of the fatty, calcified material known as *plaque* at neuronal synapses, and changes in the chemical substances (neurotransmitters) that are responsible for transmitting nerve impulses across synapses.

Hardening of the arteries, arteriosclerosis, in old age affects blood circulation, and changes in the structure of collagen influences the functioning of heart, lungs, kidneys, and other visceral organs. *Collagen*, a fibrous protein material found in connective tissue, bones, and skin, becomes less elastic with aging, leading to slower responsiveness and recovery of vital systems. These visceral changes are accompanied by declines in basal metabolic rate, mean heart rate, and kidney filtration rate. Muscular strength also is reduced, and all five senses become less acute.

The age-related changes in collagen also promote osteoarthritis (inflammation of the joints) and less flexible skin. In addition to having a wrinkled appearance, the skin of an aging person becomes rougher, dryer, more easily bruised, less hairy, and more inclined to develop pigmented areas, some of which may be malignant. These changes, coupled with thickening of the eyelids and hollowing of the eye sockets, can greatly alter one's facial appearance. Behavior and appearance are also affected by

---

1. Although heart disease is the major cause of death in the United States, people also die of many other diseases and conditions. Thus, it has been estimated that the complete elimination of heart disease would increase the average life span by less than 10 years (Kohn, 1963).

the stiffening of hip and knee joints and compression of the spinal discs. This compression, which results from loss of collagen between the spinal vertebrae, causes a stooped posture and makes older people look shorter than they really are.

Because aging produces losses in all body systems, actions that require the cooperation of several systems are most likely to be affected. For example, complex motor skills involving the coordination of sensory, neural, and motor systems manifest a greater age-related decrement than simple well-learned or automatic responses. In general, however, older people do everything more slowly (or perhaps "deliberately") than they did when younger. If anything is characteristic of growing older, it is acting more slowly. This slowing-down process is revealed in a wide range of physical and mental activities (Botwinick, 1978).

Individual Differences in Aging

Despite the significant alterations in bodily structure and function with aging, parallel changes in behavior do not necessarily occur. People can compensate for disability by exercising good judgment about their health and capabilities and pacing themselves accordingly. Many older victims of serious disease or disability "bounce back" and continue functioning quite effectively for years (see Report 2-1). Furthermore, there are wide individual differences in aging. At the lowest extreme are the young victims of progeria, a rare disorder that mimics premature aging. Children with progeria typically begin to look old as early as age four, and they usually die in their teens. Another disorder related to premature aging is Werner's syndrome, whose victims develop greying and loss of hair, deteriorating skin, cataracts, tumors, and arteriosclerosis in their twenties and thirties.

The victims of disorders such as Alzheimer's, Pick's, and Creutzfeldt-Jakob diseases are older. In Alzheimer's disease, the most common of these disorders, the brain begins to atrophy and the patient manifests progressive cognitive and emotional deterioration as early as the fifth or sixth decade of life. The exact cause of Alzheimer's disease is not known, but the fact that the disease tends to run in families suggests a genetic basis, or at least an inherited susceptibility. Research has found evidence for a gradual depletion of an enzyme (Galton, 1979) and an accumulation of aluminum (Neustatler, 1982) in the brains of Alzheimer's patients, but the evidence is not conclusive. It has also been theorized that the disease, which affects three to four million old people in the United States, is due to a slow-acting virus or is an autoimmune condition in which the body turns against itself (Freese, 1980). Efforts to isolate such a virus have failed, however.

Even among so-called normal people, there is a wide range in longevity and functional efficiency in old age. Only about 13 percent of

REPORT 2-1 _____

Age, Heart Attack No Deterrent

Clarence C. Chaffee, at 80, Is Still Winning Tennis Titles

WILLIAMSTOWN, Mass. (AP)—Doctors were skeptical when Clarence C. Chaffee resumed training for the national Super Seniors tennis championships a few weeks after suffering a heart attack.

"They made me cut out the jogging, but doctors can't tell how I feel. Only I can do that," said the 80-year-old former Williams College coach.

Five months later he had captured seven of the eight national tennis titles in his age class, including a "Grand Slam" of the singles competition, with hardcourt victories indoors and out plus the grass and clay court titles.

After his heart attack April 29, a pacemaker was implanted in Chaffee's chest, but he said recently, "I don't even know it is there. If I thought about it during a tournament, I'd have too many (mental) blockages."

A Former Coach at Brown
Chaffee, an all-around athlete at Brown University, coached tennis, squash and soccer for 33 years at Williams. He didn't begin competing nationally until he was 70. Since then he has collected 41 national seniors titles.

"I never had the time to play around when I was young, because I had a job and family," he said. "And later on I wasn't eligible for the amateur tournaments. They called me a professional, because I was a coach. I lost 10 years of my best play because of that rule."

But a relaxation of the U.S. Tennis Assn.'s eligibility rules for amateurs in the 1970s turned Chaffee loose. And Super Senior tennis, a special category for those over age 55, hasn't been the same since.

Won in Los Angeles
In mid-August, Chaffee, ranked fourth in the country, took the USTA hardcourt singles championship in Los Angeles for players 80 to 85. A week later he won the U.S. indoor hard court title in San Francisco.

In the next two weekends he took the national grass court championships in East Providence, R.I., and the clay court championships in Charlottesville, Va.

With partner Clarke Kaye, 80, of Louisville, Ky., he also won the national doubles crown on three of the surfaces and finished second in the indoor doubles.

From *Los Angeles Times,* October 18, 1981, p. III-9. Used by permission of The Associated Press.

the noninstitutionalized elderly population of the United States has some limitation in activities (Bouvier, Atlee, & McVeigh, 1977), but even within this group the sense of well-being and the range of activities vary greatly. In a sense, old age and the structural and functional changes accompanying it can be viewed as simply another source of stress in an individual's life—a stress that some people cope with quite effectively, but that devastates others.

The results of an investigation by Osterfeld (1968) indicate that the majority of old people continue to believe in their abilities to cope with the physical stresses of old age. Although the physicians consulted in this study maintained that a majority of the nineteen hundred elderly participants needed treatment, fewer than 20 percent of the participants themselves reported having "health problems." And as Shanas and Maddox (1976) pointed out, the evaluations made by older people of their own health tend to be a better indicator of how they feel about themselves and how well they are functioning than ratings made by physicians.

For most people, the combined effects of natural aging, disease, and trauma begin to take their toll by the eighth decade of life. The ability of various body organs to compensate for losses caused by aging, disease, and trauma declines, and in very old age the process of coping with everyday stress and strain is beyond the capacity of most people. However, a fortunate few continue even into the ninth and tenth decades feeling chipper and functioning effectively. There are also many centenarians who seem intent on living their lives to the maximum span. One must look askance, however, at those who claim to be 130–170 years old, as do a few residents of Soviet Georgia.

Factors Affecting Aging

A number of demographic variables associated with mortality were discussed in Chapter 1. It is not surprising that many of these same factors—sex, marital status, and socioeconomic status, for example—are related to aging. Women, in many respects, age less rapidly than men, and people of higher socioeconomic status age less rapidly than those of lower status. Other variables that have some relationship to aging are nutrition (diet), climate, prenatal environment, exercise, heredity, and psychological characteristics.

Nutrition. Studies of the effects of nutrition on aging and longevity have been concerned with both the amount and type of food ingested. The results of experiments on underfeeding rats and other small animals suggest that starving young animals may increase their lifespan somewhat, but the starved animals appear to remain sexually immature (Rockstein, Chesky, & Sussman, 1977).[2] Although it is considered wise not to overeat at any age, dramatic restriction of food intake, especially after infancy, does not appear to have a significant effect on human lifespan.

Conclusions pertaining to the importance of specific types of food are also not completely clear. It is a generally accepted fact that too much salt and too many fatty or sweet foods can contribute to a variety of

---

2. Related to this finding is the observation that castrated mice live longer than non-castrated mice (Muhlbock, 1959). But the effects of castration on human longevity are not conclusive (Hamilton, Hamilton, & Mestler, 1969; Moment, 1975).

diseases, but nutritionists do not always agree on the best overall diet for promoting a long life. Observational studies of the Abkhasians of the Soviet Republic of Georgia and other long-living peoples have promoted the following dietary rules for those who wish to improve their chances of living a long time.

- Lower protein intake and more protein from vegetables (grains, legumes, cereals), and less from animal products (red meat, whole milk, eggs).[3]
- Less fat, especially animal fat.
- Fewer calories—enough to satisfy energy requirements but no more.
- Skim-milk instead of whole-milk products.
- Chicken and fish more often and red meats only three or four times a week.
- Greater portions of whole grains, beans, rice, nuts, fresh fruits, and vegetables that provide essential vitamins, minerals, and fiber. (Aiken, 1982, pp. 14–15)

Unfortunately, most information on the relationship of nutrition to aging and longevity is based on anecdotes and observations rather than scientific experiments. There is some experimental evidence on the effects of dietary supplements of antioxidants such as vitamins C and E, but it is not conclusive (Harman, Heidrick, & Eddy, 1976; Packer & Smith, 1977).

Prenatal Environment. Not only the what, but also the when of the effects of nutrition on aging and longevity must be considered. This is also true of the effects of many other factors—smoking, pollution, stress, and even exercise. Thus, after reviewing evidence concerning the effects of nutrition and pollutants on life span, Birren and Renner (1977) concluded that environmental conditions during infancy and early childhood were much more influential than those of later childhood and adulthood. Even more important than the child's postnatal environment are the mother's and perhaps the grandmother's nutritional state and life situation at the time they were pregnant with the child and mother, respectively! Other evidence, although indirect, of a relationship between the prenatal environment and longevity is the finding that the offspring of younger mothers tend to live longer than those of older mothers (see Rockstein et al., 1977).

Exercise. The importance of exercise to aging is documented by the results of numerous studies, including those in which the physiological effects of immobility and enforced bed rest were measured. For example, an investigation by Saltin and Grimby (1968) found a 26 percent decrease in maximum cardiac output, a 30 percent decrease in oxygen uptake, and a 30 percent decline in maximum breathing capacity in subjects after three

---

3. In old age, the percentage of protein in the diet should be higher and the percentage of fat lower than before.

weeks of bed rest. Also indicative of the effects of inactivity are the findings of a study of women aged 20–69 (Wessel & Van Huss, 1969). The researchers discovered that age-related declines in physiological measurements made on these women were more closely related to their degree of inactivity than to chronological age. Other investigators (e.g., Brody, 1979) have also found that exercise, particularly during middle age, improves cardiac and respiratory efficiency, reduces body fat, and slows down the deterioration of muscles and joints. Reports such as these provide support for the belief that the typical sedentary lifestyle of modern man contributes to cardiovascular disease and a shorter life span (see DeVries, 1977).

Heredity.　There is humorous truth in the saying that if you want to live a long life, you should select your own grandparents. Both casual observation and systematic investigation point to the fact that rate of aging and longevity tend to run in families (Kallmann & Jarvik, 1959): long-living parents tend to have long-living children. Heredity is, undoubtedly, one of the most important factors in aging, but it is an after-the-fact variable from the person's own viewpoint and hence not under his or her control.

Psychological Factors.　Somewhat more directly controllable, or at least subject to personal influence, are an individual's outlook and attitude toward life. The importance of such psychological factors to survival is supported by the results of various investigations. Granick and Patterson (1972), for example, found that although a number of physiological measures did not predict survivorship very well over a period of 11 years in their sample of elderly patients, the degree of resourcefulness shown by the patients and the amount of social support given to them correlated positively with length of survival.

　　　Another important psychological variable is the degree of control or personal responsibility felt by the individual. For example, any sudden change in the lifestyle of an older person—retirement, the death of a loved one, hospitalization, being placed in an institution, being moved from one place to another—is always stressful. The individual is much more able to cope with the stress of change, however, if the change is voluntary and planned with his or her cooperation. In contrast, a significant change in a person's life over which he or she exercises no control leads to a sense of helplessness, hopelessness, and, under certain circumstances, death (Seligman, 1975).

Biological Theories of Aging

Research on the aging process has been pursued for many years, but a comprehensive explanation of why and how biological aging occurs has not yet been formulated. What has been offered is a collection of theories, or perhaps "pre-theories," that attempt to account for aging at various organismic levels. At the organic or systemic level are theories that propose to explain aging in terms of the effects of wear-and-tear or stress on the individual. Body organs are seen to wear out with usage and exposure to various types of environmental stress. One argument against this *wear-and-tear theory* is the fact that exercise, which constitutes active usage of body organs, improves physiological functioning and longevity rather than the reverse. Hans Selye's (1976) *stress theory* that every person inherits a fixed amount of adaptation energy at birth and that the rate of aging varies directly with how liberally this energy is expended can be criticized on similar grounds.

The *homeostatic imbalance theory* of Alex Comfort (1964) is related to the wear-and-tear and stress theories of aging. According to Comfort, aging is a result of an accumulation of homeostatic errors or faults and a consequent loss of the ability to maintain a steady, homeostatic internal balance. Support for this idea is found in the observation that as human beings age, they take progressively longer to readjust physiologically after physical exertion.

Also of interest at the systemic level are *immunological theory, autoimmunity theory,* and *hormonal theory*. It is a biological fact that the immune system of the body deteriorates with aging, lowering its level of protection against foreign substances and mutant cells and raising the chances of disease and cellular dysfunction. Autoimmune reactions, which also increase with aging, occur when body systems are no longer able to distinguish between normal and abnormal body cells and consequently reject the body's own tissues. Hormonal theories believe aging is caused by a decline in the secretions of one or more hormones by the thyroid gland, pituitary gland, the hypothalamus, or some other glandular structure. Denckla (1974) maintained, for example, that certain antithyroid hormones secreted by the hypothalamus inhibit the absorption of thyroxin (thyroid hormone), thus interfering with cell metabolism and function and resulting in the deterioration characteristic of aging.

Theories at the tissue level emphasize changes in substances such as collagen and the proliferation of mutant cells. As was noted previously in the chapter, cross-linkages in the strands of the connective tissue protein known as collagen change with aging, resulting in less elasticity or resilience in visceral organs, slower healing, and other bodily changes described earlier. The number of mutant cells in the body also increases with age, raising the likelihood of cancerous growths; the decline in the body's immune system obviously contributes to the growth of these mutations.

Waste products of body metabolism, many of which are poisonous and can interfere with normal cell function, build up with aging. Cell deterioration also occurs when there are failures in the delivery of oxygen and nutrients to the cells, as is the case in atherosclerosis. Within the cytoplasm of the cell are little energy "machines" known as *mitochondria* that are composed of highly unsaturated fats combined with sugar and protein molecules. According to one theory, aging is caused by oxidation of the fat molecules in the mitochondria, which interferes with the energy-releasing function of these structures. Research findings have suggested that the oxidation process can be delayed by antioxidants such as vitamin E, but the findings are not consistent (Packer & Smith, 1977). Also related to aging at the cellular level is the accumulation of *free radicals*, chemical "garbage" that consists of highly reactive molecules or parts of molecules that can connect to and damage other molecules. Vitamin E, in its role as an antioxidant, is thought to be an effective agent in neutralizing the effects of free radicals.

At the lowest level, that of the cell nucleus, aging is conceived of in terms of cross-linkages among DNA molecules and mutations within those molecules. *Error catastrophe theory* (Orgel, 1973) emphasizes the impairment in cell function and division that result from errors in the transfer of DNA by messenger RNA. *Cross-linkage theory* sees aging as the result of linkages among DNA molecules that prevent the cell from correctly reading genetic information.

Genetics and Aging

These brief descriptions hardly exhaust or do justice to the various theories of aging. Many of them have empirical support, but most authorities on aging recognize that almost all of the theories deal with events that are at least one step removed from the basic cause of aging—heredity. The work of Franz Kallmann and his associates on population genetics (e.g., Kallmann & Jarvik, 1959) was cited earlier as evidence for a hereditary basis of aging and longevity. Likewise, the research of Leonard Hayflick (1980) and other experimental geneticists has led to the conclusion that there is a kind of genetically programmed clock in every individual, or perhaps a multitude of such clocks, one in each cell. Each clock is a kind of prewired program that, when it runs down or stops, causes cells to break down and die.

The breakdown of body cells with aging may be the result of the cells' DNA being used up. As Hayflick's experiments have shown, human cells can divide only about 50 (plus or minus 10) times before they die. The maximum number of cell divisions is less in elderly people, in victims of progeria, and in animals with shorter life spans than humans. The upshot of Hayflick's research, and that of other experimental geneticists, is that there is a genetically transmitted, species-specific upper limit to longevity. Precisely how an aging or longevity "program" could be genetically blueprinted on the DNA molecules is not known, but research on the matter and on other aspects of biological aging continues.

Fatal Diseases

As we have seen, the complex interactions among biological aging, disease processes, and environmental trauma make it difficult to isolate the effects of any one of these three factors on the physiological decline of the human body. Furthermore, most common diseases have a multifactor causation, that is, they are the results of a combination of many different influences. Due to their multifactor causation, such diseases as the common cold have proven more resistant to treatment than disorders with more specific causes. Infectious diseases that have a single identifiable cause have yielded much more readily to the efforts of medical science. Examples of the latter are measles, diphtheria, poliomyelitis, and influenza, the epidemic diseases of yesteryear that have dramatically declined in incidence and fatality rate during the past half century. Unfortunately, these communicable diseases have been replaced on the mortality scale by heart disease, cancer, stroke, and other chronic degenerative disorders.

People can also be afflicted with several different diseases simultaneously. This is particularly true in the case of elderly individuals who may have arthritis, rheumatism, heart disease, and influenza at the same time, and eventually die of pneumonia. The first three of these are chronic diseases of long standing, whereas the last two are acute illnesses of short duration from which the individual either gets well or dies. The most common acute disorders among the elderly are respiratory ailments; accidental injury is second, and digestive disorders third. Acute illness is less common in later life, however, which is dominated by chronic disorders such as arthritis, rheumatism, heart disease, and hypertension (Hendricks & Hendricks, 1981). Acute illnesses are more common during childhood, but it is to be hoped that the high death rates from acute infectious diseases in infants and children are a thing of the past. Although chronic illnesses are not as frequent among children as among older people, the former are not immune to them. The most common chronic disorders in childhood are hay fever and asthma.

Age-specific death rates for the twelve most common fatal diseases in the United States during 1982 are listed in Table 2-1. Observe that the death rate is higher in later life (age sixty-five and above) for every disease listed in the table, except for liver diseases and congenital anomalies.

Demographic Variables and Lifestyle

The incidence and type of illness vary not only with chronological age, but also with sex, race, socioeconomic status, geographical region, and lifestyle. In general, men have poorer health than women, and working-class people have poorer health than those higher up the socioeconomic

TABLE 2-1
Age-Specific Death Rates for the Twelve Leading Fatal Diseases

Cause of Death	Under 1	1–14	15–24	25–34	35–44	45–54	55–64	65–74	75–84	85 & Over
					Age (years)					
Heart diseases	19.8[a]	1.2	2.9	7.7	41.7	169.3	463.4	1160.1	2808.3	7473.2
Malignant neoplasms (cancer)	2.2	3.7	6.5	12.8	45.7	179.0	443.2	834.5	1230.6	1598.0
Cerebrovascular disease (stroke)	3.8	.2	1.0	2.3	7.9	24.2	57.2	195.3	678.6	2056.4
Chronic obstructive pulmonary diseases and allied conditions	2.2	.2	.6	.6	1.5	9.9	41.0	132.1	235.8	281.4
Pneumonia and influenza	20.3	.7	.9	1.7	2.2	7.3	17.2	50.8	191.3	748.5
Diabetes mellitus	.8	.1	.3	1.3	3.1	9.1	25.1	56.0	124.6	194.3
Chronic liver disease and cirrhosis	1.1	.1	.2	3.5	10.8	24.1	36.7	38.8	31.1	14.3
Atherosclerosis	—	—	—	.1	.2	1.2	3.7	21.2	103.7	548.5
Certain conditions originating in the perinatal period	565.9	.2	—	—	—	—	—	—	.1	—
Nephritis, nephrotic syndrome, and nephrosis	6.3	.1	.2	.8	1.2	4.1	9.2	25.6	68.3	190.6
Congenital anomalies	241.1	2.8	1.4	1.1	1.3	1.1	1.8	2.7	4.9	4.1
Septicemia	7.4	.2	.2	.5	.7	2.4	6.9	16.4	39.5	104.3

Source: National Center for Health Statistics. (1983). *Monthly Vital Statistics Report, 31* (13). Washington, D.C.: U.S. Dept. of Health and Human Services.

a. Rates are per 100,000 population.

scale (Dingle, 1973). Socioeconomic status also is related to a number of other variables, including ethnicity and lifestyle.

Some of the lifestyle or pattern-of-living factors that have been found to be associated with death rate are cigarette smoking, improper diet, alcohol and drug abuse, inadequate exercise, and loneliness. Research has revealed a connection between these conditions and diseases such as arteriosclerosis, cancer, diabetes, and liver disorders (Pomerleau, 1979; Siegler, Nowlin, & Blumenthal, 1980).

Death rate varies from nation to nation and from state to state within the United States, as we learned in Chapter 1. In addition, the incidence of death due to a specific disease is greater in some states than in others. This is probably due to a complex result of selective migration, environmental differences, and differences in lifestyle from one region to another. The importance of lifestyle is suggested by the observation that death rates in California and other western states are higher than those of most eastern states for alcohol-caused cirrhosis of the liver and for venereal disease. On the other hand, death rates for diabetes and heart disease are significantly higher in the eastern United States than elsewhere in the nation (Nelson, 1982).

Cardiovascular Diseases

Cardiovascular diseases (diseases of the heart, hypertension, cerebrovascular disease or stroke, atherosclerosis, etc.) are, as a group, the leading cause of death in the entire world. An estimated 759,050 people in the United States alone died from heart diseases, 159,630 from cerebrovascular diseases (stroke), 26,550 from atherosclerosis, 7,830 from hypertension, and 20,550 from other cardiovascular diseases in 1982 (National Center for Health Statistics, 1983). Because the heart is the key organ involved in cardiovascular diseases, it is important to have some knowledge of the structure and functioning of the human heart in order to understand these diseases.

The Human Heart. The human heart is divided in half longitudinally by a band of muscle known as the *septum.* On either side of the septum is a lower chamber, or *ventricle,* and an upper chamber, or *atrium.* Blood returning to the heart from various parts of the body flows into the right atrium by way of two large veins, the *superior and inferior vena cava.* When the right atrium has filled, it contracts and the blood, which contains carbon dioxide, is pushed through the interconnecting tricuspid valve into the right ventricle. When the right ventricle is full, it contracts, the tricuspid valve closes, the semilunar valve between the right ventricle and the pulmonary artery opens, and the blood is pumped through that artery into the lungs. After being oxygenated in the lungs, blood flows through the pulmonary veins into the left atrium, which, when full, contracts and squeezes the blood through the *mitral valve* into the left ventricle. Contraction of the filled left ventricle then forces the blood through the *aortic valve* into the *aorta,* the artery whose numerous branches carry blood to all parts of the body except the lungs (DeBakey, 1983).

The relaxing and filling, or *diastolic,* phase of heart action takes place in both sides of the heart at the same time, as does the contracting and emptying, or *systolic,* phase. The alternate diastolic and systolic phases are carefully timed in the normal heart to produce a periodic beating or rhythm. The number of beats per minute (pulse rate) varies with the individual and the oxygen needs of the body, but it is around seventy per minute in an average man.

Arteriosclerosis.   Heart disease and subsequent heart failure have been known at least since the time of the Pharaohs. They can be caused by blood clots, "holes" in the chamber walls of the heart, and defective heart valves. A stationary blood clot, *thrombus,* or moving blood clot, *embolus* in an artery is caused primarily by *arteriosclerosis,* an abnormal hardening and thickening of arterial walls produced by deposits of fatty substances and calcium known as *plaque.* Arteriosclerosis usually affects the coronary arteries that carry blood to the heart muscle. The narrowing in arterial channels caused by plaque deposits increases blood pressure and the likelihood of blood clot formation. By making the heart work harder, the narrowed channels can also produce heart pains, *angina pectoris.*

Hypertension.   Increased blood pressure can also arise from constriction of the small arterioles, a condition referred to as *hypertension.* The condition is called *essential hypertension* when there are no other signs of disease, and *malignant hypertension* when the disease shows a rapid progression. Hypertension is sometimes associated with a cardiac problem (*hypertensive heart disease*) or with both heart and kidney problems (*hypertensive heart and renal disease*).

Other Heart Diseases.   A leading cause of heart disease in children is *rheumatic fever,* a streptococcal infection. A child may also be born with a defective heart (*congenital heart disease*), but death due to this condition and rheumatic heart disease is not common. Much more common, particularly in older adults, is *ischemic heart disease*—the number one cause of death in the United States. Ischemic heart disease is an anemic condition of the heart caused by an obstruction in the arteries, which reduces blood flow to the heart. The usual consequence of the ischemic condition is a destruction of heart muscle known as a *myocardial infarction.*

Heart Attack and Stroke.   In advanced cases of cardiovascular disease, the heart fails, producing a heart attack or stroke (*cerebrovascular accident,* or CVA). Heart attacks are almost always caused by clots in coronary arteries, whereas strokes result from clots or hemorrhages in cerebral (brain) arteries. In a heart attack, there is a sudden dull pain and a feeling of heaviness in the chest that may move down the arms. Associated symptoms are unrelieved indigestion, pain in the jaw or shoulders, and shortness of breath. The specific symptomatic picture, however, varies with the age of the victim, severe chest pains being less common in elderly people. The symptoms of stroke, which may be even more disabling than a heart attack, are unconsciousness and partial paralysis.

Approximately 30 percent of the victims of heart attack die immediately, and another 20–30 percent die within 24 hours of an attack. The survival of the remaining 40–50 percent of victims depends to a great extent on the severity of the attack and the ability of the victim to cope with the fear and anxiety precipitated by it. The age and overall health of the victim are also quite important to the speed of recovery from a heart attack (Hendricks & Hendricks, 1981).

Demographic and Environmental Variables. The incidence of cardiovascular disease is related to age, sex, race, heredity, geography or nationality, and lifestyle. The significance of heredity is seen in the fact that people with a family history of cardiovascular disorder are more likely to contract the disease than people with no family history of cardiovascular problems. Heart disease and stroke are also more common in men than in women, in blacks than in whites, and in North Americans and Western Europeans than in Africans and Asians (Hendricks & Hendricks, 1981). The situation among the Japanese, who eat a lot of salted fish but little meat, is enlightening. The heavy vegetarian diet of the Japanese keeps their blood cholesterol, and hence the incidence of heart disease, low, but their high salt intake raises their blood pressure and the incidence of hypertension.

Smoking and Exercise. Heavy smoking and lack of exercise also play a role in heart disease and stroke. Physiological responses associated with cigarette smoking include increased heart rate and blood pressure, constriction of peripheral blood vessels, and reduced cardiac output. Even among people who smoke one pack or less of cigarettes a day, the incidence of heart attack and stroke is above average. But among those who smoke more than one pack a day the frequency of heart attack is double the national average, and the incidence of stroke five times the average (American Heart Association, 1977).

Moderate exercise is important for optimal physiological functioning, as indicated by a higher resting heart rate and a reduction in the number of arteries and their interconnections in bedridden individuals. Exercise by itself will not prevent coronary heart disease. Still, regular exercise does improve the prognosis after a heart attack (Medical Electronics and Data, 1977).

Psychological Factors. Regarding the effects of psychological factors in heart disease, the results of research on the relationship of coronary heart disease to the behavioral pattern designated as Type A is particularly interesting (Rosenman et al., 1975). A Type A individual is characterized as "driven, aggressive, ambitious, competitive, preoccupied with achievement, impatient, restless in his movements, and staccato-like in his speech." The contrasting behavioral pattern is that of a Type B individual, who is described as more relaxed, easy-going and patient, speaking and acting more slowly and evenly. Compared with Type Bs, Type A individuals manifest a significantly higher incidence of heart attacks, even when differences in age, serum cholesterol level, smoking frequency, and blood pressure are taken into account.

The findings of a study by Lynch (1977) underscore the importance of psychological factors in heart attacks. It was found that single, widowed, and divorced people have significantly higher death rates due to heart attacks than married people, regardless of race, sex, or age. Apparently, the marital relationship creates a healthier, more therapeutic environment by providing emotional support, feelings of belonging, and a sense of control over one's life, and hence promotes greater recuperative power after a heart attack.

Treatment. The treatment of cardiovascular diseases involves drugs, diet, a prescribed combination of rest and exercise, and a reduction in psychological stress. Depending on the history and severity of the condition, a variety of surgical and mechanical procedures may also be necessary to treat heart disease. These include coronary bypasses, heart valve replacements, arterial "cleaning," the installation of electronic pacemakers and mechanical pumps, and (rarely) heart transplants.

Cancer

Cancer is a disease process in which there is uncontrolled cell growth that results in a neoplasm, or tumor. The tumor is *benign* if it is restricted to a particular clump of cells, but many tumors are malignant or *metastatic* and spread not only to surrounding tissue but also to distant parts of the body. Cancer is the second most common cause of death in the United States. An estimated 435,550 people in the United States alone and over five million worldwide died of the disease in 1982 (National Center for Health Statistics, 1983). Furthermore, unlike that for cardiovascular diseases, the death rate from malignant neoplasms (cancer) has been increasing in recent years.

Cancer is usually classified by the body organ or organ system in which it arises: a *carcinoma* originates in the skin; a *sarcoma* in the bone, muscles, and connective tissue; *leukemia* in the bone marrow; *lymphoma* in the lymph nodes. Not all types of cancer are equally serious. Cancer of the skin, for example, can usually be treated effectively and is not usually fatal if not metastatic. As indicated in Table 2-2, the highest 1982 death rates due to cancer were for cancer of the digestive organs and peritoneum and cancer of the respiratory and intrathoracic organs.

Age Differences. As was the case with cardiovascular disorders, there are age, sex, socioeconomic, and geographical differences in the incidence and type of cancer.[4] Table 2-2 shows, for example, that the death rate for all types of cancer is greater among the elderly than in younger people; it increases gradually to middle age and then accelerates rapidly to old age. The age-specific incidence of various types of cancer is not the same as the death rate, however. Although cancer is more common after age 40, there is also a sharp peak in the frequency of the disease between the ages of five and 10. Cancer kills more children than any other disease, but it is less likely to be fatal in childhood than in later life. Among children with cancer, leukemia and brain tumors are more common; cervical, lung, and stomach cancer increase in the middle thirties; and cancers of the breast, uterus, colon, stomach, and liver are more common among older adults (Krakoff, 1983).

Sex Differences. Age differences in the incidence of cancer are not the same for both sexes; the frequency of cancer in women is greater during their childbearing years. It is the second most frequent cause of death for all women, and the most common cause for women aged 35–54 ("Women Are Still . . . ," 1982). Another sex difference is shown by the incidence of lung cancer; approximately 90,000 people in the United States die of lung cancer each year, and the large majority of them are men. The frequency of lung cancer among women is rising at a rate of 5 percent annually, however, and it may soon surpass breast cancer as the number one killer of U.S. women (Bryce, 1982). This statistic is due not only to the increased frequency of lung cancer among women, but also to advances in the detection and treatment of breast cancer.

Ethnic Differences. With the exception of breast cancer, blacks tend to get cancer at an earlier age than whites. A greater percentage of blacks than whites are also affected by and die from cancer. These ethnic-group differences are undoubtedly a result of socioeconomic or cultural differences rather than race per se. Not only are blacks more likely than whites to live and work in physically hazardous surroundings, but they are less likely to seek medical assistance and more likely to delay seeing a physician. Even

---

4. As suggested by the observation that cancer tends to run in families, heredity is also an important variable. A predisposition to certain kinds of cancer appears to be inherited, but the exact genetic mechanism remains unknown.

TABLE 2-2
Death Rates for Specific Types of Cancer

Malignant Neoplasm (Cancer)	Age (years)										
	Under 1	1–14	15–24	25–34	35–44	45–54	55–64	65–74	75–84	85 & Over	All Ages
Lip, oral cavity, and pharynx	—ᵃ	—	—	.2	1.0	5.1	11.4	15.6	16.5	22.9	3.6
Digestive organs and peritoneum	—	.1	.6	1.6	7.8	34.4	102.4	214.2	371.8	554.2	48.5
Respiratory and intrathoracic organs	—	—	.1	.6	8.2	58.7	150.7	254.1	265.3	178.3	50.2
Breast	—	—	—	1.6	9.1	22.5	44.0	61.1	79.7	127.2	16.2
Genital organs	—	—	.3	1.5	3.6	12.5	35.2	90.8	173.9	260.9	20.6
Urinary organs	.3	.1	.1	.3	1.1	5.3	15.1	36.3	63.3	106.3	8.1
All other and unspecified sites	.8	1.4	2.7	3.6	8.9	24.5	54.6	94.8	141.1	191.4	23.7
Leukemia	1.1	1.6	2.0	1.7	2.5	5.4	10.1	27.5	49.9	88.3	7.4

Source: National Center for Health Statistics. (1983). *Monthly Vital Statistics Report, 31* (13). Washington, D.C.: U.S. Dept. of Health and Human Services.

a. Rates are per 100,000 population.

when they obtain medical help, the diagnosis and treatment of black patients are usually done less competently than in the case of whites (Kitagawa & Hauser, 1973).

Geographical Region. The frequency and type of cancer also vary with geographical region. For example, cancer of the stomach is more prevalent in Japan and certain Scandinavian countries, whereas cancer of the liver is found more often in certain sections of Asia and Africa (Krakoff, 1983). The reasons for these geographical differences are not completely understood, but ethnicity, nutrition, and differential exposure to certain infectious conditions (e.g., liver parasites in China) are believed to be important factors.

Carcinogenic Agents. A number of physical and chemical agents are considered to be significant carcinogenic (cancer-producing) agents. Examples of carcinogens found in industrial environments or products and the types of cancer associated with them include: vinyl chloride with liver cancer, industrial tars and oils with skin cancers, and aniline dyes with cancer of the bladder. Other cancer-producing substances or conditions and their related diseases include cigarette smoking and lung cancer, excessive alcohol drinking and cancer of the larynx, overexposure to sunlight and skin cancer, nutritional deficiencies and cancer of the esophagus and liver, excessive intake of fats and breast cancer, and certain hormones and cancer of the uterus and vagina (Krakoff, 1983; Power, 1982).

Psychological Factors. The results of observation and research suggest that psychological variables, such as an attitude of passivity and hopelessness in the face of stress, can affect the growth, if not the genesis, of cancer cells (Schmale, 1971). Convinced of the importance of psychological factors in the prognosis of cancer, Carl and Stephanie Simonton (Simonton, Matthews-Simonton, & Creighton, 1978) have supplemented physical treatment methods (surgery, radiation, chemotherapy) with psychological techniques. Their purpose is to get patients to think positively and confidently about their ability to control their illness and to stimulate their immune system by way of their thoughts. Relaxation to control anxiety and visual imagery, in which patients imagine that their white blood cells are attacking and destroying cancer cells, are among the techniques employed. Significant results have been reported using these methods, but most physicians remain skeptical. In general, oncologists (physicians specializing in the treatment of cancer) seem to feel that psychological treatment in conjunction with physiochemical treatment is worth trying. But they caution against the danger and cruelty of raising the hopes of cancer patients too high.

Early Detection. Cancer has often been referred to as the "silent killer," because it often remains undetected until well advanced. Because treatment is usually more effective in the beginning stage of the disease, early detection and diagnosis are emphasized and encouraged. All adults, and especially those over age 40, are urged to be aware of the following seven warning signs of cancer.

- A sore that does not heal.
- A change in a wart or mole.
- A lump or thickening in the breast or elsewhere.
- Persisting hoarseness or cough.
- Chronic indigestion or difficulty swallowing.
- Unusual bleeding or discharge.
- A change in bowel or bladder habits.

The presence of one or more of these symptoms should prompt the individual to make an appointment with a physician immediately.

Other Fatal Diseases

After cardiovascular diseases and cancer, chronic pulmonary diseases, pneumonia, and influenza have the highest death toll among the disorders listed in Table 2-1. Next in order are diabetes, liver diseases, conditions in the perinatal period, kidney disease, congenital anomalies, and septicemia (blood poisoning). Only those diseases with a 1982 death rate of 10 or higher per 100,000 will be discussed here.

Chronic Obstructive Pulmonary Diseases. The several disorders classified under this label—emphysema, chronic bronchitis, asthma, and related respiratory conditions—are similar in many respects and are often confused with one another. They involve interference with the normal breathing pattern, expectoration of mucus or sputum, wheezing (emphysema and asthma), and coughing (chronic bronchitis and asthma). The causes of these diseases are not well understood, but heredity plays a role in asthma and one type of emphysema. Smoking and air pollutants are important predisposing factors in emphysema and chronic bronchitis.

Emphysema has the highest fatality rate of the three disorders; the rate has increased fifteen-fold since 1950 (Raleigh, 1982). The largest number of victims are men over 40 years of age. Emphysema, which is highly disabling even when not fatal, involves the destruction of millions of little air sacs (alveoli) in the lungs. The patient experiences great difficulty exhaling and may develop a barrel-chested appearance.

Chronic bronchitis is a progressive inflammation of the bronchial tubes. Like emphysema, it is most common in men who are over 40. Both emphysema and chronic bronchitis can lead to heart failure, and chronic bronchitis can also progress to emphysema or pneumonia. Furthermore, chronic bronchitis and asthma can lead to each other.

The fatality rate of asthma is substantially lower than that of emphysema, but asthma attacks can be quite impressive to observe. These attacks, in which the bronchioles constrict spasmodically and the bronchial tubes swell, can be precipitated by a variety of substances (certain foods, drugs, and inhalants), as well as affective or psychological stimuli.

Influenza and Pneumonia. Influenza, which was once a lethal disease of epidemic proportions, is not usually considered life-threatening today. But in older people who have several chronic disorders, influenza can cause death—if not directly, then indirectly by making the patient less resistant to cardiac disorder or pneumonia. Inflammation of the lungs, which characterizes pneumonia, can be produced directly by a flu virus or by the uncontrolled growth of bacteria during a bout of influenza.

Diabetes. Diabetes mellitus, the symptoms of which include abnormally large amounts of sugar in the blood and urine, is caused by a malfunctioning pancreas. Although the symptomatic picture varies from person to person, the typical diabetic manifests persistent thirst and frequent urination combined with a loss of strength and weight. The disease also makes the patient more susceptible to infection and produces varying degrees of blindness. There is no known cure for diabetes mellitus, but insulin injections and strict adherence to a prescribed diet can control it (Best, 1983).

Cirrhosis of the Liver. In cirrhosis of the liver, regenerative nodules (groups of hard cells) replace the normal spongy tissue of the liver, resulting in the formation of scar tissue throughout the organ. Cirrhosis can be caused by excessive alcohol consumption, by deficiencies in diet, by inhaling certain chemicals, and by hepatitis (inflammation of the liver) (Holmes, 1983).

Infant Death. Infants die from many of the same conditions as adults—heart disease, accidents, and pneumonia, to name a few. However, the most common causes of death in children under one year of age are congenital anomalies and a kind of catch-all category known as "certain conditions originating in the perinatal period" (see Table 2-1). This group of disorders includes birth trauma, intrauterine hypoxia (deficiency of oxygen in the fetus), asphyxiation at birth, and respiratory distress syndrome. An even more common condition originating in the perinatal period is a phenomenon referred to as "sudden infant death syndrome (SIDS)." It is estimated that more infants in the United States die of SIDS each year—approximately 7,000—than all other diseases combined. These infants apparently do not die from suffocation, neglect, or changing modes of infant care; for some unknown reason, their lungs and hearts suddenly stop functioning. A susceptibility to SIDS can often be identified from observing the sleeping, crying, sucking, breathing, swallowing, and cuddliness of the infant. Infants receiving positive diagnoses can then be monitored at home during their sleep by electronic equipment that senses heartbeat and breathing rate (Hines, 1980).

Accidents

Accidents, defined as unplanned events that result in bodily injury and/or property damage, claimed 93,000 lives, injured more than nine million people, and cost over $88 billion in the United States in 1982.[5] Despite the seemingly large number of deaths, the accidental death rate in the United States has declined significantly during this century. The decline in the accidental death rate is due in large measure to the efforts of the National Safety Council and related organizations. Nevertheless, accidents still rank fourth as a cause of death among all age groups combined and first among younger age groups.

How and Where Do Accidents Occur?

Accidents are grouped according to type and class. The type of accident is determined by *how* the accident occurs, or by *what* causes it. Various types of accidents and the corresponding numbers and percentages of fatalities in 1982 are listed in Table 2-3. Over 49 percent of the accidental deaths in the United States during that year were caused by motor vehicles, over 12 percent by falls, and nearly 7 percent by drownings. Other causes of accidental death include fires, poisoning, suffocation, and firearms.

TABLE 2-3
Statistics on U.S. Accident Fatalities in 1982 by Type

Type of Accident	Number of Deaths	Death Rate
Motor vehicles	46,000	19.9
Falls	11,600	5.0
Drowning	6,200	2.7
Fires, burns, and associated deaths	5,000	2.2
Suffocation from ingested object	2,900	1.3
Poisoning by solids and liquids	3,000	1.3
Firearms	1,900	.8
Poisoning by gases and vapors	1,400	.6
Other types of accidents	15,000	6.5
Total accidental deaths	93,000	40.2

Source: National Safety Council. (1983). *Accident facts, 1983 edition.* Chicago, Ill.: Author.

5. The statistics cited in this section were taken from the following sources:
Encyclopedia Americana (1982, Vol. 1). Danbury, Conn.: Grolier.
Metropolitan Life Foundation. (1983). *Statistical Bulletin, 64* (1). New York. Author.
National Center for Health Statistics. (1983). *Monthly Vital Statistics Report, 31* (13). Washington, D.C.: U.S. Dept. of Health and Human Services.
National Safety Council. (1983). *Accident facts, 1983 edition.* Chicago, Ill.: Author.

The class of an accident is determined by *where,* or in what location, the accident takes place. Accidents are usually categorized into four classes: motor-vehicle accidents, injuries in and about the home, public accidents (other than motor vehicles), and work-related accidents. As shown in Table 2-4, nearly half the fatal accidents in the United States during 1982 involved motor vehicles, approximately one-fifth took place in the home, and another one-fifth in public; the remaining accidents occurred in work-related situations.

Motor vehicles have held the number one position as a cause of accidental death for over 50 years. The causes of motor-vehicle accidents are well known to traffic safety officials: improper driving in 90 percent of the cases, alcohol consumption in 50 percent of the cases, and vehicle defects in 10 percent of the cases.

Falls are the top-ranking cause of accidents in the home, followed by fires, poisoning, suffocation, firearms, and drowning, in that order. Within the house itself, more accidents occur in the bedroom than any other room. The reason why the bedroom is so dangerous is not, as some may surmise, because lovers' quarrels are more common there. Rather, it is because elderly people and infants, the two age groups with the highest non-motor-vehicle accident rates, spend most of their time in the bedroom. The yard and kitchen rank as places where home accidents are most likely to occur. The reasons for this should be fairly obvious, considering the machinery, tools, and other potential hazards in these two locations.

Among public accidents other than motor-vehicle accidents, drownings are most common, followed by falls. Falls are also the second-ranked cause of death from job-related accidents, with handling of objects ranked first and falling objects third. An important reason for the relatively low incidence of job-related accidents, considering the high potential for injury and death around industrial machinery, is the great attention paid to safety rules and practices in job situations. Accident rates and fatalities are also

TABLE 2-4
Statistics on U.S. Accident Fatalities in 1982 by Class

Class of Accident	Number of Deaths	Death Rate
Motor-vehicle accidents	46,000	19.9
Injuries in and about the home	21,000	9.1
Other than motor vehicle	20,900	
Motor vehicle	100	
Public accidents	19,000	8.2
Work-related accidents	11,200	4.8
Other than motor vehicle	7,100	
Motor vehicle	4,100	
Total accidental deaths	93,000	40.2

Source: National Safety Council. (1983). *Accident facts, 1983 edition.* Chicago, Ill.: Author.

relatively low in other organizational settings, such as schools. In general, people tend to be more observant and careful in situations where safety practices are strongly enforced and rewarded.

Catastrophes, accidents in which five or more lives are lost, are also classified according to *what* causes them and *where* they occur. Some of the more highly publicized catastrophes of 1978–82, in which 25 or more lives were lost, are described in Table 2-5. The most frequent causes of these catastrophes were nature (floods, tornadoes, blizzards), fires, and airplane crashes; collisions and structural failures also took many lives. Note that although airplane, train, and bus catastrophes are usually more publicized than automobile accidents, the death rate per million passenger miles is substantially higher in automobiles and motorcycles than in other means of transportation.

When Do Accidents Occur?

The simplest answer to the question of *when* accidents are most likely to occur is when prevailing conditions are unsafe. The following findings that pertain to fatal motor-vehicle accidents should provide some clues about when prevailing conditions are unsafe. In general, the death rate due to motor-vehicle accidents is:

- Higher at night than during the day.
- Higher from Friday through Sunday than from Monday through Thursday.
- Higher during holidays than at other times.
- Higher during the summer and fall months (especially July and August) than during the winter and spring months.
- Higher during times of economic expansion than during economically recessed times.

Among the conclusions that may be drawn from this list are that lower illumination and more vehicles on the road contribute significantly to vehicular accidents and fatalities. It also may be inferred that careless driving, alcohol consumption, and drugs are associated with fatal motor-vehicle accidents. The major careless driving practices that lead to fatal accidents are speed, failure to yield the right-of-way, and driving on the wrong side of the road (over the center line).

A list of unsafe conditions that lead to fatal accidents at home, in public, and at work can also be prepared. Studies in industry, for example, have demonstrated that lighting and temperature affect the accident rate on the job. Interestingly enough, the accident rate is lower among night workers than day workers, presumably because the artificial illumination used at night is better than daylight for performing job-related activities.

TABLE 2-5
Major Catastrophes in the United States, 1978–82

Accidents Taking Twenty-five or More Lives

Date	Place	Type of Accident	Number of Lives Lost
1982			
July 9	Kenner, La.	Crash of scheduled plane	154
January 13	Washington, D.C.	Crash of scheduled plane	78
January 3–5	Northern California	Floods and mud slides	36
April 2	Arkansas, Mississippi, Missouri, Northern Texas	Tornadoes	30
March 19	Near Chicago, Ill.	Explosion and crash of military plane	27
1981			
July 17	Kansas City, Mo.	Collapse of two aerial walkways in hotel	114
October 26	Off Hillsboro Beach, Fla.	Sinking of boat	33
January 9	Keansburg, N.J.	Fire in rest home for aged	31

50

TABLE 2-5 (continued)

Accidents Taking Twenty-five or More Lives

Date	Place	Type of Accident	Number of Lives Lost
		1980	
November 21	Las Vegas, Nev.	Fire in hotel	85
May 18	Mount St. Helens, Wash.	Volcanic eruption	60
May 9	Tampa Bay, Fla.	Collision of ship with bridge during rainstorm	35
February 13–21	Southern California	Rain, floods, and subsequent mud slides	30
		1979	
May 25	O'Hare Airport, Chicago, Ill.	Crash of scheduled plane	273
April 10	Wichita Falls, Tex.	Tornado	42
November 1	Gulf of Mexico	Collision of tanker and freighter	32
April 2	Off Galveston, Tex. Farmington, Mo.	Fire in retirement home	25
		1978	
September 25	San Diego, Calif.	Collision of scheduled and private planes	144
January 25–27	Midwest	Blizzard	80
April 27	Willow Island, W.Va.	Collapse of scaffolding inside cooling tower of power plant under construction	51
February 5–7	Northeast	Severe snowstorm	50
August 2–3	Texas	Floods	27

Source: Metropolitan Life Foundation. (January–March 1983). *Statistical Bulletin, 64* (1), 11. New York: Author.

Who Has Accidents?

Unsafe conditions do not, by themselves, usually lead to fatal accidents. Unsafe conditions must combine with unsafe acts committed by people to produce accidents. One of the factors related to unsafe acts is chronological age. Motor vehicles are the top-ranked cause of accidental death prior to age 74, but the peak occurs in the late teens and early twenties (see Figure 2-1). These are the ages (15–24) when young people are learning to drive, and lack of caution is added to inexperience. Drownings are the second most common cause of accidental death until the early forties, falls are second from age 45 to 74, and motor-vehicle accidents are second after age 74. The death rate due to accidents other than those involving motor vehicles is particularly high in old age, when sensory defects and motor incoordination are typical, and individuals spend more time at home. The very old are less likely to perceive dangerous conditions, such as a small object left on the floor, an open door or other projecting object, or something burning. Even when the danger is sensed, the response of an elderly person is usually slower and less precise. Like the elderly, infants have a relatively high death rate from home accidents, but for somewhat different

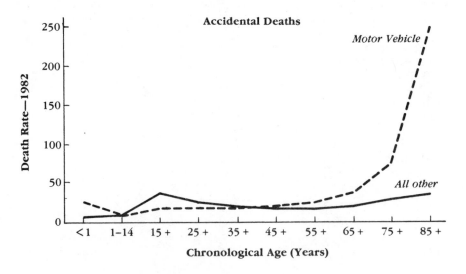

Notes: Age 15 + on horizontal axis means 15–24;
25 + means 25–34;
etc.

FIGURE 2-1
Death rates for accidents and adverse effects in thirteen age groups in the United States in 1982. (Data from National Center for Health Statistics. (1983). _Monthly Vital Statistics Report, 31_ (13). Washington, D.C.: U.S. Dept. of Health and Human Services.)

reasons. Infants suffer more home accidents than other children because of helplessness and lack of knowledge.

Due to a combination of unsafe acts and greater exposure to unsafe conditions, boys and men are more likely to have accidents, including fatal accidents, than girls and women. It also seems plausible that individual differences in physical condition, intelligence, and personality can be correlated with accident rate. There is good evidence that health and fatigue are associated with accident rate, but the results of studies on the relationship of intelligence to accidents are not clear. Inexperience in performing a task is likely to lead to an accident, but below-average intelligence appears to be a significant factor in accidents only on jobs that require judgment (Schultz, 1982).

Findings on the relationships of personality characteristics to accidents are even less conclusive than those pertaining to intellectual abilities. Some years ago, public attention was focused on the so-called accident-prone individual who, because of some quirk of temperament or faulty habit pattern, was believed to be more likely to have accidents. Interest in accident-proneness was prompted by the observation that a small percentage of people seem to have a large percentage of the accidents. Subsequent research, however, revealed no real evidence that accident-proneness is a consistent characteristic of personality. This does not mean that temporary emotional states such as anger or depression cannot increase the chances of an accident. Obviously, as with any mental state that distracts the individual or causes him or her to take unwarranted risks, they can and do.

SUMMARY

Senescence, the physical deterioration associated with aging, is caused by disease, physical trauma, psychological stress, and the biological aging process. Declines in body structure and function with aging occur at all levels—systemic, organic, and cellular. Changes in the skin and skeletal structure affect one's physical appearance, and the neuromuscular changes accompanying aging affect the speed and accuracy of responses.

Characteristics of premature aging are seen in progeria, Werner's syndrome, and, at least in the mental sphere, in Alzheimer's disease. Even among people who age normally, there is a wide range in the rate of senescence. The effects of psychological variables may be observed in the extent to which people can compensate for physical deterioration and continue their activities despite these changes.

The factors associated with aging are heredity, prenatal environment, nutrition, exercise, environmental pollution, and psychological variables. Various theories of aging consider a number of these factors. Wear-and-tear theories emphasize the effects of lifestyle and environment.

REPORT 2-2

Choice of Death

Last night I dreamed a ghost came by.
It looked at me and then
Said, "You decide how you will die,
'Though not precisely when."

Although it now seems strange to me,
I really felt no fear,
But spoke right up quite thoughtfully,
As I relate it here.

"I don't desire a heart attack,
Nor sickness of the liver.
Courage I clearly do not lack,
But 'cancer' makes me quiver.

"I really do not wish to see
Myself die from the flu.
And if pneumonia's offered me,
I shall reject it too.

"I guess I'll not get sick to death,
'Cause being ill's no fun.

If something has to take my breath,
Let it be quickly done.

"I might be shot in a world war,
Or drown out on the sea,
Or fall beneath a speeding car
That's bearing down on me.

"But being killed is too unkind
To me and those I know.
I'd better think and try to find
Another way to go.

"If I could die just as I please,
I'd go quite painlessly.
Shunning accidents and disease,
I'd age so gradually.

"And when the knock of death at last
I heard at my life's door,
I'd say, 'Please sir, forget the past
And let me live some more!'"

L. R. Aiken

Homeostatic imbalance theory, immunological theory, autoimmunity theory, and hormonal theory highlight changes in the body's internal environment. Theories that emphasize the breakdown of mitochondria and the role of free radicals and cross-linkages (error-catastrophe theory) concentrate on changes at the cellular level. Most of these theories deal with the *effects* of the genetic aging process, however, rather than the *cause* of the process itself. Research on the genetics of aging has revealed an inborn upper limit to the number of cell divisions in the human species, but precisely how the biological aging "clock" is represented in the structure of the DNA molecule is not yet known.

Scientific medicine has been more successful in combatting diseases that have a single identifiable cause (e.g., infectious diseases) than multifactor diseases produced by a combination of causes (heart disease, cancer, etc.). Cardiovascular diseases (heart disease and stroke) kill more people in the United States each year than all other diseases combined. It is clear that the lifestyle, or pattern of living, that characterizes a given cultural group, combined perhaps with a hereditary predisposition, affects cardiovascular diseases or other disorders prevalent in that culture. Many demographic variables (socioeconomic status, ethnicity, sex, etc.) correlated with death rate due to specific diseases are also related to background causes such as poor nutrition, smoking, alcohol and drug abuse, lack of exercise, and psychological factors.

Among the cardiovascular diseases listed as causes of death are arteriosclerosis, hypertension, cerebrovascular disease, rheumatic fever, congenital heart disease, and, most frequently, ischemic heart disease. Any of these disorders that result in a block (thrombosis) or break (hemorrhage) in an artery can cause heart failure. A clot in a coronary artery leads to a heart attack, and a clot or hemorrhage in a cerebral artery causes a stroke. The incidence of heart disease is related to heredity, sex, ethnicity, nationality, and lifestyle. A diet high in cholesterol, for example, is associated with greater risk of heart disease, and a high salt diet is related to hypertension. Psychological factors (e.g., Type A behavioral pattern) can also contribute to coronary heart attacks.

Cancer—uncontrolled cell growth—is not a unitary disease, and its increased incidence is considered to be a consequence of conditions produced by modern industrial society. There are age, sex, ethnic-group, and geographical differences in the frequency of cancer. The emphasis in controlling and treating cancer, however, has been on carcinogenic agents such as tobacco smoke, industrial wastes, ingested substances (e.g., fats), and overexposure to the sun and other radiation sources. Psychological variables, such as loneliness and alienation from the larger society, are also related to cancer and shortened life span, but the biological mechanisms by which these factors assert their influence are not understood. Significant results have been reported in treating cancer by means of psychological methods, but physicians remain skeptical.

Among other disorders recorded as causes of death are chronic obstructive pulmonary diseases (emphysema, chronic bronchitis, asthma, etc.), influenza and pneumonia, diabetes, and cirrhosis of the liver. Death in infancy is being studied extensively, especially sudden infant death syndrome, the basic cause of which is unknown.

Accidents killed 93,000 in the United States in 1982 and are the fourth leading cause of death in the nation. Grouped according to type, the main causes of fatal accidents in the United States in 1982 were, in order of frequency: motor vehicles, falls, drownings, fires, poisoning, suffocation, and firearms. Grouped according to class of accident, the four main causes of accidental death were, in order of frequency: motor-vehicle accidents, injuries in and about the home, public accidents, and job-related accidents.

Fatal motor-vehicle accidents are more likely to occur at night, on weekends and holidays, during the summer and fall, and during periods of economic upswing. Although elderly people have more accidents than other age groups, young people in the 15–24 year age bracket lead the list for motor-vehicle fatalities. Accidents and accident fatalities are more common among males than females and more common among those whose physical condition is poor (due to illness, fatigue, alcohol, or drugs) than among the physically fit and alert. The relationships of intelligence and personality to accidents are not highly significant, but it is recognized that an individual's mental state is an important variable to be considered.

SUGGESTED READINGS

De Vries, H. A. (1975). Physiology of exercise and aging. In D. S. Woodruff & J. E. Birren (Eds.), *Aging: Scientific perspectives and social issues.* New York: Van Nostrand.

Gould, S. J. (1978). Our allotted lifetimes. *Natural History, 87,* 34–41.

Lynch, J. J. (1977). *The broken heart.* New York: Basic Books.

Palmore, E. B. (1981). *Social patterns in normal aging: Findings of the Duke Longitudinal Study.* Durham, NC: Duke University Press.

Retherford, R. D. (1975). *The changing sex differential in mortality.* Westport, Conn.: Greenwood Press.

Rowland, K. F. (1977). Environmental events predicting death for the elderly. *Psychological Bulletin, 84,* 349–372.

Shock, N. W. (1977). Biological theories of aging. In J. E. Birren & K. W. Schaie (Eds.), *Handbook of the psychology of aging.* New York: Van Nostrand Reinhold.

Simonton, O. C., Matthews-Simonton, S., & Creighton, J. (1978). *Getting well again.* Los Angeles: J. P. Tarper (distributed by St. Martin's Press, New York).

Wantz, M. S., & Gay, J. E. (1982). *The aging process: A health perspective.* Cambridge, Mass.: Winthrop.

3 Murder and Suicide

Questions answered in this chapter:

- How common is murder, and how is it differentiated from other types of homicide?
- How, by whom, why, where, and when are murders committed?
- What roles do biological, psychological, and cultural factors play in murder?
- What are the characteristics of mass murderers and political murderers?
- How does the suicide rate vary with time, place, and person?
- What explanations or interpretations have been offered for suicidal behavior?
- Why is suicide a serious problem among today's youth?
- How can suicidal behavior be predicted and prevented?

Suicide and homicide were the eighth and eleventh leading causes of death, respectively, in the United States in 1982. An estimated 27,860 persons committed suicide, and another 22,320 deaths were attributed to homicide and legal intervention during that year. The suicide rate was 12.0 and the homicide rate 9.6 per 100,000 people, both of which represented decreases from the previous year. The rates of homicide and suicide were even higher for youths and young adults (ages 15–34), exceeded only by accidents as a cause of death in that age range (National Center for Health Statistics, 1983) (see Figure 3-1).

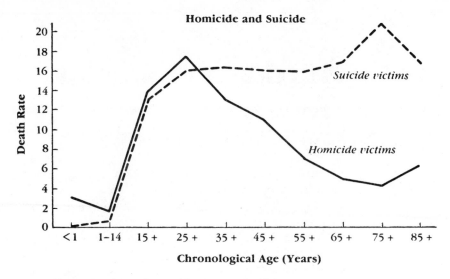

Notes: Age 15 + on horizontal axis means 15–24;
25 + means 25–34;
etc.

FIGURE 3-1
Estimated age-specific homicide and suicide rates in the United States for 1982. (Data from National Center for Health Statistics. (1983). *Monthly Vital Statistics Report, 31* **(13). Washington, D.C.: U.S. Dept. of Health and Human Services.)**

The homicide rate has increased much more rapidly than the suicide rate in the United States during the last two decades. Prior to 1960, approximately twice as many persons committed suicide as were victims of homicide. But the mortality statistics for 1980 revealed that the two rates had become almost equal during the intervening 20 years. In fact, the murder rate was higher in 1980 than it had ever been before.

Although murder is a more critical problem than suicide in the United States, concern over both of these causes of death is sufficient to stimulate a constant flow of newspaper and magazine articles, television and motion picture films, and professional research reports and books. Discovering the reasons for the high rates of self-inflicted or other-inflicted death is not simple, and many questions remain unanswered. Furthermore, it is not always easy to differentiate between murder and suicide. In cases of "victim-precipitated homicide," for example, what looks like murder on the surface may actually be a subtle form of self-destruction. Murder and suicide can also be masked as accidental death, as when a person "accidentally" falls (or is pushed) in front of an automobile. In any event, the speculations, theories, and research findings on murder and suicide are interesting, informative, and perhaps even a bit fascinating.

Murder

The term *murder* is often used interchangeably with homicide, but the latter term has a broader meaning than the former. *Homicide,* the killing of one human being by another, includes a variety of criminal and noncriminal acts. A homicidal act may be *justifiable,* as when killing in self-defense or to protect other people; it may be *excusable,* as in accidents or other misfortunes where neither negligence nor unlawful intent was involved; it may be *felonious,* in which case either negligence, unlawful intent, or both were present. Felonious homicide, in turn, is classified as *manslaughter* when negligence but not malice was involved, or *murder* when there was "malice aforethought" (an intent to kill). Manslaughter itself may be either *voluntary,* when committed during the heat of passion, or *involuntary,* when the killing takes place during the commission of a misdemeanor (e.g., reckless driving). Although legally viewed as a lesser crime than murder, manslaughter is a serious criminal offense; depending on the circumstances and the jurisdiction, manslaughter is punishable by 1–15 years imprisonment.

The most serious type of homicide is *murder,* in which case the killer intended to kill the victim(s). A deliberate and premeditated (cold-blooded, or planned) killing is referred to as *first-degree murder,* and a deliberate but not premeditated killing is classified as *second-degree murder.* An exception to this rule is when a killing takes place during the course of a robbery, rape, or kidnapping. Even when not deliberate and not premeditated, such a killing is classified as *first-degree murder.* The distinction between first- and second-degree murder is especially important in sentencing: the former crime is punishable by life imprisonment or death, whereas the latter crime carries a sentence of five years to life with the possibility of parole. However, a person who has been legally tried for murder and found to have committed the crime will not necessarily be sentenced. The defendant may be judged not guilty of murder by reason of insanity and given an open-ended commitment to a mental institution rather than a fixed prison sentence.

The United States has one of the highest murder rates in the world, a rate that has doubled since 1965. There were 20,053 reported murders in 1981 and 19,485 in 1982 (U.S. Dept. of Justice, 1983). How, why, when, and where were all these people killed, and who were the killers and their victims?

How Murders Are Committed

People kill each other with guns, knives, icepicks, clubs, bare hands, poisons, fire, gas, by drowning, and in a variety of other ways. As shown in Table 3-1, handguns were the most popular murder weapon in 1982 in the

TABLE 3-1
Types of Weapons Used in Murders in the United States in 1982

Weapon	Number of Murders	Percent of Total
Total firearms	11,721	60.2
Handgun	8,474	43.5
Rifle	1,017	5.2
Shotgun	1,377	7.1
Other gun	38	.2
Firearm not stated	815	4.9
Cutting or stabbing instrument	4,065	20.9
Blunt object (club, hammer, etc.)	957	4.9
Personal weapons (hands, fists, feet, etc.)	1,298	6.7
Poison	19	.1
Explosives	12	.1
Fire	279	1.4
Narcotics	16	.1
Drowning	52	.3
Strangulation	359	1.8
Asphyxiation	108	.6
Other weapon or weapon not stated	599	3.1

Source: U.S. Department of Justice. (1983). *Uniform crime reports: Crime in the United States* (p. 10). Washington, D.C.: U.S. Government Printing Office.

United States, followed by cutting or stabbing implements. A smaller but substantial number of people were killed by rifles, shotguns, clubs, poisons, and, when the murderers were strong enough, by beating, choking, or throwing the victim across a room or out of a window.

Guns are the most common murder weapon in the United States. Nearly one million civilians have been killed by guns since 1900, a figure greater than the total number of military personnel killed in all wars that this country has fought. Understandably, the number and rate of people killed with guns are highest in those areas with the largest per capita ownership of guns.

Since guns are so much more lethal than other weapons and they are employed so frequently in criminal activities, why hasn't greater legal control been exercised over the sale and use of these weapons? The answer to this question has two parts: (1) strict gun control is probably impossible to enforce, and (2) people who own guns form a powerful lobby against gun control. Imagine the difficulties of disarming a population of 225 million people with 50–200 million guns in their possession! An estimated 30–50 million handguns alone are on the streets and in residences, and another 2.2 million new guns are sold every year ("Surge in Murders. . . ," 1980). Even the relatively tame Federal Gun Control Act of 1968, which prohibits mail-order and over-the-counter sales of guns and ammunition to certain groups of people (out-of-state residents, convicted felons, juveniles, mental defectives, mental hospital patients, drug addicts) has proven difficult to enforce. In addition to the Federal Gun Control Act, all states have laws that limit the sale and use of guns. New York and Massachusetts, for example, limit gun possession to adults with no criminal record who can demonstrate a legitimate need for a gun. Many other states deny guns only to mental patients and paroled felons. None of these laws is very effective in limiting the acquisition and use of guns. Additionally, the National Rifle Association and certain other influential organizations have mounted stiff opposition to laws that would prohibit the manufacture or importation of guns and their purchase by ordinary citizens.

Who the Murderers and Their Victims Are

In 1982 approximately 75 percent of murder victims in the United States were male, 55 percent were white, 42 percent were black, and 2 percent belonged to other races. Forty-nine percent of those arrested for murder were white and 49 percent were black; over 83 percent were males. The majority was of lower socioeconomic status and had not finished high school (U.S. Dept. of Justice, 1983).

In 90 percent of the murders committed in 1982, the offender and the victim belonged to the same ethnic group and were usually acquainted with each other. In nearly half the murders committed in this country, black people kill black people. This fact, combined with the youthfulness of most offenders and their victims, results in murder being the number one cause of death in young black men (WGBH Educational Foundation, 1981).

Why, Where, and When Murders Are Committed

The vast majority of murders are not carefully planned, complex crimes of the sort described by Agatha Christie or solved by Sherlock Holmes. Murder is usually an impulsive, spur-of-the-moment occurrence that stems from an argument or another felony. A typical murder situation involves two young working-class males under the influence of alcohol or drugs who begin arguing about something and, to demonstrate their toughness, resort to physical violence.

In the majority of murders, both the killer and the victim had been drinking (Lunde, 1976). In fact, the larger the volume of alcohol consumed, the greater the chances of a violent crime occurring. Drinking, of course, may be a contributing factor in accidental death. Other drugs, such as amphetamines, can also lead to accidents and outbursts of violence.

The most common location for murder is in the home, especially in a bedroom. More women than men are murdered in bedrooms, and more men are murdered in kitchens; the kitchen is the second most lethal room in the home and the living room is the third. Outside the home, murder occurs most often in the streets, followed by bars and other commercial establishments in terms of frequency.

Murder rates are higher in large cities than in suburbs or rural areas, and within large cities there are a few sections with exceptionally high murder rates. These are usually areas of high population density, high unemployment, substandard housing, poor health-care services, and a generally low educational level among residents. In the national United States, the southern states have the highest murder rate (12 per 100,000 in 1982) and the western states second (9 per 100,000); the northeastern and north central states have the lowest rates (7 per 100,000 in 1982) (U.S. Dept. of Justice, 1983). That the murder rate increases with decreasing geographical latitude has been observed on the national level, and is seen to some extent on the international scene. Countries such as Colombia, Mexico, South Africa, Guatemala, and Nicaragua, which are closer to the equator, have even higher murder rates than the United States (Lunde, 1976).

Murder rates show temporal as well as spatial variations. For example, murders are more common on weekends, holidays, vacations, and during times of economic prosperity.[1] The greatest number of murders are committed during July and December, when large numbers of people are on vacation, and large amounts of money are visible (see Figure 3-2). Although no relationship has been found between murder rate and weather conditions, nighttime murders are more common during a full moon. But in a study conducted in Florida (see Lunde, 1976), it was found that more murders occurred during the dark phase of the lunar cycle. It has been speculated that this phenomenon is due to the gravitational pull of the moon on the mind; however, this explanation is a bit far-fetched, considering the extremely small effect of the moon's gravity on human beings. Simpler explanations are also given for the slight correlation between the rate of murder and the earth's magnetic fluctuations. If a person accepts these correlates and their explanations, he or she would find it inadvisable to argue with a young whiskey-drinking gun-toting acquaintance at home or in a bar on a Saturday night in July or December when the moon is full and there is plenty of money around![2]

---

1. The significant relationship between alcohol consumption and murder rate may be due in part to the fact that both alcohol consumption and murder increase during times of prosperity (Lunde, 1976).

2. It might also be added that the potential for trouble is greater when a heavyweight prizefight is being shown on a television set in the home or the bar. According to statistics compiled by Phillips (1983), homicides in the United States increased by an average of 12.46 percent after heavyweight championship prizefights during 1973–78. Apparently heavyweight prizefights stimulate fatal aggressive behavior in some individuals.

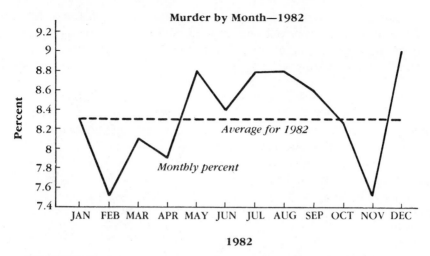

FIGURE 3-2
Murder rate by month as a percentage of annual total in 1982.
(From U.S. Dept. of Justice. (1983). *Uniform crime reports:
Crime in the United States.* Washington, D.C.: U.S. Government
Printing Office.)

Cultural Factors in Murder

The relationships of murder rate to geography, nationality, ethnicity, sex, religion, and many other demographic variables can be interpreted to a large extent in terms of cultural differences. For example, the dominant culture of the southern United States has historically been characterized by firearms, duels, militia, military training, military titles (e.g., Colonel), and vigilante groups (Franklin, 1956). The maintenance of extreme social class differences in that geographical region required the use of violent punishment to control troublemakers and rebels against the system. This latter-day feudal system persisted even after the Civil War, when the South continued to resist industrialization, defended local ownership and control, and reacted suspiciously to strangers. The affinity for guns, manifested by both southern whites and blacks, was correlated with the murder rate. Given the central role of guns and militarism in southern history, it is not surprising that the incidence of murder is higher in states that were settled primarily by southerners in the westward expansion of the nation (e.g., Louisiana and Texas) than in states settled predominantly by northerners (e.g., Wisconsin and Minnesota) (see Lunde, 1976).[3]

---

3. Three of the four states with the highest homicide rates in the nation are southern (Louisiana, Texas, and Georgia). However, the highest homicide rate in the entire United States is found in Washington, D.C. (Unpublished data, courtesy of National Center for Health Statistics.)

The use of violence and firearms to settle disputes is found in many subcultural groups, especially among individuals belonging to lower socioeconomic strata. Members of the "subculture of violence" that characterizes certain sections of large U.S. cities are likely to subscribe to the macho ethic that one should carry a weapon and be prepared to use it when one's status is questioned or threatened. Such a person may become sensitized to any real or imagined insult and be prepared to attack on a moment's notice. Furthermore, those who do not conform to this ethic of machismo are usually ostracized or victimized.

Violence and murder are actually condoned in certain countries and during certain historical periods. The murder rate in Mexico, a country in which the dominant majority subscribes to the macho ethic, is three times that of the United States. By way of contrast, the murder rate in Canada, a nation that absorbed the British emphasis on order and self-control, is only one-fifth that of the United States.

The fact that Mexico and other Latin American countries with high murder rates (e.g., Nicaragua, Colombia, Guatemala) also have quite low suicide rates may be interpreted in terms of the effects of religion on behavior. Although the Bible enjoins that "thou shalt not kill," the four recorded incidents of suicide in the Bible are described without comment. The Koran, on the other hand, strongly forbids suicide but is less vehemently opposed to murder. The teachings of both the Bible and the Koran obviously have been interpreted somewhat differently by different cultural groups. Homicide is not necessarily a mortal sin in Roman Catholic theology, but suicide is.[4] Judaism does not sanction suicide, but it is less strongly opposed to it than to murder. Consistent with these religious differences are the observations that the murder rate is relatively high and the suicide rate low among Moslems and Catholics; the reverse is true among Jews. In general, Protestant theology is less opposed to suicide than Catholicism and less opposed to homicide than Judaism. Predictably, the rates of murder and suicide among Protestants fall between those for Catholics and Jews (Lunde, 1976).

The seeming tendency for homicide and suicide rates to vary in opposite directions over time and across different cultural groups has intrigued many social scientists. In an early study, Porterfield (1949) found that cities with high suicide rates had low murder rates, and cities with high murder rates had low suicide rates. Following up on Porterfield's research, Henry and Short (1954) pointed out that suicide decreases and homicide increases during economically prosperous times, but the reverse is true during economically depressed periods. In addition, suicide is more common than

---

4. A murderer can confess and receive absolution for his sins, but a person who has succeeded in committing suicide is obviously unable to do so. But Catholicism has changed in recent years, and the Catholic Church now permits the Mass of Christian Burial as well as burial in consecrated ground in the case of suicide victims.

murder among higher social classes, but the opposite situation prevails among the lower social classes. It is tempting to conclude, as do Henry and Short, that a sociological law underlies these findings: there appears to be a relatively fixed level of "violent energy" in any given culture or society, the expression of which depends on the relative strength of the restraints imposed on individual behavior by social forces outside the person (external restraints) and the restraints imposed from within the person himself (internal restraints). The extent to which this violent energy is expressed in homicidal or suicidal behavior depends not only on the relative strengths of the external and internal restraints, but also on the degree to which homicide and suicide are culturally prohibited. When homicide is more severely prohibited than suicide, the murder rate will be low and the suicide rate high; when suicide is more strongly prohibited, the reverse will occur. Furthermore, if there are strong external restraints on group members and suicide is strongly forbidden, then the murder rate will be higher than the suicide rate, as in the lower social classes. But if internal restraints on group members are strong and murder is more severely censured than suicide, as in the upper social classes, then the suicide rate will be higher than the murder rate. Unfortunately, the results of more recent statistical studies fail to support such a law. Both the murder and suicide rates have risen in recent years, and both are now higher in the lower social classes than in the higher social classes (Lunde, 1976).

Murder, suicide, and other violent behaviors are culturally conditioned reactions to specific situations. But modern-day cultures are not static; they change rapidly in many instances, being influenced by information and techniques communicated by interactions with people from other cultures. Children see murders in the street and murder in war zones almost every night on their home television sets. Socially condoned violence in the Middle East results in the social acceptability of violence as a means of handling disputes elsewhere in the world. People become conditioned to guns as symbols of violence and react violently to them (Berkowitz, 1968). They learn to murder by mail, by bombs, and by means of other weapons provided by modern technology. Techniques of killing are not restricted to a specific culture; they are there for all unhappy, frustrated people to observe and employ.

Psychological Factors in Murder

Criminology, the study of criminal behavior, has traditionally been the province of sociologists, whose primary explanation of the cause of criminal behavior has been the *principle of differential association.* A modified version of this principle states that:

> Overt criminal behavior has as its necessary and sufficient conditions a set of criminal motivations, attitudes, and techniques, the learning of which takes place when there is exposure to criminal norms in excess of exposure to corresponding anticriminal norms during symbolic interaction in primary groups. (DeFleur & Quinney, 1966, p. 7)

According to the principle of differential association, a necessary and sufficient condition for murder is prolonged exposure to a subculture of violence and violent role models without compensating exposure to nonviolent situations and models. The principle does not take biological variables into account. However, it does consider learning, a process of great interest to psychologists, to be crucial in the development of criminal behavior in general and homicidal behavior in particular.

Many anthropologists and biologists have been concerned with the possible influences of such biological variables as body build (somatotype), hormones, brain waves, and abnormal chromosomes or genes in the determination of criminal behavior. The nineteenth-century notion of the "bad seed" continues to influence speculations about the causes of murder and other crimes (see Yochelson & Samenow, 1976). Although they do not deny the importance of environment, supporters of a genetic basis of criminality maintain that a predisposition to such behavior, manifested in temperamental characteristics such as impulsiveness or low frustration tolerance, is inherited. In recent years, for example, the XYY, or so-called supermale, chromosomal pattern has received a great deal of attention as a possible biological basis for aggressiveness and impulsive murder. Other theorists believe that, although criminal behavior is not strictly determined by heredity, one may inherit a characteristic such as an athletic (mesomorphic) body build that makes violent activity more likely or rewarding (Glueck & Glueck, 1956).

Unfortunately, no single theory of criminal behavior in general or of homicide in particular can account for the variety of crimes and their antecedents. Not all murderers have biological abnormalities, not all come from deprived backgrounds or have criminal associates, and not all possess low IQ's or the same personality traits. Even Guttmacher's (1973) classification of murderers into four groups—normal, sociopathic, alcoholic, and avenging—does not do justice to the range of characteristics and motives found in individuals who kill.

There is some evidence that the greater the impulsiveness and violence of a murderer, the more likely the murderer is to be rather shy, inhibited, and, in the case of a male, more feminine in his interest pattern (Lee, Zimbardo & Bertholf, 1977). The overcontrol normally exhibited by such individuals breaks down when the core of the person's identity is threatened and he or she is no longer able to deny intense feelings of anger. In contrast to the overcontrolled, impulsive murderer is the more common undercontrolled, macho individual who acts out his aggressions with little restraint. In either case, the violent act of murder releases feelings of frustration and tension and, in some cases, fear, on the part of the murderer. The murderer views the victim as well as himself or herself with a sense of detachment. The victim becomes a dehumanized object, to be exploited and destroyed. The detached self of the murderer looks on as the lethal weapon is employed, and the killer experiences an emotional release.

A link between murder and suicide has been noted by many authorities. According to Halleck (1971), both of these violent actions may represent efforts to cope with feelings of helplessness, hopelessness, hostility, and depression. Halleck reports that murder can be an act of self-preservation: the murderer kills another person to keep from killing himself or herself. This self-protective gesture fails, of course, when a murder is committed and the murderer immediately commits suicide.

Murder and Insanity

Any discussion of psychological factors in murder requires some consideration of the popular assumption that many murderers are insane. Most law-abiding citizens probably find it impossible to identify with or even understand a person who commits a particularly violent murder in which the victim is ravished or mutilated, for example. Therefore, it is natural to conclude that anyone who would commit such a crime is deranged. This point of view is perhaps more common in countries such as England, where the murder rate is lower than that of the United States and one-fourth of the apprehended murderers are declared legally insane. Although social supports for murder and efficient means of committing it are less common in England, the rate of mental illness is just as high as it is in the United States. In addition, murder is more often followed by suicide in England than in the United States (Lunde, 1976).

The mentally ill are often feared, but in actual fact mentally ill people in general are less likely to commit murder than so-called normal people. Those few mentally ill individuals who do commit murder usually provoke dramatic, frightening stories in the media that stimulate the public's fear of mad dogs on the loose and monsters in the streets. This fear becomes particularly intense when a mass murderer such as the Boston Strangler or the Son of Sam is depicted as stalking unsuspecting, innocent victims. These mass murderers are usually either paranoid schizophrenics, as in the case of David Berkowitz, the Son of Sam, or sexual sadists such as Jack the Ripper. The paranoid mass murderer typically has a history of psychiatric treatment, but the sadist—who derives sexual pleasure from killing, abusing, and mutilating his victims—usually does not. The killings of a mass murderer may all be committed in a relatively short time period or serially over several weeks, months, or years. It is noteworthy that alcoholic and drug intoxication are not involved in mass murder to the extent that they are in other types of murder (Lunde, 1976).

A special type of mass murder known as *collective crime* is represented by the killings committed by the Manson family, the American soldiers led by Lt. William Calley in Viet Nam, and the Lebanese Christian Falangists. When such killings, which are sanctioned by a particular social subgroup or group, occur on a sufficiently large scale and are directed at a specific group of people, they are referred to as genocide. In *genocide,* an attempt is made to exterminate an entire ethnic, national, or religious group. The victims of genocide are almost always viewed as subhuman or nonhuman objects by the murderers, as in the shooting and gassing of millions of Jews by the Nazis during World War II.

Genocide is sometimes referred to as *political murder.* War is also a kind of political murder, in which case an entire nation is dehumanized and categorized as bad or evil. On a much more limited scale is the assassination of a political or religious leader such as the president or the pope. Although political assassins are popularly viewed as deranged or crazy, many of them act from rational motives. Clarke (1982) has theorized that there are actually four types of political assassins. Type I is extreme, but rational, selfless, principled, and without perversity; Type II kills for revenge or to gain acceptance or recognition from a "significant other"; Type III is a psychopath who views life as meaningless and purposeless, and the destruction of society (including himself or herself) as desirable for its own sake; Type IV is a "real crazy." Not all of the 17 political assassins considered by Clarke fell into one of these four categories, but the great majority (15) did. Finally, whatever his or her personality characteristics and motives may be, a political assassin's task is made easier by the ready availability of guns and explosives. The majority of successful and unsuccessful assassins also have received military training in the use of lethal weapons.

Murder in the Home

As noted previously, more murders occur in the home than in any other location. This is where parents kill their children, husbands kill their wives, and wives kill their husbands. The fragility of young children, coupled with the demands they make on immature parents, make them prime targets for overwrought mothers and fathers.

It is frequently the case that parents who abuse and murder their children were themselves abused during childhood. Such parents are also often unrealistic in their expectations of their offspring. In the great majority of cases the parents do not intend to kill their children, but the stress and frustration of coping with them becomes too great and the parents vent their rage in child abuse and murder. As in other murders, the child-victim is perceived as a demanding, dehumanized "thing" that is interfering in some way with the parent's emotional gratification (Kastenbaum & Aisenberg, 1976).

The motives of people who kill their spouses vary with the sex of the killer. Wives are more likely to kill their husbands because of bruised bodies, whereas husbands are more likely to kill their wives because of bruised egos. A wife will usually kill her husband only as a last resort, after she has been verbally and physically brutalized for a prolonged period of time. But a husband who kills his wife usually does so in an impulsive response to a walkout, a demand, or a threat of separation; these acts represent rejection, abandonment, or desertion to the male (Barnard et al., 1981).

The murder of a spouse in the home is frequently victim-precipitated, in the sense that the victim either knowingly or unknowingly contributes to his or her own death (Lester, 1973). In general, victim-precipitated murders are more commonplace in lower socioeconomic classes and when the victim and offender possess similar characteristics. Homicide victims may contribute to their own deaths in a variety of ways and circumstances—by habitually exposing themselves to danger, by arguing heatedly with a drunken person, by being indiscriminately seductive, and even by striking the first blow. In such instances it seems as if the victim actually harbored a secret suicidal wish and encouraged murder as an indirect form of self-destruction. A similar psychological process is seen in individuals who commit "senseless" murders in order to receive the death penalty. In these cases, the murderer consciously or unconsciously believes that being killed by some other person or agency is more socially and morally acceptable than direct suicide (Wolfgang, 1969; Abrahamsen, 1973).

Apprehending Murderers

The rate of arrest, or *clearance rate,* is higher for homicide than for any other crime. In approximately two-thirds of the cases, the killer, who typically goes to no great pains to escape or avoid detection, is in police custody within 24 hours after the crime has been committed. For whatever reason—fear, tension, a feeling of helplessness—murderers frequently act in such a way as to assure their own detection and capture. The desire to be caught, which was dramatized in Fyodor Dostoyevski's *Crime and Punishment,* is most apparent in impulsive murders committed by quiet, nonviolent people with no previous arrest record. If a suspect has not been apprehended within 48 hours, however, the odds against detection and capture increase markedly (Lunde, 1976).

The arrest of a homicide suspect does not, of course, ensure a conviction. Only about 60 percent of those charged with murder or voluntary manslaughter in the United States are actually convicted and sentenced.

The severity of the sentence depends on a variety of mitigating circumstances, for example, whether the defendant expresses remorse over the crime. The death penalty is rarely used, and even a person who is sentenced to life imprisonment is usually eligible for parole in seven years or so. On the average, those convicted of first-degree murder in the United States spend about 10½ years in prison; those convicted of second-degree murder are in prison for approximately 5 years, and those convicted of voluntary manslaughter about 3½ years. Many observers feel that stiffer prison sentences and a more liberal application of the death penalty are needed to curb the rise in murder and other violent crimes in the United States.[5] We shall return to this topic in Chapter 6, but let us now examine another kind of unnatural death.

Suicide

Over the years, this writer has occasionally asked large groups of high school and college students whether or not they have ever seriously thought of committing suicide. When able to answer anonymously, over half the students in several groups replied affirmatively. At first it seemed surprising that so many healthy, attractive young people in the spring of life with presumably so much to live for had thought of killing themselves. But it is less surprising when one realizes that pain and sadness are no respecters of youth, beauty, ability, or affluence. Even the most physically and socially favored persons can hurt, and occasionally desire to end their sufferings by destroying themselves.

Until the last two decades or so, suicide was somewhat of a taboo topic that many people thought about but few discussed. The situation has changed markedly during the past few years, and *suicidology,* the study of suicide, has become almost popular. Research on the demographics and dynamics of suicide has accompanied the growth of suicide prevention centers, prescriptions for committing suicide, and university courses and course units on the topic. Although the greater openness with which the topic is now discussed has led to some rather bizarre notions, the situation is certainly healthier than it used to be.

Demographics of Suicide

There were 27,860 reported suicides in the United States in 1982, an average of one every 19 minutes. If one considers the undoubtedly large number of suicides that are "hushed up" or disguised as accidents, an

---

5. Interestingly enough, the recidivism rate for convicted murderers is lower than that for any other crime. Fewer than two percent of the murderers who are placed on parole kill again.

estimated 60,000 actual suicides and 100–200 thousand suicide attempts occur annually in the United States. Despite these seemingly large numbers, the U.S. suicide rate (12.0 per 100,000 in 1982) is by no means the largest in the world. Hungary has the highest reported suicide rate (43 per 100,000), Denmark has the second highest (26 per 100,000), followed by Austria, Czechoslovakia, Finland, Sweden, and West Germany, all with rates around 20 per 100,000. The suicide rate of Canada is approximately the same as that of the United States, but the rate in England and Wales (8 per 100,000) is lower (Follett, 1980). Even lower suicide rates are found in predominantly Roman Catholic countries such as Ireland, Italy, Mexico, and the Philippines (1–2 per 100,000). The lowest rates of all (near 0) are found in Iceland, the Faeroe Islands, and among the aborigines of western Australia. Nevada has the highest suicide rate of all the states (22.9 per 100,000 in 1979), Wyoming the second highest (19.0), and New Mexico the third (18.7) (unpublished data supplied by National Center for Health Statistics).

As shown in Figure 3-1, the U.S. suicide rate increases steadily from near zero in early childhood to over 16 per 100,000 population in the 35–44 year age bracket. The rate remains fairly constant during middle age, but rises again after age 65. The high suicide rate during later life is caused primarily by the large number of suicides among elderly men rather than elderly women.

More women than men attempt suicide in the United States, but men succeed three to four times as often as women do before old age and ten times as often after age 85. The greater number of male suicides is due largely to the fact that men employ more lethal methods. The number of people who committed suicide in the United States in 1980 and the various methods they used are listed in Table 3-2. On a worldwide scale, the preferred methods and their usage vary not only with sex but also with nationality. Perhaps because of their ready availability, suicide by firearms is

TABLE 3-2
Methods Used to Commit Suicide in the United States in 1980

Method	Number of Suicides		
	Male	*Female*	*Total*
Drugs, medicaments, and biologicals	1,142	1,619	2,761
Other solid and liquid substances	183	91	274
Gases and vapors	1,672	746	2,418
Hanging, strangulation, and suffocation	2,997	694	3,691
Handgun	1,633	476	2,109
Other and unspecified firearms	11,304	1,983	13,287
All other means and late effects of self-inflicted injury	1,574	755	2,329
Total	20,505	6,364	26,869

Source: Data provided by National Center for Health Statistics.

most common in the United States, whereas domestic gas is the most popular method in the United Kingdom ("Suicide," 1983).

In the United States, the suicide rate is higher among Caucasians and Orientals than among Blacks (see Figure 3-3). However, the rate for Blacks, particularly males, has increased steadily during the past 35 years. The rising suicide rate for Blacks since World War II has been attributed to the vertical social mobility of this ethnic group, the consequent role changes, and the accompanying high degree of psychological stress (Woodford, 1965). The social changes during the 1950s, 1960s, and 1970s created high expectations in people who had for generations been resigned to low social status. When people do not know what they are missing, or when opportunities for acquiring something do not exist, they usually adjust and resign themselves to their situation. But frustration inevitably follows when hopes and expectations are raised and not fulfilled quickly enough. Such frustration then leads to anger and depression, and, in certain instances, to violence and suicide (Simpson, 1979).

The suicide rate is higher for city-dwellers than for country-dwellers, and higher for people of lower socioeconomic status and those who are downwardly mobile. Nevertheless, suicide is no respecter of social class; it is relatively high among physicians (especially psychiatrists), dentists, and lawyers, but low among teachers and clergymen. Understandably, the rate of suicide is also a function of the availability of means

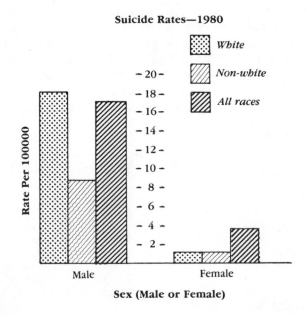

FIGURE 3-3
U.S. suicide rate by race and sex in 1980. (From data supplied by National Center for Health Statistics.)

for committing it. Physicians can easily obtain lethal drugs and instruments; soldiers and police officers, among whom the suicide rate is also high, have easy access to firearms. The fact that all three of these occupations can be highly stressful also contributes to the high suicide rate (Cavan, 1982).

Suicide rates are related to mental and physical health, family history, marital status, and religious affiliation. As would be expected, the suicide rate is highest for people who are likely to have serious problems—the chronically ill or violent, alcoholics, drug addicts, and the mentally ill. Suicide also runs in families, not through the genetic transmission of a potential for self-destructive behavior, but because the suicide of a relative acts as an example of an acceptable way of resolving personal problems. The suicide rate is also high among the childless and those from broken homes. With respect to marital status, the rate of suicide is highest for divorced persons, next highest for the widowed, next highest for singles, and lowest for married people (Simpson, 1979). Among religious groups, the rates for Jews and Protestants are higher than those for Roman Catholics and Moslems (Dublin, 1963; Farberow, 1975).

The suicide rate varies with time as well. It is higher during the spring than at other times of year, and higher during periods of economic recession, depression, and social unrest (Coleman, Butcher, & Carson, 1980). Interestingly enough, the rate declines during wartime and during times of natural disasters (e.g., earthquakes). There is also a contagious or epidemic quality to suicide; the rate increases after the suicide of a famous person such as Marilyn Monroe or Freddie Prinze. Statistics also indicate that the number of suicides increases significantly after a "TV suicide," so even fictional suicides can trigger imitative deaths (Phillips, 1979).

Sociocultural Factors in Suicide

Despite occasional attitudes of tolerance and even admiration, suicide was generally opposed in ancient Greece, Rome, and other early Western nations. Orthodox Jewish law and early Christianity also condemned it. As mentioned earlier in the chapter, the Bible does not explicitly condemn suicide, but the Christian church in the Middle Ages viewed the taking of one's own life as a violation of the commandment "thou shalt not kill." Consequently, the penalties were severe, including denial of Christian burial, degradation of the corpse, confiscation of the deceased's possessions, and censure of the survivors. Many of the penalties were codified into civil as well as church law. Early English law, for example, required that a stake be driven through the heart of a person who committed suicide and that the body be buried at a crossroads ("Suicide," 1983; Coleman, Butcher, & Carson, 1980). Suicide was, and continues to be, most severely condemned in Islamic countries.

73

Antisuicide laws continued to be on the judicial books of Western countries until the late eighteenth century, when they began to be repealed. France was the first (1789) and England the last (1961) European nation to repeal antisuicide legislation. In both England and most of the United States, suicide itself is no longer illegal, but aiding and abetting it remains a felony. In addition, suicide attempters and survivors of people who take their own lives are still socially censured ("Suicide," 1983).

Far Eastern cultures in which Hinduism, Buddhism, and related religions predominate have traditionally been tolerant of suicide. Both Hinduism and Buddhism condone suicide under certain conditions, as when it serves religion or country. *Suttee,* an ancient Hindu custom in which a devoted wife voluntarily was cremated on the funeral pyre of her husband, was practiced in northern India until it was outlawed by the British in the nineteenth century.[6] And *seppuku,* or *hara-kiri,* a ritual in which a disgraced samurai disemboweled himself with a knife, was considered an honorable way to die in medieval Japan. A more modern form of ritual suicide was committed by Japanese kamikaze pilots during World War II. Even today, the Japanese, whose language contains 58 different phrases pertaining to suicide, remain sympathetic toward hara-kiri as an honorable way to die under certain circumstances (Jameson, 1981).

Hara-kiri, suttee, and other conventional suicides were labeled *altruistic suicides* by Emile Durkheim (1897). Durkheim, who provided the first systematic sociological interpretation of suicide, also described two other types—anomic and egoistic. *Anomic suicide* is a personal response of the individual to loss of social equilibrium; for example, the stock market crash of 1929 precipitated many anomic suicides. *Egoistic suicide* is a selfish act committed by an individual who, through failure to become socially integrated, lacks social supports to help him through a crisis.

Durkheim's theory views suicide not as a medical problem but rather as caused by the failure of individuals to become adjusted to society and to absorb its values and norms. Hence individuals with strong group ties are less likely to commit suicide, according to Durkheim. They are more sensitive to the standards and expectations of the group, which include opposition to group dissolution and suicide, and more susceptible to the enforcement of those standards. As pointed out earlier, married people, who presumably have stronger group (i.e., family) ties than divorced, widowed, and single people, are less likely to commit suicide. In addition, people whose relationships with others are stable and satisfying are less likely to kill themselves than isolates, loners, or those whose social relationships are unrewarding (Farberow, 1974). Although findings such as

---

6. It was customary among the Vikings and other early northwestern European groups for the wife or concubine of a slain warrior to commit suicide or be killed in order to serve the deceased in the afterlife.

these would appear to lend substance to Durkheim's theory, the current scientific viewpoint on suicide is more holistic; it includes not only sociological factors but biological and psychological variables as well.

Psychological Factors in Suicide

As suggested by the large number of people who admit to having contemplated suicide, there are no invariant traits of personality that consistently differentiate between the potentially suicidal and the nonsuicidal individual. All kinds of people kill themselves, and for a variety of reasons. The reasons include rejection by or the death of a loved one, failure to attain a desirable professional or social position or the loss of same, chronically poor health and physical pain, a desire for revenge, or even altruism. The accompanying emotional reactions include depression, guilt, anger, hopelessness, and despair. Depression is the most common emotion in suicide, and mental disorders in which depression is a primary symptom (e.g., involutional melancholia, manic-depressive psychosis) carry the highest risk of suicide (Leonard, 1974).

Whatever the reason or emotion associated with their decision, the majority of suicidal individuals communicate their intentions, directly or indirectly, to at least one other individual (Farberow & Litman, 1970; Rudestam, 1971). These communications range from subtle hints that one may not be around very long to clear-cut threats to kill oneself. Although suicidal individuals are frequently ambivalent about taking their own lives, suicide threats should never be taken lightly. "Would you like to borrow my gun" is no fit response to a person who admits to thinking about shooting himself or herself.

Psychoanalytic Theory. Because so many personal and situational factors contribute to a decision to take one's own life, no single theory of personality or behavior can explain all suicides. The classical psychoanalytic interpretation views the act of suicide as an internalization of anger that the person is unable to express externally. Freudians believe that the destructive instinct, *thanatos,* is always present in an individual, and it gains the upper hand in suicide. The suicidal person has not lived up to his ego ideal, and the pressure of the superego becomes intolerable, driving the person to make an attempt to destroy the self ("Suicide," 1983).

Humanistic and Behavioristic Perspectives. The humanistic perspective considers a good life to be one that is meaningful and self-actualizing; therefore, suicide represents a waste or defeat. By destroying himself or herself, an individual fails to fulfill his or her potential, and consequently life becomes meaningless. According to the behavioristic analysis of suicide, a person attempts to self-destruct only when there is a real or

75

imagined loss of reinforcers (health and vitality, love, success, etc.). By committing suicide, the person fancies that he or she will move from a position of no reinforcement to a position in which pity, attention, revenge, and other possible consequences of the suicide provide reinforcement (in absentia) (Bootzin & Acocella, 1980).

Suicidal Modes of Thinking.   From a more cognitive perspective, Shneidman and Farberow (1970) conceptualize suicide as an action that results from particular modes of thinking. *Catalogical thinking* is described as despairing and destructive; the individual feels helpless, fearful, and pessimistic about becoming involved in personal relationships. In *logical thinking,* on the other hand, the person's thought processes are rational, as in an elderly individual who, after enduring long years of physical suffering or loss, decides to release himself or herself. *Contaminated thinking,* as represented by hara-kiri, perceives suicide as a way of saving face or as a transition to a better life. For these individuals, death is a religio-cultural ritual with a deep personal significance. In the final type of suicidal thinking, *paleological thinking,* the individual responds with the act of suicide to accusatory delusions or hallucinations that involve shame and promise redemption only through death.

Suicide in the Young

Although suicide is more common among older than younger people, it is the third leading cause of death in individuals aged 12–20 in the United States. There were only 150 reported suicides in children under age 15 in 1982, but the suicide rate in the 15–24 year age bracket had tripled from 1965 to 1982. Over 5,000 people in the United States between the ages of 15 and 24 were reported to have committed suicide in 1982, and there were probably at least 5,000 more that were disguised as accidental deaths (data provided by National Center for Health Statistics).

Today's youth appear more confused and frightened about the future than ever before. Feelings of anonymity and alienation, insecurity, and pressure to grow up too soon or to become popular and successful overnight, are widely expressed by teenagers and young adults. Children may reach the point at which they feel that nothing is fun anymore, that they are loved by no one and must reciprocate by loving no one and nothing. The failure to live up to parental expectations and the resulting loss of a sense of belonging and self-esteem act as predisposing conditions for anger and depression. The danger signals of potential suicide then appear.

Some indicators of suicidal intentions among young children are a decline in school performance, insomnia, irritability, and mishaps of various kinds. Young boys are more apt to have temper tantrums, engage in violent actions, and run away from home; young girls are more likely to become deeply depressed and develop psychosomatic symptoms (headaches, nervous quirks, excessive weight gains) ("Children Who Want to Die," 1978). In addition to a decline in academic achievement, older youths may exhibit depression, deterioration in personal care and hygiene, withdrawal and isolation, and self-criticism indicative of reduced self-esteem (Coleman, Butcher, & Carson, 1980). The person may increase his or her consumption of alcohol or drugs, talk about methods of committing suicide, and even threaten to kill himself or herself. Such behavior is most likely during a crisis or transition period in a young person's life—the breakup of a romance, parental divorce or death, academic failure, or when the person is forced to rely on his or her own resources for the first time.

Suicide Prediction and Prevention

People who are thinking about suicide usually fail to realize that they need help, and consequently do not seek it. Interested family members, friends, and associates must be aware of and alert for the danger signs of potentially suicidal behavior. Because prediction facilitates prevention, a great deal of attention is paid by suicidologists to indicators such as those listed in the last paragraph. Many of these symptoms are also evident in adults who are contemplating suicide (Coleman, Butcher, & Carson, 1980).

The results of research studies have suggested that it may be possible to predict suicidal behavior by means of psychological or biochemical tests ("Am I Suicidal?," 1978; "The Suicide Factor," 1982), but the responsibility for determining if a person is considering suicide usually lies with his informal contacts. Consequently, Shneidman (1980c) advised those who wish to prevent suicides to be particularly alert for such cues as heightened anxiety, expressions of hopelessness, a seeming tendency to act against one's own best interests, and a narrowing of focus ("tunnel vision"). Threats to commit suicide, even when made in a jocular manner, as well as actual suicide attempts, should be taken seriously. A sizable percentage of people who threaten to take their own lives actually make an attempt, and many of those who try and fail try again.

The prevention of suicide is important not only to the victim but also to the survivors. Perhaps not the most important reason, but certainly a serious one, is the fact that insurance companies are usually not required to pay death benefits to the survivors of suicide victims. Over three-quarters of a million people in the United States are affected each year by someone else's suicide, not just economically, however, but also psychologically. The grief, guilt, blame, and feelings of helplessness experienced by these survivors are incalculable.

The need for a professional approach to suicide prevention has led to the establishment of clinics devoted to this task in many countries. One of the first formal organizations established to help prevent suicide was the Samaritans, which was founded by an Anglican minister, Chad Varah, in 1953 in London, England. The first suicide prevention clinic in the United States was opened a few years later in Los Angeles, and currently there are over 200 such clinics throughout the nation. These clinics, which are geared mainly toward crisis intervention, provide psychological first aid and support to thousands of lonely, desperate people every year. Clinic staff members try to help suicidal individuals cope with immediate crises in their lives.

Long-term programs for treating suicidal individuals emphasize helping them realize the possibilities that remain open and giving them hope and courage to make their lives meaningful and worth living. The following procedures are employed by counselors of suicidal persons.

1. Urge the person to speak frankly, no matter how negative his or her statements may seem.
2. Listen carefully and demonstrate genuine interest, concern, and caring.
3. Assess the person's internal and external strengths and resources.
4. Assist the person in clarifying his or her problem(s) and formulating a plan of action.
5. Arrange for psychiatric hospitalization when the situation is highly lethal, even if legal commitment becomes necessary. (Altrocchi, 1980)

These procedures, when applied by trained, empathic counselors, are effective in a large percentage of cases. Unfortunately, they don't always work, and a counselee ultimately may decide that suicide is the only reasonable solution to an intolerable situation.

Euthanasia

Many people question whether a person who has decided to take his or her own life, after examining the various alternatives in detail, should be permitted to do so and even assisted in making it less painful. *Euthanasia* (easy death) is the act of painlessly putting to death an individual who is suffering from an unbearably painful incurable disease or condition. Simply letting a terminally ill person die without applying "heroic measures" to keep him or her alive is called *passive euthanasia. Active euthanasia,* on the other hand, entails using active measures to end a suffering person's life.

Throughout human history, active euthanasia sporadically has been practiced on certain groups of people (infants, the elderly, the chronically ill, the physically or mentally deformed, and even certain unpopular or "socially undesirable" ethnic or religious groups). The "mercy killing" of infants, for example, was common in ancient Greece and certain other Middle Eastern countries. Historically, euthanasia has been opposed by Christianity, Islam, and Judaism, but its practice in moderation has been supported by a number of eminent philosophers, scientists, and other famous individuals. For example, Plato, Aristotle, David Hume, and Immanuel Kant all endorsed euthanasia under certain circumstances. In our own time, euthanasia has sometimes been associated with *genocide,* as in the extermination of millions of European Jews by the Nazis during World War II. Genocide is not only active, however, but also involuntary because it is done without the consent of the subject.

Active euthanasia, is a criminal offense in both the United States and Great Britain. Organizations such as the Euthanasia Society of America and the Voluntary Euthanasia Legalization Society of Great Britain have lobbied for legislation that would legalize active euthanasia with the consent of the person whose life is at issue (*voluntary euthanasia*). These organizations have gained many supporters, but, no matter how humane their reasons may be, aiding and abetting suicide, which is how the law interprets voluntary active euthanasia, remains a crime (Eaton, 1982). Passive euthanasia, on the other hand, is not illegal under certain circumstances.

SUMMARY

Suicide and homicide were the eighth and eleventh leading causes of death, respectively, in the United States in 1982. Suicide is more common than homicide in old age; homicide is most common in young adulthood. The death rates due to both causes have increased during the past 20 years, the homicide rate twice as rapidly as the suicide rate.

Legal distinctions are made among justifiable, excusable, and felonious homicide, and among involuntary manslaughter, voluntary manslaughter, first-degree murder, and second-degree murder. Manslaughter involves criminal negligence but not malice. Second-degree murder involves malice but not premeditation. First-degree murder is both malicious and premeditated.

Firearms are the most popular murder weapon in the United States, accounting for 60 percent of all murders in 1982. Unlike the situation in other countries with stricter gun-control laws, firearms are relatively easy to obtain in the United States. Cutting and stabbing instruments are the second most popular weapon, accounting for 21 percent of U.S. murders in 1982.

Over four-fifths of the murderers and three-fourths of the murder victims in the United States are male. Approximately half of all murderers and slightly over half of their victims are white. In terms of both victim and offender, murder is more common in lower socioeconomic than in upper socioeconomic groups. It is the number one cause of death in young black men.

Alcohol and arguments are associated with murder, which, in the majority of cases, is impulsive rather than planned violence. Homes are the most popular places for murder, followed by streets and bars. The murder rate is higher in cities than in small towns and rural areas, and higher in the southern and western states than the north central and northeastern states. The murder rate is also relatively higher in countries closer to the equator. The frequency of murder is usually greater during July and December and during holidays and vacations. Among the major religious groups in the United States, the murder rate is highest among Roman Catholics, intermediate among Protestants, and lowest among Jews.

The principle of differential association attempts to explain criminal behavior, including homicide, as a natural result of living in a subculture of violence and around violent role models. Biologically based explanations of violent behavior point to the inheritance of aggressiveness and other temperamental and structural characteristics that predispose human beings to violence. Psychological theorists emphasize specific personality traits and the learning process in their analyses of violent behavior.

The great majority of murderers are not legally insane, and the murder rate is actually lower than average among the mentally ill. Mass murder is rare, and mass murderers usually are paranoids or sexual sadists. Collective crime, genocide, and war are types of mass murder that are sanctioned by a social group or society. Such homicides are usually politically motivated, as are many assassinations of public figures. Political assassins, however, greatly vary in their motives and personalities.

Women who murder their husbands most often do so because of bruised bodies, whereas men who murder their wives do so because of bruised egos. Mothers and fathers also abuse and murder their own children, the usual causes being frustration coupled with emotional immaturity and/or psychosis. In these murders, as in almost all murders, the murderer perceives the victim as a dehumanized, impersonal object to be destroyed.

The clearance rate, the percentage of perpetrators who are apprehended, is higher for homicide than for any other crime, but being arrested for murder does not ensure conviction or sentencing. Murderers who are paroled from prison, however, rarely kill again.

The annual suicide rate in the United States of 12–13 per 100,000 inhabitants is about average for the world. The world rate varies from approximately zero in Iceland and western Australia to 24 + in Hungary and Denmark. The suicide rate increases with chronological age and is higher in males than in females, higher in Caucasians and Orientals than in Blacks, higher in Jews and Protestants than in Catholics, higher in city-dwellers than in country-dwellers, higher in lower-class than in upper-class people, and higher in divorced than in married people. It is also higher during economic recessions than during economic upswings, and after the suicide of a famous person, real or fictional.

Suicide is opposed in most Western and Middle Eastern countries, especially those that are predominantly Catholic or Moslem. It is viewed with less disfavor in the Far East, where conventional suicides such as suttee in India and hara-kiri in Japan were practiced for generations. The act of suicide is no longer a criminal offense in most Western countries, but it is generally disapproved by society. Helping a person commit suicide is illegal.

A principal sociological theory of suicide is Emile Durkheim's classification of suicides into three types—altruistic, anomic, and egoistic. Psychological theories of suicide include the psychoanalytic notions of thanatos and self-directed aggression, the behavioristic view of suicide as an attempt to attain positive reinforcement, and the cognitive conception of catalogical, logical, contaminated, and paleological thinking.

An increase in the incidence of suicide among teenagers and young adults during recent years has been attributed to their feelings of anonymity, alienation, and uncertainty. Young people who are contemplating suicide, and suicidal individuals in general, usually show changes in behavior and other indications of their intentions. Suicidologists and suicide prevention clinics are making efforts to predict and prevent suicide in all age groups.

Interest has been growing in voluntary euthanasia and the right of the individual to terminate his own existence. Active euthanasia is illegal, whether voluntary or not, but passive euthanasia is legal under certain circumstances.

SUGGESTED READINGS

Alvarez, A. (1974). *The savage god.* New York: Bantam.

Choron, J. (1984). Philosophers on suicide. In E. S. Shneidman (Ed.), *Death: Current perspectives* (3rd ed.). Palo Alto, Calif.: Mayfield.

Clarke, J. W. (1982). *American assassins: The darker side of politics.* Princeton, N.J.: Princeton University Press.

Danto, B. L., Bruhns, J., & Kutscher, A. H. (Eds.). (1982). *The human side of homicide.* New York: Columbia University Press.

Farberow, N. L. (Ed.). (1979). *Indirect self-destructive behavior.* New York: McGraw-Hill.

Lunde, D. T. (1976). *Murder and madness.* San Francisco: San Francisco Book Co.

Plath, S. (1971). *The bell jar.* New York: Harper & Row.

Portwood, D. (1978). A right to suicide. *Psychology Today, 11*(8), 66–76.

Shneidman, E. S. (1980). *Voices of death.* New York: Harper & Row.

PART II

Cultural Beliefs and Practices Concerning Death

4 Funerary Rituals and Religion

Questions answered in this chapter:

- What are the origins and characteristics of death rituals and beliefs?
- What purposes have been served by funerary rites and customs?
- What factors have played a role in methods of treating and disposing of corpses and in selecting and designing graves?
- What have been the major differences in Eastern and Western attitudes toward death and related customs?
- What are the relationships between myth and religion, and what purposes do these cultural belief systems serve?
- What are the differences between Eastern and Western religions in conceptions of life after death, and how did these differences arise?
- What are the similarities and differences among the major religions of the world in eschatological beliefs (final battle between good and evil, appearance of savior figure, last judgment, etc.)?

*T*he topic of death and dying is not something that has been of interest only to writers and scholars in the late twentieth century. From the earliest beginnings of civilization, people have been faced with death and the questions of why it occurs, what it means, and how to cope with it. Primitive man encountered death almost daily, and every member of early human societies was probably aware that he or she would die someday. Because one's life expectancy at birth was less than 20 years, that day was usually not long in coming.

Death is an event experienced by an individual, but it is also a social event. People did not have to wait for John Donne's time to realize that "no man is an island" and "each man's death diminishes me." In ancient times, the death of a member disrupted the order of a social group, forcing a readjustment in roles and feelings. (The same is true today.) The societal disruption and consequent readjustment caused by a person's death did not have a uniformly negative effect on other members of a tribe or clan. Rather, in most cases it probably served to increase group cohesiveness, adaptability, and growth. The death of a fellow member was an emotional experience for the group, however. Not only did it remind the other members of their own mortality, but collective ignorance about the causes and meanings of life and death led to a fear of dying and of the dead themselves—*thanaphobia.* This fear undoubtedly contributed to the invention of a variety of methods for dealing with death and efforts by the living to gain some control over it.

The great diversity in the modern world of cultural rituals and customs concerning death originated from both a psychological need to cope with thanaphobia and a practical need to dispose of the deceased and his or her belongings. According to anthropologists, these death rites may either relieve or intensify anxieties about death. Anxiety concerning immortality and the afterlife may be decreased, but the loss itself, the need for social readjustment, and the possible existence of spirits and ghosts may precipitate additional anxieties in the living (Lessa, 1976).

Although the beginnings of death customs and rituals were associated with magic, myth, and religion, to some extent they have become self-perpetuating and continue to exist even in the absence of strong religious feelings. For example, just as Moslems make pilgrimages to Mecca and Christians and Jews make the journey to the Holy Land, nonreligious Communists attach great importance to traveling long distances to visit the graves of Marx and Lenin. Even when they involve no true religious sentiment, such rituals serve to strengthen the feeling of belongingness or togetherness with other devotees.

Research on the anthropology of death, which is the subject of this chapter, requires the services of archaeologists, linguists, theologians, and psychologists, as well as cultural anthropologists and historians. Information is obtained from relics and documents discovered in archaeological digs of ancient graves, tombs, churches, and other structures, from manuscripts and records preserved by monasteries and in other ancient collections, and by anthropological studies of primitive cultures that continue to exist in out-of-the-way places of the world today. The findings thus far have revealed a kaleidoscope of practices and beliefs concerning death. Each culture has, to use Kastenbaum and Aisenberg's (1976) term, its own *death system,* a conglomerate of rituals and beliefs by means of which a society attempts to cope with death and come to terms with it. Many of the elements of any death system are oriented toward the seemingly universal and timeless belief that the dead do not cease to exist, but rather continue to function in some kind of afterlife.

Funerary Rites and Customs

Strictly speaking, humans are not the only creatures known to bury their dead. Elephants have been observed burying dead elephants and other animals with mud, leaves, and earth (Douglas-Hamilton & Douglas-Hamilton, 1975). Large quantities of food, flowers, and fruit are sometimes included in these elephant graves. Burying behavior has also been observed in other animals; in fact, it has been speculated that early humans may have observed and copied the burying behaviors of animals (Siegel, 1980).

Be that as it may, no other animal buries its dead with as much deliberation and detail as man. In a typical modern funeral, for example, the grave is carefully prepared and the corpse is scientifically treated and neatly groomed. One or more services or events, at which the behavior of participants and spectators is carefully prescribed, are performed. As we shall see, the funeral rituals of individuals of rank were even more elaborate and painstakingly planned in ancient times.

Purposes of Funerary Customs

Social customs associated with burying and mourning the dead serve a variety of purposes. Among these are disposing of the body, assisting the deceased in afterlife activities, and reaffirming or rearranging the surviving social group. Archaeological evidence suggests that these purposes applied in ancient as well as modern times. For example, the presence of food, tools, and ornaments in the graves of Neanderthals who lived over 50,000 years ago suggests a belief in an afterlife (Williamson, Evans, & Munley, 1980).

Observations of funeral customs among primitive peoples living today, coupled with the archaeological evidence, lead to the conclusion that some kind of burial rites have existed since Lower Paleolithic times (circa 500,000–250,000 B.C.) (Middleton, 1982). Rather than being motivated by hygienic considerations, about which early man knew nothing, these burial ceremonies were undoubtedly prompted by fear of the supernatural. The ceremonies were used as a means of placating the ghosts of the deceased by facilitating their journey to the spirit world and their existence therein. Funerary rites also served in later time to honor the dead and find favor with the gods. The rites and customs became more elaborate as time passed, and in certain instances were set down in writing, as in the Egyptian and Tibetan versions of The Book of the Dead. These books provide detailed outlines of the death systems of their respective cultures, including instructions for treatment of the deceased in accordance with specific views of the afterlife.

Funerary rites and customs served not only religious purposes, but they also became occasions for artistic, engineering, and even scientific achievements. The seemingly magical creative endeavors of the tomb and monument builders of Egypt, Greece, and other ancient cultures undoubtedly contributed to the feeling that mankind was not utterly helpless in the face of death. The construction and decoration of these structures also provided occasions for cooperative action, thus reaffirming the vitality and permanence of the community.

Disposal of the Corpse[1]

Human beings, both ancient and modern, have shown an almost obsessive concern with proper disposal of the dead. There are sound hygienic reasons for this concern, but these were not the primary historical aims of corpse disposal. In the main, people have been anxious to get rid of corpses as quickly as possible in order to circumvent the activities of ghosts and to assist the dead in finding peace.

Interment (Inhumation). Burial of the corpse in a covered or enclosed pit, cave, or other structure, in which it eventually decomposes, probably has been the most common method of disposal (Middleton, 1982). It is also the most ancient method, dating back to the Paleolithic era. Among certain ancient peoples, such as the early Egyptians and Peruvians, the body was specially treated with preservatives before interment, a process known as *mummification.* Similarly, in the modern world the corpse is often chemically treated or embalmed before interment to preserve it for a time. Another practice was to bury the body, wait until the flesh had decomposed, and then exhume the bones for cleaning and a second burial in a final resting place.

Open-Air Disposal. Not all cultures buried their dead, of course. Some simply let the corpse rot on the ground, in a tree, or on a specially constructed scaffold. Such was the practice among certain Australian aborigines and American Indian tribes. Even today, the Parsee people of India practice the ancient Zoroastrian rite of placing their dead on scaffolds

---

1. The material in this section was abstracted from a variety of sources, including *Encyclopedia Americana* (1982, Vol. 8), *Encyclopaedia Britannica* (1983, Vol. 5), *Chamber's Encyclopedia* (1976, Vol. 4), and *The World Book Encyclopedia* (1983, Vol. 7).

known as high *dakhmas* ("towers of silence"), where the bones are eventually picked clean by vultures. Zoroastrians believe that other methods of corpse disposal defile the basic elements of nature (earth, air, fire, water).

Water Burial. Certain Pacific Island and early northwestern European cultures did not share the Zoroastrians' concern that dead bodies would contaminate the water. To these seafaring folk, water burial seemed the natural way to dispose of a corpse. Water burial also occurs in modern times whenever a person dies at sea and his body cannot be preserved until land is reached.

Cremation. Burning of the corpse is a common burial practice, dating back to antiquity. It was the primary method of corpse disposal during the Bronze Age, especially among the Hindus, Buddhists, and Romans. The Roman practice of *os resectum,* in which a severed finger joint was buried after cremation of the body, was probably a symbolic representation of the earlier custom of interring the entire body ("Death Rites & Customs," 1983). The rise of Christianity, which, together with Judaism and Islam,[2] opposed cremation, put a stop to the practice in western Europe for a time. Until the Second Vatican Council (1962–63), canon law of the Roman Catholic Church forbade cremation as a proper form of disposing of the dead. However, cremation of Catholics is now permitted, and Roman Catholic priests can take part in services for cremated persons.

Cremation has grown in popularity in recent years, especially in predominantly Protestant countries. In a typical cremation, a gas or electric crematory is heated to 2,000–2,500° F, the coffined body is placed inside, and is reduced to five pounds or so of ash (actually, calcified material) in approximately 80 minutes. The ashes are then disposed of in various ways, for example, by scattering them on a holy river (in the manner of the Hindus) or some other natural formation, storing them in a special vault, or keeping them in an attractive urn.

Cremation possesses a number of advantages over other methods of body disposal, including space conservation and public health considerations. But there are legal complications in certain cases, in addition to religious opposition. Murder is more easily concealed by cremation than burial, and therefore the cause and circumstances of death must be carefully determined before a body is cremated.

Mortuary Cannibalism. Among the most distasteful ways of disposing of a dead body is by eating it. The corpse may be eaten by other animals, as

---

2. The ancient Hebrews considered burial to be the only proper manner of disposing of a corpse, a practice which influenced Roman Catholic doctrine and remains the custom among Jews and Catholics today. Moslems oppose cremation, because Islamic doctrine holds that the dead, like the living, feel pain (Bardis, 1981).

in the Zoroastrian rite, or, in whole or part, by other humans. In *endocannibalism,* the deceased was consumed by a member of his or her own family. Archaeological evidence of mortuary cannibalism has been found in Peking man of 500,000 years ago and in Neanderthal man. In more recent times, certain Australian aborigine tribes and the Luiseño Indians (southern California) were mortuary cannibals.

Mortuary cannibals believed eating a portion of the deceased's body endowed them with the virtues (and vices) of the deceased, thus uniting the dead with the living. This magical feature of mortuary cannibalism has been incorporated into various religions. For example, the Christian sacrament of communion (Eucharist) and the associated ritual changing of the bread and wine into the body and blood of Christ, *transubstantiation,* has been interpreted as having a symbolic connection with mortuary cannibalism (Lessa, 1976).

Grave Sites and Structures

In very ancient times people were frequently buried where they fell or, if that was inconvenient, in some randomly selected spot. Stone Age man had special burial sites, mounds, or pits that often became associated with magical and religious rites and beliefs. Fear of spirits and ghosts frequently led to efforts to keep these burial places secret. Then as now, a person's status or wealth influenced the location of his burial place. Selection of a burial site also varied with religious beliefs.

The first known use of coffins and the construction of stone tombs took place in the Near East, particularly Egypt and Sumer, during the third millenium B.C. As time passed, more elaborate stone coffins, *sarcophagi,* were constructed. These sarcophagi had various shapes—oval, curved, houselike, humanlike—and were decorated with symbols and pictures of gods to protect the deceased. During Egypt's first dynasty (circa 3000 B.C.), the earlier burials in graves and caves gave way, at least in the case of royalty and priests, to tombs of massive size. The walls of these tombs were decorated with writings and pictures of various kinds, depicting the life and beliefs of the deceased (Seele, 1983).

Pyramids. The ancient Egyptians became most famous for those wonders of the ancient world, the pyramids. The oldest known structure of this kind, the Step Pyramid, was built around 2650 B.C.[3] The most widely known, however, are the three pyramids of Giza, which were constructed 150 years later. These three structures and the surrounding pyramids com-

---

3. Contemporaneous with, and in some instances predating, the Egyptian pyramids were the Sumerian *ziggurats,* temples built in a pyramidal shape as a series of terraces.

prise a *necropolis,* a City of the Dead; other necropolises are at Memphis and Thebes.

Each pyramid was actually designed to be the tomb of a pharaoh or other royal personage. In addition to housing the mummy of the deceased, it contained precious objects, foodstuffs, and other materials to ease the deceased's life in the next world. The pyramidal shape presumably assisted the *Ka,* or soul, of the dead person in climbing up the sun's rays to join the gods in the sky (Mertz, 1983). An inspection of the interior of a pyramid reveals a complex maze of numerous passageways and blind alleys to confuse grave robbers. Nevertheless, the robbers (and Egyptologists!) eventually succeeded in relieving all the known pyramids and other Egyptian tombs of their treasures.

Greek Tombs.[4] Decorative sarcophagi and tombs were also constructed by other ancient peoples. Most early Greek corpses were placed in simple sepulchers (tombs) cut out of rock or in graves similar to those in use today. However, as seen in the Tomb of Mausolus at Halicarnassus in Caria, the tombs of royalty or heroes during the classical Greek period were often quite impressive and artistic. The art of *sepulchral iconography* rose to a high peak in such monuments. In addition to a brief inscription, a sepulchral iconograph depicts the deceased carrying out some action for the last time and the grief of the survivors. The ancient Greeks believed, as did other ancient peoples, that such sepulchers had magical powers and hence should be treated as shrines.

Roman Tombs. The Etruscans, whom the Romans displaced as rulers of the Italian peninsula, were constructing stone tombs and terra cotta sarcophagi around 600 B.C. The Romans were also great builders of tombs. Because burial in the city was forbidden, tombs lined the Appian Way and other roads leading in and out of Rome. The ruins of many of these early tombs, including those of Gaius Cestius, Caecilia Metella, Hadrian, and the tombs at Pompeii, are popular tourist attractions today.

The early Roman Christians had no elaborate tombs, but they had the catacombs, a system of underground passageways on the outskirts of the city that were used for burial purposes. According to Roman law, such burial places were sacred sanctuaries; the early Christians could take refuge in the catacombs without being pursued inside by the authorities.

Jewish, Christian, and Moslem Tombs. Like the Greeks, the Jews during Christ's time usually cut tombs out of rock. This practice was followed in early Christian tombs, which were fairly simple structures. Christianity subsequently made up for the simplicity of these funerary monuments, and

---

4. The sections on tombs were abstracted from various sources, especially *The World Book Encyclopedia* (1983, Vol. 19).

many of the Christian tombs of later centuries were quite rich and elaborate. But perhaps none can compare with the Taj Mahal, the famous Islamic tomb built by Shah Jahan in Agra, India, between 1630 and 1652.

Contemporary Tombs. Almost every modern nation has one or more famous tombs that attract thousands of visitors annually. In the United States are the Tomb of the Unknown Soldier, Grant's Tomb, and the Tomb of George and Martha Washington. The most famous sarcophagi are those of George Washington (United States), Napoleon Bonaparte (France), the Duke of Wellington (Great Britain), and V. I. Lenin (Soviet Union).

Treatment of the Corpse

Several ancient methods of treating corpses (cremation, eating, etc.) already have been discussed. The corpse may also have been dismembered, and each of the resulting parts buried in a different place. Such was the case with William the Conqueror. The body was buried at Saint-Etienne, the heart in Rouen Cathedral, and the entrails in the Church of Chalus. More typically, a corpse was groomed and adorned before disposal. It was usually cleaned, anointed, and covered with some colored substance. Among certain primitive European peoples, it was customary to cover or bury the corpse in ochre (iron pigment), perhaps because of the belief that the red color would revitalize the dead. In addition, the various body openings were often plugged and the eyes closed. Early Christians perfumed the body, after which it either was covered with a shroud or left naked. Depending on the individual's social status and wealth, ornaments might be added to the body as well as a more expensive covering, for example, linen. The Chinese pared the corpse's nails, shaved its head, and dressed it according to rank ("Death Rites and Customs," 1983).

Mummification. As in life, wealth had its privileges in death.[5] In ancient China, for example, dead men of higher social rank were buried in better suits (with several spare suits!) than those of lower social rank. But no cultural group spent more of its material and human resources on deceased persons of high rank than the early Egyptians. The elaborate treatment accorded a dead pharaoh and the expense of his funeral preparations have seldom been duplicated. Other nations have constructed magnificent tombs for their leaders, but none like the pyramids. And other peoples have embalmed their royalty, but none as expertly nor on such a scale as

---

5. Just as high social status had its advantages in death and life, low social status had its disadvantages in both situations. In every culture, there have been groups of people who at death were not accorded special rites or ceremonies. Among these individuals were infants, slaves, criminals, suicides, heretics, and victims of violent death or illness.

the early Egyptians. Consider the following description of embalming and mummifying a deceased Egyptian royal personage.

> First, a metal hook was used to remove the brain. This process was completed by means of encephalic drainage (dissolving the remainder with drugs). Then, with an Ethiopian stone, the side was cut and the viscera were removed (evisceration). After filling the abdomen with palm oil, spices, and aromatic powders, the body was sewn up. Thus, mainly the less corruptible skin, cartilages, and bones remained. These were dehydrated by immersion of the corpse in salt of natron for 70 days. Hundreds of yards of fine gauze and bandages, protective amulets, stone eyes, and more aromatic substances completed mummification. At each stage, which symbolized a step in the death and resurrection of Osiris, the priests recited passages from the sacred texts—for instance: "You will live again, you will live again forever! Behold, you are young again forever!" (Bardis, 1981, p. 20)

Not included in this description is the rite of opening of the mouth of the mummy, which was done to restore the mummified body's ability to breathe, see, and take nourishment. Another important procedure was hiding the mummy in the tomb to protect it from grave robbers and other ne'er-do-wells.

Other Cultures.   Unlike the Egyptians, the Greeks of Homer's time never embalmed corpses. Rather the corpse was washed and perfumed and, in the case of a hero, cremated together with several servants. Whether or not the deceased was a hero, a coin (*obolus*) was placed in the mouth of the corpse to pay Charon, ferryman on the river to Hades.

Moslems, who have traditionally opposed both embalming and cremation, pour a mixture of sugar and water into the mouth of the deceased. Then the mouth is tied shut, the two great toes are tied together, and the body is cleaned and perfumed before burial (Bardis, 1981).

Posture and Orientation of the Buried Corpse

Traditionally, graves have been dug rather deep, usually six feet or so, to avoid seepage, odors, and exhumation of the dead by animals or other grave robbers. In Western cultures, the pit is dug wide enough for the body to lie horizontally, although certain cultures have interred the body in a sitting position or even upright. Some Australian aboriginal tribesmen bury their dead in a vertical position with a space above the head, and dead Japanese are buried seated in tublike coffins.

During primitive times the corpse was typically buried in a fetal position. Jonas (1976) maintained that Cro-Magnons were buried in this position because of their belief that it would facilitate rebirth. However, the fetal posture of the skeletal remains of many ancient people is probably due to binding the arms and knees of the corpse to the chest. The purpose of binding the corpse in this fashion was presumably to keep the soul of the deceased from "walking" and hence disturbing the living. In later times, the body was buried in a horizontal position.

With respect to the directional orientation of the corpse, the face in horizontal burials was usually turned toward the west, perhaps emphasizing the death (of the sun). In ancient Egypt from 2500 B.C. onward, however, the body was placed with its head to the north and its face to the east. This easterly orientation of the face was presumably chosen to indicate rebirth (of the sun) (Lessa, 1976). Early Christian burial was with the feet to the east, a position in which it was believed that the "last trumpet" could best be heard and responded to.

In modern times, the custom of directing the feet eastward continues in modern England, although some Christians are buried with their feet pointed toward Jerusalem. The associated belief is that, with their feet pointed toward the Holy City, the dead will be more ready to rise up and meet Christ there on Judgment Day. Other religions dictate other body orientations. Moslems are buried lying on the right side, head toward the north and feet toward the south, with the face turned toward Mecca. Buddhists are buried on their backs with the head facing north, which is believed to have been the Buddha's dying position ("Dead, Disposal of the," 1976).

Grave Goods

The presence of various kinds of valuables and other goods found in prehistoric graves suggests a belief in an afterlife. For example, the grave of a Neanderthal man who lived approximately 70,000 years ago in what is now southwestern France also contained a leg of bison with the flesh still attached. The implication of this finding seems to be that the leg was buried to provide meat for the deceased in the next life. The goods accompanying the dead in later graves included not only food and drink, but ornaments, weapons, and implements of various kinds. Occasionally the objects were quite large, such as those discovered in the Sumerian city of Ur. Excavators of one of the 5,000-year-old graves found in this city, which is located in modern Iraq, discovered, in addition to the skeleton of a king, a chariot,[6] the remains of a donkey to pull the chariot, various weapons, tools, valuables, and 65 members of the royal court! Apparently

---

6. On a similar scale were ship burials, which occurred in northern and western Europe during the pre-Christian era. Ship burial is based on the belief that the deceased must make a sea journey to the land of the dead. The deceased is buried in a boat, which may or may not be burned, and then an earthen mound is raised over the ashes or unburned boat ("Dead, Disposal of the," 1976).

the ladies, soldiers, and grooms who made up this entourage had taken a lethal drug, marched to their assigned positions, and died (Woolley, 1965).

The killing of wives and servants to accompany the deceased also occurred among the Scythians, a nomadic people who lived in southern and eastern Europe from 600 B.C. to 100 A.D. This ancient practice also occurred in more modern times in the *suttee* custom (northern India) of cremating alive the wife of the deceased. The early Egyptians followed a similar practice, but *paddle dolls* later replaced people in these rites. These dolls, shaped from thin strips of board into small canoe paddles, were placed in Egyptian tombs to act as servants and friends to the deceased in the spirit world. The tombs also contained household furnishings and food, the latter presumably being replenished periodically by attending priests.

The practice of burying goods in graves continued during the time of ancient Greece and Rome and down through the Middle Ages. In addition to boat fare for Charon, a dead Greek was provided with honeycakes for Cerberus, the three-headed dog that guarded the entrance to Hades. Even today, modern African societies and other cultural groups place grave goods alongside the dead body. The practice in many of these contemporary societies, however, does not imply a belief in an afterlife, but rather is a custom signifying the termination of the social position occupied by the deceased.

Prefunerary Rites

Today's emphasis on dying and death as essentially private affairs to be kept from public view, and on rationality and efficiency in dispatching the dead, contrasts sharply with the social nature and extensive preparations for death that characterized previous times. Woodcuts of death scenes in medieval Europe depict crowded rooms, with friends, servants, clergymen, and even animals attending the dying person.

Throughout history, many cultures have placed a great deal of emphasis on both the dying person and his associates being properly prepared for his death. Buddhist teaching, as described in the Tibetan Book of the Dead,[7] provides details on how a dying person should concentrate on the experience in order to have a good reincarnation or to become free of the birth-death cycle. Traditional Jewish teaching encouraged the dying person to put his or her spiritual life in order by confessing and repenting. By expressing personal fears in open communication with loved ones, the dying person obtained social as well as spiritual support. In addition, the

---

7. A similar purpose was served by the *Ars Moriendi (The Art of Dying)*, a book written in the late Middle Ages. It contained advice for both the dying person and his or her relatives, as well as religious sayings, prayers, and answers to questions about salvation.

survivors received instructions from the rabbi on how the dying person should be treated and how his or her affairs should be handled. Dying persons of the Roman Catholic faith were administered the sacrament of *extreme unction,* now called "anointing of the sick." In this ritual, which was performed as much in the hope of curing the sick or injured person as in preparing his or her soul for the next world, the person's eyes, nose, mouth, ears, hands, and feet were anointed with sacred olive oil while prayers were said for his or her health. In addition to this sacrament, it was very important to confess one's sins to the priest. It was believed that, if the last rites were not performed, the unconfessed or otherwise unprepared soul would be seized immediately by demons as soon as the dying person took his last breath. On the other hand, a properly prepared soul would be taken by the angels.

In medieval and Renaissance Europe, a continuous vigil known as a *deathwatch* was usually maintained beside the bed of the dying person, and a death knell (bell) sometimes sounded as soon as the person died. In some societies, the deathwatch continued even after the person had expired, perhaps in the hope (or fear) that he might return to life. The modern-day Irish wake harks back to the earlier custom of filling the hours of the deathwatch with entertainment to "rouse the ghost."

Other prefunerary practices in medieval Europe, some of which have continued into modern times, include opening all doors and windows, turning mirrors toward the wall, stopping clocks, removing tiles from the roof, and either emptying all water receptacles or filling them for use by the deceased. The exact origins of many of these customs are unknown, but they presumably had to do with superstitious beliefs concerning the activities of ghosts. As archaic and quaint as these practices may seem to us, they did provide people with ways of coping with their fears of death. They also brought individuals closer together, creating a sense of community that is often lacking in the practices of today (Lessa, 1976).

Funeral Transports and Processions

In addition to methods of disposing of the corpse, funeral rites and customs include special ways of transporting the corpse to the grave, the apparel and treatment of mourners, and their behavior in the funeral procession and afterward. Great care has often been taken to make certain that the spirit of the dead does not return to haunt the living. For example, the corpse may be blindfolded, taken from the house by a special door that is later sealed, and carried to the grave by an indirect route; thorns may then be strewn along the path from the grave back to the house or town. Loud sounds and bad odors, or in exceptional circumstances, dismemberment of the corpse, have also been employed to ensure the nonreturn of the spirit.

Finally, in some instances it was considered taboo to speak the name of the deceased for fear that it might arouse his ghost from sleep (Lessa, 1976).

The funeral custom of walking in procession was introduced by the Romans into Britain when they invaded the British Isles in 43 A.D., but it did not originate with them. A highlight of a Roman funeral procession was the parade of the death masks of the deceased ancestors. Today people of many different religions—Hinduism, Judaism, Christianity, Islam—march in procession to the place of burial, or in the case of Hindus, to the place of cremation. The Romans also introduced into Britain the funerary practices of wearing black and raising a mound over the grave (Hambly, 1974). Mourners in other cultures might wear black or white, but their garments were typically colorless. It is also of interest in this connection that the older practice among Roman Catholic priests of wearing only black to funerals and using black candles gave way to white vestments and white candles after the Second Vatican Council (1962–63) ("Death Rites and Customs," 1983).

The funerals of pharaohs in ancient Egypt also included a journey by the deceased, first to the river and then across the river in a boat. A gathering of people on the west bank then voted to decide whether the deceased had been a good or a bad king. If the decision was "good," his body was buried in a tomb. But if the decision was "bad," the body was simply dumped into the river (Hardt, 1979).

Lamentations

The behavior of mourners during and after funerals has often been quite impressive and dramatic. Mourners may cover their faces with mud (ancient Egypt), tear their clothing (Jews, Moslems), let their hair become unkempt (Moslems), turn their clothing inside out and walk backwards (Australian aborigines), and even mutilate themselves (various cultures). They may wail, shriek, and engage in other wild actions. Since ancient times, societies have also hired professional mourners—usually women who are highly gifted in simulating hysterics—to walk and otherwise "perform" in funeral processions (Lessa, 1976).

In addition to the hysterical wailings of professional mourners, lamentations may be expressed in dirges (funeral songs and songs commemorating the dead), dances, art, and writings. The ancient Greeks and Romans also honored the dead by means of funeral games and banquets.[8] Chinese and Irish cultures, to name just two others, have also emphasized the more optimistic aspects of death, celebrating it on occasion with

---

8. Jewish custom also prescribes a "meal of recuperation" for mourners, a practice also followed by certain Christian groups.

festivity and revelry. To add to the festivities, animal and even human sacrifice was a funerary practice in certain ancient cultures (Lessa, 1976).

Although living in a world where death was ever-present, and realizing that all people die, primitive man was not ready to accept death as the end of personal existence. Being close to nature, and therefore aware of seasonal cycles in which death in winter is followed by rebirth in spring, was undoubtedly a factor in the interpretation of death as a transition from one stage of life to another (Cavendish, 1977). Thus death was viewed as a kind of rite of passage from this world to the next. In fact, many early customs and myths characterize life and death as a cyclic process similar to the growth, death, and revival of plants.

Religious Beliefs

Myths, Religion, and Death

Every culture has had *myths*, which are stories that concern the creation of things (e.g., the world, human beings, gods) or explain events (sickness, death, etc.). To people outside the culture, these myths are viewed as interesting but fanciful folk tales and legends. But the myths are sacred and true to members of the culture in which they originated. Consequently, myths are a significant part of the religious life of many societies and a forerunner of institutionalized religion. The majority of myths concern the actions of supernatural or divine beings, who possess human characteristics as well as superhuman powers. These beings may even look human, at least in part or in idealized form, and they interact (both socially and sexually) with real people. The actions of these godlike creatures frequently go back to primordial time, as in myths concerned with the creation of the world from a primal substance (Babylonian and Hebrew myths) or from a giant egg (Chinese and Hindu myths). Supernatural beings are viewed as responsible not only for creation, but also for death: people die because of the actions of mythical beings (Long, 1982).

Unlike the modern scientific view of death as a natural event that signals the end of an individual's existence, most religions, like the mythologies that preceded them, have depicted death as an unnatural occurrence resulting from the actions of supernatural beings. Also unlike the scientific viewpoint, religions do not consider death to be final or complete; the body dies, but the soul continues to exist.

Concern about death and about life after death has varied extensively with culture and religion. The early Sumerians (circa 5000 B.C.), for example, were more interested in life than in life after death. They believed that, since the gods had assigned death to man when he was created, they would not help him in death. As we have seen, the ancient Egyptians gave much more attention than the Sumerians to death. The Egyptians enjoyed life, but sadness and tears accompanied the death of a loved or revered person. They thought of death constantly, and although they had no god of death as such, two Egyptian goddesses (Sekmet and Bastet) were associated with death. The ancient Greeks, on the other hand, placed the responsibility for death squarely on the shoulders of a single male deity—Thanatos (Bardis, 1981).

Like the ancient Egyptians, the early Chinese enjoyed life and were simultaneously concerned about dying. Historically, the Chinese valued longevity, and the death of an elderly person was as much an occasion for rejoicing as for mourning. Consistent with their reverence for long life was the Chinese belief that the death of a young person is a sign of an evil spirit at work, and hence a threat to other people. They also believed that, at death, the body-soul system is dispersed and the dead person becomes a sacred ancestor.

On the more modern scene, Islam is fatalistic about death. The time of a person's death, it is believed, is fixed in advance. Mohammed taught that because a person's death is predetermined, it should be accepted joyfully and without fear. In fact, those who die in defense of Islam are guaranteed a place in heaven. This credo, of course, is similar to the early Greek and Viking beliefs that warriors who die in battle go to a special place (Elysian Fields or Valhalla, respectively). Islam has many other beliefs and teachings in common with those of other cultures and religions. Moslems believe, for example, that death is caused by a supernatural being—the Angel of Death—who steals the soul of the deceased (Adams, 1983; Bardis, 1981).

The Judeo-Christian view of death and life after death developed over many centuries. In actuality, both the Old and New Testaments have relatively little to say about death and afterlife. Furthermore, interpretations of Old Testament statements such as "a time to be born, and a time to die" (Eccles. 3:2) must consider the historical context in which the statements were written. In the New Testament, there is no specific passage in the synoptic Gospels (the first three Gospels) in which Jesus Christ discusses the subject of death (Gatch, 1980). Rather, it is in the writings of Paul of Tarsus that death is described as man's last and greatest enemy, an enemy whose power results from man's sinfulness (1 Cor. 15:50–57). Paul taught that, except for the intervention of Christ, who died on the cross to atone for man's sins, death would mean obliteration. By the resurrection of Christ, Paul preached, man has attained victory over death. In Paul's words, "Christ was raised up from the dead by the glory of the Father, even so we can also walk in newness of life" (Rom. 6:4). Several centuries later, St. Augustine in *The City of God* interpreted Paul's writings on the subject as meaning that death is a punishment for sin and that only divine grace can free man from the fear of death.

Immortality and the Soul

As witnessed in the elaborate process of mummification and writings in the Egyptian Book of the Dead, the ancient Egyptians believed in a life after death. This belief is indicated in the myth of Osiris, the god of the underworld, who was reassembled and came back to life after being cut up into 14 pieces. Henceforth, immortality was assured by the intervention of Osiris. The ancient Greek and Roman myths also describe a life after death, and even earlier peoples, e.g., Neanderthals, apparently believed in immortality. In fact, such a belief is much older than the concept of personal extinction. The latter notion, that individual identity ceases to exist at death, appeared first in early Buddhism (sixth century B.C.) and two centuries later in the writings of the Greek philosopher Epicurus (341–270 B.C.). The concept of personal extinction maintains that after death a person no longer exists as a distinct personality but becomes, as before birth, one with nature or the cosmos (Bardis, 1981).

The Soul. All religions teach that something of the individual survives death, but they differ on what it is that survives. The early Egyptians did not clearly distinguish a person's mind or soul from his physical structure, as revealed in their attempts to ensure immortality for the pharaohs by preserving their bodies. Although the Egyptians had a word, *Ka,* roughly equivalent to the English *soul,* the Ka lived in the person's mummy after death. In contrast, the dualistic concept of a discardable physical body and an inner, immortal soul, which was proposed in the ancient Greek philosophy of Orphism, greatly influenced Greek thought and religious beliefs.[9] The Orphists taught that the personality of the deceased is retained in an immortal soul.

The ancient Hebrew Bible contains no specific discussion of personal immortality or the concept of soul. The book of Genesis can be interpreted as implying that either (1) man's mortality was part of God's original plan of creation, or (2) man was originally created as immortal, but God took away the immortality as punishment for man's disobedience. In any case, man is mortal and whatever immortality he may attain is collective rather than personal. Jehovah did not promise Abraham personal immortality but rather perpetuation of his line through a multitude of descendants. Thus, in ancient Judaism there is no such thing as a personal afterlife, and the individual's life acquires meaning only in its contribution to the mission of the People of the Covenant (Gatch, 1980). Social or national immortality was the dominant theme among the Jews well into the time of Christ. But during the second century B.C., due to the influence of Zoroastrianism, the belief in personal immortality of the soul gained

---

9. People in many primitive societies have believed in *animism,* the doctrine that every natural object in the universe, and even the universe itself, has a soul.

strength among the Pharisaic Jews. After the destruction of the temple at Jerusalem in 70 A.D., the concept of resurrection of the dead became a part of orthodox Jewish faith.

Like the Old Testament, the synoptic Gospels of the New Testament contain no specific reference to a soul or nonphysical aspect that survives death. Again, it is in the writings of Paul, who was greatly influenced by Greek thinking on the matter, that the idea of a soul is enunciated. Expanding on the concept, Paul and other early Christian thinkers saw damnation and salvation of the soul as determined by the actions of a person during his or her lifetime. However, even a sinner can be saved by the unmerited favor and love bestowed by God on human beings (God's *grace*).

Reincarnation. The single physical lifetime of Christian doctrine contrasts with the multiple lifetimes conceptualized by Eastern religious thinkers. In many religions, especially Hinduism and Buddhism, life and death are likened to points on a constantly moving wheel. Each person has a succession of lives, being reborn or reincarnated after death into a life form determined by his or her character and actions (*karma*) during his or her previous lifetime. According to the doctrine of *reincarnation,* the soul is born again as another human being or animal. Each successive life form is determined by the lessons that a person has not learned during his or her previous life. For example, if one behaves like an animal and fails to learn obedience, then he or she may be reincarnated as a dog. Both Hinduism and Buddhism teach that only when the soul is purified and the individual finds identity and unity with the cosmos (Nirvana, Enlightenment, Brahman, the Universal Power) can it break the continuous cycle of life, death, and rebirth (Bouquet, 1982).

Although it was more time-consuming to travel between East and West during ancient times, there was still some communication between Far Eastern and Mediterranean cultures. Consequently, it is not surprising to find the influence of the Eastern concept of reincarnation, or transmigration of souls, in Plato's writings. And, as we have seen, the doctrine of immortality and rebirth of the soul espoused by Plato had a profound influence on Paul and Christian theology.

Resurrection. The concept of reincarnation in Hinduism and Buddhism is not a resuscitation of the dead in the same form, but rather a metamorphosis. The belief in physical *resurrection,* or the return of the dead to life in bodily form, existed in part among the ancient Egyptians, however. The process of mummification and associated rites were supposed to enable the deceased to live forever in his well-equipped tomb. The Zoroastrians of ancient Persia also believed in resurrection of the dead, a belief that was communicated to and absorbed by Pharisaic Judaism and subsequently by Christianity and Islam (Toynbee, 1980). It was Paul's message that Christ's resurrection in both body and spirit holds out the promise of personal resurrection of body and soul to all who believe in him and have attained salvation. As Christ said, "and whosoever liveth and believeth in me shall never die" (John 11:26).

The Land of the Dead

Many myths and religious stories describe the soul after death as traveling to a land of the dead. This realm may be in the sky, deep within the ground, on top of a high mountain, inside a mountain, in the ocean, or in some unspecified place. Belief in the first two locations prevailed in ancient Egypt. The sun god Ra lived in the heavens, and the god Osiris ruled in an underworld that was entered by way of the grave. At night, the soul (Ka) either followed Ra on his journey across the sky or, according to the dominant viewpoint, remained in Osiris's underground fields. But at dawn Ka returned to its mummy and spent the day in the tomb.

Wherever the land of the dead might be, the journey to it was often fraught with obstacles and dangers—rivers to be crossed by bridge or barge, monstrous animals to be faced, and personal humiliation or pain to be endured. The gradual unfrocking of the goddess Ishtar of Babylonian mythology as she descended to the land of the dead and the labors of Hercules in Hades are cases in point (Bardis, 1981).

Hades. On arriving in the land of the dead, the ancient traveling soul was likely to find it a dreary abode of shadows where the spirit-residents would rather not be. The most detailed description of this land was given by the ancient Greeks. Their land of the dead, which was ruled by the god Hades (Pluto) and his queen Persephone (Proserpina), was a dreadful place that had to be approached by a river, Styx or Acheron. The fee paid to the boatman Charon to ferry a soul across the river was an obolus (coin) carried in the mouth of the deceased. The deceased also brought along some honeycakes to bribe the ferocious, three-headed dog Cerberus that guarded the entrance to the underworld. After passing through the gates of Hades and being judged, the soul was assigned to one of three sections—Tartarus (the worst section), the Plains of Asphodel (an intermediate section), or the Elysian Fields (the best section). The Elysian Fields, or Isles of the Blessed, was the abode of heroes and others favored by the gods.[10] Despite his assignment to the Elysian Fields, the Greek hero Achilles described it as unpleasant compared to life on earth. Nevertheless, his dissatisfaction was nothing compared with that of Sisyphus, who, as punishment for having fooled the god Hades, was condemned forever to Tartarus. There Sisyphus must spend eternity rolling a huge stone to the top of a high hill, at which

---

10. Similar to the Greek Elysian Fields is the Scandinavian Valhalla, a great hall in the sky reserved for those who died in battle.

point the stone rolls back down the hill and he must start all over ("Death Rites and Customs," 1983).

Heaven and Hell.   Somewhat similar to the model of Greek mythology, the great religions of the world describe the land of the dead as consisting of two, three, or even more sections. Comparable to the Greek Hades are the Mesopotamian *Land of No Return,* the Hebrew *Sheol,* and the Scandinavian *Hel.* The sorrows and tortures endured by residents of Tartarus are shared by those forced to abide in the Moslem and Christian hell. These tribulations of the damned in hell are vividly and fearfully described in Dante's *Inferno.* In contrast to the sufferings of the souls of sinners, however, are the delight and peace experienced by those who have attained salvation and gone to heaven. Both Christian and Islamic texts describe heaven as a gardenlike paradise permeated by the spirit of God (Allah).

Purgatory.   Early Protestant theologians (Martin Luther, John Calvin) maintained that the dead, depending on how they are judged, are consigned to either heaven or hell. However, both Catholic and Moslem theology maintain that there is a third region—*purgatory*—for souls about whom a final judgment has not been made. The existence of such an intermediate zone was not original with Christianity or Islam. Dante's Purgatorio is reminiscent of the Plains of Asphodel of Greek mythology and the ten hells of Chinese Buddhism. But Christianity and Islam tied the notion of purgatory to that of the last judgment. Whereas those who had committed mortal sins went directly to hell, persons judged guilty of venial (pardonable) sins could atone for those sins in purgatory while awaiting final judgment.

Testing and Judgment

Both Eastern and Western religions view life as a time of testing for the individual; a person's actions in this life determine what becomes of him or her in the next. But the standards according to which a person's life is evaluated vary from religion to religion. In general, Christianity and Islam have demanded a more ascetic (austere) life,[11] whereas Hinduism and Buddhism have stressed the importance of contemplation and mysticism. Furthermore, except for the existence of purgatory, the outcome of the test is final in the case of Christianity. In Eastern thought, however, a failed life test can be taken again in a subsequent reincarnation. The outcome of the test might be described as "pass/fail" in the case of Christianity, compared

---

11. As in Christianity, asceticism in Islam varies with time and sect. In general, Moslems believe that a person should do his or her best to be good and helpful to others, while trusting in the justice and mercy of Allah to decide his or her fate (Adams, 1983).

with "pass/try again" in Hinduism (Pardi, 1977). Zoroastrianism also subscribes to a pass/fail system, but the test is less difficult than that of Christianity. The prophet Zoroaster taught that a moral life is sufficient to attain life after death and that it is not necessary to live an ascetic life.

Asceticism or Damnation. Eastern religions do not necessarily deny the importance of asceticism and individual suffering. Certain sects of Buddhism, for example, are quite stern in their belief that bodily deprivations and pain are important to moral uprightness. The emphasis on asceticism in Christianity also varied with the particular sect and time period. The belief reached a high point during the late Middle Ages, when life was characterized as a "place of trials" that one must endure and a "veil of tears" through which one must pass stoically in order to achieve a heavenly reward. The consequences of failure to follow the teachings and ascetic example of Christ, whatever the personal cost, were vividly described as endless torment and mortification in hell. There one would suffer not only severe physical punishment but would be forced to listen to his or her evil deeds gleefully and perpetually recounted by a horde of devils. Because eternal damnation was likely if one were deprived of the last rites of the Church, a sudden death was to be avoided at all costs and was constantly feared during the Middle Ages (Aries, 1974).

Battle of Good and Evil. Many ancient myths influenced the development of the world's great religions. One of these myths is that a last great battle will be fought between good and evil before the world ends (God vs. Satan, Ahura Mazda vs. Ahriman). Revelation 16 describes this final battle as occurring at a place in central Palestine known as Armageddon. Once the battle is joined, a savior figure will arise to save the day for the forces of good. Then, as described in Zoroastrian, Hebrew, Christian, and Moslem myths, the living and the dead will be judged and consigned to either heaven or hell.

Last Judgment. The belief in a judgment after death, the outcome of which determines whether the soul goes to heaven or hell, existed among the Egyptians, Persians, Greeks, Hebrews, and many other ancient peoples. The Egyptian judge was Osiris—god of the underworld—and the Zoroastrian judge was Ahura Mazda—the god of light. The three judges of Greek mythology were Minos, Aeacus, and Rhadamanthys, divine residents of Hades. The biblical Old Testament proclaims a day of coming of the Lord (Amos 5:18–20), at which time the Israelites will be called to task for their sins, and Israel and other nations of the world will be judged.

Early Christian theology described judgment in two stages—an initial judgment immediately after the death of the person, and a final judgment after the second coming of Christ. At the time of the last judgment, when the world has ended, souls will be reunited with their bodies and a final decision will be made to consign the individual to heaven or hell. Similar to the Christian belief is the Moslem credo that on the last (judgment) day of the world, everyone will be given a record of his earthly deeds. If the record book is placed in the individual's right hand, he or she has been adjudged good and will go to heaven. But if the record book is placed in the left hand, he or she has been deemed bad and will be sent to hell (Adams, 1983).

SUMMARY

Historically, death has been both a personal and a social event. Death produces existential anxiety and fear of the supernatural, but also leads to group reorganization and increased cohesiveness. The death system of a society consists of a composite of rituals and beliefs by which the society attempts to cope with death.

Perhaps human beings are not the only creatures to bury their dead, but they certainly do so more painstakingly than other animals. Funeral customs or rites, which go back to antiquity, serve a threefold purpose: disposing of the corpse, helping the corpse to find peace, and reaffirming the social group. The primary methods of corpse disposal are inhumation (burial) in the ground or caves and cremation. However, water burial and eating by other humans or animals have also been practiced. The use of coffins and tombs probably began prior to the third millenium B.C. The most elaborate stone coffins and tombs in ancient times are the sarcophagi and pyramids of Egypt. Many of these structures, including the sarcophagi and tombs designed later by the Greeks, Romans, Christians, and Moslems, were elaborately and beautifully decorated. The ancient Egyptians also practiced mummification of the corpses of royal persons and priests, as did the ancient Peruvians.

The position in which the body is placed in the grave has varied with religious beliefs and social customs. It has also been the practice since Neanderthal times to bury various objects (food, weapons, ornaments, other people, etc.), referred to collectively as *grave goods,* with the corpse.

In addition to religious sacraments, prefunerary rites have included a variety of superstitious rituals to pacify or confuse the ghost of the deceased person. Funerary rites such as transporting the corpse and marching in procession to a holy place or burial site are found in many different cultures. These rituals have also included lamentations, religious services, and, in some cases, festivities (games, banquets, etc.).

As suggested by the presence of grave goods and other indicators, primitive man apparently believed in a life after death. The later development of myths is based on this early belief, in addition to other beliefs about the creation of the world, phenomena of nature, and death. Cultural myths, which are concerned with the activities of superhumans or gods, were the antecedents of formal systems of religious beliefs. Like myths, religions offer explanations of natural phenomena, including the origin and fate of the cosmos, and man in particular, as well as guidelines for human conduct.

Although the Sumerians, Egyptians, Greeks, and other ancient peoples had many myths and associated religious beliefs, the principal religions have been Hinduism, Buddhism, Judaism, Christianity, and Islam. The teachings of these religions developed and changed over the centuries, influencing each other and hence having many elements in common. One shared belief is that human beings have immortal souls. Hindus and Buddhists, however, subscribe to the doctrine of reincarnation, whereas Jews, Christians, and Moslems believe in resurrection.

The location and character of the land of the dead also varies with the particular mythological or religious system. Best known to people in Western culture are the Hades of ancient Greek mythology and the heaven (paradise)-purgatory-hell (inferno) complex of medieval Christianity. Each of these designs, as well as the land of the dead in other mythologies and religions, consists of several sections or zones reserved for souls of different character.

Both Eastern and Western religions teach that life is a time of trial or testing, with an individual's actions in life determining his or her next condition or destination. Hinduism and Buddhism maintain that after death a person is reincarnated as an animal or another human, depending on how the individual behaved in his or her previous existence; the cycle continues until the person finds identity and unity with the cosmos. Christianity and Islam, on the other hand, hold that the soul goes to heaven, hell, or purgatory, depending on its record of sins.

The eschatology, or doctrine of last things, in many religions maintains that the world will end with a final battle between good and evil, in which a savior figure will appear to lead the forces of good to victory. After the battle is won, a last judgment of souls—both living and dead—will be made when every person is consigned to either heaven or hell.

SUGGESTED READINGS

Aries, P. (1981). *The hour of our death* (H. Weaver, Trans.). New York: Knopf.

Choron, J. (1963). *Death and Western thought*. New York: Collier.

Huntington, R. & Metcalf, P. (1979). *Celebrations of death: The anthropology of mortuary ritual*. Cambridge: Cambridge University Press.

Leca, A. P. (1981). *The Egyptian way of death*. (L. Asmal, Trans.). Garden City, N.Y.: Doubleday.

Lifton, R. J. (1977). The sense of immortality: On death and the continuity of life. In H. Feifel (Ed.), *New meanings of death*. New York: McGraw-Hill.

Long, J. B. (1975). The death that ends death in Hinduism and Buddhism. In E. Kübler-Ross (Ed.), *Death: The final stage of growth.* Englewood Cliffs, N.J.: Prentice-Hall.

Siegel, R. K. (1980). The psychology of life and death. *American Psychologist, 35,* 911–931.

Toynbee, A. (1984). Various ways in which human beings have sought to reconcile themselves to the fact of death. In E. S. Shneidman (Ed.), *Death: Current perspectives* (3rd ed.). Palo Alto, Calif.: Mayfield.

Turner, A. W. (1976). *Houses for the dead.* New York: McKay.

5 Death in the Arts and Philosophy

Questions answered in this chapter:

- What role does the awareness of death play in artistic accomplishments?
- What are some of the death themes expressed in the nonverbal and verbal arts, and how has the emphasis on different themes varied with the historical era?
- How has the figure of death been represented in the nonverbal arts and literature? Why?
- What are the differences between realism and romanticism, as expressed in the verbal and nonverbal arts since ancient times?
- What are some of the ways in which immortality is treated in literature, and how has the treatment varied with the specific culture and historical period?
- What are some of the similarities and differences in attitude toward death and belief in immortality expressed by the great philosophers?
- In what ways have Eastern religious writings influenced the thinking of Western philosophers on the topics of death and immortality?

*H*uman beings are restless, striving organisms whose activities over the past 5,000 years have altered the shape of this planet. Evidence of these changes, this manipulation of the environment, can be seen almost everywhere. Many factors—economic, political, social, personal—motivated these human efforts and productions. The awareness of personal impermanence and the associated fear of death are not the least of these.

The realization that their days are numbered and that death may be lurking just around the corner has challenged people since antiquity to make the most of their lives and leave their marks on the world. The awareness and fear of death also prompted attempts to understand the human condition and to find some meaning in existence. As we saw in Chapter 4, the uniquely human struggle to find purpose and meaning in life contributed to the great religions of the world. These theological systems are the products of human discovery and creativity, just as the arts and philosophy are.

Sigmund Freud believed many achievements of human culture, including the arts and sciences, philosophy and religion, and even civilization itself, stemmed from the operation of the psychological defense mechanism of *sublimation,* the channeling of (sexual) energy into socially acceptable forms (Lindzey, Hall, & Manosevitz, 1973). Freud emphasized the central role of sexual energy, *Eros,* in all seemingly higher-order activities; interpreted in its broadest sense, *sexual* means *life* or *creative energy.*

As recognized by Freud and other influential thinkers, the creative impulse is the opposite of the death instinct, *thanatos.* Death means destruction, and, unless one is convinced of a life after death, individual death implies personal extinction. In any case, creative artists and philosophers have been concerned with death; they have theorized about it; constructed funerary monuments, painted, sculpted, and etched death scenes; composed elegies, requiems, and tales about death; and staged dramas concerned with death and dying. In fact, it is interesting to speculate whether many famous artists, composers, and writers would have reached such high levels of creativity and productivity without an awareness of death (Goodman, 1981). Knowing that their time was limited perhaps served as a stimulus to action, an impetus toward greater exploration and achievement. Thus, it can be argued that the awareness of death prompted them to make something special of their lives, to convert their potentialities into actualities. As a consequence, they were able to reach the end of life with fewer regrets about what they had not accomplished. To the creative person even greater than the fear of death is the fear of living an incomplete life, a life that is too short or time-consuming to do the things that he or she is capable of doing (Goodman, 1981). This feeling is obviously not unique to artists and philosophers, but rather something they have in common with all people who strive toward self-actualization.

Death in the Nonverbal Arts

The depiction of death in the nonverbal arts (visual designs and musical compositions) is at least as ancient as the Stone Age drawings on cave walls. The themes of death and life after death, for both religious and commemorative purposes, have been represented in painting, sculpture, architecture, and music for thousands of years. Mythological beings and their activities provided the stimuli and content for much of the world's art, inspiring masterpieces in painting, sculpture, music, and poetry. Many works of art also stemmed from religious motives and therefore contain religious themes. In addition, they express the living person's fear of death, the democracy of death, and other more secular (and moralistic) themes. These works range from the sublime to the ridiculous and from the inspirational to the obnoxious, depending on the tastes of the viewer or listener. But they also reveal something about the artist and his or her time, especially the fears of annihilation and punishment, the hopes for an afterlife, and the desires to represent and understand the human condition.

Funerary Monuments

Tombs, sarcophagi, and the associated art of sepulchral iconography were discussed briefly in Chapter 4. From the time of ancient Egypt and Greece, down through the Middle Ages, and into the modern era, many of the sculptured scenes on tombs and caskets have been essentially com- memorative. They were designed to keep alive the memory of the dead in the minds of the living. In other instances, funerary monuments were con- structed to serve magical or religious purposes.

One common scene that appears on funerary monuments, both an- cient and medieval, depicts the deceased performing some activity. The deceased is usually shown as in life, healthy and dressed according to social standing. But in the *memento mori* tombs of the late Middle Ages (thirteenth–fifteenth century), an effigy of a naked, decaying corpse or skeleton is shown below the figure of the deceased as he or she appeared in life. The purpose of this double image was to illustrate the corruption of death and perhaps its equalitarianism ("Death," 1983).

Themes of Death

Memento mori tombs are only one indicator of the preoccupation or obses- sion with death that characterized the late Middle Ages. The obsession is not surprising, considering that the period from the thirteenth through the fifteenth century in Europe was a time of almost continuous conflict, star- vation, and disease, in which death and destruction were common sights. It has been estimated, for example, that during the fourteenth century the population of Europe was reduced by one-fourth because of the ravages of the Black Death (bubonic plague) alone (Tuchman, 1978). Death was everywhere. Since it was nearly impossible to live the ascetic life they had been taught would merit a heavenly reward, people were threatened by an afterlife in hell that was even worse than what they were experiencing on earth. Themes and scenes of the Last Judgment and the tortures inflicted on sinners in hell were common in painting and sculpture, especially during the early part of the period. Such scenes exerted a powerful effect on the public fear of eternal damnation, and undoubtedly assisted the Church in its efforts to dominate human thoughts and actions. Nevertheless, after a thousand years of almost uncontested control over the religious beliefs of Western society, the hold of the Roman Catholic Church in Europe was beginning to weaken during this period.

In addition to the memento mori tombs, the late Middle Ages was a time when the *triumph of death,* the *danse macabre* (dance of death), and the *Ars Moriendi (Art of Dying)* were featured in all the arts (Tuchman, 1978). The first of these features is represented in Francesco Traini's (1350) fresco entitled *The Triumph of Death.* The painting shows three young knights on horseback who encounter three coffins containing corpses at progressively greater stages of decay. This fresco and similar works of art (e.g., the Tomb of Cardinal Lagrange in the Musée Calvet, Avignon) were concerned with the *vanity theme.* The message is that no matter how attractive a person may be or how high his or her station in life, he or she will soon be a rotting corpse. Another representation of the vanity theme is found in a painting of a beautiful young girl staring at her skeletal reflection in a mirror.

The theme of the danse macabre, or dance of death, found in medieval art refers to an allegorical dance in which Death leads a group of people to their graves. The fact that many of the followers are high-status members of the nobility or clergy demonstrates again the vanity theme. By illustrating the democracy of death—the proud and humble, rich and poor, good and bad, are all equal in death—the vanity theme in medieval art was interpreted in somewhat secular fashion as implying that one's situation or conduct in life has no bearing on his or her fate.

The *Ars Moriendi* is a written treatise, apparently prepared by German monks, that provides details on how to die in a dignified, holy manner. The scenes of devils, fornication, murder, and robbery with which the treatise was illustrated, however, whetted and/or satisfied the appetites of people of the time for ghoulish, macabre art. Despite the fact that actual death was visible almost everywhere one went, the artists of the time dwelled on the themes of violence and mortuary putrescence. Popular paintings showed corpses being mutilated, worms crawling through decaying bodies, and ugly bulbous toads squatting on glassy human eyeballs. It was, indeed, a time of artistic preoccupation with death that has not been equaled since, and that stands in stark contrast with the beautification, romanticism, and denial of death that characterized later times.

The obsession with death during the late Middle Ages was not limited to famous works of art. Death also became a popular art theme depicted on jewelry, in woodcuts, statues, poems, and dramas. In ancient Egypt and Rome, silver skeletons and miniature coffins were sometimes presented to the diners at feasts to remind them of their mortality and encourage them to enjoy themselves while they still could. But such party antics were not representative of the public feeling in ancient times and were not indicative of a general "cult of the dead" of the sort that existed in Europe during the late Middle Ages (Boase, 1972; Tuchman, 1978).

Similar memento mori and "playing with death" antics are found in certain modern cultures (see Report 5-1). In a historical sense, such bravado in the face of death often has been the stuff of which heroes are made. Daring or challenging death is socially admired behavior—at least up to a point—in many cultures. But beyond that point, taking unnecessary chances ("laughing in the face of death," "spitting in the eye of the devil") is considered extremely foolish or insane.

The Middle Ages obviously was not the only historical period in which death influenced art. Representations of death in the visual arts and poetry were commonplace in early Greece (Vermeule, 1979), and, as in the Middle Ages, these representations were not merely symbolic. Early Greek art depicts the dead undergoing horrifying physical tortures in the underworld, humans and deities being raped and slaughtered, and heroes being mutilated in battle. Nevertheless, the general atmosphere in early Greek art is heroic rather than necrophilic. The early Greek theme of human fortitude and competence in the face of mortality became fashionable again during the Renaissance period (sixteenth–seventeenth centuries). New geographical and scientific discoveries led people to believe once again that they could prevail against nature, an optimism that was reflected in all art forms.

The theme of death appears extensively in the nonverbal arts, albeit often in romanticized form, down through the nineteenth century. Unlike their counterparts in previous centuries, twentieth-century painters have dealt with the subject of death rather sparingly. This is a reversal of the popularity of the theme during the Middle Ages, which has in common with the twentieth century the slaughter of millions of people. Even when twentieth-century painters deal with the subject of death, unlike the reality of the nineteenth century, it is typically indirect or symbolic (Gottlieb, 1959).

Representations of Death and Immortality

From the Bronze Age to the Atomic Age, death has been personified and symbolized in a variety of ways in art. The most widely known personifications are the Angel of Death, the Rider on a Pale Horse, the Grim Reaper, and the Twin Brother of Sleep. Death may be a skeleton, a mummy, a shrunken body, or an old man or woman. It may be naked, covered with a white or black shroud, or dressed in some other distinctive attire. It may be

REPORT 5-1

The Mexican Way of Death

by Ron Arias

Poet Octavio Paz writes that Mexicans are seduced by death. They defy it, mock it, play with it, and in some stories they even make love to the figure of death. Not that Mexicans, he adds, are unafraid of death, but they must try to touch it, for in that touch life is given its truest meaning. It's the ultimate act of selfhood, an attempt to transcend life and the solitude of human existence.

To most Americans this may sound cultish, morbid. Here in North America we prefer to elevate life and serenely usher death into tiny boxes that are carried to precisely cut rectangles in the ground. Nothing messy, no residues of what death really is—a few bones, stillness, perhaps an afterlife, perhaps oblivion. Grief should be shortlived, get on with life. Tough it out. I once heard an Englishman say, "dwelling on it only retards health and progress."

These two ways of coping with death—one sprung from Indian-Catholic roots, the other from an Anglo-Protestant past—admittedly are extreme, as I've described them. Most urban dwellers, whoever they are, probably approach death in similar urban ways—with funeral parlors, graveside prayers, consolations. We do what the system allows.

Still, there's one time of the year when the difference between north and south surfaces. In the United States it's Halloween, in Mexico the Dia de los Muertos, or Day of the Dead (actually two days, November 1 and 2).

In this century, Halloween marks but almost never celebrates the eve before All Souls Day, since remembering the dead doesn't seem to mesh well with a night of pumpkin lanterns and giggly, costumed children. The Day of the Dead, on the other hand, is just as festive yet quite different in purpose and expression. Even if Mexicans and by extension Chicanos, don't openly celebrate this holiday, the everpresent display of barrio skulls and skeletons in the form of masks, candies, bread, cookies, and papier-mâché figures underscores a typically Mexican closeness or familiarity with death. Behind the parades, the laughter, church Masses, and a profusion of cemetery flowers lurks the very real grimace—some say entreaty—of one's own death, not just that of those already buried.

I'll explain. About five years ago my six-year-old son was killed in a stupid freak accident. He was hit by a car that jumped the sidewalk and swept him under its tires, lacerating his liver. A few hours later he died.

The following week Benito, a Mexican friend of mine in Aguascahentes, Mexico, sent my family some toy plaster skulls. He hadn't known of my youngest son's death. The gifts, all with our names boldly written across each bony forehead, were a mischievous—you might say affectionate—reminder of our mutual humanity, our own common mortality. Benito meant nothing morbid. I told myself, it's a Mexican custom. The toys were simply folk products of a city known throughout Mexico for its enthusiastic celebration of the Day of the Dead. He even sent them in March in a show of his year-round playfulness. Aguascahentes, by the way, was the home of Jose Guadalupe Posada, a turn-of-the-century caricaturist whose skulls and skeletons (calaveras) later influenced the paintings of such muralists as Diego Rivera and David Alfaro Siquieros.

At the time, I shrugged off the grim coincidence of Benito's gifts and my

113

son's death. Yet, strangely, we kept those skulls around the house and in view. They weren't obvious, but they were there. My other son and I even fiddled with the string that pulled the flapping jaw up and down. We never talked about it, but I'm sure my wife—from a Jewish family but quite familiar with everything Mexican—understood what was really at play with these reminders that Benito had innocently sent us. Looking back, I see them now as embodiments of a presence that came crashing into our lives, stealing our will to live in the present yet shoring us up for the future. Paradoxically, Benito's lighthearted gesture—along with the embrace of almost everyone else we knew—helped us through the worst of times.

No, I don't celebrate the Day of the Dead in the Mexican way. A second generation Chicano, I was raised literally and figuratively between Glendale's predominantly Anglo Forest Lawn and East Los Angeles' mostly Mexican (at least in recent years) Evergreen Cemetery. Thus, I had two choices for coping with death, and I chose neither. Instead, like so many urban Chicanos, I've worked out a blend of two traditions, two emotions. My behavior isn't entirely Mexican, yet I haven't completely entered the controlled mechanistic world of Anglo answers to grief, fear, and the unknown.

An Aztec poem says the following:

Must I go like the flowers that die?
Won't anything be left of my name,
Nothing of my life here on Earth?
At least flowers
At least songs.

It's an ambivalent view of death, one certainly not endorsed by the friars who converted the Aztecs, at least nominally, to a belief in immortality. But this very ambivalence is what most often is misunderstood by those outside the Mexican culture, and it is what Octavio Paz and others try to explain. We may believe in an afterlife, we may even be good Catholics, yet an uneasiness toward death persists. So why not celebrate it, play with it, mock it, challenge it? Outsiders may call it fatalism, bravado. But for Mexicans and many Chicanos this careless defiance, when carried to an extreme, is a matter of affirmation, even ecstasy.

An Anglo friend of mine recently witnessed a scene that shocked and puzzled him. In a California bar patronized mostly by Mexican farm workers, a group of men were gathered around a table covered with broken glass. Two of the men, one at a time, were competing in a bloody contest to see which man could smash down more empty bottles than the other. The bottles were gripped by the throat, pointed upward and brought down hard, resulting in quite a few glass-skewered palms and fingers. The men, of course, had drunk much and my Anglo friend was told that this was the kind of contest that frequently took place in some parts of Mexico. These men were just having a go at it here.

I explained to my head-shaking friend what I knew and felt of Mexican death, of defiance, of a damn-it-all approach to life, of moments of truth and selfhood. All academic, he couldn't quite grasp its meaning—perhaps something to do with sacrifice—any more than many of us can fathom what occurs in the minds of gang members when bullets and knives shatter a closed-in desperation.

Myself, I prefer a milder approach to death. It's part practical American, part Mexican grandmother, my own. She was realistic and, it seemed to me, amused to the end. About 80 years old and dying, she could clown about her wasted appearance, her toothless mouth, her skeletal hands. Not long before she died she motioned for me to come close to her bed. At the time, I was young, impatient. Life was all. Shakily, she touched my hand, winked one glaucous eye and said: "Asi como me ves, te veras"—as you see me now, so you will see yourself.

Even today, years later, her words won't leave me. They are stronger, far more insistent than Benito's toy skulls. In this sense I am familiar with death. At times, I joke about it, and luckily I have not yet needed to defy death. There is no desperation in my voice, so I can now whisper—but warily—that I don't intend to be seduced.

From Arias (1981). Reprinted by courtesy of Ron Arias.

standing menacingly, riding a horse, or lying in a coffin, often grinning or leering. It may be carrying a scythe, sword, dart, bow and arrows, or some other weapon to deliver the mortal stroke that severs a life.

Death has also been represented symbolically, usually by obvious symbols such as coffins, cemeteries, amputated limbs, deathbeds, skulls, and bones. Other easily understood symbols for death are an inverted torch and a clock set at the "hour of death" (12:00 P.M.–1:00 A.M.). The association of death with time is also seen in Holbein's painting *Dance of Death,* in which Death is depicted as a skeletal figure holding an hourglass. In another painting, Dürer's *The Knight, Death, and the Devil,* the figure of Father Time carries a scythe. Other common symbols of death are environmental scenes such as winter landscapes, ruins, leafless trees, trees struck by lightning, dead birds, and vultures (Gottlieb, 1959). One of the earliest representations, which was found in a Neolithic settlement located in modern Turkey, shows gigantic, black, vulture-like birds attacking headless human corpses (Cavendish, 1970).

Birds and certain insects (butterflies, beetles) have also been used since ancient Egyptian and Greek times to represent the soul and immortality. The butterfly and beetle (scarab) symbolized the soul (Ka) and immortality (resurrection) to the ancient Egyptians, and the "soul bird" was a common symbol in early Greek art. Reptiles that shed their skins, and are consequently presumed to be immortal, are symbols of immortality in certain, primitive cultures. The Judeo-Christian tradition, of course, views snakes as symbolic of evil rather than immortality. Another lower animal, the fish, was a symbol of early Christianity. The symbol was presumably derived from the Greek letters for Christ, which somewhat resembled a fish; the symbol is also related to Christ's injunction that the apostles be "fishers of men." The cross, however, is the most time-honored symbol of the Christian religion and resurrection.

Some famous works of art and the death symbols used in them are Francesco Traini's *Triumph of Death,* corpses; Hans Baldung Grien's *Three Ages of Woman and Death,* skeletal figure with hourglass; Albrecht Dürer's *Four Horsemen* and *Knight, Death, and the Devil,* rider on a pale horse; Marc Chagall's *Gate to the Cemetery,* cemetery; Albert Ryder's *Death Bird,* dead bird; Pablo Picasso's *Vanities with Skulls,* human skulls,

115

and *Woman Kissing a Crow,* crow; and Salvador Dali's *Persistence of Memory,* broken watches (Gottlieb, 1959).

Music

As with funerary monuments, the role of music in death has been closely associated with religion throughout human history. The masses of Johann Sebastian Bach, several of George Frederick Handel's oratorios, requiems such as the one by Wolfgang Amadeus Mozart, the hymns of Charles Wesley, and many other musical compositions are sacred in nature. Thousands of chants, dirges, and songs have been composed to express sorrow, longing, and love for the dead. Funeral music is common throughout the world, assuming different forms in different cultures. Like poetry, music has a peculiar ability to strike the emotional chords that are associated with death and dying and to make life and death seem meaningful.

Death in Literature

Beginning with the oldest known poem, the *Epic of Gilgamesh,* death has been an enduring topic in literature throughout human history. Transcending both time and place, poems, stories, essays, and other written compositions on death and dying have been exceeded in popularity only by works concerned with love. These two themes are universal; they appeal to the emotions of readers of all ages and in every walk of life. Both love and death transport the reader through the entire range of human moods, from ecstasy to despair. They have also inspired the noblest and vilest of human actions, ranging from heroism to cowardice and from altruism to greed. And in many enduring favorites, such as the story of Romeo and Juliet, the themes of love and death are blended together into a single romantic tale.

Mythological Origins

Mythology has served as a source of inspiration for much of the world's great art and literature. The *Epic of Gilgamesh,* which has been preserved since ancient Babylonian times (circa 2000 B.C.), deals with the activities of mythological beings, both human and divine. The hero of the epic, Gilgamesh, is initially an oppressive Sumerian king. The gods send the champion Enkidu to challenge him in battle, but the two men become friends and share many adventures. After Enkidu dies, Gilgamesh searches for the secrets of knowledge and immortality. He is successful in obtaining a branch of the tree of knowledge and another branch from the tree of immortality. Unfortunately, he drops the second branch while crossing a river. The branch is eaten by a water snake, so mankind gains knowledge but loses immortality. Note the obvious similarities between this story and the biblical tale of Adam and Even in the Garden of Eden. (There is also a great flood in the *Epic of Gilgamesh,* like the one experienced by Noah in the Bible (Kramer, 1982; Weir, 1980).)

Other mythological tales also attempt to explain how death came to mankind. Many cultural groups have believed that people were originally meant to be immortal and that death is an unnatural intruder. According to myth, death arrived as the result of a mistake—a message wrongly delivered; a punishment for human disobedience, ingratitude, or stupidity; the outcome of a debate or contest between divine beings or the first humans. Common in Africa is the myth that God sent the chameleon to tell human beings that they were immortal, but the chameleon dawdled along the way and the lizard—the messenger of death—arrived first (Cavendish, 1970).

Primitive people, who undoubtedly observed snakes shedding their skins and seemingly rejuvenating themselves in this manner, presumably came to the conclusion that people originally possessed the same ability. According to one African myth, a serpent was sent by God to deliver the message to human beings that all they had to do to be young again was to shed their skins. The serpent repeated the message to a bird, but the bird failed to deliver the correct message. In similar myths, insects or other animals are told to inform people of their immortality, but the messengers go astray or the messages are garbled in some way. In another skin-changing story, a child sees its mother changing her skin. According to different versions, the mother either dies immediately or climbs back into her old skin when the child cries, thus losing the opportunity for immortality.

As seen in the Old Testament story of Adam and Eve, death may be viewed as a punishment for human transgression. A similar explanation is found in an Australian aborigine myth. A tribe of aborigines was forbidden by God to steal honey from a beehive located in a certain tree. The men obeyed God, but the women approached the tree and one hit it with an axe; out flew the bat of death! A Blackfoot Indian myth tells of a debate between the first old man and the first old woman. The man wanted people to live forever, but the woman argued that this would result in more people than the world could hold. They agreed to settle their dispute by a game of chance. If a piece of buffalo meat thrown into the water floated, then humans would be immortal. But the old woman used her magical powers to change the meat into stone, which, of course, sank. Human beings thereby were condemned to mortality (Cavendish, 1970).

Tales such as these formed the basis of oral stories, and ultimately literature, in ancient cultures. Explanatory myths concerned with the origin of death and the destination of the dead, for example, were the sources of much Greek poetry and art (Vermeule, 1979). As seen in the poetry and sculpture of Greece during the Bronze Age, memories and tales of dead ancestors and heroes had a significant influence in early Greek civilization. It would be incorrect to characterize these effects as a cult of the dead, but the dead were revered and featured extensively in stories and poems. The resulting classical literature not only reflected but also helped determine Greek interest in death. For example, the scenes of the underworld and its tortures described in Homer's *Odyssey* undoubtedly had a profound effect on the attitudes and behavior of the ancient Greeks.

Personifications of Death in Literature

Death in ancient Egyptian literature was occasionally represented as a jackal-headed god named Anubis. Homer used another animal—the mythological winged Harpy—to depict death in the *Iliad.* The jackal and other animals with pointed ears, horns, long snouts, and splayed tails also represented evil, and death sometimes intermingled with evil in the same form.

A connection between death and the Devil is seen in the myth of Christ's descent into Hades; Death is often depicted as a skeletal figure prostrate beneath the victorious Christ (Cavendish, 1970). In the literature of certain cultures, death is described as a monster with multiple heads and hands, a villain who uses a built-in flamethrower or other weapon to attack humans. Such a monstrous death god was referred to (perhaps appropriately) as Uggae in ancient Mesopotamia.

As in the nonverbal arts, personifications of death in the ancient literature of both the Occident and the Orient include a humanlike individual dressed in black or red and carrying a scythe, spear, rope, timepiece, and so on. Later Greek mythology presented death as a winged youth with a sword, and the literature of the Vedic period of Hinduism (1500–450 B.C.) describes death as Yama, the first man. In a Hindu poem of a somewhat later period, the *Mahabharata,* death is characterized as a beautiful, dark-eyed woman, Mara (or Mrtya). According to the poem, Mara came from within Brahma, creator of the world, and was ordered by him to kill all the world's creatures. Due to the intercession of the god Shiva, the deaths were not made permanent; the slain individuals were reincarnated as other forms of life. Another deathlike figure in Hindu literature is the goddess Kali, the consort of Shiva, a black person with three eyes and four arms who gorges herself on the blood of her victims.

Ancient Persian literature associates death with time, so the god of time, Zurvan, is also the god of death.[1] In Hebrew literature, death is an

---

1. Although the Koran refers to an Angel of Death, Islam strictly forbids depicting death as a person in painting or sculpture. In fact, it forbids artists from making images of any human or animal, living or dead. It is reasoned that an artist who paints or forms something lifelike is trespassing on the divine right of Allah (Ettinghausen, 1983).

angel known as Sammael (the drug of God). In the New Testament, death is described as the "last enemy that shall be destroyed" (1 Cor. 15) and as riding on one of the baleful horses (Rev. 6) (Cavendish, 1970).

Death has been personified in modern Western drama and literature as a pale-faced man in a long, black cloak (*The Seventh Seal,* by Ingmar Bergman), a hunter who stalks human beings (*Journey to Ixtlan,* by Carlos Casteneda), and a blundering fool dressed in a black-hooded cape and skin-tight black clothes (*Death Knocks,* by Woody Allen) (Weir, 1980).

The Inevitability and Universality of Death

Many death themes and scenes have appeared in literature, including the inevitability of death, the universality of death, the fear and love of death, murder and suicide, romanticized death, deathbed scenes, bereavement, and immortality. Interestingly enough, primitive peoples frequently appear to have been unaware of the naturalness and inevitability of death. When one lives in a culture in which people usually die of accidents or diseases rather than old age, it is understandable how death could come to be viewed as an unnatural consequence of something gone wrong. Even in more developed cultures, there is a pronounced tendency to act as if death were not inevitable—at least not for "me"—until something happens to shake one's feeling of invulnerability.

Although writers have been tempted by the human tendency to deny the inevitability of death, many playwrights, poets, and novelists have succeeded in directing the reader's attention to the fact that death comes to all (see Weir, 1980).[2] The realization of the certainty of death, as enunciated in Thomas Gray's "Elegy Written in a Country Churchyard" and Jean-Paul Sartre's *The Wall* and *The Victors,* is a disturbing, or at least sobering, experience. The inevitability of death can be a source of death anxiety, but it can also stimulate individuals to make the most of the time they have.

Realism and Romanticism

Historically, the fear induced by the realization of death has been handled in a variety of ways, for example, by reveling in or laughing at death, by romanticizing it, and by denying or suppressing thoughts of death. None of these solutions is completely objective, but each has been emphasized in the art and literature of different periods. As in the nonverbal arts, emphasis on the physical aspects of death—blood, decaying flesh, worms, and

---

2. Refer to the quotations from poems by Henry Wadsworth Longfellow and Edna St Vincent Millay at the beginning of Chapter 1.

other "realistic" images—was an obsession in the literature of the Middle Ages. The memento mori, the dance of death, and the preoccupation with the "maggotry" of death can be interpreted as a kind of psychological extinction process: by absorbing oneself in the paraphernalia of death, one gradually becomes less terrified or anxious about it. Such wallowing in death is exemplified by the illustrations from the *Ars Moriendi* treatise of the late Middle Ages—emotional deathbed scenes, grave diggers uprooting bones, vicious black devils fighting with angels over the naked corpse or soul of the deceased. Other indicators of this cult of the dead in literature were scenes in plays and mysteries in which, for example, Christ's body is viciously hacked by Roman soldiers, a mother roasts and eats her own child, or a woman's belly is sliced open so an emperor can see the place where children are conceived. In addition to the maggotry and decomposition of death, an erotic-morbid theme in which the ecstacy of orgasm is combined with the agony of death is seen in some of the poetry of the time (Tuchman, 1978).

Tuchman (1978) argues that anxiety over the expected end of the world was associated with the cult of the dead during the Middle Ages. A belief in the approach of Judgment Day was prompted not only by the massive number of deaths caused by war, disease, and famine during the fourteenth and fifteenth centuries, but also by a widespread feeling that sin was becoming rampant and the human soul was aging. The maggotry of death, of course, was not unknown in other historical periods. The theme of the "conqueror worm" was still very much in evidence in the nineteenth century:

> It writhes!—it writhes!—with mortal pangs
> The mimes become its food,
> And the seraphs sob at vermin fangs
> In human gore imbued.
> —Edgar Allan Poe

For the most part, however, eighteenth and nineteenth century literature expressed a hatred for the ugly, violent death and a preference for the beautiful, tame death. The great romances of the Middle Ages (*Chanson de Roland, Le Morte d'Arthur, Tristan and Iseult*) had emphasized the acceptance of death and the proper way to die. But the romantic poets of the eighteenth and nineteenth centuries pictured death as a bittersweet or even attractive destiny, and occasionally expressed a desire for it (Simpson, 1977). The romantic view of death seen in poems by William Wordsworth, Stéphane Mallarmé, Lord Byron, Percy Bysshe Shelley, and the younger Johann Wolfgang von Goethe is also a kind of denial of mortality: the poet will join his lady love in the hereafter.

The denial of death was difficult to maintain in real life, however. Goethe, for example, was actually quite anxious about death, avoiding deathbeds and funerals, and indeed any contact with death whenever possible (Simpson, 1977). The fear of death during the eighteenth and nineteenth centuries was also related to the fear of premature burial, as seen in many stories of the time. Aries (1981) describes the "shelters of doubtful life," or funeral parlors, in nineteenth century Germany. Bells were attached to the extremities of the deceased, who was kept for several days until there was no possibility of reanimation.[3]

Death scenes have figured prominently in both ancient and modern literature (*Epic of Gilgamesh,* Eric Segal's *Love Story*) and in many different cultures (*Dream of the Red Chamber* in Chinese literature). Especially popular in the literature of the Romantic Era were scenes of the death of a beautiful young woman, a child, a wife, or other loved one, and the resulting grief that stressed the sweet sadness and poetic nature of an attractive death. However, deathbed scenes, elegies, and the topic of death in general went out of fashion in Anglo-American culture during the twentieth century. Whereas sex was an unmentionable topic in polite Victorian and Edwardian society (later nineteenth century) and death scenes were popular set pieces, sex has become more popular during the twentieth century and death themes have been muted in art, literature, and drama. The ugly facts of death were disguised and cosmetized during the early twentieth century: people "passed on" rather than died, and they went to rest in lovely gardens rather than being buried (Gorer, 1980).[4]

Despite the tendency to deny, or at least avoid, the subject of death in the twentieth century, it has proven difficult in a time of millions of victims of war and genocide. Whatever theme of romanticism remained in poetry written during the early part of World War I, for example, was extinguished by the reality of wholesale human slaughter in the trenches of Europe. The time-honored belief that it is gallant and noble to die for one's country and the associated chivalrous images of warrior knights battling for honor, country, and ladies fair, gave way to the anger, bitterness, and sorrow of soldier-poets such as Robert Graves and Wilfred Owen:

> If you could hear, at every jolt, the blood
> Come gargling from the froth-corrupted lungs
> Bitter as the cud
> Of vile, incurable sores on innocent tongues—
> My friend, you would not tell with such high zest
> To children ardent for some desperate glory,
> The old lie: *Dulce et decorum est*
> *Pro patria mori.*[5]

---

3. A similar practice is described in *The Great Train Robbery* (Crichton, 1975). Coffins were equipped with bells on the outside and pull-chains on the inside; the chain could be pulled and the bell rung by the "deceased" if he or she happened to regain consciousness.

4. More recently, there has been increased interest in death and horror themes, at least among young people. This is seen in the spate of gory movies and in the names of rock groups such as The Grateful Dead.

5. Reprinted from *The Collected Poems of Wilfred Owen.* Copyright 1946 © 1963 by Chatto & Windus, Ltd. Reprinted by permission of New Directions and the Owen estate.

The realism in literature engendered by the events of World War I has persisted in twentieth century poetry with modifications. Many poets, especially those of the "Confessional School" (Robert Lowell, Sylvia Plath, Ann Sexton), have revealed a fascination with death and especially suicide. Much of their poetry is autobiographical and self-centered, occasionally bordering on the pathological. Theirs is a subjective art form that describes universal truths in terms of the poet's own experiences and expresses little social conscience or concern for other people. This is especially true of the poems of Plath and Sexton, both of whom committed suicide (Simpson, 1977).

Immortality

There are those who end their lives voluntarily, but there is a much larger number of people who wish to live forever. Both the religious and secular literature of Eastern and Western cultures have developed the theme of immortality. The earliest written story concerned with immortality was the *Epic of Gilgamesh*. The associated doctrine of the soul (Ka) also appeared in writing in the Egyptian Book of the Dead at about the same time (circa 2000–1800 B.C.). Plato's philosophical writings on the soul (*psyche*) exerted a greater influence on Western religion and literature, however. The dualistic position proposed in Plato's dialogues describes the body as material and terminating in death, but the soul as immaterial and everlasting. Although Epicurus and certain other philosophers and writers in ancient Greece and Rome questioned Plato's dualistic doctrine, it remained a major influence into the Christian era (Choron, 1963).

The Jewish tradition regarding immortality, as expressed in the second book of Samuel of the Old Testament, is different from that of the Greeks. To the ancient Jews, who perceived death as a "draining away of the body's aliveness," the afterlife kingdom of Sheol was only a land of shadows. The dominant Jewish viewpoint on immortality changed over the centuries, however. During the first century A.D., it shifted from belief in collective, or social, immortality to belief in personal immortality. The early Christian perspective on immortality, reminiscent of Plato's dualism, was stated by Paul in his letter to the Corinthians; the spiritual, but not the physical, body is restored after death (Weir, 1980).

Hindus and Buddhists have no single sacred text such as the Bible that explains the nature of their beliefs in reincarnation. Ancient Hindu scriptures are contained in the Vedas, at least one part of which—the Upanishads—influenced the thinking of a number of Western philosophers and writers. The Hindu conception of reincarnation is best explained in the sacred writings known as the Puranas. Two other sacred writings in Hinduism, the *Ramayana* and the *Mahabharata,* are long epics that contain mythical stories and philosophical principles. Unlike Christianity and

Hinduism, one theory of Buddhism is the "no-soul doctrine" that at death both the mind and the body disintegrate, leaving only a "stream of life" or character disposition, but not a permanent soul, that is reborn in another living being. The stream of life continues until nirvana, a state of eternal bliss and oneness with the cosmos is attained (Weir, 1980). One Buddhist treatise, the Tibetan Book of the Dead, provides minute details on the state of consciousness that exists between death and reincarnation.

In the West, epic stories such as Homer's *Odyssey,* Virgil's *Aeneid,* and Dante's *Divine Comedy* expressed and helped determine conceptions of immortality and the afterlife. On the more modern scene, a belief in immortality is expressed in Goethe's *Faust,* Alfred Lord Tennyson's "Crossing the Bar," Robert Browning's "Prospice," Miguel de Unamuno's fiction, Federico Lorca's dramas, and many other poems, stories, and plays. Perceptions of life after death are provided in D. H. Lawrence's "Ship of Death," Thornton Wilder's *Our Town,* and Amos Tutuola's *The Palm-Wine Drunkard* (see Weir, 1980, Ch. 10 for further details and illustrative selections).

Many Western poets, Emily Dickinson, for example, have revealed a conflict over the notion of personal immortality in their work. The general hope, particularly among those who have been deeply frustrated in their own lives, is for a life after death, but they are not completely confident. Certain poets stress the attainment of biological immortality through one's descendants. Others, in a manner reminiscent of early Judaism, write of social immortality through the enduring influence of one's work on the memory of one's life and personality in the minds of the living. Still others appear to be content with a perhaps more scientific conception of immortality through the survival of the basic elements comprising one's body (Simpson, 1977).

Death in Philosophy

Philosophy, which literally means *love of wisdom,* originally encompassed all fields of human intellectual endeavor. There was *natural philosophy* that included what are now referred to as the natural sciences, *mental philosophy* that dealt with psychological topics, and *moral philosophy* that was concerned with ethics and religion. During the Renaissance and the Industrial Revolution, many specialized areas of knowledge separated from the parent discipline of philosophy and formed their own fields of study (physics, biology, psychology). However, the academic discipline of philosophy is still concerned with questions about the nature of reality, *metaphysics;* the basis of human knowledge, *epistemology;* the principles of right and wrong human conduct, *ethics;* the principles of valid inference, *logic;* and the nature of beauty and judgments of it, *aesthetics* (Lewis, 1982).

Philosophy is similar to literature because it is a creative field, and the results of philosophical analysis are usually recorded in written form. Furthermore, many creative writers are, like philosophers, careful observers and thinkers who desire to understand and explain some phenomenon of nature or human action. Literary writers, however, focus more than philosophers on entertaining, or at least interesting, their readers in what they have to say. In addition, poets, novelists, and other creative writers are usually less concerned with the logic and reality of their works than philosophers, concentrating as much on the form as on the substance of a written composition.

Philosophical Interest in Death

Whereas death and immortality have been the subjects of almost continuous interest by literary writers in all countries and cultural periods, the concern with these topics shown by philosophers has varied greatly with time and place. There was certainly no lack of interest in death among the philosophers of ancient Greece and Rome, but philosophical writing on the topic declined after the fall of the Roman Empire. It was apparently assumed by European philosophers of the Middle Ages that questions pertaining to death and immortality had been solved by Christianity and were consequently the province of religion rather than philosophy (see Choron, 1963; Bardis, 1981).

Even during the Renaissance Period, when the power of the Church began to weaken, philosophers continued to devote relatively little thought to matters of human mortality and immortality. Certain influential figures, such as Benedict de Spinoza, included almost nothing on the topic of death in their formal writings. Spinoza disposed of the topic in one sentence: "A free man thinks of nothing less than of death, and his wisdom is not a meditation upon death but upon life" (*Ethics* IV, 67). In fact, not until the nineteenth century was death once again viewed as a suitable subject for philosophical analysis. Arthur Schopenhauer was the first famous philosopher in modern times to give serious attention to death in his writings, which provided a background for discussions by the late nineteenth and early twentieth century existentialists (Bardis, 1981).

Interested philosophers, or anyone else, might wish to consider the following questions about death.

1. How does a fear of death originate, and how can it be conquered, or should it be conquered?
2. Does death imply permanent extinction, or does something of the individual survive in an afterlife? If something survives, what is it and what is the nature of the afterlife?
3. Does God exist, and if so, how do human beings become aware of him and why should he care about humanity?

4. How should one live life, knowing that death is certain to occur sooner or later?
5. Under what circumstances, if any, is taking one's own life or the life of another person justifiable and acceptable?

Some of these questions are metaphysical, others are epistemological, and still others are moral in nature. Consequently, the search for answers involves a number of philosophical (and nonphilosophical) fields.

Greek and Roman Philosophers

Among the philosophers in ancient Greece who had something to say about death were Pythagoras, Socrates, Plato, Aristotle, and Epicurus. Very brief descriptions of the attitudes toward death espoused by several of these philosophers and their successors are given in Table 5-1. Despite their interest in death, the ancient Greek artists, poets, and philosophers believed in enjoying life while it lasted (not necessarily in a hedonistic fashion). This was specifically the philosophy of Epicurus, the first Western philosopher to conclude that death means personal extinction.

TABLE 5-1
Philosophical Attitudes Toward Death

Socrates (469–399 B.C.): Death may be better than life, and the true philosopher is cheerful in the face of it.
Plato (427–347 B.C.): Death is the release of the soul from the body.
Epicurus (341–270 B.C.): Death is personal extinction, but it should not be feared.
Zeno of Cyprus (335–263 B.C.): We should never oppose unavoidable evils, including death.
Lucius A. Seneca (4 B.C.–65 A.D.): The best way to diminish the fear of death is by thinking about it constantly.
Leonardo da Vinci (1452–1519): Just as a happy day ends in a happy sleep, so a happy life ends in a happy death.
Michel de Montaigne (1533–1592): One learns how to die properly by living properly.
Benedict de Spinoza (1632–1677): A free man meditates on life rather than death.
George W. F. Hegel (1770–1831): Death is the reconciliation of the spirit with itself, a reuniting of the individual with cosmic matter.
Arthur Schopenhauer (1788–1860): Death is the true aim of life and the muse of philosophy.
Ludwig A. Feuerbach (1804–1872): Life must be lived fully in spite of death.
Bertrand A. Russell (1872–1970): When I die, I shall rot and nothing of my ego will survive.
Martin Heidegger (1889–1976): A person's life becomes more purposeful when he faces his own death.
Jean-Paul Sartre (1905–1980): Constant awareness of death intensifies the sense of life.

Source: Adapted from material presented in Choron (1963) and Bardis (1981).

Unlike his more famous predecessors (Socrates, Plato, Aristotle), Epicurus did not believe in a soul, a position also adopted over two centuries later by the Roman philosopher-poet Lucretius (Toynbee, 1980).

Both the Epicurean and the Stoic philosophers were interested in how the fear of death can be overcome. Epicurus taught that freedom from the fear of death can be attained by seeking moderate pleasures, especially the pleasures of friendship, and avoiding pain.[6] Zeno of Cyprus, the first Stoic philosopher, advocated a life based on reason and self-control in the face of death. A later Stoic, the Roman statesman Lucius Seneca, maintained that only by thinking about death constantly can we be prepared for it. Somewhat fatalistic in their outlook, the Roman Stoics Seneca and Marcus Aurelius believed that preparation for death was the only proper goal of philosophy. The Stoics did not place much faith in an afterlife, but rather emphasized the importance of living a satisfying life with no regrets, a life that would not bring shame upon one's family (Bardis, 1981). Understanding how nature works and that human beings are a part of nature presumably facilitates a stoical attitude toward death. This outlook is similar to the Taoist principle in Buddhism, which states that human beings can find happiness and completeness in life only when they discover "the Way" (*Tao*) of nature and surrender to it (Pardi, 1977).

Schopenhauer and the Existentialists

As indicated previously, very little philosophical writing on death appeared from the decline of the Roman Empire until the nineteenth century. One can find statements pertaining to death in the writings of Michel de Montaigne, Spinoza, René Descartes, Gottfried Wilhelm Leibniz, Immanuel Kant, and George W. F. Hegel (see Bardis, 1981), but the topic did not receive serious philosophical attention until Schopenhauer's time. There was, to be sure, a concern with immortality, especially during the eighteenth century (Choron, 1963),[7] but even the great eighteenth century philosophers Kant and Hegel had little to say about death. The precedent established by Spinoza during the seventeenth century was that there are

---

6. The philosophy of hedonism, "eat, drink and be merry, for tomorrow we die," was not precisely what Epicurus had in mind and is wrongly attributed to him. The Epicureans, as well as the Stoics, preached and practiced moderation in all things and did not approve of the notion that one should have fun at all costs (Pardi, 1977). Certainly the drabness with which the afterlife was depicted by the ancient Greeks and Romans made hedonism and the idea of *carpe diem* (seize the day) popular, but it was not due specifically to Epicurus.

7. It was during the seventeenth century that the French mathematician Blaise Pascal proposed his famous "wager" concerning the existence of God (and hence immortality). If you bet that God exists and he actually does not, then you have lost nothing. But if you bet that God does not exist and he actually does, you have lost everything. Therefore, given no choice but to bet, the wiser thing to do is bet that God exists and behave accordingly.

much more interesting philosophical questions, and these do not invade the domain of the theologians or step on the toes of the ecclesiastics.

Arthur Schopenhauer, the nineteenth century philosopher who made the awareness of death a central part of his system, was a pessimistic atheist who viewed life as dominated by pain. In a fashion reminiscent of the Stoics, Schopenhauer maintained that the solution to life's pain is indifference facilitated by an awareness of death. But one cannot be indifferent to death itself, which every animal "instinctively" fears and which Schopenhauer called the "muse of philosophy." Although he characterized life as a struggle for existence—a struggle that must be lost—and did not believe in personal immortality, he maintained that the idea or "will" of the species survives death. Thus, Schopenhauer taught that the species is indestructible and that there is an immortality of nature. This conclusion, of course, is reminiscent of the philosophy of Buddhism, which influenced Schopenhauer's thinking (Choron, 1963).

Other philosophers succeeded Schopenhauer, some agreeing and others disagreeing with his point of view concerning death. Friedrich Nietzsche attacked the idea that death is the muse of philosophy, but the existentialists believed Schopenhauer was correct. Many of the philosophers and philosopher-scientists who came after Schopenhauer and were interested in the problem of death were also atheists or, at most, agnostics. Nietzsche was an admirer of Zoroastrianism, whereas Sigmund Freud, Bertrand Russell, and Jean-Paul Sartre were acknowledged atheists (Bardis, 1981).

Existentialism was the first philosophical school to make a detailed study of death and its meaning to the individual. Existentialists such as Martin Heidegger, Jean-Paul Sartre, and Albert Camus stressed the fact that the awareness of mortality makes people anxious and concerned about whether their lives have any significance. From the existentialist viewpoint, real human happiness is not possible to attain. But the meaningfulness of an individual's life develops from the awareness of its inevitable termination. While admitting that death is absurd—a kind of "cosmic joke" on thinking humanity—existentialism maintains that people do not fear death so much as a meaningless, valueless life. In any case, death loses much of its terror for the person who sees his or her life as having been productive and meaningful.

Sartre did not believe that there is a providential order in nature or a personal immortality; however, he did accept the notion of social immortality and the fact that the individual life can contribute to that immortality. And how does the individual come to make such a contribution? Faced with the inevitability of a personal ending, the individual is spurred into action to live a life that will have some social significance (Bardis, 1981).

Thus, we have come full-circle in this chapter on creativity and death. We began with Goodman's (1981) conclusion from interviewing almost 700 prominent artists and scientists that the fear of living an incomplete life, a life in which one has not had the opportunity to experience or accomplish all that he or she wishes to, is greater than the fear of death. If we accept the conclusion that life must be experienced and acted upon to the limit of one's potential in order to be most meaningful, then the parallel between Goodman's research findings and the conclusions of existential philosophers is apparent. But prominent artists, scientists, and philosophers are not ordinary people, and perhaps they cannot speak for the feelings and attitudes of the average person. Indeed, as we shall see in Chapter 8, there is more to attitudes toward death than is perhaps dreamt of in a great man's philosophy.

SUMMARY

Research findings suggest that the awareness of their finitude has prompted the efforts of creative individuals to achieve something of lasting value. They fear not so much the fact that they are going to die, but rather that they may die without fulfilling their potentials.

The dual themes of death and immortality have been expressed in all art forms. Tombs, sarcophagi, and other funerary art forms have served magical, religious, and memorial functions. Particularly noteworthy in the sepulchral iconography of medieval times are memento mori tombs that depict the deceased in both living and dead images. These images were designed to reveal the corruption of death and to suggest its equalitarian nature (the great leveler). Other artistic themes that illustrate the preoccupation with death during the late Middle Ages are the triumph of death, the danse macabre, and the *Ars Moriendi.*

Death has been personified and symbolized in art in a multitude of ways since the Bronze Age. Common personifications are the Angel of Death, the Rider on a Pale Horse, and the Grim Reaper. Common symbols of death are cemeteries, skulls, clocks, and dead birds.

The origins of much of the nonverbal art and literature concerned with death are found in mythology. One of the earliest mythical stories was the *Epic of Gilgamesh,* an ancient tale of a Sumerian king and his search for immortality. Many myths in primitive cultures attempt to explain how humans became mortal—as the result of a mistake, as a punishment inflicted on humans by deities, or as the outcome of a great debate.

Representations of death in Western literature include grotesque animals and monsters, and a humanlike individual dressed in black and carrying a scythe, another weapon, or a timepiece, and perhaps riding a horse. Similar personifications are found in the literature of the Middle and Far East.

Death has been a popular topic in literature, particularly the themes of the inevitability and universality of death, the beautiful and romantic death, deathbed scenes, grief, immortality, and unnatural death (murder,

128

suicide, death in combat). The obsession with death that characterized the arts during the late Middle Ages is seen in the preoccupation with the maggotry of death in painting, poetry, and drama. A romantic view of death typified the literature of the eighteenth and nineteenth centuries, giving way to a denial of death and then greater realism during the twentieth century.

Ancient Greek and Roman philosophers (Plato, Epicurus, Seneca) were quite interested in the topics of death and immortality, but interest waned during the Middle Ages. Not until the nineteenth century was death once again considered a topic worthy of philosophical analysis. Arthur Schopenhauer was the first modern philosopher to give serious attention to the topic, a precedent that greatly influenced the philosophical school of existentialism in the late nineteenth and early twentieth centuries. Heidegger, Sartre, Camus, and other existentialists agreed with Schopenhauer that death is the muse of philosophy. Expanding on this theme, the existentialists argued that the awareness of death gives meaning to life. The realization that he or she must eventually die motivates a person to strive to live a meaningful, self-actualizing life.

SUGGESTED READINGS

Aries, P. (1981). *The hour of our death.* (H. Weaver, Trans.). New York: Knopf.

Boase, T. S. R. (1972). *Death in the Middle Ages: Mortality, judgment, and remembrance.* New York: McGraw-Hill.

Choron, J. (1963). *Death and Western thought* (I. Barea, Trans.). New York: Macmillan.

Goodman, L. M. (1981). *Death and the creative life.* New York: Springer.

Gottlieb, C. (1959). Modern art and death. In H. Feifel (Ed.), *The meaning of death.* New York: McGraw-Hill.

Hoffman, F. J. (1959). Mortality and modern literature. In H. Feifel (Ed.), *The meaning of death.* New York: McGraw-Hill.

Scholl, S. (1984). *Death and the humanities.* Lewisburg, Pa.: Bucknell University Press.

Simpson, M. A. (1977). Death and modern poetry. In H. Feifel (Ed.), *New meanings of death.* New York: McGraw-Hill.

Tolstoy, L. (1971). *The death of Ivan Ilych and other stories* (L. & A. Maude, Trans.). London: Oxford University Press.

Tuchman, B. W. (1978). *A distant mirror: The calamitous fourteenth century.* New York: Knopf.

Vermeule, E. (1979). *Aspects of death in early Greek art and poetry.* Berkeley, Calif.: University of California Press.

Weir, R. F. (Ed.). (1980). *Death in literature.* New York: Columbia University Press.

6 Legal Aspects of Death

Questions answered in this chapter:

- What are the major legal issues concerning death?
- Why is it important to determine an exact moment of death, and how is the determination made?
- What functions are served by a death certificate, and what information does it contain?
- When are abortion and euthanasia legal, and what are some of the issues connected with these matters?
- What are natural death acts and their merits and shortcomings?
- What are the origins of capital punishment statutes in the United States?
- What are the arguments for and against capital punishment?
- What is the history and nature of the will as a legal document?
- What are death taxes, and what purposes do they serve?

*T*he survival of individuals and groups demands that certain basic needs be satisfied. Human beings have known for thousands of years that both competition and cooperation play a role in need satisfaction, but these complementary processes are much more effective for society as a whole when they take place in an orderly fashion. The existence of order, of course, implies rules and sanctions that, when formalized and codified, are called *laws.*

Although people in Western countries, in particular, are proud of their individuality and freedom, much of their behavior is governed by customs, mores, and laws. There are laws concerning almost every aspect of one's interactions with other people, whether they be living, dying, or dead. Dead, of course, generally means biologically dead, although society and its laws have also differentiated civil death and presumptive death. *Civil death* is a term in English common law formerly applied to label the legal status of a person who had lost his or her civil rights for some reason. Legally *presumptive death,* on the other hand, refers to a situation in which a person has been physically absent from his or her place of residence and out of contact with family and acquaintances for some unexplained reason for several years (usually seven). The legal determination of death in such a case is made by a court of inquiry, after which the property and the familial rights and duties of the missing individual become those of a dead person. For example, a soldier who has been missing in action for seven years is presumed dead. Consequently, the survivors of this presumptively dead individual are entitled to the same legal rights (inheritance, remarriage, etc.) as they would be if direct proof of death were available (Kalven, 1974).

In the great majority of deaths, direct proof of the person's demise exists. The major legal issues that pertain to a death in the usual situation are:

1. Determining when death occurred and what caused it.
2. Taking or shortening human life for medical or legal reasons.
3. Disposing of the decedent's property.

The first two matters are of concern to both medicine and law, whereas the third is primarily of legal interest. The three matters are not necessarily independent; the manner in which a decedent's property is disposed of, for example, may be affected by how and when death occurred. Be that as it may, the legal procedures connected with death and dying have developed over the centuries to protect individuals from untimely death and improper burial, and to make certain that estates are disposed of according to the desires of the decedents (Schroeder, 1982).

Cause of Death and Disposal of the Corpse

The exact moment of death must be known in a number of legal situations, for example, in civil and criminal liability lawsuits, in processing insurance claims and determining survivors' benefits, and in matters of inheritance (see Report 6-1). When two people have died, it may be necessary to determine which one died first ("Death," 1983). Furthermore, in cases of body organ donations, it is important to know when the donor has actually died to ensure a viable organ.

REPORT 6-1

Repayment Sought on Last Social Security Check
Retiree Died 37 Minutes Too Soon, Widow Told

OMAHA (AP)—Shortly after Roy Gillespie died May 31, his widow got a certificate, signed by President Reagan, lauding his military service and promising the country would never forget him.

It didn't. The next day, she got a letter from the Social Security Administration that demanded the return of Gillespie's last Social Security check, for $358.60, because he died 37 minutes too soon to qualify for it.

Kay Gillespie is furious. She says she spent the money on funeral expenses and will not repay it.

Gillespie, a 72-year-old retired airplane mechanic, died at 11:24 p.m. May 31. He would have had to have survived until 12:01 a.m. June 1 to qualify for the May check, Darrell Gray, district manager of the Council Bluffs, Iowa, Social Security office, said. Gray and other Social Security officials said a person must be alive for every second of a month in order to collect benefits for it.

"I am not a chronic complainer," Gillespie, 71, of David City, Neb., told the Omaha World-Herald in an interview published Sunday after she had written the newspaper about her problem. "But I was just so outraged that I had to do something."

She wrote to state Sen. Loran Schmit. He replied, "I certainly wouldn't return any money to them."

In a letter to Sen. Edward Zorinsky (D-Neb.), she asked, "I realize the Social Security system is in trouble, but is this the way to solve the problem?"

Gillespie said her husband's May check was deposited directly in their joint account at the First National Bank of David City on June 3—the day he was buried.

Contacted by Phone
In addition to the letter from Social Security, Gillespie got a telephone request to repay the money.

Next, officers of First National Bank got a letter telling them to take the money out of Gillespie's account and send it to the Social Security Administration. The account was short, so a bank officer called Gillespie. She told him not to pay the government's claim.

Tom O'Connor, operations analyst in Social Security's Norfolk, Neb. office, said the death benefit—$255 meant to defray burial costs—could be withheld. Gillespie has not received that check and said she suspects it is being held up because she will not repay the May check.

O'Connor said the government could also take the money out of Gillespie's own monthly Social Security checks of approximately $360.

However, Gillespie said she will not willingly repay the money and will work to change the law. One alternative, she suggested, is prorating benefits for a person who dies. That way, for example, the spouse of a person who lived until the 15th of a month would collect half of the regular benefits for that month.

From *Los Angeles Times*, August 24, 1982, p. I-15. Reprinted by permission of The Associated Press.

It would appear to be a fairly straightforward task to determine when a person is dead, except that death can be defined in so many ways and different parts of the body "die" at different times. Among the physiological indicators of death are a drop in body temperature, stiffening and rigidity of the muscles (rigor mortis), and the presence of a waxy substance known as adipocere in the blood. Unfortunately, these indicators are rather crude and do not fix an exact moment of death.

Ambiguity in the definition of death and the consequent uncertainty of establishing a precise time of death have prompted many states to adopt the concept of brain death. According to this concept, death occurs when electrical activity of the brain ceases—as indicated by a flat electroencephalogram (EEG). But for legal purposes in most states, the older definition of death as the cessation of all vital functions, in particular, heartbeat, breathing, and reflexes, is still followed.

The Death Certificate

Not only must a moment of death be specified, but a cause of death must also be identified. Both the time and cause of death are indicated on a *death certificate,* a medico-legal document that must be completed and signed by a physician before the death can be registered. Death certificates, which are fairly uniform throughout the United States (see Figure 6-1), constitute legal proof of death in a host of situations concerned with burial, insurance payments, inheritance claims, and prosecution of homicides. A copy of the death certificate is filed with the local and state vital statistics branches of the Department of Health and Human Services. Filed in this manner, the death certificate constitutes official registration of the death and is a necessary preliminary to disposal of the corpse (Schroeder, 1982).

As shown in Figure 6-1, the death certificate has a place for filling in the cause of death. Causes that may be indicated are accident, suicide, homicide, undetermined, or pending investigation. A natural death is assumed if none of these terms is entered on the form. This classification system has been criticized as too simplistic (see Shneidman, 1980a), but it is fairly standard throughout the United States and Europe. Legal problems are most likely to arise when the identified cause is either accident, suicide, or homicide. In cases of accidental or homicidal death, for example, the survivors may have a legal claim against the person or persons who are responsible for the mishap or crime.[1] Certain insurance clauses

---

1. These rights stem from "Lord Campbell's Acts" (1846) in British law, which legally entitled the surviving kin to monetary benefits from the guilty party equal to those they would have received if the decedent had lived.

(PHYSICIAN, MEDICAL EXAMINER OR CORONER)
U.S. STANDARD
CERTIFICATE OF DEATH

Form Approved
OMB No. 68R 1901

LOCAL FILE NUMBER — STATE FILE NUMBER

TYPE OR PRINT IN PERMANENT INK FOR INSTRUCTIONS SEE HANDBOOK

DECEDENT

DECEDENT—NAME FIRST MIDDLE LAST 1.			SEX 2.	DATE OF DEATH (Mo., Day, Yr.) 3.
RACE—(e.g., White, Black, American Indian, etc.) (Specify) 4.	AGE—Last Birthday (Yrs.) 5a.	UNDER 1 YEAR MOS. 5b. DAYS · UNDER 1 DAY HOURS 5c. MINS.	DATE OF BIRTH (Mo., Day, Yr.) 6.	COUNTY OF DEATH 7a.
CITY, TOWN OR LOCATION OF DEATH 7b.	HOSPITAL OR OTHER INSTITUTION—Name (If not in either, give street and number) 7c.			IF HOSP. OR INST. Indicate DOA, OP/Emer. Rm., Inpatient (Specify) 7d.
STATE OF BIRTH (If not in U.S.A., name country) 8.	CITIZEN OF WHAT COUNTRY 9.	MARRIED, NEVER MARRIED, WIDOWED, DIVORCED (Specify) 10.	SURVIVING SPOUSE (If wife, give maiden name) 11.	WAS DECEDENT EVER IN U.S. ARMED FORCES? (Specify Yes or No) 12.
SOCIAL SECURITY NUMBER 13.	USUAL OCCUPATION (Give kind of work done during most of working life, even if retired) 14a.		KIND OF BUSINESS OR INDUSTRY 14b.	
RESIDENCE—STATE 15a.	COUNTY 15b.	CITY, TOWN OR LOCATION 15c.	STREET AND NUMBER 15d.	INSIDE CITY LIMITS (Specify Yes or No) 15e.

IF DEATH OCCURRED IN INSTITUTION, SEE HANDBOOK REGARDING COMPLETION OF RESIDENCE ITEMS

PARENTS

FATHER—NAME FIRST MIDDLE LAST 16.	MOTHER—MAIDEN NAME FIRST MIDDLE LAST 17.
INFORMANT—NAME (Type or Print) 18a.	MAILING ADDRESS STREET OR R.F.D. NO. CITY OR TOWN STATE ZIP 18b.

DISPOSITION

BURIAL, CREMATION, REMOVAL, OTHER (Specify) 19a.	CEMETERY OR CREMATORY—NAME 19b.	LOCATION CITY OR TOWN STATE 19c.
FUNERAL SERVICE LICENSEE Or Person Acting As Such (Signature) 20a.	NAME OF FACILITY 20b.	ADDRESS OF FACILITY 20c.

CERTIFIER

To be Completed by CERTIFYING PHYSICIAN Only

21a. To the best of my knowledge, death occurred at the time, date and place and due to the cause(s) stated. (Signature and Title)

DATE SIGNED (Mo., Day, Yr.) 21b.	HOUR OF DEATH 21c. M
NAME OF ATTENDING PHYSICIAN IF OTHER THAN CERTIFIER (Type or Print) 21d.	

To be Completed by MEDICAL EXAMINER or CORONER Only

22a. On the basis of examination and/or investigation, in my opinion death occurred at the time, date and place and due to the cause(s) stated. (Signature and Title)

DATE SIGNED (Mo., Day, Yr.) 22b.	HOUR OF DEATH 22c. M
PRONOUNCED DEAD (Mo., Day, Yr.) 22d. ON	PRONOUNCED DEAD (Hour) 22e. AT M

NAME AND ADDRESS OF CERTIFIER (PHYSICIAN, MEDICAL EXAMINER OR CORONER) (Type or Print) 23.

REGISTRAR 24a. (Signature)	DATE RECEIVED BY REGISTRAR (Mo., Day, Yr.) 24b.

CAUSE OF DEATH

CONDITIONS IF ANY WHICH GAVE RISE TO IMMEDIATE CAUSE STATING THE UNDERLYING CAUSE LAST

25. IMMEDIATE CAUSE (ENTER ONLY ONE CAUSE PER LINE FOR (a), (b), AND (c).)

PART I
(a) — Interval between onset and death
DUE TO, OR AS A CONSEQUENCE OF
(b) — Interval between onset and death
DUE TO, OR AS A CONSEQUENCE OF
(c) — Interval between onset and death

PART II OTHER SIGNIFICANT CONDITIONS—Conditions contributing to death but not related to cause given in PART I (a)	AUTOPSY (Specify Yes or No) 26.	WAS CASE REFERRED TO MEDICAL EXAMINER OR CORONER (Specify Yes or No) 27.

ACC., SUICIDE, HOM., UNDET., OR PENDING INVEST. (Specify) 28a.	DATE OF INJURY (Mo., Day, Yr.) 28b.	HOUR OF INJURY 28c. M	DESCRIBE HOW INJURY OCCURRED 28d.
INJURY AT WORK (Specify Yes or No) 28e.	PLACE OF INJURY—At home, farm, street, factory, office building, etc. (Specify) 28f.		LOCATION STREET OR R.F.D. No. CITY OR TOWN STATE 28g.

HRA-162-1
Rev. 1/78

FIGURE 6-1
U.S. standard death certificate. (National Center for Health Statistics, U.S. Department of Health and Human Services.)

and benefits are also activated in cases of accidental death (e.g., double indemnity provisions, worker's compensation death benefits). In the case of any voluntary and unlawful taking of life, the guilty party is not entitled to benefits that he or she might have received from the victim's death.

Coroners and Autopsies

Three additional items of interest on the death certificate are the coroner's certification, an indication of whether or not an autopsy was performed, and information on how, where, and by whom the corpse was disposed of.

In medieval England, *coroners* were agents commissioned by the king to determine the cause of death and, in cases of murder, to collect revenues from forfeiting the property of the murderer (Schroeder, 1982). The U.S. coroner of today is usually an elected official who may or may not be a medical doctor. Functions similar to those of coroners are performed by medical examiners—physicians usually trained in forensic pathology and appointed to their jobs by a government official or commission.

The task of the coroner or medical examiner is to examine deaths with unclear causes, that is, either the cause of death is unknown or unnatural—accident, suicide, homicide. The coroner or medical examiner may conclude that sufficient doubt as to cause exists to make a post-mortem examination, an *autopsy,* necessary. An autopsy, which involves dissection of the body, traditionally required permission from the next of kin. But a coroner can now order an autopsy whenever it appears that the deceased was in good health before his or her demise, or in other instances in which the death has not been satisfactorily explained. The results of the autopsy, conducted by a pathologist, are then recorded on appropriate legal documents. In certain cases, this may be followed by a legal inquest in which witnesses are heard and other evidence pertaining to the cause of death is presented.

Corpse Disposal and Disinterment

Burial of corpses was traditionally controlled by the Church, and not until the seventeenth century did the legal concept of a right to a decent burial develop (Schroeder, 1982). Although no one actually "owns" a dead human body, the law now requires that the next of kin or executor/executrix of the decedent's estate make arrangements to dispose of the body. The cost of burial is charged to the estate, except when the deceased is destitute or the relatives have authorized use of the body for scientific or educational purposes. In the usual situation, the next of kin obtains a burial permit when the death is registered and then engages a funeral director or mortician to take care of the details of the funeral and disposal of the corpse.

A dead body may be embalmed, cremated, or treated in other ways, for example, frozen; the laws pertaining to treatment vary from state to state. *Embalming,* which entails removal of the blood and injection of a special preservative mixture into the arteries, retards putrefaction for only a few days and is not usually required by law. However, it may be legally required whenever the body is to be transported for a long distance before burial.

Because cremation can be used to conceal a crime, a more detailed legal inquiry usually precedes issuance of a permit to cremate than a permit to bury. There are also laws pertaining to exhumation or disinterment of a buried body. In general, it is a misdemeanor to either mistreat or disinter a corpse, but certain officials can authorize disinterment in order to obtain legal evidence for prosecuting civil or criminal cases.

Abortion and Euthanasia

A decision by a lawfully constituted authority that a death is natural makes it legally, if not always personally, acceptable. Unnatural death due to accident, homicide, or suicide may also be legally sanctioned under certain conditions that vary with time and place and the specific circumstances of death. Like every aspect of human culture, laws are a function of the changing needs and tolerance of society. Laws and law enforcement pertaining to unnatural death caused by abortion, euthanasia (mercy killing), or capital punishment, for example, have not always been consistent or just. Nevertheless, there are indications of greater reasonableness and fairness in contemporary attitudes and legislation that apply to these issues. Fair or not, laws concerning these matters, as well as the interpretation and enforcement of the laws, continue to be reexamined and debated in the legal community and among the public at large.

Abortion

The most general definition of *abortion* is any procedure that results in the death of an unborn child. An abortion may be *spontaneous,* in which case it is known as a *miscarriage,* or it may be *induced* by some external agent. Abortions can be induced by either chemical or surgical techniques. The usual medical procedure employed through the twelfth week of pregnancy consists of either scraping the fetus from the uterus (dilatation and curettage) or aspirating the fetus from the uterus by means of a special suction pump. After the first 12 weeks of pregnancy, aborting the fetus becomes increasingly more hazardous to the health of the mother. The usual abortion technique in these cases consists of injecting a salt solution into the amniotic fluid surrounding the fetus (Callahan, 1983).

The controversy over induced abortion revolves around the issue of taking a human life. Taking its position from the Sixth Commandment (Thou shalt not kill.), organized Christianity has historically opposed induced abortion. Similar opposition has been expressed by Buddhism, Hinduism, and Judaism. British common law and that of many other countries also considered abortion to be a crime when induced after the onset of "quickening" (fourth–fifth month of pregnancy), because the fetus was regarded to be a legal person after it began to move (Williams, 1982).

The Protestant and Jewish positions on abortion have become less conservative during the twentieth century, and abortion to save the life or preserve the health of the mother is now generally acceptable to those religions. The Roman Catholic Church, however, continues to oppose abortion. Public opposition to abortion, of course, is not restricted to the religious community; many professional and lay groups are also against it. Whoever the opponent may be, the major point in opposition to abortion is that an unborn child is actually a human being and, hence, abortion is murder. Antiabortionists believe that this is certainly true of the fetus (third month to term), and, according to some opponents, even of the embryo and the fertilized egg.

Organized opposition to induced abortion is not as strong in other countries as it is in the United States. For example, abortions by qualified physicians are performed with virtually no restrictions in eastern Europe, the Soviet Union, and Japan. In the United States, it is legal in many states to abort for reasons of health of the mother or fetus, or when pregnancy is caused by rape or incest. But the great majority of the estimated 200,000–1,200,000 abortions that take place in the United States every year are prompted by reasons other than health or unlawful sexual intercourse. Consequently, most abortions are illegal (Williams, 1982). Pressure on state and federal legislators to liberalize abortion laws continues, however, especially by women's rights groups. One argument of these groups is that the fetus is part of a woman's body and that a woman has a right to control her own body.

Euthanasia and Natural Death

Euthanasia, the practice of putting to death people who suffer severe, unremitting pain, disease, or handicaps, was covered briefly in Chapter 3. As discussed, the distinction between *active* and *passive* euthanasia, which is not always clear, pertains to whether positive action is taken to hasten a person's death or whether extraordinary, heroic measures to save a dying person's life are merely withheld. Euthanasia is *voluntary* if the person whose life is in question voluntarily decides to die; it is *involuntary* if death occurs against the person's will. Despite the support of many famous people, the history of euthanasia has been at least as stormy as that of abortion (Eaton, 1982). The debate has not centered on the voluntary-involuntary distinction, since it is generally conceded that involuntary euthanasia is merely a euphemism for murder. Rather, the most frequently debated issue is whether active and/or passive euthanasia are morally and legally justifiable. The laws of the United States, Canada, and most European countries define active euthanasia—taking active measures to shorten the life of a person whether or not that person approves—to be a crime. Shortening one's own life is defined as suicide, and shortening the life of another is defined as murder.

Certain organizations (e.g., Exit in England and Concern for Dying in the United States[2]) have been established to lobby for changes in those laws, so far without notable success. Concern for Dying also distributes a

---

2. Formerly known as the Voluntary Euthanasia Legalization Society and the Euthanasia Society of America, respectively.

"Living Will" that expresses the patient's wish that extraordinary medical techniques not be utilized to keep him or her alive when the situation becomes final and hopeless (see Figure 6-2). Although not legally binding, this document is honored by certain physicians. Furthermore, some progress has been made toward legal acceptance of passive euthanasia, or *natural death* as it is called by proponents.

Religious Opposition. Christianity, Judaism, and Islam have traditionally opposed both suicide and euthanasia, the objections being directed more toward active than passive euthanasia. Roman Catholic opposition to euthanasia stems not only from the Sixth Commandment but also from St. Augustine's maxim that the Scriptures do not authorize man to destroy innocent human life, so man may not authorize himself to do so. But as seen in the *Ars Moriendi* treatise and the "double effect" principle of the Middle Ages, Roman Cathoic theologians have traditionally been more interested in saving souls than in preserving lives. According to the double effect principle, an action that has the primary effect of relieving human suffering may be justified even when it shortens human life (Eaton, 1982).

Modern Catholic theologians have also addressed the question of passive euthanasia, for example, when a respirator should be turned off or heroic medical measures on behalf of a patient should cease. Dealing with the question of whether the respirator should be turned off in the case of a patient who is in an irreversible coma, Pope Pius XII concluded in a 1957 statement that there is no moral obligation to keep the respirator turned on in such a situation. A case in point is that of Karen Ann Quinlan, an irreversible coma patient since 1975, whose Roman Catholic parents— presumably after Church consultation— decided to have the respirator turned off. Despite disconnection of the respirator, Karen continues to live and breathe. The parents decided against the removal of the feeding tube, however, which would have guaranteed the termination of Karen's life.

The Karen Quinlan case is not unique. Doctors are confronted almost daily with irreversible coma patients, and there has been much debate over the moral and legal implications of deciding when to remove artificial life-support systems and let patients die. The President's Commission on Medical Ethics recommended in 1983 that the family be permitted to decide whether to maintain the life of a coma patient or other seriously ill but incompetent individual who is incapable of making that decision. Competent and informed patients, on the other hand, would have the right to decide for themselves whether to die or be sustained by artificial life-support systems (Cimons, 1983).

Natural Death Act. Physicians' concerns over medical malpractice suits, coupled with the efforts of those who support passive euthanasia, have resulted in so-called natural death legislation in 15 states and the District of Columbia. California's Natural Death Act, which became law in 1977, was

138

To My Family, My Physician, My Lawyer and All Others Whom It May Concern

Death is as much a reality as birth, growth, maturity and old age—it is the one certainty of life. If the time comes when I can no longer take part in decisions for my own future, let this statement stand as an expression of my wishes and directions, while I am still of sound mind.

If at such a time the situation should arise in which there is no reasonable expectation of my recovery from extreme physical or mental disability, I direct that I be allowed to die and not be kept alive by medications, artificial means or "heroic measures". I do, however, ask that medication be mercifully administered to me to alleviate suffering even though this may shorten my remaining life.

This statement is made after careful consideration and is in accordance with my strong convictions and beliefs. I want the wishes and directions here expressed carried out to the extent permitted by law. Insofar as they are not legally enforceable, I hope that those to whom this Will is addressed will regard themselves as morally bound by these provisions.

(Optional specific provisions to be made in this space — see other side)

TO MAKE BEST USE OF YOUR LIVING WILL

You may wish to add specific statements to the Living Will *in the space provided for that purpose above your signature*. Possible additional provisions are:

1. "Measures of artificial life-support in the face of impending death that I specifically refuse are:
   a) Electrical or mechanical resuscitation of my heart when it has stopped beating.
   b) Nasogastric tube feeding when I am paralyzed or unable to take nourishment by mouth.
   c) Mechanical respiration when I am no longer able to sustain my own breathing.
   d) _____ "

2. "I would like to live out my last days at home rather than in a hospital if it does not jeopardize the chance of my recovery to a meaningful and sentient life or does not impose an undue burden on my family."

3. "If any of my tissues are sound and would be of value as transplants to other people, I freely give my permission for such donation."

If you choose more than one proxy for decision-making on your behalf, please give order of priority (1, 2, 3, etc.).

Space is provided at the bottom of the Living Will for notarization should you choose to have your Living Will witnessed by a Notary Public.

Optional proxy statement: I hereby designate _____
to make treatment decisions for me in the event I am comatose or otherwise unable to make such decisions for myself.

Optional Notarization:

"Sworn and subscribed to

before me this _____ day

of _____, 19_____ ."

_____
Notary Public
(seal)

Signed_____

Date _____

Witness_____

Witness_____

Copies of this request have been given to _____

_____   _____

(Optional)   My Living Will is registered with Concern for Dying (No, _____)

FIGURE 6-2
A living will. Prepared by Concern for Dying, it expresses the signer's wish to avoid the use of heroic measures to preserve his or her life in the event of irreversible disease or injury. (Used by permission of Concern for Dying, 250 West 57 Street, New York, NY 10107.)

the first of these. The California law permits a patient who has been diagnosed by two physicians as terminally and incurably injured or ill to sign a directive stating that life-sustaining procedures not be used to prolong his or her life when death is imminent (see Figure 6-3). The law does not provide for or permit active steps to end life, but only to terminate treatment that is prolonging the dying process.

The patient who signs the directive in Figure 6-3 must be emotionally and mentally competent to make the decision, which is effective for five years and can be revoked by him or her at any time. The directive must be executed 14 days after the patient has been diagnosed as having a terminal condition; otherwise it is only advisory and need not be complied with by the attending physician. As with any legal procedure, the patient's signature must be witnessed by two other people.

Natural death legislation has not been without problems and critics (e.g., Meyers, 1977). Nowhere in the California statute, for example, is the word *imminent* defined. Furthermore, a terminal patient in a comatose state obviously cannot make or sign such a declaration. Relying on guidelines prepared by the Harvard Medical School Ad Hoc Committee in 1968, California law permits physicians (at least two) to declare a patient dead when there is an absence of brain waves for 24 hours; there must also be no spontaneous breathing and no response to external stimulation. Once the patient has been declared dead, the physicians can "pull the plug" on life-sustaining machinery. Because the law is not clear in all situations, most physicians lean toward the conservative side and consult with the patient's family and legal counsel before making a final decision.

Another problem has arisen in attempting to implement the California Natural Death Act and similar laws, because many doctors are opposed, on ethical or religious grounds, to any form of euthanasia. Physicians may also view the demand for "death with dignity" as romantic nonsense contrary to their own experiences with dying patients. In the eyes of these doctors, terminally ill patients are usually frightened, suffering people who do not really want to die. A patient may state in a moment of despair that he or she wishes it (life) were all over and may even sign a legal form requesting that extraordinary life-sustaining procedures not be used. But the patient often changes his or her mind when something hopeful or pleasurable occurs (see Report 6-2).

The legalization of passive euthanasia also poses other problems for the medical profession. Some officials of the American Medical Association fear, justifiably or not, that legalized euthanasia might result in the corruption of physicians by relatives who stand to gain financially from the patient's death (Williamson, Evans, & Munley 1980). It is also possible that in a case of body organ donation, overeagerness to obtain a transplant organ as quickly as possible could lead to a premature decision to stop life-support systems. Consequently, the restriction that no member of the

CALIFORNIA NATURAL DEATH ACT

DIRECTIVE TO PHYSICIANS

Directive made this_____day of_____(month, year).

I,_____, being of sound mind, willfully,
and voluntarily make known my desire that my life shall not be artificially prolonged
under the circumstances set forth below, do hereby declare:

1. If at any time I should have an incurable injury, disease, or illness
certified to be a terminal condition by two physicians, and where the application
of life-sustaining procedures would serve only to artificially prolong the moment
of my death and where my physician determines that my death is imminent whether or
not life-sustaining procedures are utilized, I direct that such procedures be
withheld or withdrawn, and that I be permitted to die naturally.

2. In the absence of my ability to give directions regarding use of such
life-sustaining procedures, it is my intention that this directive shall be
honored by my family and physician(s) as the final expression of my legal right
to refuse medical or surgical treatment and accept the consequences from such
refusal.

3. If I have been diagnosed as pregnant and that diagnosis is known to my
physician, this directive shall have no force or effect during the course of my
pregnancy.

4. I have been diagnosed and notified at least 14 days ago as having a
terminal condition by_____, M.D., whose
address is_____, and whose
telephone number is_____. I understand that if I
have not filled in the physician's name and address, it shall be presumed that
I did not have a terminal condition when I made out this directive.

5. This directive shall have no force or effect five years from the date
filled in above.

6. I understand the full import of this directive and I am emotionally and
mentally competent to make this directive.

Signed_____

City, County and State of Residence_____

The declarant has been personally known to me and I believe him or her to be of
sound mind.

Witness_____

Witness_____

FIGURE 6-3
A natural death directive. (Used by permission of Concern for
Dying, 250 West 57 Street, New York, NY 10107.)

REPORT 6-2

"Death with Dignity": Should Patients Decide?

BOSTON (AP)—Doctors should be reluctant to accept the requests of sick persons for "death with dignity," because their desire to die may change, be based on needless fears or be a quest for attention, two physicians say.

In recent years, doctors have paid increasing attention to patients' wishes for quiet death as the development of respirators and other advances allowed them to keep people alive long after they lost consciousness.

A team of physicians who treat people with bad burns recently recommended that patients be allowed to make life-and-death decisions, because "who is more likely to be totally and lovingly concerned with the patients' best interests than the patient himself?"

Now, two Cleveland doctors say this view "may be somewhat naive and, in certain clinical situations, potentially dangerous."

In today's New England Journal of Medicine, the doctors said that before pulling the plug, doctors should make sure the patient who seeks death really means what he says.

"Physicians who are uncomfortable or inexperienced in dealing with the complex psycho-social issues facing critically ill patients may ignore an important aspect of their professional responsibility by taking a patient's statement at face value without further exploration or clarification," they wrote.

The doctors, David L. Jackson and Stuart Younger, described six cases they encountered in the intensive care unit at University Hospitals of Cleveland.

In one case, an 80-year-old man with lung disease at first said he did not want to be kept alive by a respirator. However, later, he changed his mind several times. The case, they said, shows that "one must be cautious not to act precipitously on the side of the patient's ambivalence with which one agrees, while piously claiming to be following the principle of patient autonomy."

In another case, a 52-year-old man with multiple sclerosis said he did not want doctors to try to save him if he developed serious complications. However, he later admitted he was upset with his family for not paying attention to him.

An 18-year-old woman with chronic asthma resisted treatment with a respirator. But after she was questioned by doctors, she said she was afraid of the hospital equipment. Her fears were calmed and she was discharged eight days later.

A 56-year-old woman with cancer urged doctors to do all they could to help her because she wanted to live long enough to see the birth of her first grandchild. When her condition worsened and she lost consciousness, her family asked that treatment be stopped. But the doctors refused, and the woman recovered enough to go home and see the child.

The doctors said they hoped their experience would help other physicians cope with situations in which "superficial and automatic acquiescence to the concepts of patient autonomy and death with dignity threaten sound clinical judgment."

transplant team should be involved in the terminal care or death determination of the patient is a reasonable precaution.

Although laws governing anatomical donations vary from state to state, the Uniform Anatomical Gift Act of 1968 provides guidelines for donor laws in every state. These guidelines dictate who can donate, to whom the donation can be made, and what can be donated. In general, a donor must be at least 18 years old, and, although the survivors may act to donate if the owner has not, the latter's request supercedes all others. The donor may also revoke the gift, and it may be refused by the intended recipients. Eyes, kidneys, the liver, and certain other organs can be donated for transplant purposes, and the pituitary and other glands can be donated for hormone extractions. The entire body also can be donated for educational or research uses.

Capital Punishment[3]

Another controversial legal issue concerned with actively taking a person's life is that of capital punishment. The death penalty has been applied to hundreds of different crimes since ancient times. During the Middle Ages, capital punishment was widely employed for crimes against church and state. Even as late as 1819, British law listed 223 different capital crimes (Radzinowicz, 1948). The list of 13 capital crimes in Massachusetts in 1636 indicates the influence of religion on legal punishment: adultery, assault in sudden anger, blasphemy, buggery, idolatry, manstealing, murder, perjury in a capital trial, rape, rebellion, sodomy, statutory rape, and witchcraft (Haskins, 1956). The American colonies had no uniform system of criminal justice, however, and whether or not an offense was deemed a capital crime depended to a great extent on the locality in which it occurred.

Number of Executions

Although the total number of crimes warranting the death penalty in this country has declined since colonial days, people have been executed during the current century for armed robbery, kidnapping, rape, treason, and military desertion. As might be expected, most of the executions in the United States since 1900 have been for the crime of murder. But even in more recent times, the number of executions for capital crimes has varied widely from state to state (see Figure 6-4). Approximately 60 percent of the executions in the United States from 1930 to 1981 took place in the South, 9½ percent occurring in Georgia alone (U.S. Department of Justice, 1982).

---

3. The author wishes to express his gratitude to Dr. Ola Barnett for her invaluable assistance in sharing much of the information in this section with him.

Number of persons executed, by jurisdiction, 1930–81 (total 3,863)

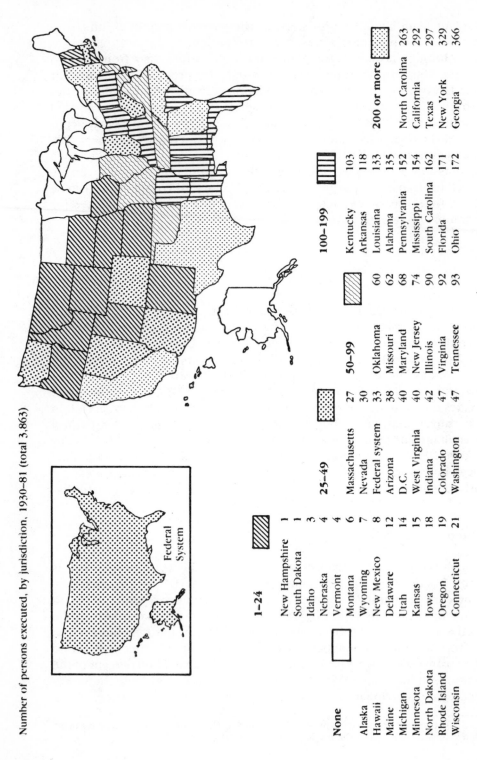

	1–24			25–49			50–99			100–199			200 or more	
None				Massachusetts	27		Oklahoma	33		Kentucky	103		North Carolina	263
Alaska	New Hampshire	1		Nevada	30		Missouri	38		Arkansas	118		California	292
Hawaii	South Dakota	1		Federal system	33		Maryland	40		Louisiana	133		Texas	297
Maine	Idaho	3		Arizona	38		New Jersey	40		Alabama	135		New York	329
Michigan	Nebraska	4		D.C.	40		Illinois	42		Pennsylvania	152		Georgia	366
Minnesota	Vermont	4		West Virginia	40		Virginia	47		Mississippi	154			
North Dakota	Montana	6		Indiana	42		Tennessee	47		South Carolina	162			
Rhode Island	Wyoming	7		Colorado	47					Florida	171			
Wisconsin	New Mexico	8		Washington	47					Ohio	172			
	Delaware	12												
	Utah	14												
	Kansas	15												
	Iowa	18												
	Oregon	19												
	Connecticut	21												

Federal System

FIGURE 6-4
Number of prisoners executed by state in the United States from 1930–1981. (From U.S. Department of Justice, Bureau of Justice Statistics, 1982, p. 9.)

Between 1930 and 1968, an average of more than 100 people were executed in the United States every year. As indicated in Figure 6-5, murder and rape have accounted for the greatest number of executions since 1930. Over 86 percent of these executions have been for murder, approximately 12 percent for rape, and less than 2 percent for all other offenses. Approximately 50 percent of those executed for murder, 90 percent of those executed for rape, and 54 percent of all those who were executed were black (U.S. Department of Justice, 1982).

Methods of Execution

As illustrated by the following death sentence imposed in England in 1812, the method of execution in earlier times could be quite cruel and unusual.[4]

That each of you, be taken to the place from whence you came, and from thence be drawn on a hurdle to the place of execution, where you shall be hanged by the neck, not till you are dead; that you be severally taken down,

---

4. Another intricate example of cruel and unusual punishment is that prescribed in ancient Roman law for the crime of parricide (kin killing). The person found guilty of this crime was bound and sealed in a sack also occupied by a dog and a chicken. The sack was then tossed into the water, and the person drowned if he wasn't scratched to death by the animals (Rosenblatt, 1982). A dog also figured in a 1906 execution in Switzerland. The animal, along with several people, was executed for its participation in a robbery and murder (Gambino, 1978).

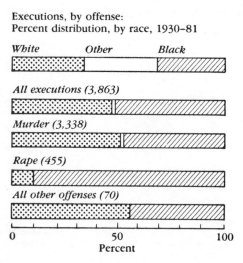

Executions, by offense:
Percent distribution, by race, 1930–81

FIGURE 6-5
Number of prisoners executed by offense in the United States from 1930–1981. (From U.S. Dept. of Justice, Bureau of Justice Statistics, 1982, p. 9.)

145

while yet alive, your bowels be taken out and burnt before your faces—that your heads be then cut off, and your bodies cut into four quarters, to be at the King's disposal. And God have mercy on your souls. (Scott, 1950, p. 179)

Five different methods of execution are now lawful in the United States, depending on the particular state—electrocution, lethal gas, hanging, lethal injection, and firing squad. The first two methods have been the most common, accounting for 75 percent of the total number of executions since 1930. As seen in Figure 6-6, however, none of these methods has been used extensively since 1968. Because of U.S. Supreme Court decisions, there were no executions in this country from 1968 through 1976, three in the late 1970s, and 16 more by June, 1984. Further Supreme Court decisions in the early 1980s designed to speed up the appeals process by death row inmates resulted in an increase in the number of executions.

Court Decisions

A landmark U.S. Supreme Court decision on capital punishment was handed down in 1972 in the case of *Furman v. Georgia.* By a vote of five to four, the court judged Georgia's death penalty law to be unconstitutional according to the Eighth Amendment prohibiting cruel and unusual punishment. The effective result of this judgment and subsequent Supreme Court

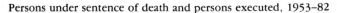

Persons under sentence of death and persons executed, 1953–82

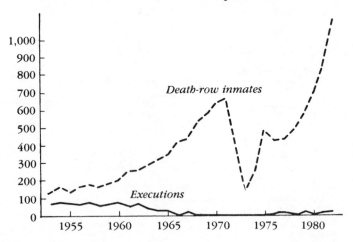

FIGURE 6-6
Persons under sentence of death and persons executed in the United States from 1930–1982. (From U.S. Dept. of Justice, Bureau of Justice Statistics, 1983, p. 3.)

decisions pertaining to capital punishment was to strike down existing capital punishment statutes. Laws that made capital punishment mandatory for certain crimes, that eliminated the discretion of the judge and jury in setting penalties, were declared unconstitutional (*Roberts v. Louisiana, Woodson v. North Carolina,* 1976). Laws making rape a capital crime (*Coker v. Georgia,* 1977) and laws specifying a limited number of mitigating circumstances in deciding punishment (*Lockett v. Ohio,* 1978) were also invalidated. Other laws declared unconstitutional were those excluding prospective jurors who admit that the possibility of capital punishment would make their decision difficult (*Adams v. Texas,* 1980).

On the side of capital punishment, three separate Supreme Court decisions rendered in 1976 (*Gregg v. Georgia, Jurek v. Texas, Profitt v. Florida*) upheld state laws providing for guided discretion in setting capital punishment sentences. Thus, the court concluded that when applied thoughtfully, carefully, and under the right circumstances, capital punishment is not unconstitutional. As a result of these decisions, by 1981 a total of 36 states had revised capital punishment statutes on their books.

The U.S. Supreme Court, of course, has not been the only judicial body concerned with capital punishment. Noting that a disproportionately large number of minority group members, especially blacks, had been executed in this country since 1930, the Massachusetts Supreme Court in 1979 ruled that a law reinstating capital punishment in that state during the preceding year was invalid. The court argued that not only was capital punishment cruel and unusual but that it had not been applied fairly to all ethnic groups and was therefore racially discriminatory. In fact, the Massachusetts court came very close to concluding that capital punishment was unjust under any circumstances (U.S. Department of Justice, 1981).

Death Row Inmates

The number of prisoners awaiting execution has increased sharply since 1973, while the states awaited Supreme Court decisions on capital punishment and drafted new legislation to conform to those decisions. As of August 20, 1983, there were 1,230 persons on death row in the United States, approximately 98 percent of whom were men and 51 percent white (Noffsinger, 1983). The typical death row prisoner is a white or black man in his late twenties who has less than a high school education and has been married at least once. In approximately three-fourths of the cases, he is imprisoned in the South and probably in Florida, Georgia, or Texas (see U.S. Department of Justice, 1982).

Life during the average stay of over two years on death row has been characterized as legalized torture, to such an extent that several men executed in the United States since 1976 chose not to appeal the death sentence rather than be forced to remain in that oppressive atmosphere.[5] As one prisoner stated, "A maggot eats and defecates. That's all we do: eat and defecate. Nothing else. They don't allow us to do nothing else" (Johnson, 1982).

In addition to eating, sleeping, and performing other natural functions, death row inmates spend much of their time thinking. What do they think about? From an analysis of letters and other documents written by people awaiting execution, Shneidman (1980c) concluded that they think intensively about themselves and what it will be like when they are dead. Knowing that one is about to die results in focusing on the self, to such an extent that the person literally begins to mourn or grieve for himself. Shneidman's sample of written documents is probably not representative of death row inmates in general, but many of the letters demonstrate a nobility of sentiment and concern about other people in the face of death. Thus, the execution notes that Shneidman analyzed reveal an increased compassion for loved ones and a feeling of inner peace as the end of life approached. Many death row inmates also develop strong religious convictions and beliefs in reincarnation or other forms of afterlife.

Pros and Cons of Capital Punishment

The United States is one of the few Western nations that has not abolished the death penalty, although many prominent citizens have opposed it for over 200 years.[6] Among European countries, only France, Ireland, Spain, and the Soviet Union still employ the death penalty. It has also been abolished in most Latin American countries, and Canadian federal law uses capital punishment only when police officers or prison guards have been murdered. Although a mere handful of people have been executed in the United States during the past few years, public sentiment in favor of the death penalty remains high. In a 1980 public opinion poll, for example, 59 percent of those questioned approved of capital punishment (Ellsworth & Ross, 1980). Why might this be so?

There are at least three community services that the death penalty might be expected to perform (Sellin, 1980, p. 6):

1. Satisfaction of the demand for retribution by making the criminal pay with his or her life.

---

5. Under a 1983 Supreme Court ruling designed to speed up the appeals process, federal judges can use special procedures to handle appeals by death row inmates. Furthermore, stays of execution are now not automatically granted in order for those appeals to be heard.
6. Benjamin Rush, the father of psychiatry in the United States, is also credited with being the father of the U.S. movement to abolish capital punishment (Post, 1944).

2. Discouraging others from committing capital crimes, that is, general deterrence.
3. Removal of the danger that the criminal's survival would pose to society, that is, prevention.

In general, decades of empirical research has provided no conclusive evidence in support of capital punishment for retribution, general deterrence, or prevention.

There is no evidence that murderers, who typically act impulsively, are deterred by the legal consequences of their actions before killing. The correlation between the threat of the death penalty and the homicide rate is not significantly different from zero. Rather than the threat of punishment, it is the swiftness with which punishment is applied that deters crime (Felkenes, 1983). The recidivism rate for murder parolees is extremely low, so it would appear that capital punishment cannot be credited with prevention. With respect to retribution, it may be considered sufficient that capital punishment serves as an expression of community outrage and the moral right of society to retribution. This position stems from Hammurabi's Code (the talion principle of "an eye for an eye") and the Mosaic Law, but it is at odds with the positions of many religious organizations (National Interreligious Task Force on Criminal Justice, n.d.). Nevertheless, Christians who favor capital punishment point out that the Scriptural prohibition against killing should be interpreted as applying only to the actions of persons acting solely on their own. Even Christ, it is pointed out, accepted his execution because it was ordered by legally constituted authority.

Whether or not a society feels that capital punishment is justifiable on the grounds of social retribution, it would seem necessary for the sentence to be imposed fairly, without regard to race, sex, socioeconomic status, or special influence. But law enforcement with respect to capital punishment has been very inconsistent. For example, only about half of willful homicides lead to murder charges, and only about half of those charged with murder are prosecuted for capital murder (Sellin, 1980). It is usually impossible in retrospect to determine all the factors that led to a capital murder charge and to the imposition of a capital sentence, but the fact that justice has been applied unequally should cause us to question whether capital punishment is administered fairly. After examining the roles of sex and other factors in sentencing for capital cases, Sellin (1980) concluded that not only has the death penalty failed as an agent of retribution, but the selective application of capital punishment has grossly distorted justice.

Another unfortunate effect of capital punishment is in making people believe that they have done something constructive about crime, whereas in reality they are probably only making matters worse. As Albert Camus declared, the sanctioning of official killing as a response to private killing only adds a second defilement to the first (Kerby, 1982).

Bequests and Taxes

Another matter pertaining to death and dying that is of concern to the legal profession is the disposition of estates. Not everyone who dies leaves behind an appreciable amount of property. Many people die poor, and a few even manage to "take it with them." For example, there are no wealthy people in a certain Arizona Indian culture, because a dead person's possessions are buried with the corpse (Shaffer & Rodes, 1977). The old saying that "you can't take it with you" is, in a sense, untrue in this culture. Since the dead take their possessions with them into the next world rather than leaving them to the living, those left behind are materially poor and remain that way except for what they can earn or what they are given by others.

Burying a dead person's possessions with the corpse is not unique to these Indians. As noted in Chapter 4, it has been practiced since Stone Age times and reached its height in the opulent grave goods of the Egyptian pharaohs' tombs. However, even the dead pharaohs did not take everything with them; some of the royal treasury was left for future pharaohs.

Wills in the Middle Ages

Throughout history, the usual practice of disposing of one's property at death has been to leave it to family, friends, and institutions. As far back as ancient Rome, the manner in which a decedent's property was to be distributed was frequently recorded in a legal document known as a *will.* In medieval Europe, under the direction of the Church, the preparation of a will prior to death became an obligatory sacrament, even for the poor. Like the confession of sins, the disposal of one's worldly property served as a form of redemption, as long as it was given to pious causes. A person who did not make a will could be excommunicated, and those who died intestate (no will) were presumably not buried in sacred ground (Aries, 1981).

Despite the shortness of life and the weak condition of entrepreneurship during the Middle Ages, many people managed to accumulate property and other holdings. They were proud of their possessions, but they also had strong beliefs in an afterlife. And here arose the conflict—a conflict of love of life and material things versus the paralyzing fear of eternal damnation and hell. The resolution of this conflict in many cases was to give all one's worldly goods, or at least a substantial portion of them, to the poor, to hospitals, and to churches and religious orders. In response to this generosity, which often left the benefactor's family almost penniless, the Church issued a kind of passport to heaven to the benefactor, agreeing to have Masses, services, and prayers said in perpetuity for his or her soul. As for the living, having little or no legacy made it even more difficult to accumulate the fortunes required for successful capitalistic endeavors.

By the middle of the eighteenth century, charitable contributions and the endowment of Masses were no longer the primary reasons for the last will and testament. What had been a philanthropic religious document during the Middle Ages now focused more on family management (Aries, 1981). Ambivalence between love of life and desire for salvation was still expressed in the wills of the Renaissance and Enlightenment, often in poetic or at least literary fashion. But the hold of the Church on the human mind and spirit had weakened, and the influences of more practical economic and legal factors began to manifest themselves.

Modern Wills[7]

Drawing up of wills is a big business in the modern world. It is estimated that 70 percent of the elderly population and 25 percent of all adults in the United States have made wills (American Bar Foundation, 1976). Although most states have a common procedure for implementing a written, attested will, there is actually no standard legal form on which a will must be drawn up and no universally required procedure for making a will. In fact, certain states accept an unwitnessed will prepared in the testator's[8] (legator's) own handwriting, *holographic will,* or even an oral will, *nuncupative will.* A nuncupative will, however, is permitted only under the most limited circumstances and can only be used by a person in fear of imminent death from an injury sustained on the same day.

Included in a will are the testator's name, address, and age, followed by a statement of the testator's capacity to make a will—*testamentary capacity*[9]—and voluntariness of the action. Next comes a listing of the disposition of specific items in the estate and the names of the heirs (distributees, legatees). The name of the appointed executor of the will or estate should also be given, followed by the dated signature of the testator and the signatures and addresses of two witnesses. The will may be altered, added to by means of a codicil, or destroyed by the testator at any time.

---

7. The material in this section was critically reviewed and supplemented by Professor Charles I. Nelson, J.D., of the Pepperdine University School of Law.

8. Throughout this section the masculine noun forms testator, legator, and executor will be used to refer to both men and women. The comparable female nouns are testatrix, legatrix, and executrix.

9. Testamentary capacity is possessed by a testator who knows (1) the nature of his or her property ("bounty"), (2) that he or she is making a will, and (3) who his or her natural beneficiaries are. A testator's testamentary capacity is not the same as the competency to handle his or her life and property. A person's competency, if questioned by relatives or heirs, must be determined by a separate legal hearing from that required to establish testamentary capacity.

Laws concerning inheritances and wills vary from country to country and from state to state within the United States. Most states, however, require that either a will be filed or the nonexistence of a will be disclosed to a probate court within 10 days of a death. Certain procedural matters pertaining to the legality of a will are usually resolved fairly easily. If a person names an executor of the estate, that executor serves under the jurisdiction of a local probate court. But if no executor is named by the testator or if a person dies *intestate* (no valid will having been located), the court appoints an administrator to handle the distribution of the decedent's property. Probate courts also become involved in disputations about whether a will is valid or which of several wills takes precedence (usually the most recent).

One of the most common disputes regarding bequests and wills has to do with the question of legal heirs or beneficiaries. British law historically subscribed to the rule of primogeniture, in which the male was preferred over the female line and the eldest over the youngest in the distribution of real property. A decedent's personal property, however, went to the next of kin. Furthermore, illegitimate children had no rights of inheritance under English common law (Arenson, 1982). Such distinctions have largely disappeared in modern inheritance laws, and, depending on the particular state, anyone—relative or not—can be a legal heir to an estate.

Death and Gift Taxes

Shaffer and Rodes (1977) describe three purposes of a legal system of inheritance:

1. To maintain order in dividing the decedent's property.
2. To support the decedent's dependents.
3. To inhibit the growth of private wealth and raise revenues for governmental purposes.

It is the third purpose that has prompted the levying of *death taxes.* These kinds of taxes are not new; they existed in ancient Egypt, Greece, and Rome, and continued to be levied during the Middle Ages (Mercer, 1982).

There are two kinds of death taxes, *estate taxes* on property left at death and *inheritance taxes* on property acquired from a person who has died. The United States has both state and federal death taxes. Pennsylvania was the first state to impose death taxes (1826), and today all states except Nevada have estate and/or inheritance taxes ranging from 3 percent to 23 percent of the taxable property. Recently, however, several states have moved away from inheritance taxes, effectively abolishing them in some instances (e.g., California).

The United States government levied its first death tax, a one-half of one percent stamp tax on the transmission of estates, in 1797. The current system of federal estate taxation, however, began in 1916. The rates were raised in 1924, lowered in 1926, raised again in 1932, and finally raised to their present levels in 1941. The current federal tax rate progresses steeply with the value of the estate, the rates in the middle and upper brackets being higher than those in the lower brackets. The rates are even higher in Great Britain, where they have served to break up large landed estates (Sennholz, 1976).

The U.S. Internal Revenue Service requires IRS Form 706, along with a check for the tax due, to be filed within nine months after the death of a person whose estate exceeds $60,000. It is wise to compute and file state inheritance tax before paying the federal tax, because the state tax is usually credited to the federal tax. In addition, federal and state income taxes must be filed for the deceased at the next filing period.

Despite their apparent magnitude, only about 2 percent of the total tax collections by the U.S. government come from estate taxes. The availability of many tax dodges, such as trusts and foundations, results in the payment of relatively small estate taxes by affluent people. Furthermore, even those who inherit modest estates in the $100,000 range are not taxed severely. In addition to the $60,000 exemption, a surviving spouse is entitled to an exemption of one-half the decedent's estate. And if the survivor owns half the estate to begin with, obviously only the decedent's half is taxable (Sennholz, 1976).

As indicated, one way to avoid large estate taxes is to set up a trust that spans one or more generations. For example, if a husband's property is placed in trust, his wife can avoid inheritance taxes by living only on the income from the estate after his death. At her death, the estate either remains in trust or goes to the surviving children. In the former case, the children also avoid taxation; in the latter case, the estate is now taxed. However, the appreciated property that remains in the estate is free of capital gains, and the estate tax is now probably less than it would have been previously.

In addition to death taxes, gifts made by a person before death may also be taxed (gift taxes). But gifts of certain amounts during a specified time period are not taxed. Thus, a person can distribute $30,000 during his or her lifetime, in addition to as much as $3,000 a year to as many people as he or she desires, without paying any taxes on the gifts. A husband and wife may reduce their estate for tax purposes by giving their children a lump sum of $60,000 plus $6,000 to each child during every year. The largest tax savings on gifts, however, come from property, cash, or stock given to a private foundation. Nonvoting stock given to a charitable foundation is not taxed, but the gift enables the benefactor to retain control of the company by means of his or her voting stock. It is understandable why numerous private educational, medical, and charitable institutions owe

153

their very existences to the dislike of the wealthy for taxes (Simpson, 1979).

There are so many opportunities and intricacies in death tax law that finding ways to avoid these taxes has become a full-time occupation for some lawyers and accountants ("Death and Gift Taxes," 1983). In fact, the money spent collecting death taxes and attempting to take advantage of loopholes in the tax laws is nearly equal to the amount of tax actually collected. This situation has prompted a variety of suggestions for modifying the death tax system. For example, integrating income, capital gains, death, and gift taxes into a single tax might simplify matters and make the system fairer to all concerned. But whether or not changes in the laws occur, those who understand the tax structure or possess the wherewithal to buy the services of someone who does will probably continue to be most effective in avoiding heavy taxation.

Considering the complexities of federal and state laws pertaining to inheritances and gifts, it would be well for anyone planning a bequest to consult an attorney. Estate planning, of which the will is only a part, is itself only one aspect of planning for death. In addition to preparing a will and understanding death taxes, it is wise for both benefactor and beneficiaries to be familiar with the language and laws pertaining to insurance policies, joint bank accounts, safe-deposit boxes, social security benefits, veterans benefits, and civil service benefits (see Simpson, 1979).

SUMMARY

The major legal issues pertaining to death are determining when death occurred and what caused it, taking or shortening human life for medical or legal reasons, and disposing of the decedent's property. The various legal procedures associated with death and dying are designed to protect people from untimely death and improper burial, and to make certain that estates are disposed of according to the decedents' wishes.

The concept of brain death is now accepted in many states, but the definition of death as the cessation of all vital functions is still applied in others. All states require a death certificate that contains identifying data and information on the time and cause of death; the death must be registered and a burial permit issued after the death certificate is completed. Special legal problems occur when a death is not natural, that is, when it is due to accident, homicide, suicide, or undetermined cause. In such cases, the coroner or medical examiner may decide to conduct an autopsy to isolate the cause of death.

Induced abortion is illegal in most states, except in special circumstances, namely, rape, incest, or to preserve the health of the mother. Aborting a fetus becomes increasingly more hazardous to the health of the mother after the twelfth week of pregnancy. Opposition by the Roman

Catholic Church and other organizations has made induced abortion illegal in most Western countries, but there are virtually no restrictions on abortions performed in Eastern European countries, the Soviet Union, or Japan. The number of illegal abortions performed in the United States is estimated to be as high as one million annually.

Euthanasia, or mercy killing, may be voluntary or involuntary, active or passive. The debate over euthanasia has centered on voluntary euthanasia (with the patient's consent) of the active or passive sort. Despite strong religious opposition, public approval of euthanasia—especially passive euthanasia—has increased during recent years. The Roman Catholic Church now accepts passive euthanasia as morally defensible in certain cases, for example, turning off the respirator in a case of irreversible coma. Some states have passed natural death acts pertaining to medical responsibilities and procedures with regard to terminal patients, but the wording of these laws is not always legally or medically clear.

Nearly 4,000 people were executed in the United States between 1930 and 1980, the great majority for murder (86 percent) or rape (12 percent). They were electrocuted, gassed, hanged, shot, or, more recently, injected with a lethal substance. There were no executions in this country from 1968 to 1976, but since the Supreme Court decisions in 1976, 19 men had been executed by mid-1984. In August, 1983, there were 1,230 inmates on the death rows of this nation, living in an environment described as legalized torture.

The United States is one of the few Western nations that has not abolished the death penalty, although much care is now being exercised to make certain that prisoners' legal rights are not violated. Proponents of capital punishment argue that it fulfills its purpose of retribution, general deterrence, and prevention. The results of research on the effects of capital punishment, however, do not support any of these arguments.

The last will and testament has changed from a primarily religious document in the Middle Ages to a legal document for family and estate management. Wills are usually written and witnessed by two persons, but oral and unwitnessed wills are legal under certain conditions. Questions concerning the authenticity or conditions of a will must be resolved in a probate court.

There are two kinds of death taxes—estate and inheritance—and they may be assessed by both state (except Nevada) and federal governments. The federal estate taxation rate is relatively low on small estates, but it increases rapidly as the dollar value of the estate rises. Setting up a trust and/or giving property to a foundation are ways of avoiding large estate taxes. A person can avoid death taxes on a certain amount of money while still alive by giving the money to a number of individuals, although gift taxes are assessed when the amount becomes large. Preparing a will and being knowledgeable about death taxes are essential to estate planning, but planning for death goes beyond estate planning.

SUGGESTED READINGS

Behnke, J. A., & Bok, S. (Eds.). (1975). *The dilemmas of euthanasia.* Garden City, N.Y.: Doubleday.

Clark, M. et al. (1977). A night to die. In S. H. Zarit (Ed.), *Readings in aging and death: Contemporary perspectives.* New York: Harper & Row.

Devins, G. M., & Diamond, R. T. (1977). Determination of death. *Omega, 7,* 277–296.

Lippett, P. E. (1979). *Estate planning: What anyone who owns anything must know.* Reston, Va.: Reston.

Rupert, M. K. (1976). Death and its definitions: Medical, legal, and theological. *Michigan Academician, 8*(3), 235–247.

Russell, O. R. (1977). *Freedom to die: Moral and legal aspects of euthanasia* (rev. ed.). New York: Human Sciences.

Sellin, T. (1980). *The penalty of death.* Beverly Hills, Calif.: Sage Publications.

Sennholz, H. F. (1976). *Death and taxes.* Washington, D.C.: The Heritage Foundation.

Shapiro, M. (1978). Legal rights of the terminally ill. *Aging, 5*(3), 23–27.

Shneidman, E. (1980). *Voices of death* (Chap. 4). New York: Harper & Row.

PART III

Attitudes toward Death and Treatment of the Dying and the Dead

7 Children and Death

Questions answered in this chapter:

- Why are children today less familiar with death than were children in previous generations?
- How do children's conceptions and feelings about death change as they grow older?
- What are the causes and correlates of fears of death in children and adolescents?
- How do death rates and causes of death vary as a function of age in childhood and youth?
- What are the effects of terminal illness on the understanding and feelings of dying children and their families?
- What counseling techniques are employed by health personnel who work with dying children and their parents?
- What effects does the death of a parent have on children?
- How does death education, both formal and informal, vary with the age and background of the student?
- What is the recommended structure of a curriculum in death education at the grade school level?

hildhood is supposed to be a happy time, a time when one's thoughts and feelings are focused on living, learning, and having fun. Therefore, *children and death* may appear to be an unkind, or at least an unfortunate, combination of words. Death is seen as a more appropriate companion of old age than of childhood. Certainly children in industrialized nations today seem to be less familiar with death than sex, the opposite of what was true for children of yesteryear.

Why are today's children less acquainted with death than those of earlier generations? One reason is a lack of exposure to death at an early age. It is not unusual for people today to reach their late teens or even twenties without directly experiencing the death of a single friend or family member. In fact, it has been estimated that during the first half of life the average American attends only one funeral every 15 years (Whitley, 1983). For most people, death is an unwelcome stranger who finds them emotionally and intellectually unprepared.

Death wasn't any more welcome in previous times, but it was no stranger. Children lived with death, and it was an exception if a child reached adolescence without having witnessed the death of a sibling, a grandparent, or other close relative or friend. Many of those who died were young people. At the beginning of this century, death was almost as common in infancy as in old age (Morison, 1973). In addition, many of those who escaped death from some contagious disease in infancy or early childhood became orphans when one or both of their parents succumbed.

There is another reason why children of today are less familiar with death than those in previous generations. Dying has now become less public. People who in former times would have died at home, surrounded by young and old family members and friends, are now more likely to expire in antiseptic, electronically equipped hospitals or nursing homes. Consequently, children are spared the unpleasantness and, unfortunately, the growth experience, of observing the death of a grandparent or other relative. The relative simply "passes away" or "goes directly to Heaven" without saying goodbye to the child. Even dead animals are something to be disposed of quickly, before children see them and ask embarrassing questions.

The isolation and rapid disposal of the dead has been interpreted by thanatologists as indicative of a denial of death that was ushered in with the beginning of the century (Aries, 1962). Death became what sex was in Victorian times, an unavoidable process but unsuitable for public viewing or discussion. In a turnabout from the Victorian era, modern children are permitted to ask questions about where they came from but not where they are going.

There are many signs that death has become rather distant from everyday life. Even the funeral has changed from a home-based event in which the deceased was laid out in the living room for all to see, to a professionally orchestrated affair designed to maximize the efficiency of corpse disposal and minimize the public display of grief. Also unlike previous times, particular efforts are now made to isolate children from the dying process and exclude them from participating in funerary rites. Children typically are viewed as fragile, impressionable little creatures who cannot cope with death and might be traumatized by it. Even the discussion of death with children, a process that makes adults uncomfortable and anxious, is taboo in many families.

The conception of childhood as a special stage of human development is actually a fairly recent occurrence in Western history. Until the eighteenth century, young people who were not yet fully grown typically were dressed the same as adults, participated in most of the same activities as adults, and shared many of the responsibilities of their full-grown elders. The concept of *child* was much less age-related then than it is today. No matter what his or her chronological age, anyone who, because of limited ability or misfortune, was dependent on other people was labeled a child (Aries, 1962). One explanation why children were treated more as adults in earlier times is that people in general were less educated, and children were more likely to contribute to family survival than they are today. Consequently, differences between adults and children in knowledge and ability and, therefore, the behaviors expected of the two age groups were less extreme in those days (Stillion & Wass, 1979).

Whatever the reasons for historical variations in the treatment of children may be, there are indications that, after over a half century of denying death and attempting to isolate young people from it, a different viewpoint is beginning to prevail. Research on topics such as the development of ideas and feelings about death, the effects of terminal illness in children on both the child and the family, and the effects on children of the loss of a parent is providing information and guidelines for death education and counseling. One result of these efforts has been the introduction of death and dying units and courses, not only at the senior high and college levels but throughout the school grades. Much of the material used in these courses is also of value to parents who want to answer more meaningfully children's questions about dying and prepare them for the death of a family member, a friend, or even a pet.

Developmental Changes in Conceptions and Fears of Death

Despite the attitude of many adults that children who think about death are abnormal in some way, death is a part of human development and a subject of interest to normal children. Parents cannot shield their children from death forever; it will be encountered in nature, in the media, and in conversations with other children and adults. What parents can do is deal with death and the child's questions about it in a natural manner suitable to the child's level of cognitive and emotional development.

Nagy's Developmental Stages

Jean Piaget's theory of stages in cognitive development has provided a starting point for much psychological research on children during the past

161

40 years, including their conceptions of death. Some 35 years ago, Maria Nagy (1948) conducted a study of 378 Hungarian children aged 3–10 that has become a classic in the psychology of death. All the children were questioned on their ideas about death, and those aged 6–10 also made drawings to represent their ideas. Following Piaget's theory of cognitive development, Nagy found evidence for three stages in the growth of children's conceptions about death.

Children in the first stage (ages three–five) usually did not distinguish death from separation. People who died were believed to be asleep or on a journey, from which they would awaken or return in time. Death to these young preschoolers was not a final or permanent condition, and a dead person might very well come back to life at any moment. The person who was dead was less "alive" than an alive person, but he or she could still breathe, eat, and drink in a coffin or wherever he or she was. Illustrative of the thinking of children in this preoperational stage is the following excerpt from a child's conversation with her 84-year-old great-grandmother.

> You are old. That means you will die. I am young, so I won't die, you know. . . . But that's all right. Grandmother, just make sure you wear your white dress. Then, after you die, you can marry Nomo (great-grandfather) again, and have babies. (Kastenbaum, 1977, p. 280)

Children in the second of Nagy's stages (ages five–nine) saw death as related to age, as did the child in the cited quotation; it is something that happens to old people. At this second stage, in which children are capable of concrete operational thinking and understanding the concept of conservation, death was seen as irreversible but avoidable. Only bad people or those who have accidents die, but death can be outwitted if you're good, cautious, and fast. Therefore, one must be careful not to eat or drink too much, catch a disease, or get hurt. And what is this thing called *death?* Depending on the child, death was personified by these children as an angel, a bogey man (monster), or the death man. Children in the second stage also had difficulty understanding the difference between life and death. They were apt to view moving things as alive—whether or not those things moved by themselves—and nonmoving things as dead.

Nagy's stage-three children (ages 10 +) had a more realistic, adultlike view of death. Note that this stage overlaps Piaget's stage of formal operations, implying the ability to think abstractly. To these children, death was the real, inevitable, and irreversible destruction of body life, a fate that is yours even when you're careful. The following conversation reported by Lifton (1979) reveals the more mature level of questioning and thinking about death in a stage-three child. A 10-year-old girl and her father are discussing the death and cremation of their pet dog, which took place while the girl and her brother were away at camp.

DAUGHTER: Daddy, Ken (her brother) and I were talking—why did you and Mommy spread Jumblie's ashes without us?

FATHER: Well, you and Ken were at camp, so Mommy and I thought we should go ahead and do it.

DAUGHTER: What were the ashes in?

FATHER: They were in a jar.

DAUGHTER: All of them?

FATHER: Yes, all of them.

DAUGHTER: Well, how big was the jar?

FATHER: It was round like a bottle and about six or eight inches high.

DAUGHTER: But where was Jumblie?

FATHER: The ashes were all that was left of Jumblie after he was cremated.

DAUGHTER: But what about his bones?

FATHER: They were all burned down to ashes.

DAUGHTER: But what about the rest of him? What about his ears?

FATHER: Everything was burned to ashes.

DAUGHTER: Daddy, are you and Mommy going to have your ashes spread out on the dunes when you die?

FATHER: I think so—that's our plan now. What do you think of that plan?

DAUGHTER: I don't know. Who will spread them?

FATHER: Well, it depends on who dies first—whoever dies first, the other will spread them, and maybe you and Ken.

DAUGHTER: But what if you die together?

FATHER: Then I guess you and Ken will spread them. But that isn't very likely. Anyhow, we don't plan to die for a while.

DAUGTHER: Daddy, do you believe that when you die you are reborn again?

FATHER: No, dear, I don't. I believe that when you die, that's the end.

DAUGHTER: I don't think Mommy believes that.

FATHER: Well, maybe not. But that's what I believe.

DAUGHTER: Then how could it be the *end?* You must feel *something*.

FATHER: No, not after you're dead.

DAUGHTER: But what happens to *you?*

FATHER: Well, when you die, there is only your body left—not really you— and you can't feel anything at all anymore.

DAUGHTER: Does it hurt?

FATHER: Not after you're dead.

DAUGHTER: But you can still *dream,* can't you?

FATHER: No, not after you're dead. You can't dream either. You just don't have any feeling at all. That must be pretty hard to understand, isn't it?

DAUGHTER: Yeah, it is.

FATHER: Well, even adults like us have a hard time understanding it.[1]

_____

1. From THE BROKEN CONNECTION: *On Death and the Continuity of Life,* by Robert Jay Lifton. © 1979 Robert Jay Lifton.

Effects of Culture and Experience

As with the Piagetian stages of cognitive development, not all children of a specific chronological age fit into the stage prescribed by Nagy's schema. Cultural factors, for example, have a great influence on the development of death concepts. Children in the United States today do not personify death to the same extent as Nagy's stage-two children, and they also understand the organic basis of death at an earlier age (Childers & Wimmer, 1971; Melear, 1973). Nevertheless, understanding the finality and universality of death, as Nagy's research suggests, has been shown by subsequent investigations to be related to chronological age (White, Elson, & Prawat, 1978).

Nationality differences are not the only cultural factors that affect ideas about death. Social class differences within the same country are also influential. Young lower-class people are more likely to associate death with violence, whereas middle-class children in the United States tend to associate death with disease (Tallmer, Formaneck, & Tallmer, 1974). In addition to cultural differences, specific experiences in the family, such as the death of a pet, affect a child's knowledge and feelings about death and dying. From her work on terminally ill children, Bluebond-Langner (1978) found that all views of death can be expressed at any stage of development. The particular view expressed by a child of a given age depends on the psychosocial stimulation and concerns that the child is experiencing at the time.

Death Concepts in Infancy

One of Nagy's conclusions that has been extensively criticized is that infants and toddlers have no conception of death. The observations of several investigators (Anthony, 1972; Fraiberg, 1977; Maurer, 1966; Pattison, 1977) suggest that rudimentary conceptions of death begin to form as early as the first year of life. It is proposed that the infant's awareness of dichotomous states such as here-gone (as in the game peek-a-boo or in separation from the mother), sleeping-waking, and other alternating internal states become the basis for object constancy and the me–not-me distinction. The infant's experiments with states of being and nonbeing, as in peek-a-boo, are believed to provide a conceptual foundation for later thinking about death. Anthony (1972) maintains that observations of the growth and deterioration of things, the one-directional nature of time, and the many linguistic referrents to death also play a role in the young child's understanding of death. Thus, these psychologists see the child as perceiving and understanding more about death than he or she is capable of expressing to researchers such as Maria Nagy.

Children's Games and Sayings about Death

Peek-a-boo, which is derived from an old English word meaning *dead or alive,* is only one of the many games that assist young children in developing a concept of being versus nonbeing. Other popular children's games that help instill this concept are hide-and-go-seek, I spy, and ring-around-a-rosy. The chant "ashes, ashes, all fall down" in an older version of ring-around-a-rosy came from the reactions of children during the Middle Ages to the Black Plague.

The children's prayer:

> Now I lay me down to sleep,
> I pray the Lord my soul to keep.
> If I should die before I wake,
> I pray the Lord my soul to take.

is also a holdover from a previous time, a time when many children died at night and parents were often fearful that a young son or daughter would not be alive in the morning. Unfortunately, this prayer may now serve no better purpose than to needlessly frighten young children. With this in mind, one objector changed the last two lines of the prayer to

> Thy love guard me through the night,
> And wake me with the morning light.
> (Pardi, 1977, p. 119)

Many other sayings (and jokes) quoted by children probably assist them in coping with the idea of death. The common threat of the elementary school child that "I'll kill ya" is a case in point, having the effect of putting the child rather than death in control.

Death Concepts in Adolescence

Nagy did not carry her research beyond 10-year-olds, but other investigators have questioned older children, adolescents, and adults on their ideas and feelings about death. As do younger children, adolescents are likely to view death as something that happens to old people. It is a distant, abstract event, although sometimes tinged with romance. Adolescents come to accept death as something that happens eventually to everyone, but, with respect to themselves, it tends to be associated with fate or violent circumstances (Ambron & Brodzinsky, 1979). Those who have a religious background are more likely to think about heaven, hell, and the hereafter, but religious doubts are also more common at this time (Hogan, 1970). As one survey (McIntyre, Angle, & Struempler, 1972) discovered, however, adolescents do not necessarily accept the finality of death. In fact, the seven- to nine-year-old children who were questioned in this study accepted the finality of death more readily than the adolescents did.

Children's Fears of Death

Cursory observations of the behavior of a typical infant or young child show that separation from the mother or other nurturing person causes the child to respond in a fearful manner. Many authorities believe that the fear produced by such separations lays the groundwork for later fears of death ("Death: 2. Psychological Aspects of Death," 1982). A very young child probably does not remember being separated from its mother, but frequent or prolonged separations at a critical stage of development can lead to a high level of anxiety, depression, and emotional overactivity in the child (Fraiberg, 1977).

Most normal children, depending on their stage of development, are afraid of some things,[2] but they are not generally fearful nor are they intensely afraid of a specific object or situation. For example, children do not normally develop a pathological fear of death (*thanaphobia*); they do not dwell on the topic, but they can handle it. On the other hand, many emotionally disturbed children are abnormally afraid of death, among other things. And many of the fears of these children are related to the more general fear of separation.

Fears of dying and death are usually associated with other problems in the child's life. These problems naturally are influenced by the child's experiences, particularly those occurring in the home situation. Physical separation from the parents through death or divorce, or emotional separation through lack of understanding and outright rejection of the child, are important home-related factors in emotional disturbance in childhood. One symptom of severe emotional disturbance in children is death anxiety. Unlike the leveling off of death anxiety that occurs as emotionally healthy children grow older, death anxiety in disturbed children tends to increase steadily with age (Von Hug, 1965). The level of death anxiety is also related to the self-perceptions of the child, that is, children with higher self-concepts tend to be less anxious about dying (Wass & Scott, 1978).

Parents are important in many other ways in shaping a child's attitudes and feelings toward death. By means of the identification process, fearful parents tend to produce fearful children—just as suicidal parents are more likely to produce suicidal children (see Templer, Ruff, & Franks, 1971). On the other hand, the children of adults who approach the topic and actuality of death in a calm, accepting manner tend to be less afraid of

---

2. Very young children, for example, may express fears of being sucked in by a vacuum cleaner or bathtub drain, or even being flushed down a toilet.

it. The following conversation illustrates a rational parental approach to a young child's concerns about death (Rust, unpublished study).

CHILD (four-and-one-half-years-old): Mummy, what means a dead mother?
MOTHER: A woman that has died and does not walk or talk anymore.
CHILD: But what will the children do?
MOTHER: Well, if a mother should die, the father would take care of them and maybe an aunt.
CHILD: Will you be a dead mother some day?
MOTHER: Why yes, though I don't expect to be for a long time.
CHILD: A *very* long time?
MOTHER: Yes.
CHILD: But I don't want you to die; I want you here like this.
MOTHER: Well, you will probably be quite grown-up before that happens.
CHILD: A *long* time?
MOTHER: Yes.
CHILD: But what means dead, mummy?
MOTHER: Well, your heart stops beating and you lie still without breathing.
CHILD: And what do you do with the talking part—you know, the inside talk?
MOTHER: I'm not sure, but some people think you live in another world and, of course, some don't.
CHILD: I guess we do (excitedly). Yes! And then you die in a *long,* long time—a *very* long time, and then I die and we both hug each other and then you won't have any wrinkles. . . .

It is suggested that adults be natural, but thoughtful, in answering a child's questions about death, trying to see beneath the surface of the questions and responding in words the child understands. However, it is not advisable to lie to the child by professing beliefs one really doesn't have (Gordon & Klass, 1979). Using euphemisms such as "gone away" or "gone to sleep," rather than "dead" to explain what happened to a relative are also confusing to young children. Saying that grandmother is "in heaven with the angels," where she is "watching over you" is especially inappropriate if the parent does not believe in these things. Furthermore, as Stein (1974) points out, the child might not like to have grandmother watching all the time, observing not just the good things but also the bad things that the child does.

Adolescent Fears of Death

Like their younger counterparts, emotionally healthy adolescents are able to cope with death more effectively than adolescents who have emotional problems. Maurer (1964) found that adolescents who were low academic achievers, for example, had stronger fears of death than those who were normal achievers; the former also showed greater separation anxiety and a

167

greater tendency to believe in ghosts. Poor academic achievers also usually have lower intellectual ability than high achievers, so the lower achievement and greater fearfulness on the part of the poor achievers may both have been due to lower ability. Support for this interpretation is provided by the results of a study by Chalmers and Reichen (1954). These investigators found that intellectually subnormal high school girls were more likely to show fears of death in their expressed thoughts and feelings than intellectually normal girls.[3]

Children whose parents have prepared them for the changes and challenges of adolescence can cope more effectively with the problems of identity and status that characterize this period of development. Needing to maintain the illusion of invulnerability, adolescents usually reject thoughts of death (Kastenbaum, 1959). But the rapid changes of adolescence tend to increase anxiety levels. Adolescent girls who have not been informed about the physical changes of puberty, for example, may imagine that they are dying when they first begin to menstruate. And all the media talk about nuclear war may lead adolescents to believe that they will never grow up, never get jobs, and never marry or have children (Caldicott, 1982).

Death of a Child

Mortality rates for young Americans have declined dramatically during this century, but even in highly industrialized nations such as the United States children still die in sizable numbers. During 1982, an estimated 41,700 infants, 7,620 children in the 1–4 year age range, and 9,450 children in the 5–14 year age range died in this country (National Center for Health Statistics, 1983). Although the infant mortality rate of 15.4 per 100,000 live births was higher than the rates for older children, it was the lowest ever recorded in the United States. The major causes of infant death in 1982 are listed in Table 7-1. Nearly half of the deaths were due to three causes—congenital anomalies, respiratory distress syndrome, and sudden infant death syndrome.

Congenital anomalies in internal body organs and tissues, the leading cause of death in infancy, are often treatable. The cost of infant care in an intensive care unit is quite high, however, averaging around $25,000 and ranging up to $350,000 for the total period. Because a large percentage of infants who are treated in these facilities survive, the high

---

3. A significant negative relationship between mental ability and fear of death is also suggested by the findings of Wass and Scott's (1978) study of children aged 11 and 12. Children whose fathers were college-educated showed less fear of death, although they theorized about death and verbalized thoughts concerning death more, than children whose fathers had only completed high school.

TABLE 7-1
Major Causes of Infant Mortality in the United States in 1982

Cause	Death Rate Per 100,000 Births
Congenital anomalies	237.0
Respiratory distress syndrome	107.2
Sudden infant death syndrome	127.2
Disorders relating to short gestation and unspecified low birth weight	98.8
Intrauterine hypoxia and birth asphyxia	39.7
Pneumonia and influenza	20.0
Birth trauma	15.4
Certain gastrointestinal diseases	7.3
Other conditions originating in the prenatal period	295.1
All other causes	177.1
All causes	1124.5

Source: Adapted from National Center for Health Statistics. (1983). *Monthly Vital Statistics Report,* 31(13). Washington, D.C.: U.S. Dept. of Health and Human Services.

cost is usually considered justified. But the decision about whether to continue the hospital care or to give up is not always easy for parents to make. Not only is the cost a strain on the typical family budget, but the child (and the family) may be forced to endure a severe physical handicap.

Sudden infant death syndrome, also known as *crib death,* has received a great deal of attention in the media during the past few years. Public interest has been prompted not only by the frequency of crib deaths, but also because the causes are unclear. For some reason, the sleeping infant simply stops breathing. The condition is rare during the first month after birth, increases gradually to a peak at about 10 weeks, and then declines until it becomes rare again after six to eight months (Hines, 1980).

Occasionally associated with death in the fetus or newborn is death in the mother due to complications during pregnancy, childbirth, or the postchildbirth period (the *puerperium*). Like infant mortality, the maternal mortality rate has declined steadily during recent years. As indicated in Table 7-2, both the infant and maternal mortality rates in the

TABLE 7-2
Maternal Deaths and Mortality Rates by Race in the United States in 1979

Race	Number of Deaths	Death Rate Per 100,000
White	180	6.4
Black	145	25.1
Other	11	10.0
Total	336	9.6

Source: Adapted from National Center for Health Statistics. (1982). *Monthly Vital Statistics Report,* 31(6). Washington, D.C.: U.S. Dept. of Health and Human Services.

United States are related to ethnicity, a demographic variable associated with maternal health and prenatal care. The 1979 death rate for black infants was almost twice that for white infants; the death rate associated with pregnancy, childbirth, and the puerperium was almost four times higher for black women than for white women.

Statistics on the leading causes of death in children during 1979 are listed in Table 7-3. Many of these fatal disorders are chronic conditions, involving a long period of home care and hospitalization before the child expires. Such disorders, referred to as *terminal* or *catastrophic* illnesses, usually demand a great deal of physical and emotional investment—not only by the patient but by the entire family. There are extraordinary medical measures, such as liver and bone marrow transplants, that can be taken to arrest or retard certain conditions, but the financial costs often run into hundreds of thousands of dollars. Because insurance companies often refuse to pay for "experimental" treatments, whether a child with a catastrophic illness lives or dies frequently hinges on the affluence of the family or the generosity of the public.

Rick and Pat Escalambre know that all too well. Everyone who meets their three-year-old Rachel agrees that she is an adorable child. While her cancer was in remission, she giggled, she smiled, she danced for strangers. She jabbered on about Donald Duck. Dark-eyed and button-nosed, she stole hearts with the finesse of a jewel thief. The only reminder of her life-threatening illness was the soft covering of down on her head, the aftermath of chemotherapy that caused the loss of her long dark hair.

"You were told she was sick, and you knew it, but she is very bright and personable and gregarious," said Jennifer Foote, a reporter for the San

TABLE 7-3
Leading Causes of Death in Children in the United States in 1979

Cause	1–4 Years		5–14 Years	
	Number	Rate	Number	Rate
Accidents and adverse effects	3,349	27.1	5,689	16.5
Malignant neoplasms	578	4.7	1,552	4.5
Congenital anomalies	1,021	8.3	578	1.7
Cardiovascular disease	321	2.6	417	1.2
Homicide	314	2.5	394	1.1
Infectious and parasitic diseases	311	2.5	219	.6
Pneumonia	250	2.0	204	.6
Meningitis	183	1.5	56	.2
All causes	8,108	65.6	11,146	32.2

Source: Adapted from National Center for Health Statistics. (1982). *Monthly Vital Statistics Report, 31*(6). Washington, D.C.: U.S. Dept. of Health and Human Services.

Francisco Examiner, which published more than 30 articles about Rachel and helped raise $250,000 for a bone marrow transplant.

"So you had this winning kid juxtaposed with this terminal illness, and it creates this real desperation to want to defeat the illness and save the winning kid."[4]

The three leading causes of death in adolescence are accidents, homicide, and suicide, although cancer and cardiovascular diseases also claim their share of victims in this age category. The loss of an adolescent son or daughter, bright with promise and full of great expectations, can be particularly heartrending for a parent. The loss of a friend or sibling in adolescence can also place a heavy burden on a person and act as a damper on his or her enthusiasm and hope.

Feelings of Dying Children

Based on Nagy's (1948) research with normal children, the assumption was made at one time that the majority of dying children, and particularly those below the age of four or five, had no real understanding of impending death. It was obvious that terminally ill children were made anxious, depressed, and even angry by the pain and treatment connected with illness and by the social separation of hospitalization, but so were children whose illnesses were not terminal (Yudkin, 1967). The results of later studies, however, revealed that fatally ill children were made even more anxious than other sick children by hospitalization and the treatments associated with it (Waechter, 1971; Spinetta, Rigler, & Karon, 1973). In Waechter's (1971) investigation, dying and nondying hospitalized children between the ages of six and 10 years were administered an anxiety inventory and asked to make up stories about pictures they were shown. The fatally ill children scored significantly higher on the anxiety inventory and told more stories associated with dying than the nonfatally ill children. Many of these stories expressed concerns about mutilation or loss of body functioning. Similarly, Spinetta, Rigler, and Karon (1973) found that children with leukemia were more anxious than other chronically ill children about being injured or unable to function normally, even when both groups had received the same number and duration of medical treatments.

The nature of the anxiety or fear experienced by a terminally ill child varies, of course, with the chronological (and mental) age of the child. Spinetta (1974) found that what three- to five-year-old dying

---

4. From *Los Angeles Times,* July 17, 1983, p. 1B. Reprinted by courtesy of The Associated Press.

children feared most about death was separation from their parents, grand-parents, and playmates. Children of this age are primarily afraid of being left all alone or abandoned, and are comforted by frequent attention and reassurance that mommy and daddy will never leave them. In contrast, the five- to nine-year-olds in Spinetta's (1974) study were more afraid of death as the end of life and of body mutilation.

One of the most important investigations concerned with the feel-ings of terminally ill children was conducted by Bluebond-Langner (1977, 1978). She concluded from her observations that not only fatally ill children younger than four or five years, but even those as young as 18 months can understand that they are dying and that the process cannot be reversed. This understanding does not come all at once, but progresses through a series of five stages. In each stage, the child acquires a little more information about the illness and its prognosis and alters his or her self-concept in accordance with that information. In the first stage, after the initial diagnosis is made, the child is concerned about the seriousness of the illness and with feeling so sick; the self-concept is *seriously ill.* In the second stage, after experiencing his or her first remission of symptoms, the child becomes interested in the medicines, their side effects, and names; the self-concept is changed to *seriously ill, but will get better.* In the third stage, after the first relapse or return of symptoms, the child begins to feel that he or she will always be ill but continues to hope for improvement; the self-concept is modified to *always ill, but will get better.* In the fourth stage, the illness has continued and the child wonders if he or she will ever improve; the self-concept changes to *always ill, and will never get better.* In the fifth and final stage, the child comes to realize, after observing the death of a fellow patient, that he or she too is going to die; the self-concept changes to *dying.*

Family Reactions to the Death of a Child

The death of a child can be emotionally devastating to a family. This is especially true when the death is unexpected, as in an accident, a suicide, or a sudden fatal illness. Even in the case of an infant who is aborted, still born, or dies shortly after birth, the mother's emotional attachment to the child has already started forming (Grobstein, 1978). The loss is usually even more difficult to bear when the child has developed to the point at which he or she can interact socially with the parents. Coupled with the guilt and depression experienced by the parents are feelings of impotence, frustration, and anger that this should happen and at being unable to do anything for the fatally ill or dead child. The anger may be directed toward anyone who seems responsible for the tragedy—the hospital staff, the parents themselves, and even God. These feelings are so intense in many cases that the parents never fully recover; the emotional problems associated with the death may still be present a decade or more after the death of the child. When one or both of the parents are unable to work through their grief, family life becomes disrupted. Alcoholism, sexual dysfunctions, sleep and eating disturbances, and other symptoms of emotional disorder are commonplace, indicating a need for psychological counseling or psychotherapy. If untreated, these parental reactions often lead to separation and divorce (Simpson, 1979).

Not only the parents, but all members of the family are affected by the fatal illness and death of a child. Grandparents grieve in a threefold sense—for the grandchild, for their son or daughter, and for themselves (Hamilton, 1978). Furthermore, the parents are frequently so preoccupied with their own thoughts and feelings and with attending to the dying or dead child that they neglect their other children. The siblings of dying and deceased children often feel anxious, deprived, confused, and socially isolated. The physical and behavioral changes that occur in a dying child as the illness progresses can also be frightening to a young brother or sister. And when the child dies, the surviving children are not only sad, as everyone else in the family is, but they may also feel guilty for having mistreated the dead sibling or having wished he or she were dead. They may also show regressive behavior and develop an unreasonable fear of doctors, hospitals, and of dying themselves. If ignored by the parents, these feelings can persist and influence the child's future emotional behavior and mental stability. A number of writers (Rosenzweig & Bray, 1943; Green & Solnit, 1964; Pollock, 1978) have described the psychological vulnerability of such children and their greater than average tendency to have emotional problems lasting into adulthood.

On the other hand, the attitudes of children with terminally ill or dead siblings are often healthier than those of their parents. Childhood is a time of flexibility, a time when losses and frustrations are usually adjusted to rather quickly. What seems like a traumatic experience to an adult is typically not as disturbing to a growing child, who is full of energy and keen on living and learning. However, children do need reassurance and a sense of being included, both during the fatal illness and after the death of a brother or sister. They should be made to feel that they are important and needed at all stages of the illness. They can be permitted to visit the hospital, provided with details on their brother's or sister's illness, and encouraged to express their feelings and thoughts—especially any feelings of guilt—about the dying child (Stillion & Wass, 1979). After the death, the surviving siblings should not be excluded from the funerary rituals or postmortem discussions. Those in middle childhood (6–10 years) can certainly understand the significance of death and loss and the meaning of a funeral, so adults should take time to explain to them, at their own level, the cause of the death and what it means. Consider the following conversation between a small girl and her mother after the child's recently deceased brother had been cremated.

"I will keep your ashes, Mom (after you die), but who will keep mine?"
I say, "Your kids will, if you have kids. Or your best friend."
"Who will keep the ashes of the last person in the world?"
"God will," I say.[5]

Even children as young as five or six can cope with a funeral and, to some extent, understand its significance. Therefore, they should be encouraged, but not forced, to participate. In any event, the key to how the surviving siblings deal with the death is almost always in the hands of the parents or other significant adults. Clearly then, it is important for the parents to work through their own problems associated with the death as quickly as possible (Stillion & Wass, 1979).

Working with Terminally Ill Children and Their Parents

Physicians, nurses, and other health workers usually recognize the importance of being fairly open and truthful in responding to dying children. They also recognize the cruelty of repeatedly encouraging the child to minimize the seriousness of his or her illness or of pretending that a severe loss is not being suffered. On the other hand, complete candor and a failure to offer some hope is inadvisable and unrealistic. After all, over one-third of the approximately 2,500 U.S. children who are stricken with leukemia each year survive more than five years and many are able to live normal lives ("What Does Cancer Do . . . ?," 1982). What health workers and counselors are advised to do is listen to these children and remain open to their questions. These questions are usually not highly technical queries about disease or afterlife, but rather questions indicating a need for reassurance, companionship, and assistance. Green (1966) noted, for example, that three questions are of most concern to terminally ill children in the 6–12 year age range: Am I safe? Will there be a trusted person to keep me from feeling helpless, alone, and to overcome pain? Will you make me feel all right? It takes patience and experience to respond to these questions in a manner appropriate for a particular child, but love and understanding, combined with adequate training, can help.

Hospitals are not the only community agencies that are concerned with fatally ill children. Various organizations provide books, toys, and other materials for young, catastrophically ill patients. Every year, the Sunshine Foundation, which is based in Philadelphia, sends a number of dying or chronically ill children and their families on expense-paid trips to athletic events, amusement parks, and other places of interest to children. Information on various services that are available to sick children and their parents can be obtained by writing to the addresses given in Appendix B.

---

5. Excerpts from "When Wendy's Brother Died," by Marty Keyser, Reader's Digest, July, 1977.

One of the most important contributions that health workers can make in treatment programs for terminally ill children is in making suggestions and giving advice to the parents. As shown by the fact that calm acceptance on the part of the parents leads to a better prognosis for the child (see Morrissey, 1963), parents are a significant part of the total treatment program for fatally ill children. Health workers should begin by recognizing the cognitive, emotional, and social needs of the parents. On the cognitive side, the parents require clear explanations of the child's diagnosis (nature and type of disease), the type of therapy or treatment to be undertaken, and the prognosis (probable outcomes). On the emotional side, health workers must be aware of the depth of shock and despair felt by the parents.

Parents' emotional reactions to terminal illness in their child are normally a three-stage process (Natterson & Knudson, 1960). The stages are:

1. Shock and denial, frequently accompanied by anger, frequent weeping, and overprotection of the child.
2. Acceptance of the child's illness, and a willingness to search for ways to save the child.
3. Defensively sublimating parental feelings by directing energy toward other sick children.

Health workers must be prepared to discuss and help relieve any guilt felt by the parents and to emphasize any possible hope.

On the social side, health workers should be ready to assist parents with any problems in telling other people about the illness and in maintaining continuity in rearing the sick child. Effective parent counselors will also want to assess the capacities of the family for coping with the child's illness and to encourage building on the family's strengths. A final parent conference after the death of the child is recommended to provide an opportunity for the expression of postmortem feelings and to achieve closure (Stillion & Wass, 1979).

Futterman and Hoffman (1970) concluded that parents who are able to deal successfully with the death of a child usually progress through a series of five emotional stages, collectively described as *anticipatory mourning.* These stages are:

1. Acknowledging that the child's illness is terminal.
2. Grieving in response to this knowledge.
3. Becoming reconciled to the child's death by finding meaning in it and in the child's life.
4. Becoming somewhat emotionally detached from the child.
5. Memorializing the child by forming a lasting mental image of him or her.

175

Death of a Parent

It is the natural order of things for parents to precede their children in death, and this usually occurs after the children have grown up. It is estimated, however, that 5 percent of U.S. children experience the death of at least one parent (Stein, 1974). Young children, as noted previously, are usually quite resilient when faced with upsetting situations, but the death of a parent can be a real tragedy for a child. The death of a sibling, another relative, an acquaintance, or even a pet is disturbing enough, but usually does not compare with the child's emotional reactions to the death of a close parental figure. The effects of parental death on the child are indicated by the fact that adults who, in childhood, have lost a parent are more likely to have psychiatric problems. These problems include depression and suicidal behavior (Brown, 1961; Beck, Sethi, & Tuthill, 1963; Crook & Eliot, 1980), schizophrenia (Blum & Rosenzweig, 1944), antisocial behavior (Barry, 1939), and even physical disorders such as cardiovascular disease (Lynch, 1977).

The normal grief responses of children who have lost parents are similar to those seen in anyone who has suffered a severe loss. As described by Bowlby (1974), the grieving child begins by refusing to believe that the parent is actually dead, protests vigorously, and tries to find a way to get the parent back. When these efforts are unsuccessful, the child's behavior becomes disorganized and genuine grief sets in. Eventually the child accepts the reality of the loss and begins to reorganize his or her life. These stages are less intense when the child has alternative sources of emotional support and understanding. In fact, the process of grieving can be eased even before the death by offering the child a role in caring for the sick parent. No matter how minor the role may seem, it can give the child a feeling of contributing to the well-being of the parent. One child may be comfortable in the role of practical nurse to the parent, whereas another would rather talk to the parent or simply listen to music with him or her (Pier, 1982).

Death Education

Death, like sex, is a part of life about which children and adults need to know. Nevertheless, as with sex education, introduction of the topic of death into school and college curricula has sometimes been met with cries of alarm about the potentially damaging effects of lessons on death and dying. Some people have voiced concerns that discussions of mortality will make children and youth anxious, depressed, and callous, in addition to increasing the rates of suicide and homicide and decreasing religious faith. The fact that such fears are unwarranted is seen in the results of studies of changes occurring in children and adults who have been exposed to educational experiences and courses concerned with thanatology. Rather than wreaking emotional havoc, the typical result of a discussion or course on death and dying is a moderate improvement in participants' attitudes and knowledge about death (see Leviton, 1977).

Units, courses, and entire curricula on death and dying have been designed for schools, colleges, senior citizens organizations, and many special interest groups. The basic goals of these educational efforts are both theoretical and practical. Because people frequently lack accurate information on death and dying, one important goal is to increase the student's knowledge about death, as well as the professions and organizations (medical, governmental, funeral, etc.) that are concerned with it. Another goal is to help students learn to cope, in an emotional sense, with the deaths of loved ones and associates. Beyond these two very concrete goals is the more abstract goal of helping students understand the social and ethical issues concerning death, and particularly the value judgments involved in discussions of these issues (Gordon & Klass, 1979).

College and Adult Death Education

Because formal education in death and dying was first offered at the college level, a brief look at the activities of higher education programs is perhaps in order before discussing our main topic of death education for children. Leviton (1977) describes a number of these programs and the organizations that helped structure the curricula. The addresses of several such organizations are listed in Appendix B at the end of this book. These organizations are hopeful that carefully designed courses and curricula on death and dying will not only provide information on practical and theoretical matters pertaining to the topic, but will also contribute to the development of empathy and concern for one's fellow human beings. A successful course on death and dying should not only make students more knowledgeable but should also make them more sensitive to the feelings and needs of dying people.

In addition to readings, lectures by the course instructor, and class discussions, several special activities have become a part of college level and adult education courses on death and dying. These activities include such things as:

1. Describing one's reasons for taking the course and what is expected from it.
2. Live talks, tape recordings, and films, particularly films featuring dying people.
3. A visit to at least one death-related institution, for example, a cemetery, a funeral home, or a crematorium.

4. Drawing pictures or writing poems and stories describing one's personal feelings and ideas about death.
5. Writing one's own epitaph and obituary.
6. Role playing scenes of dying, death, and related matters.

All adults do not require a formal course in death and dying in order to become informed about the topic. Many of the books listed in the Suggested Readings list at the end of this chapter and in Table 7-4 provide useful information for both adults and children. However, parents and teachers need to make certain that they are themselves sufficiently informed before attempting to explain death to children. Adults also need to get in touch with their own feelings about death, because emotional reactions are even more easily communicated than misinformation.

Educating Children about Death

Much of the death-oriented teaching of young children is informal and impromptu, depending on what is taking place at the time and the questions posed by the child. Parents and teachers usually talk about death only when the child wants to or when the death of a pet or person indicates that a "teachable moment" has come (Leviton & Forman, 1974). The nature of the response to a child's query about death depends not only on the specific question asked or the particular situation, but also on the maturity level of the child. Preschoolers, for example, require less elaborate explanations than other children. Therefore, death can be explained in simple physical and biological terms to children in this age group without becoming too detailed or abstract. In fact, what preschoolers need, more than highly accurate explanations about death, is reassurance that they are loved and will not be abandoned. Older children, on the other hand, should be encouraged to go beyond simple notions and think a bit more abstractly about the meaning of life and death (Stein, 1974). Regardless of the child's age, adults should be honest, sensitive, and sympathetic, encouraging children to express their own feelings and ideas. Children should be told when family members or other individuals whom they know are dying, and they should be permitted to stay with their families at that time. They should also be encouraged, but not forced, to attend the funerals of family members and friends. And, if they decide to attend, they should be told exactly what to expect. Finally, when children question them about life after death, adults should express their own beliefs but admit that they do not know all the answers.

A Comprehensive School Curriculum

The degree of formality in death education at the elementary and secondary school levels varies with the school and the teacher, but a number

TABLE 7-4
Books on Death and Dying Recommended for Children and Adolescents

Preschool and Primary Grades (Ages 3–8)
Berger, T. (1971). *I have feelings*. New York: Human Sciences Press.
Bonnet, S. (1974). *About death*. New York: Stein, Walker.
Brown, M. W. (1965). *The dead bird*. Glenview, Ill.: Scott Foresman.
De Paola, T. (1973). *Nana upstairs and Nana downstairs*. New York: Putnam's.
Fassler, J. (1971). *My grandpa died today*. New York: Behavioral Publications.
Katrowitz, M. (1973). *When Violet died*. New York: Parents Magazine Press.
Miles, M. (1976). *Annie and the old one*. Boston: Little, Brown.
Shector, B. (1973). *Across the meadow*. New York: Doubleday.
Stein, S. (1974). *About dying*. New York: Walker.
Stull, E. (1964). *My turtle died today*. New York: Holt, Rinehart & Winston.
Tressalt, A. (1971). *The dead tree*. New York: Parents Magazine Press.
Viorst, J. (1971). *The tenth good thing about Barney*. New York: Atheneum.
Warburg, S. (1969). *Growing time*. Boston: Houghton Mifflin.
Zolotow, C. (1974). *My grandson Lew*. New York: Harper & Row.

Elementary Grades (Ages 8–12)
Carlson, N. (1970). *The half sisters*. New York: Harper & Row.
Corley, E. (1973). *Tell me about death, tell me about funerals*. Santa Clara, Calif.: Grammatical Sciences.
Erdman, L. (1973). *A bluebird will do*. New York: Dodd, Mead.
Farley, C. (1975). *The garden is doing fine*. New York: Atheneum.
Harris, A. (1965). *Why did he die?* Minneapolis: Lerner Publications.
Hunter, M. (1974). *A sound of chariots*. New York: Harper & Row.
LeShan, E. (1976). *Learning to say goodbye: When a parent dies*. New York: Macmillan.
Lorenzo, C. L. (1974). *Mama's ghosts*. New York: Harper & Row.
Orgel, D. (1970). *The mulberry music*. New York: Harper & Row.
Smith, D. B. (1973). *A taste of blackberries*. New York: Crowell.
Watts, R. (1975). *Straight talk about death with young people*. Philadelphia: Westminster.
White, E. B. (1952). *Charlotte's web*. New York: Harper & Row.

Junior and Senior High School (Ages 12 and up)
Agee, J. (1959). *A death in the family*. New York: Avon.
Bach, R. (1970). *Jonathan Livingston Seagull*. New York: Macmillan.
DeVries, P. (1961). *Blood of the lamb*. Boston: Little, Brown.
Greene, C. C. (1979). *Beat the turtle drum*. New York: Dell.
Hunter, M. (1972). *A sound of chariots*. New York: Harper & Row.
Klein, N. (1974). *Sunshine*. New York: Avon.
Lee, V. (1972). *The magic moth*. Boston: Houghton Mifflin.
L'Engle, M. (1980). *The summer of the great-grandmother*. New York: Seabury.
LeShan, E. (1976). *Learning to say goodbye when a parent dies*. New York: Macmillan.
Olander, J., & Greenberg, M. H. (1978). *Time of passage*. New York: Taplinger.

of curricular plans have been proposed. A comprehensive curriculum designed by Gordon and Klass (1979) is outlined in Table 7-5. Spanning the entire range of grade levels from preschool through senior high, this curriculum is based on four goals. The first goal, which is concerned with the question of what happens when people die, is attained when students

179

TABLE 7-5
Goals and Grade-Level Objectives of Death Education

Goal 1. To inform the student of facts not currently widespread in the culture.

Objectives in Preschool and Grade 1
Explore the life cycle of plants and animals in order to introduce students to birth, life, and death as part of the same cycle.
Find out what happens to dead people and pets, and explore the cemetery.
Identify various stages in the life cycle with special attention to the characteristics of old age.
Objectives in Grades 2 and 3
Include human death within the biological life cycle.
Find out what causes death.
Objectives in Grades 4 and 5
Introduce the student to factual information about the demography of death.
Introduce the student to the facts about institutions that are concerned with death.
Objectives in Grades 6 and 7
Acquaint the students with the legal and scientific definitions of death.
Students study various methods of body disposal.
Objectives in Grades 8 and 9
Cross-cultural study of beliefs and customs about death in order to acquaint students with a broad range of views and practices concerning death.
Understand the dynamics of aging and death and the social institutions that deal with them.
Explore attitudes and stereotypes about aging in the United States.
Objectives in Grades 10 and 11
Acquaint the student with current legal and medical definitions of death, and introduce the problematic character of those definitions.
Acquaint students with the legalities and problems of body and organ donation.
Objectives in Grade 12
Survey theories about suicide and its occurrence in our culture.

Goal 2. To help the student affectively deal with the idea of personal death and the deaths of significant others.

Objectives in Preschool and Grade 1
Talk about the feelings students have when they experience loss.
Objectives in Grades 2 and 3
Explore students' feelings when someone dies.
Explore students' ideas of death as expressed in the culture.
Objectives in Grades 4 and 5
Help children reflect upon their past ideas of death, and consolidate these views. (Student is in a transitional period to more mature concepts of death, and this topic will help formulate student's new ideas and acceptance of death as a final reality.)
Children begin to accept the reality and finality of their own deaths.
Objectives in Grades 6 and 7
Help the student develop a philosophy of life and death.
Students learn the appropriate social behavior at the time of death and mourning.
Maturing students identify feelings they and others have in anticipating death and feelings they might have at the time of death.

TABLE 7-5 (*continued*)
Objectives in Grades 8 and 9
Explore the students' own feelings about the aged and getting old.
Objectives in Grades 10 and 11
Make students aware of their responses to loss and ways of coping with loss.
Have the students explore decisions about death and dying as these decisions
would affect them and their families.
Objectives in Grade 12
Have students explore their own feelings about suicide.
Acquaint the student with experiences connected with the crises of death and
dying that may not fit into commonly accepted reality.

Goal 3. To make the student an informed consumer of medical and funeral services.

Objectives in Grades 2 and 3
Introduce funeral procedures and the funeral establishment.
Objectives in Grades 6 and 7
Help students clarify their value systems on the issue of body disposal.
Objectives in Grades 8 and 9
Discover the medical context of dying, and introduce the student to the tech-
nology, professional duties, and attitudes surrounding death.
Objectives in Grades 10 and 11
Acquaint students with the financial aspects of medical care for terminal illness
and life-threatening situations.
Introduce the student to a variety of methods of body disposal, current funeral
practice, and relative costs.
Objectives in Grade 12
Acquaint students with insurance and wills.

Goal 4. To help the student formulate socioethical issues related to death and define value judgments these issues raise.

Objectives in Grades 4 and 5
Explore society's values on issues related to death and dying as presented in
media ordinarily seen by young children.
Objectives in Grades 8 and 9
Introduce the students to basic ethical and social policy issues connected with
dying.
Objectives in Grades 10 and 11
Acquaint the student with the legal and moral issues reflected in the problems
of the prolongation of life and the termination of life.

Source: Adapted from the book THEY NEED TO KNOW by Audrey K. Gordon & Dennis
Klass. © 1979 by Prentice-Hall, Inc. Published by Prentice-Hall, Inc., Englewood Cliffs,
NJ 07632.

become informed about facts that are not generally known in the culture.
The second goal is concerned with how to cope with the reality of death in
a healthy way. It is reached when students have learned to deal effectively
with the idea of personal death and the deaths of people who are significant to them. The third goal is concerned with the practical matter of making students informed consumers of medical and funeral services. The
fourth and final goal, which is the most abstract of all, is to help students

formulate socioethical issues related to death and to define value judgments raised by these issues.

Each of the four goals in the Gordon and Klass curriculum is broken down into several subgoals or objectives that understandably become more complex and abstract at higher grade levels. Special methods and materials are employed in attaining each of the objectives. For example, poems, stories, and films are often useful in attaining the affective objectives listed under Goal 2. Assignments similar to several of those listed previously for college and adult education courses can also be made in teaching children about death. For example, a trip to a mortuary, a hospice, or a hospital ward for terminally ill patients can contribute significantly to children's lessons on death and dying. Despite the concerns expressed by certain adults, children rarely find such experiences frightening or distasteful. In fact, when prepared and accompanied by a sensitive, knowledgeable adult, young visitors almost always find these trips interesting and informative.

SUMMARY

Because death has become less common, less public, and a topic that is not discussed as much in the presence of children as it once was, children in the United States are less familiar with death and dying than children in previous centuries. However, there are indications that the denial of death that was characteristic of Western culture during the first half of this century is changing to a greater openness and an interest in education concerning the subject.

The findings of Nagy's classic research investigation on children's conceptions of death were interpreted as pointing to the existence of three stages: a first stage between the ages of three and five years, in which children do not distinguish between death and separation; a second stage between five and nine years, in which death is conceived of as irreversible but avoidable; a third stage at 10 years and over, in which children understand death as real, inevitable, and irreversible. Nagy has been criticized for failing to consider the effects of culture and experience on the child's conceptions of death and for her assumption that very young children have little or no understanding of mortality. Studies conducted in the United States, for example, have not found the frequent personifications of death reported by Nagy's second-stage children. Furthermore, lower-class U.S. children are more likely to associate death with violence; middle-class children are more likely to associate death with illness. From her research on terminally ill children, Bluebond-Langner concluded that rather than being restricted to a specific chronological age range, all views of death are present at every stage of child development.

Extreme fears of death in children are not normal and are usually indicative of other emotional problems. A child who is intensely afraid of death or dying is, in most cases, actually afraid of being separated from a parent or other nurturing person. A fear of death, like all fears, can also be learned from parents and others who are afraid. Whatever their origin, a child's fears and questions about death should be responded to by adults in a natural but thoughtful manner, neither lying nor denying, but answering in a way that the child is capable of understanding.

Death in infancy has declined dramatically during this century, but it is still more common than in other periods of childhood. The three leading causes of infant death are congenital anomalies, respiratory distress syndrome, and sudden infant death syndrome. The three leading causes of death in children aged 1–14 years are accidents and adverse effects, malignant neoplasms, and congenital anomalies.

Terminally ill children are usually more afraid, depressed, and angry than other hospitalized children, and they realize, in most instances, that they are dying. The fears concerning death that are expressed by dying children vary with their chronological age. In early childhood they are more afraid of separation, whereas in middle childhood they are more afraid of body mutilation and the end of their lives. Bluebond-Langner's formulation of five stages through which terminally ill children pass in their changing attitudes toward their condition and self-concepts points to a fairly high level of awareness on the part of the children.

The death of a child can be a real tragedy for the parents and other members of the family. Anxiety, depression, guilt, and anger are common parental and sibling reactions that can lead to more serious emotional problems and family disruption when unresolved. The siblings of deceased children usually adjust more readily than the adult members of the family, especially when the parents do not neglect them while caring for the dying or deceased child.

Health workers are advised to be open and truthful with dying children, not giving them false encouragement but communicating a realistic degree of hope. The dying child's questions about his or her condition and future should be answered sensitively and at a level appropriate to the child's ability to understand. Realizing that the parents must also be helped, both for the sake of the dying child and the parents themselves, health workers are advised to recognize and deal with the cognitive, emotional, and social needs of the parents as they relate to the dying child. Parents pass through a number of stages before accepting the fact that their child is dying or has died. Anticipatory mourning begins even before the child's death, and it is a positive sign that the parent is working on his or her emotional problems related to the impending death.

Parents do not always wait until their children are grown before dying. A very small percentage of newborns never know a mother and form no direct emotional attachment to her. The loss of a parent to whom the child has become emotionally attached, however, can produce an extreme psychological reaction that, if not dealt with adequately, can create an emotional disorder lasting into adulthood.

The realization that both sex and death are parts of life for which children and adults require preparation has led to increased attention to these two topics in schools and colleges in recent years. Lessons, courses, and entire curricula on death and dying have been designed for a variety of formal and informal groups, ranging from preschoolers to senior citizens. The goals of these efforts are both practical and theoretical, cognitive and affective, the overall aim being to enable participants to cope more effectively with their own deaths and the deaths of significant others. The participants in sessions or courses on death and dying are presented information and experiential opportunities by means of conventional instructional approaches (lectures, discussions, readings, writing assignments) as well as trips to hospitals, mortuaries, cemeteries, and other death-related places. A comprehensive curriculum for the school grades, encompassing a wide range of materials and experiences, has been designed by Gordon and Klass.

SUGGESTED READINGS

Bluebond-Langner, M. (1977). Meanings of death to children. In H. Feifel (Ed.), *New meanings of death*. New York: McGraw-Hill.

Bluebond-Langner, M. (1978). *The private worlds of dying children*. Princeton, N.J.: Princeton University Press.

Furman, E. (1974). *A child's parent dies*. New Haven, Conn.: Yale University Press.

Gordon, A. K., & Klass, D. (1979). *The need to know: How to teach children about death*. Englewood Cliffs, N.J.: Prentice-Hall.

Grollman, E. A. (1976). *Talking about death: A dialogue between parent and child*. Boston: Beacon.

Krementz, J. (1981). *How it feels when a parent dies*. New York: Knopf.

Lonetto, R. (1981). *Children's conceptions of death*. New York: Springer.

Rudolph, M. (1978). *Should the children know?* New York: Schocken.

Ryerson, M. (1977). Death education and counseling for children. *Elementary School Guidance and Counseling, 11*, 165–174.

Sahler, O. J. (Ed.). (1978). *The child and death*. St. Louis, Mo.: Mosby.

Schiff, H. S. (1978). *The bereaved parent*. New York: Penguin.

Ulin, R. O. (1977). *Death and dying education*. Washington, D.C.: National Education Assn.

Wolf, A. M. (1973). *Helping your children to understand death*. (rev. ed.). New York: Child Study Press.

8 Adult Development and the Dying Process

Questions answered in this chapter:

- How can fears and attitudes toward death and dying be determined?
- In what ways are fears and attitudes toward death associated with chronological age, culture, and history?
- What are near-death experiences, and how have they been interpreted?
- What is a terminal drop, and how can it be explained?
- What roles do feelings of helplessness and hopelessness play in dying, and how can they be counteracted?
- What is Kübler-Ross's stage theory of dying, and why has it been criticized?
- What are some alternative descriptions and explanations of the psychological processes involved in dying?

*C*hildren and young adults do not generally spend much time thinking about their mortality. When one is young, energetic, and full of hopes and expectations, life is just beginning, and death, if it is considered at all, is perceived as lying in the distant future. Rather than being afraid of growing older and dying, young people are more often in a hurry to grow up so they can start living their own lives and acquiring all the benefits that adulthood appears to promise.

There is no specific age at which people begin thinking more about death and dying. Tradition has it that the turning point is age 30 for women and age 40 for men. But whatever the critical age may be, there comes a time in an individual's life when he or she is more apt to measure life in terms of the number of years left to live rather than the years already passed. At this time, the reality of temporal limits on personal existence becomes of greater concern to the individual than it has been previously.

Sometime during the fourth decade of life, signs that the breaking-down processes of the body are outstripping the building-up processes become obvious. Physical deterioration caused by aging begins to show in one's own appearance and abilities as well as those of relatives and friends. The deaths of relatives and friends who are in the middle or late years of life remind a person that the chances of dying increase every year after age 45 or so. This trend is demonstrated by the age-specific death rates given in Table 8-1; the probability of dying not only increases but does so at an accelerated rate after young adulthood. Physical changes occurring in oneself reveal the unexpressed but half-believed romantic assumption that "other people may die, but I am invulnerable and hence immortal" to be untrue. Death is now recognized as something that eventually happens to everybody, including oneself.

As a person grows older and the physical deterioration of the body becomes more and more apparent, the psychological distance from death diminishes. With each passing year, people perceive themselves as getting closer and closer to the end of life. In this shifting time perspective, the personal past—the time of one's major successes and failures—is seen as being relatively long and the personal future as relatively short. People now begin to talk more and more about bygone times and "how it used to be," a tendency that may cause their younger associates to remark that their elders are living in the past. The aging process also leads people to think more about death and, it might be presumed, to be more anxious about death. As we shall see, however, the fear of death and dying is not directly related to age.

TABLE 8-1
Estimated Age-Specific Death Rates for U.S. Adults in 1982

Chronological Age (years)	Death Rate Per 100,000 Population		
	Male	Female	Total
15–24	154.5	53.8	104.7
25–34	181.7	72.7	126.9
35–44	271.6	146.3	207.9
45–54	730.2	393.8	556.4
55–59	1,376.1	728.2	1,033.5
60–64	2,119.0	1,105.8	1,574.6
65–69	3,307.0	1,691.5	2,411.7
70–74	4,846.7	2,554.7	3,516.7
75–79	7,231.7	4,040.8	5,270.7
80–84	10,714.0	6,731.3	8,107.1
85 +	18,053.9	14,042.4	15,228.6

Source: National Center for Health Statistics. (1983). Monthly Vital Statistics Report, 31 (13). Washington, D.C.: U.S. Dept. of Health and Human Services.

Attitudes and Fears about Death

Why are people afraid of death? Is it the process of dying and the associated pain and suffering that evoke anxiety? Is it a fear of abandonment, aloneness, and separation from loved ones or from life in general? Is it a fear of dying before accomplishing one's goals, or a fear of not knowing what will happen after death (the "great unknown")? Is it what the existentialists refer to as the state of nonbeing or nothingness—the loss of identity—that is feared? There are no simple answers, because people are afraid for different reasons. Furthermore, the intensity and direction of the fear vary with the person and external circumstances. Fears and attitudes toward death and dying change with culture, chronological age, sex, educational level, familial and other social supports, personal mishaps, the sense of purpose or meaning in an individual's life, and other conditions. Like all affective responses, attitudes and fears concerning death are shaped by the sociocultural context in which a person develops, and particularly in the family situation (Huyck & Hoyer, 1982).

Not all people admit to being afraid of death and dying, and some even express a wish to die. Pain, loneliness, shame, guilt, depression, and the feeling that there is nothing worthwhile to live for may all lead to a desire for death. Among elderly people, for example, only a minority report fearing death (Kalish & Reynolds, 1976; Kimsey, Roberts, & Logan, 1972). Such findings would seem to question Becker's (1973) conclusion that the fear of death is inborn rather than acquired. Perhaps the fear is present in everyone from the beginning, but not everyone recognizes or admits to experiencing it.

Assessment of Attitudes toward Death

Whatever their origin may be, fears and attitudes toward death and dying, like all human predispositions, can be measured. One common method of assessing attitudes toward anything is a simple opinion poll. For example, Shneidman (1973) asked the question "What does death mean to you?" of a large national sample of people. The percentage of respondents giving specific answers were as follows:

- The end; the final process of life. (35 percent)
- The beginning of a life after death; a transition; a new beginning. (13 percent)
- A joining of the spirit with a universal cosmic consciousness. (12 percent)
- A kind of endless sleep; rest and peace. (9 percent)
- Termination of this life but with survival of the spirit. (17 percent)
- Don't know, or other answers. (14 percent)

187

These answers do not measure the intensity of death fears, but they do reveal something of what death means to the respondents.

Somewhat more precise than a simple yes-no tabulation of responses, at least from a measurement standpoint, is to have respondents rank a series of statements in order of their perceived importance. This procedure was followed in Diggory and Rothman's (1961) study of the rankings given by 550 people to seven statements concerning death. The statements receiving the three highest rankings in order of importance to the respondents were:

1. My death would cause grief to my friends and relatives.
2. All my plans and projects would come to an end.
3. The process of dying might be painful.

Other studies (e.g., Kalish & Reynolds, 1976; Kastenbaum & Aisenberg, 1972) have also found the death of a family member or relative to be one of the most stressful events in a person's life.

More direct attempts to assess the intensity of the fear of death are represented by the administration of a death anxiety scale like those constructed by Boyar (1964) and Templer (1972). Templer's Death Anxiety Scale, including a scoring key, is reproduced in Table 8-2. Such a scale may be useful not only in research on the causes and correlates of fears of death but also in identifying extremely death-anxious individuals for counseling purposes.

TABLE 8-2
Death Anxiety Scale

1. I am very much afraid to die. (T)*
2. The thought of death seldom enters my mind. (F)
3. It doesn't make me nervous when people talk about death. (F)
4. I dread to think about having to have an operation. (T)
5. I am not at all afraid to die. (F)
6. I am not particularly afraid of getting cancer. (F)
7. The thought of death never bothers me. (F)
8. I am often distressed by the way time flies so very rapidly. (T)
9. I fear dying a painful death. (T)
10. The subject of life after death troubles me greatly. (T)
11. I am really scared of having a heart attack. (T)
12. I often think about how short life really is. (T)
13. I shudder when I hear people talking about a World War III. (T)
14. The sight of a dead body is horrifying to me. (T)
15. I feel that the future holds nothing for me to fear. (F)

Source: From Templer, D. (1972). The construction and validation of a death anxiety scale. *Journal of General Psychology, 82,* 167. Used by permission.
*The keyed answers (in parentheses) indicate high death anxiety.

Cultural Differences and Similarities

Although customs and attitudes associated with death have varied extensively with time and place, there are a number of cross-cultural similarities in practices and beliefs. Most cultures do not consider death as the end of existence. Rather, something of individual consciousness is believed to survive death and go on to a heavenly or hellish afterlife (Grof & Halifax, 1977). As among the Murngin tribe of Australia and the Gond people of India, the cause of death is often viewed as accidental or external (due to magic or demons). A similar belief that death, illness, and other misfortunes are nonrandom occurrences precipitated by forces external to the individual is found among many native African groups.

The Murngins respond with anger and fear to the death of a member of their tribe. In contrast, the Tlingit people of Alaska, who view death as a natural phenomenon, accept it calmly and even joyfully. Similarly, the Basques of northern Spain hold that death is the crowning point of life, to be anticipated and celebrated by complex mourning rites. The East African Masai are also apparently unafraid of death, but, unlike the Basques, they minimize the importance of death and practice quite simple burial rites.

Cultural differences in attitudes and beliefs concerning death are widespread within the United States. For example, Kalish and Reynolds (1976) found many differences among the responses of their samples of Blacks, Whites, Japanese-Americans, and Mexican-Americans to questions about death and dying. Larger percentages of Blacks and Whites indicated that patients should be told when they are dying. Mexican-Americans were less likely than the other three groups to believe that (1) they would let people die if they wanted to, (2) they should be informed when they are mortally ill, and (3) they would try very hard to control their emotions in public if someone close died. A greater percentage of Whites than the other groups indicated that slow death is more tragic than sudden death and death in childhood is most tragic of all; the Whites also reported having had less contact with the dead and dying and were more likely to avoid funerals. Greater percentages of both Blacks and Mexican-Americans (1) saw the death of a woman as more tragic than the death of a man, (2) admitted having experienced or felt the presence of someone who had died, and (3) wanted to live past 90. Many of the differences in the responses of the four ethnic groups declined with age, and there were noteworthy similarities. For example, large percentages of all four groups viewed the private expression of grief as appropriate.

Some of the ethnic differences in the attitudes cited are undoubtedly expressions of educational and social class differences rather than ethnicity per se. In any event, attitudes toward death and dying are related to education. Compared with those having more education, the less educated are more likely to view death negatively, as coming too soon, and as being

TABLE 8-3
Percentages of a Large Sample of People of Different Age and Educational
Levels with a High Degree of Preparation for Death

	Educational Level		
Age	Junior High School or Less	High School	College
	Percent with High Degree of Preparation for Death		
30 and under	0	1	3
31–40	2	4	8
41–50	8	14	22
51–60	8	25	40
61 and over	20	30	44

Source: From AGING AND SOCIETY, Volume I, by Matilda White Riley, Anne Foner, and Associates. © 1968 by the Russell Sage Foundation. Reprinted by permission of the publisher.

associated with suffering (Keith, 1979). People with less education are also less likely to have talked about death or to have made any plans for it, as in preparing a will or discussing funeral arrangements (see Table 8-3).

Death Attitudes in Historical Perspective

Differences in attitudes toward death and dying are obviously not unique to the present scene but have varied throughout human history. In spite of the difficulties of attempting to reconstruct the past to obtain insight into the origins of death rites and customs, the painstaking research of Philippe Aries (1981) has yielded many interesting findings. Employing a variety of historiographic methods, Aries set out to test the hypothesis of a relationship between attitude toward death and the awareness of the self, or sense of individuality. Beginning his studies with documents and artifacts from the European Middle Ages of a thousand years ago, Aries traced the evolution of attitudes toward death and their relationships to self-awareness up to the twentieth century. The following discussion is a synopsis of his conclusions.

During the *tame death* era of the Middle Ages, death was accepted and expected as a terrible but necessary human misfortune. In this group-centered, less individualistic period dominated by the Church, the dead were thought merely to be sleeping until the Second Coming of Christ. Death itself was not feared so much as the method and timing of death. Of greatest concern was a sudden death, without warning or during sleep, because it provided no opportunity for confession and absolution. Except in the case of upper-class personages, even the funerary practices were a testimonial to the unimportance of the individual. Most people were buried in common pits, their bones being removed and placed in special

190

receptacles, *ossuaries,* after the flesh had decayed. The ossuaries were tended by church workers and could be seen from the villages, where the descendants of the dead lived.

The late Middle Ages (through the fifteenth century) were, according to Aries, a time of the *death of the self,* a period when individuality was minimized even more than previously. The dead were believed to be judged at the moment of death, and hence that moment became especially feared. Deathbed confessions abounded, determining at the moment when the body died whether the immortal soul was seized by an angel or a devil.

The death of the self attitude was succeeded by the *remote death* attitude of the seventeenth and eighteenth centuries. Death was now perceived as a sorrowful but remote event. Mortality was accepted, but thoughts of personal death still made people anxious. It was also a time of romantic or macabre eroticism in which death was intermingled with sex in art and literature.

The prevailing attitude toward death had changed again by the beginning of the nineteenth century. The attitude toward death as ugly, including the belief in hell, began to diminish. During this period, which Aries sees as dominated by a *death of the other* attitude, death was considered to be a beautiful event leading to a happy reunion in paradise. According to the religious beliefs of the time, the personal self survives death and roams the earth with other disembodied spirits.

Aries is most critical of the next era, that of the *denial of death* beginning in the late nineteenth century. This was the start of what he calls *the lie* and a time when death became less visible. Dying people were hidden away in hospitals, children were "spared" the unpleasantness of viewing and knowing about death and dying, the deceased was efficiently prepared and interred by a team of professionals, and public mourning was essentially eliminated. Death was likely to be seen as either an accident or a medical failure, and, in contrast to the belief of the Middle Ages, the best way to die was during sleep.

There are indications that the denial and externalization of death, which have been so characteristic of twentieth-century Western society, have eroded somewhat in the past two or three decades. Adults and children are learning once again that death is a part of what it means to be human, and that it is inhuman for people to die all alone attached to tubes and life-sustaining machines without being given a chance to make their peace and say their goodbyes.

Attitudes and Fears in Middle and Late Life

People in early adulthood do not think very much about death and do not usually express great fears of it. A young man who has had a serious accident or a young pregnant woman may experience some death anxiety, but

191

the fear of death does not intrude upon the consciousness of most people until middle age. Cross-sectional surveys of adults are fairly consistent in showing that fear of death is more common and more intense during middle age than in later life (Bengston, Cuellar, & Ragan, 1977; Kalish & Reynolds, 1976). This fear, which has been identified as part of the "midlife crisis," is precipitated by the individual's awareness of his or her declining health and appearance, coupled with unfulfilled dreams and unattained goals. An inventory of one's assets and liabilities, combined with a reasonable assessment of the time remaining in life, frequently acts as a stimulus to anxiety, sometimes hastening the very event that the individual dreads the most. Fears of death can be particularly intense in middle-aged people who are living enjoyable, personally meaningful lives.

Compared with the middle-aged, the elderly are more likely to see themselves as having had their day and to see death in old age as only fair. Realizing that time is shorter than in earlier years, older people do not plan as far ahead and are more inner-directed or private in their activities (Kalish, 1976). The deaths of friends and relatives, a lack of satisfying social roles, health and financial problems, and increased dependency on others all contribute to the feeling of having outlived one's usefulness and resignation to one's fate. Whatever the reasons may be, Wass's (1979) review of the literature on fear of death suggests that older people are not afraid of dying as much as younger people are. This does not mean that elderly people never fear their own demise. Butler and Lewis (1977) found, for example, that although 55 percent of the elderly people whom they surveyed had realistically resolved their fears of death, 30 percent were overtly afraid of it, and the remaining 15 percent used defensive denial to cope with their fears of dying.

Fears of death and dying may be quite strong in elderly people who are in poor physical or mental health, or who have a disabled spouse, dependent children, or important goals that they still expect to attain. By and large, however, the elderly are less afraid than middle-aged adults, and those who are afraid are more likely to fear the process of dying rather than the state of death itself. Even terminally ill older people tend to be less afraid than their younger counterparts. Although terminal illness usually increases fears of dying in the young (Feifel & Jones, 1968), it appears to have no such effect on the majority of elderly people (Kastenbaum, 1969).[1]

Chronological age is not the only factor related to the fear of death, of course. The intensity of the fear is a highly individual matter and varies with a range of personal and social variables. One important variable that

---

1. Kalish (1976) argues that the "blurring of ego boundaries" in the elderly may serve as a mechanism for transcending pain, and hence contribute to the lower incidence of death fears in this age group. Also associated with the blurring of ego boundaries are "altered mind states" resulting from psychedelic drugs and psychological techniques, which have been found to reduce fears of death and dying (Peck, 1968; Kalish, 1976).

helps control the fear of death is living (and dying) in familiar and stable surroundings (Lieberman & Coplan, 1969). And a significant individual difference affecting attitude toward death is sex. Back (1971) found, for example, that in comparison with older men, elderly women tend to be more accepting and benevolent in their attitudes toward death, likening it to a compassionate mother or an understanding doctor rather than an opponent. Men, on the other hand, are more likely to see death as an evil antagonist, a grinning butcher or hangman with bloody hands, who must be combatted.

Attitudes toward death in later life are also related to emotional adjustment, socioeconomic status, and achievement. People who are emotionally and financially stable and have attained most of their life goals are typically more accepting of death. But those who have many unresolved frustrations or are extremely self-centered are more likely to view death in a negative way or, alternatively, as an escape from an unrewarding life (Hinton, 1972).

The event of death can obviously be viewed in a number of ways—as the final insult to humanity, as the last developmental task, as a rite of passage to another plane of existence. However it may be perceived, the fact remains that death comes to all and must be thought about and dealt with by everybody. Whether these thoughts produce motivational paralysis on the one hand or a beneficial or destructive change in personality on the other depends on the individual's past experiences and present social supports. The effects of increased awareness of death also depend on the person's philosophy of life, a philosophy that is shaped by the multiplicity of social interactions taking place from childhood to senescence. A part of that continually developing philosophy is concerned with a sense of purpose in life, a purpose that serves as a mainstay in coping with the problems and emotions precipitated by the inevitability of life's ending.

Religious Beliefs and Near-Death Experiences

The great majority of humankind, since time immemorial, has found a purpose in life through religious beliefs. A strong belief in conventional religious principles is not essential to a calm acceptance of death, however, and certainly does not guarantee fearlessness in the face of it. Erikson (1976) maintained, for example, that an identification with the human race is the best defense against death anxiety.

Simply professing a belief in God and an afterlife and attending church regularly are not likely to protect people from fears of death and dying. Nevertheless, studies have shown that strong religious and philosophical beliefs are frequently a comfort to dying people (Becker,

1973; Mathieu, 1972). Those who believe in some form of God and have truly integrated religion into their lives are usually better able to face death without overwhelming fears than are those who are uncertain about religion (Kübler-Ross, 1974; Nelson & Nelson, 1973). Also of interest is the fact that affirmed atheists typically profess few fears of death. The greatest apprehension about death is found among people in the middle range between the strong believers and the strong nonbelievers in religion, those sporadically religious people whose beliefs are inconsistent.

Belief in an Afterlife

Characteristics of religions that give comfort to dying people vary widely with time and culture, but all religions try to provide a purpose and meaning for human existence. Although most religious people believe in some form of personal afterlife, such a belief is not essential to facing death calmly (Kalish & Reynolds, 1976). In fact, elderly people are usually more concerned about death per se and their own demise than they are with life after death (Hurlock, 1980). It is understandable, however, that feelings of personal transcendence and belief in an afterlife often provide comfort and reassurance to dying people. Such beliefs may be interpreted as wishful thinking or defensive denial, and those mechanisms are operating in many cases. The threat of total extinction and nothingness is a fearsome prospect, and it is natural for the human ego to defend itself against that threat.

Conceptions of immortality and afterlife, heaven, and hell form a part of most religions. Christians are frequently unclear about the nature of the life to come, but a large percentage believe that something of human personality survives the death of the body. Hindus, Buddhists, and members of certain other religious groups believe in reincarnation or metempsychosis, in which the soul of the deceased passes into another living body. The particular form in which the deceased is reincarnated is determined by his or her *karma,* or actions in previous lives (Long, 1975).

The United States prides itself on being a religious nation, and belief in a hereafter is held quite strongly by many U.S. citizens. In a Gallup poll conducted a few years ago, 67 percent of those surveyed stated that they believed in life after death. However, the percentage professing such a belief varied significantly with geographical region, size of community, ethnicity, religion, and other demographic variables. Greater percentages of southerners and midwesterners than easterners and westerners, and a greater percentage of small-city dwellers than large-city dwellers, reported believing in an afterlife. Greater percentages of whites than blacks and of Protestants than Catholics also stated that they believed in an afterlife. Although a majority of all those polled reported believing in an afterlife, only 20 percent felt that life after death would ever be scientifically proved (Gallup & Proctor, 1982).

Near-Death Experiences

Despite Blaise Pascal's conclusion that it is wise to bet on the existence of an afterlife, little if any direct information on the outcome of the wager has been forthcoming. A wealth of anecdotal information has been obtained, however, from people who almost died and were actually pronounced medically dead in some instances. Based on a number of these reports, Noyes (1972) identified three experiential phases occurring at death—resistance, life review, and transcendence. During the first phase, *resistance,* the dying person is initially aware of extreme danger, which leads to fear and struggling; the person's sensations are enhanced and accelerated, and time seems to expand. During the second phase, *life review,* there is a pleasant "out-of-body" sensation of observing one's own physical being from somewhere outside; the individual's past also passes rapidly before him or her. During the third phase, *transcendence,* there is a sense of awareness of the cosmos, of being one with other people and with nature—a feeling of contentment and even ecstasy in which one is outside space and time.

Reports of such out-of-body experiences are not uncommon. For example, 15 percent of a national sample of U.S. adults polled by Gallup and Proctor (1982) reported having "been on the verge of death or had a 'close call' which involved any unusual experience at the time." Particularly influential in stimulating both popular and scientific interest in life after death has been the work of Raymond Moody (1975). Moody's research methodology, which has also been employed by Sabom (1983) and others, consists of interviewing people who have been resuscitated after having been pronounced clinically dead. Although the 150 or so individuals whom Moody interviewed had difficulty describing their experiences, there were some common features. Most people referred to a feeling of peace and quiet, a sense of floating out of and above one's own body, traveling through a dark tunnel and toward a distant white light. On approaching the light, the person had a powerful sense of love and an impression of being interrogated about his or her life and degree of satisfaction with it. At this time the person experienced a colorful, panoramic review of his or her life, which was totally accepted by the "being of light." Many of those who reported having these experiences confessed that they were reluctant to return to their physical bodies, but the need to complete unfinished earthly tasks made them do so.

According to Sabom (1983), the experiences of Moody's patients are not rare; millions of people, of all ages, cultures, religions, and educational levels have had them. The question is not whether the experiences are genuine, but rather how to explain and interpret them. Siegel (1980) admits that Moody's findings can be interpreted as demonstrating that people survive death, but he feels there is a more parsimonious explanation. Noting the similarity of these afterlife visions to hallucinations produced by drugs such as keatmine, which is related to PCP or "angel dust," Siegel

(1980) prefers to regard them as dissociative hallucinations caused by abnormal brain activity. Other parsimonious explanations have been offered by Simpson (1979) and Thomas (1975). In describing what he labels "the Lazarus syndrome," Simpson interprets near-death experiences as delirium states, romantic wish-fulfillment, or psychological attempts to survive death. Consistent with Siegel's (1980) viewpoint, Thomas (1975) suggests that these experiences are caused by the release of beta-endorphin, an opiate produced by the body, at the time of death.

Whatever their ultimate explanation may be, the occurrence of near-death phenomena has served as a consolation to many people—both those who have had such experiences and those who are mourning a loved one or anticipating death. Near-death experiences also demonstrate that the moment of death need not be feared; the pain goes away, and the feeling can be calm and peaceful. Unfortunately, it is not always so. Although these reported visits to the "other side" are generally pleasant, they have been terrifying in some instances. One physician (Rawlings, 1978) found that half of the 30 resuscitated patients whom he interviewed had unpleasant visions of hell when they were near death.

Personal Timing and Control of Death

Like other things that they do, people die at different rates. The rate of decline in functioning from health to death can be fast or slow, with many starts and stops. This *dying trajectory,* as it has been labeled, depends on the nature of the disorder, the patient's age and lifestyle, the kinds of medical treatment received, and various psychosocial factors. The effects of a specific disorder are seen in the "staircase" trajectory of multiple sclerosis, in which there are rapid declines followed by periods of remission (Glaser & Strauss, 1968). A long dying trajectory, although it gives the deceased a better chance to put his or her affairs in order and is perhaps less stressful to the survivors than a short dying trajectory, is not always desired by the dying person. Given a choice, many people would rather die quickly and avoid much pain and psychological stress for themselves and, presumably, their loved ones (Feifel, 1959).

Whether the dying trajectory is long or short, and especially when it is short, people of all ages are expected to deal with impending death in a reasonable way. What is socially accepted as reasonable, however, varies with the age of the person. It is generally expected that young people will actively and antagonistically fight against death and attempt to take care of uncompleted tasks. Elderly dying people, on the other hand, are expected to be more passive than the young and to express less anger and frustration toward death (Sudnow, 1967).

Terminal Drop

Although people are not always permitted to choose how quickly or slowly they will die, there are usually signals of impending death. Certain researchers, for example, have found evidence of a *terminal drop*—a decline in cognitive abilities (IQ, memory, cognitive organization), response time, and personality (e.g., assertiveness)—during the last few months or so of a person's life (Lieberman & Coplan, 1969; Granick & Patterson, 1972; Riegel & Riegel, 1972). To the extent that they are genuine and not simply artifacts of inadequate research methodology (Palmore & Cleveland, 1976), these declines in functioning are probably caused by cerebrovascular and other physiological changes during the terminal phase of life. Lieberman (1965) also noted that people who are approaching death become more preoccupied with themselves, not because of any conceit or egocentricity, but rather as a desperate effort to keep from falling apart psychologically. Realizing that he or she is no longer able to organize and integrate complex sensory inputs efficiently and therefore not able to cope with environmental demands, the individual experiences feelings of chaos and impending doom.

Personal Control of Death

Not all dying people manifest the sharp decline in mental functioning and behavior described by Lieberman. But whatever the explanation may be, many individuals realize when they are about to die (Kalish & Reynolds, 1976). This realization affects different people in different ways. Some who no longer wish to live may give up without a struggle and die rather quickly. Having lost the will to live, they embrace death as a solution to their personal problems. For example, Kastenbaum (1971) found that over one-fourth of a group of terminally ill patients whom he interviewed wished to die soon.

Another group of severely ill people, those who find themselves unable to cope with the pain and frustration of prolonged illness but are also afraid of death, continually vacillate between a desire to live and a wish to die. The conflict between living and dying is aggravated when the person has one or more dependents but is afraid of becoming a burden to them.

Whether they wish to die sooner or later, it is generally acknowledged that people can, through their own attitudes and efforts, either hasten or delay their own death. Evidence for this point was obtained by Kastenbaum and Aisenberg (1972), who found that cancer patients who had strong motivation to survive—as indicated by resentment against the illness and positive attitudes toward treatment—survived longer than patients whose will to live was weaker. Also associated with longer survival times is the maintenance of cooperative, happy social relationships, as opposed to the depressive reactions and destructive social relations that are associated with shorter survival times (Weisman & Worden, 1975).

Although evidence pertaining to personal control over time of death is primarily anecdotal, or at best correlational, it is undeniably intriguing. A priest (Trelease, 1975) who worked with Indians in the interior of Alaska, for example, observed that these people could, to some extent, control the time, place, and manner in which they died; the majority died shortly after they had received the last sacrament. Also supportive of the supposition that dying people can control their time of death is the finding of a significant decrease in the deaths of famous persons in the United States during the month preceding their birthdays but a significant increase in the month following their birthdays (Phillips, 1975).[2] Similar findings also apply to the less eminent (Fischer & Dlin, 1972). Other indirect evidence is provided by reports that believers in the power of the voodoo curses that are placed on them can be literally scared to death. The breaking of taboos has also apparently contributed to the deaths of violators convinced that spirits were going to kill them for their actions.

> In New Zealand, a Maori woman ate some fruit which she subsequently learned had come from a tabooed place. She explained that the sanctity of her chief had been profaned thereby and that his spirit would kill her. She apparently died within twenty-four hours.[3]

Helplessness, Hopelessness, and Choice

Deaths resulting from extreme stress and fear, as in voodoo, are referred to as *sympathetic deaths.* In these cases, extreme shock leads to excessive activity of the sympathetic nervous system. Heartrate increases dramatically, blood pressure is elevated, and finally death occurs. On the other hand, nursing home patients and other ill or otherwise desperate people who "give up" sometimes die *parasympathetic deaths.* In these cases, the parasympathetic nervous system becomes excessively active, resulting in an extreme reduction in heart action and a fatal lowering of blood pressure (Seligman, 1975).

Parasympathetic death is believed to be the result in many instances of feelings of helplessness and hopelessness. Death attributable to loss of hope and simply giving up has been observed in convicts, prisoners of war, and other institutionalized persons. For example, being forced to move

---

2. Both John Adams and Thomas Jefferson died on the Fourth of July, and Mark Twain died on the eve of the second arrival of Halley's comet—the date on which he had predicted that he would die.

3. From Barker (1968), p. 19. SCARED TO DEATH published in the United Kingdom by Frederick Muller Ltd., London.

from a more familiar environment to a less familiar one, such as a different hospital ward or institution, is commonly associated with increased rates of illness and mortality in elderly people. Lefcourt described the following occurrence in a psychiatric hospital.

This writer witnessed one such case of death due to a loss of will within a psychiatric hospital. A female patient who had remained in a mute state for nearly 10 years was shifted to a different floor of her building along with her floor mates, while her unit was being redecorated. The third floor of this psychiatric unit where the patient in question had been living was known among the patients as the chronic, hopeless floor. In contrast, the first floor was most commonly occupied by patients who held privileges, including the freedom to come and go on the hospital grounds and to the surrounding streets. In short, the first floor was an exit ward from which patients could anticipate discharge fairly rapidly. All patients who were temporarily moved from the third floor were given medical examinations prior to the move, and the patient in question was judged to be in excellent medical health though still mute and withdrawn. Shortly after moving to the first floor, this chronic psychiatric patient surprised the ward staff by becoming socially responsive such that within a two-week period she ceased being mute and was actually becoming gregarious. As fate would have it, the redecoration of the third-floor unit was soon completed and all previous residents were returned to it. Within a week after she had been returned to the "hopeless" unit, this patient, who like the legendary Snow White had been aroused from a living torpor, collapsed and died. The subsequent autopsy revealed no pathology of note, and it was whimsically suggested at the time that the patient had died of despair. (Lefcourt, 1973, p. 422)

Engel (1971) collected 170 cases of sudden death that were not medically expected and concluded that the common elements in all of them were feelings of hopelessness and helplessness. The individuals apparently resigned themselves to being unable to cope with whatever physical and psychological stress they were experiencing and simply gave up and died; to die was apparently the only choice they thought they had.

The results of Ferrare's (1962) oft-quoted study of nursing home applicants also underscore the importance of individual choice. Fifty-five women applicants to a nursing home were interviewed and classified as seeing themselves as either having no choice but to enter the nursing home, or having other alternatives. Although no medical differences between the two groups of women were observed on admission to the home, eight of the 17 women in the "no-choice" group died within four weeks and another eight died within 10 weeks. But only one of the 38 women in the "choice" group died during the initial period.

The findings of a later investigation by Langer and Rodin (1976) support and extend Ferrare's (1962) results on the importance of having choices or control over one's life. The subjects, nursing home patients between the ages of 65 and 90, were divided into three groups. One group was told by the home administrator that they still had a great deal of control over their own lives and should therefore decide how to spend their time. For example, they were encouraged to decide whether or not they wanted to see a movie that was being shown and were made responsible for taking care of a plant. A second (comparison) group of patients was assured that the nursing home staff was concerned with their well-being, but they were not encouraged to assume greater control over their own lives. They were told that the staff would inform them when they were to see the movie, and although they were also given a plant, they were told that the nurses would take care of it. A third (control) group of patients was given no special treatment. Subsequent ratings of the happiness, alertness, and activity of the residents were obtained from the nurses and the residents themselves. The results showed significant increases in the happiness, alertness, and activity of the group that was urged to assume greater control over their lives, whereas the ratings of the comparison group on these variables declined. Follow-up data obtained 18 months later (Rodin & Langer, 1977) revealed even more impressive results. Not only did the patients in the first (experimental) group continue to be more vigorous, sociable, and self-initiating than those in the comparison and control groups, but the death rate in the first group was only half that of the other two groups.

The results of studies like those of Ferrare (1962) and Langer and Rodin (1976, 1977) have been cited to support the recommendation that patients and other institutionalized people be permitted as much control as possible over their own lives, for example, planning their own meals, selecting their own clothes, deciding how to decorate their rooms, choosing whether or not to attend meetings and recreational activities, and the like. Unfortunately, these choices, often with good intentions, are sometimes taken away by institutional personnel and family members.

Psychological Stages in Dying

Elisabeth Kübler-Ross, in her writings, talks, and workshops, has probably done more than any other person during the past two decades to stimulate both popular and professional interest in death and dying. Her theory of five stages in the process of dying (Kübler-Ross, 1969) has been of particular interest (see Figure 8-1). These stages, which people are presumed to go through regardless of how slowly or quickly they die, were postulated after an analysis of interviews with over 200 dying patients. Kübler-Ross argues that it is important for health workers and families to be observant and aware of these progressive stages, because the psychological needs of patients and the appropriate responses to them vary

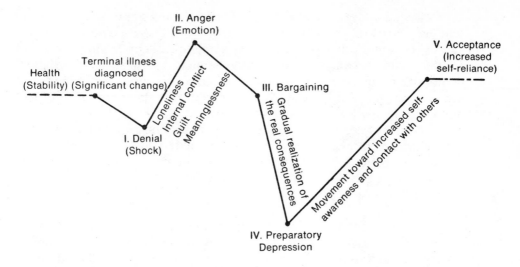

II. Anger
(Emotion)

V. Acceptance
(Increased
self-reliance)

Terminal illness
diagnosed
Health   (Significant change)
(Stability)

III. Bargaining

Loneliness
Internal conflict
Guilt
Meaninglessness

I. Denial
(Shock)

Gradual realization of
the real consequences

Movement toward increased self-
awareness and contact with others

IV. Preparatory
Depression

FIGURE 8-1
**Psychological stages in the dying process. (From the book
DEATH: The Final Stage of Growth by Elisabeth Kübler-Ross. ©
1975 by Elisabeth Kübler-Ross. Published by Prentice-Hall, Inc.,
Englewood Cliffs, NJ 07632.)**

somewhat from stage to stage. Throughout all five stages, however, efforts must be made to ensure that the patient does not lose hope or become merely resigned to death. Kübler-Ross advocates supporting the patient's feelings of hope with constant reassurance that everything medically and humanly possible is being done to help.

Kübler-Ross's Five Stages

Denial. The first stage, denial, is a common reaction to being told that one is dying. Denial, of course, is an important self-protective mechanism. It enables people to keep from being overwhelmed or rendered helpless by the frightening and depressing events of life and to direct their attention to more rewarding experiences. Certainly, a seriously ill person will do well to question a terminal prognosis and seek additional medical opinions concerning the prognosis. But denial becomes unrealistic when the patient invests precious time, money, and emotions in quacks and faith healers. These efforts are understandable, because it is difficult to face self-destruction; at an unconscious level, most people do not really believe they are going to die. By refusing to acknowledge the fact of death, people protect themselves from the anxiety generated by the realization that they will soon cease to exist.

Denial of death manifests itself in many ways. For example, patients who have been told clearly and explicitly that they have a heart disorder, cancer, or some other serious illness sometimes deny having been told anything (Aitken-Swan & Easson, 1959; Bennett, 1976). Such "oversights" demonstrate how denial operates in selective attention, perception, and memory. Denial also has the effect of minimizing the importance of bad news and dogmatically refusing to believe it.

Denial of death is not limited to dying patients. It is at least as common among medical personnel, who are trained to save lives and to whom the loss of a patient represents failure. The family and friends of dying persons also deny the inevitable, and all too often perform a disservice to patients in doing so.

Anger. Continual deterioration of the patient's health and sense of well-being makes it more and more difficult to suppress the fact that time is getting short. As the dying process continues, denial gradually fades into partial acceptance of death. But partial acceptance creates feelings of anger at the unfairness of having to die without being given a chance to do all that one wants to do, especially when so many less significant or less valuable people will continue to live. The feelings of anger experienced by the dying person are frequently nondiscriminating, being directed at family, friends, the hospital staff, and God. The direct target of the patient's anger, however, is the unfairness of death rather than other people. It is important for those who have regular contacts with dying people to be prepared for these attacks of anger and to recognize that much of the hostility represents defensive displacement.

Bargaining. In the normal course of events, the patient's anger fades and is replaced by desperate attempts to buy time, for example, by striking a bargain with fate, God, the attending physicians, or with anyone or anything that offers hope for recovery or at least a delay in the time of death. Although it is not obvious in all patients, the stage of bargaining represents a healthier, more controlled approach than denial and anger. In any event, patients in this stage make many promises—to take their medicine without fussing, to attend church regularly, to be kinder to other people, and so on. Praying for forgiveness, embracing new religious beliefs, and engaging in rituals or magical acts to ward off death are also common.

Depression. The fourth stage is depression, a stage in which the partial acceptance of the second stage gives way to a fuller realization of impending death. Denial, anger, and bargaining have all failed to stave off the demon, so the patient becomes dejected in the face of everything that has been suffered and will be relinquished in dying. Like the previous three stages, Kübler-Ross considers depression to be a normal and necessary step toward the final peace that comes with complete acceptance. She advises loved ones and medical personnel to let the patient feel depressed for a while, to share the patient's sadness, and then to offer reassurance and cheer when appropriate.

Acceptance. Kübler-Ross describes the last stage of dying, that of acceptance, as characterized by "quiet expectation," and as being the healthiest way of facing death. The weakened, tired patient now fully accepts death's inevitability and its blessings in terms of release from pain and anxiety. The patient may reminisce about life, finally coming to terms with it and acknowledging that the experience has been meaningful and valuable. This is a time of disengagement from everyone except a few family members and friends and the hospital staff. In these social interactions, old hurts become erased and last goodbyes are said. This calm acceptance of death has been immortalized in many poems, stories, and other works of art, including William Cullen Bryant's "Thanatopsis," Alfred Lord Tennyson's "Crossing the Bar," and Robert Louis Stevenson's "Requiem." More recently, the noted journalist Stewart Alsop, as he lay dying of cancer, wrote: "A dying man needs to die as a sleepy man needs to sleep, and there comes a time when it is wrong, as well as useless, to resist" (Alsop, 1973, p. 299).

Criticisms of Stage Theory

Kübler-Ross's observations and investigations of dying are important contributions to thanatology, but her stage theory of the dying process has been questioned by a number of her professional colleagues. In all fairness, Kübler-Ross has emphasized that the theory should not be interpreted as a fixed, unvarying sequence or inevitable progression, but rather as a model for understanding how dying persons feel and think. Nevertheless, the very orderly listing or sequencing of these stages has encouraged application of the theory as an exact description of how dying persons should behave and the precise order of occurrence of their reactions. Medical personnel can memorize the names and characteristics of the five stages fairly easily, and the pat descriptions make the stages seem more definite than they were perhaps intended to be. In fact, nurses and doctors have been known to chide terminally ill patients for not completing particular stages in the proper sequence and on time. As a result, dying patients are made to feel guilty for failing to accomplish the various tasks associated with specific stages at the time the theory implies they are supposed to.

Despite criticisms of her work, Kübler-Ross is correct in certain respects. For example, although there is considerable movement back and forth between denial and acceptance, denial is more common during the early part and acceptance more common during the later part of the dying trajectory (Kalish, 1976). Stage theory is also appealing from a training point of view: medical personnel are busy people who are receptive to learnable and easily applicable suggestions for dealing with terminal patients, their relatives, and close friends. As a result of the training, health personnel may also become more accepting of the full range of emotions expressed by dying people, emotions that otherwise might have been deemed inappropriate.

Other Descriptions of the Dying Process

Alternative ways of viewing the dying process have been proposed by a number of observers, including Weisman and Kastenbaum (1968), Shneidman (1976), and Pattison (1977). Weisman and Kastenbaum (1968) observed two broad patterns of response in the dying persons whom they studied. One group of individuals either seemed unaware of the fact that they were dying or they accepted it; both subgroups became less and less active as the time of death approached. A second, contrasting group of individuals remained active in hospital life up until the very day on which they died.

Referring to the dying person's task as "death work," Shneidman (1976) maintained that the person first deals with his or her impending death at a psychological level and prepares to meet the end. The dying person next readies himself or herself for death in a way that assists loved ones in preparing to be survivors. Shneidman (1976) recognizes, however, that there is a great deal of individuality in how people face death. As with any life crisis, the manner in which a person approaches death is a reflection of his or her total personality. Consequently, reactions to impending death reveal something about the personality and kind of life that the individual has lived. One person sees death as a punishment for wrongdoing; another is afraid of the separation entailed by death; still another perceives death as an opportunity to be reunited with departed loved ones.

Various emotions and concerns are expressed by dying people—fear of the unknown, loneliness and sorrow, pain and suffering, loss of body, loss of self-control, and loss of identity, to name a few. Pattison (1977) proposed a three-phase descriptive model including these reactions and other psychological responses of persons during the "living-dying interval,"—the interval between the initial death crisis and the actual time of death. In the first phase, *acute phase,* which corresponds to Kübler-Ross's denial, anger, and bargaining stages, anxiety and fear are at a peak. The high level of anxiety experienced during the acute phase is reduced by defense mechanisms and other cognitive and affective resources of the person. During the second phase, *chronic living-dying phase,* anxiety is reduced and questions about the unknown are asked: What will happen to my body, my "self," and my family and friends while I am dying and afterward? Considering my present situation, what realistic future plans can I make? It is also during the chronic living-dying phase that the person begins to accept death gracefully. During the third and final phase, *terminal phase,* the person still wants to live but now accepts the fact that death is not going to go away. Functioning at a low energy level and desiring mainly comfort and caring, the person begins a final social and emotional withdrawal from the living.

SUMMARY

Fears and attitudes toward death and dying have been assessed by means of yes-no polls, by rankings of statements concerning death, and by other psychometric questionnaires and scales. Psychometric scales, such as the Death Anxiety Scale, typically have high reliabilities but modest validities.

Fears and attitudes toward death vary with a wide range of variables, including cultural and social status, chronological age, sex, personal experiences, and religious or philosophical beliefs. Different cultures view death and dying and the practices or rituals associated with them from different perspectives. Many of these cultural variations, of course, are related to religious beliefs, socioeconomic status, and education.

Aries's historical research on the evolution of attitudes toward death since the Middle Ages points to relationships between attitude toward death and awareness of the self. From the early Middle Ages to the present, Aries characterizes the dominant attitude changes from the *tame death* to the *death of the self* to the *remote death* and, finally, to the *denial of death* in the twentieth century.

Elderly people think and talk more about death than young and middle-aged adults do, but fears of death are usually more intense during middle age. Even in old age, there are significant individual differences in fears and attitudes toward death. Older women are more likely to view death in a benevolent way, whereas older men tend to perceive it as an enemy. Furthermore, more positive attitudes toward death and dying are found in emotionally adjusted and financially stable people than among the maladjusted and the poor.

Deeply religious people and affirmed atheists tend to be less afraid of death than those who are uncertain about their beliefs. Religion, by providing a meaning for human existence and a hope for an afterlife, can provide comfort to the dying. The results of studies of people who have had near-death experiences have been interpreted either as being bona fide visits to the "other side" or as hallucinatory phenomena with a biochemical or psychological basis. Such experiences are usually reported as pleasant and therefore may provide hope and comfort to survivors.

People have different dying trajectories, depending on the specific illness, the treatment program, and the age and lifestyle of the patient. Time of death, which may be signaled by a decline in abilities and personality, *terminal drop,* can apparently be controlled to some extent by the person's attitude and desires. The results of observational and correlational research indicate that feelings of helplessness and hopelessness can contribute to a short dying trajectory, whereas permitting patients to make choices and exert other controls over their lives delays death.

Kübler-Ross described five psychological stages—denial, anger, bargaining, depression, and acceptance—through which patients are supposed to pass in the process of dying. This formulation has been criticized as implying a unidirectional, unvarying sequence, that is seldom observed in dying patients. Rather than progressing irreversibly from denial to acceptance, dying patients are more likely to fluctuate between two or more emotional states. Alternative descriptions of the dying process have been proposed by Weisman and Kastenbaum, Shneidman, and Pattison. Kübler-Ross's theory, however, has found greater favor among doctors and nurses, who consider it a useful guide in the treatment of dying patients.

SUGGESTED READINGS

Becker, E. (1973). *The denial of death*. New York: Free Press.

Kastenbaum, R. (Ed.). (1979). *Between life and death*. New York: Springer.

Kastenbaum, R., & Costa, P. A. (1977). Psychological perspectives on death. *Annual Review of Psychology, 28*, 225–249. Palo Alto, Calif.: Stanford University Press.

Kübler-Ross, E. (Ed.). (1975). *Death: The final stage of growth*. Englewood Cliffs, N.J.: Prentice-Hall.

Moody, R. (1977). *Reflections on life after life*. New York: Bantam.

Pattison, E. M. (1977). Attitudes toward death. In E. M. Pattison (Ed.), *The experience of dying*. Englewood Cliffs, N.J.: Prentice-Hall.

Rosenfeld, S. S. (1977). *The time of their dying*. New York: Norton.

Seligman, M. (1975). *Helplessness: On depression, development, and death*. San Francisco: Freeman.

Siegel, R. K. (1981). Accounting for "afterlife" experiences. *Psychology Today, 15*(1), 65–75.

Tolstoy, L. (1971). *The death of Ivan Ilych*. London: Oxford University Press.

9 Treatment of the Dying and the Dead

Questions answered in this chapter:

- What are the arguments for and against dying at home rather than in a health-care institution?
- What attitudes have hospital staff members traditionally shown toward dying patients?
- In what ways are individual differences related to efforts to sustain life and/or resuscitate?
- How do medical definitions differ from legal definitions of death?
- What are the goals of hospice treatment and the procedures used to attain these goals?
- What is a conspiracy of silence, and how should it be handled?
- What techniques are recommended for counseling dying persons?
- How do modern funerals differ from traditional funerals?
- What problems are being experienced by the funeral industry, and what are the causes of these problems?

Whether death is perceived as a normal occurrence or a tragedy depends, among other things, on the age of the dying person, his or her relationships with the perceiver and the larger society, and the length of the dying trajectory. The death of a young person, or any sudden, unexpected death, is usually more tragic than death in old age or death at the end of a long dying trajectory. In fact, when the patient has suffered extensively, death may be seen as a blessing rather than a tragedy.

In another sense, death is always something of a tragedy for the survivors, especially when the deceased was deeply loved, highly esteemed, or valued in other respects. The tragedy of death is compounded when a person dies all alone in the impersonal, unloving atmosphere that characterizes some general hospitals, nursing homes, and even private residences.

Unlike earlier days, when most of the dying was done at home, approximately 70 percent of all deaths today take place outside the home ("A Better Way . . . ," 1978). They occur in large, anonymous intensive-care units or wards of hospitals, where the emphasis is on preserving life rather than the quality of that life, or in long-term care institutions. When given a choice, however, most people, particularly young adults and the elderly, prefer to die at home (Garrett, 1978). At home in a familiar atmosphere of intimacy and loving care, the dying person is more likely to face the inevitability of death without feeling abandoned and humiliated by his or her declining physical condition and dependence on others. Be that as it may, for both humanitarian and medical reasons, home care is not always advisable. Although most family members would rather have their loved ones die at home (Cartwright, Hockey, & Anderson, 1973), attending to a dying relative can place severe physical and emotional strains on the family. A decision not to die at home may also be made when family relations are unstable or unhappy or older patients are concerned about upsetting young children in the home. Furthermore, private homes are usually poorly equipped to handle medical emergencies and other special procedures that may be required to sustain life and make dying patients comfortable.

Dying in Institutions

Despite the availability of life-saving equipment and medical "know-how," a typical hospital or nursing home is not, from a psychosocial perspective, the best of all possible places in which to die. Preoccupied with administrative and technical chores, busy physicians and nurses usually have little time to understand and deal with the emotional and social needs of dying patients (Buckingham et al., 1976). The hospital staff can be seen moving swiftly and efficiently in and out of intensive-care rooms or terminal wards, checking their watches, administering medicines, and tuning machines. If they do stop to chat with patients, it is usually only for brief moments before they are off to more pressing duties.

Training and Attitudes of Medical Personnel

Doctors and nurses are trained to save lives, so it is not surprising if they become frustrated when, in spite of their best efforts, patients die. Dying patients represent failures in the application of medical skills, and, regardless of their status, most people dislike failure and try to avoid it. Such avoidance may take the form of defensive anger at the dying patient, treating him or her differently from other patients, and staying away as much as possible. For example, research has shown that staff contact with a patient declines abruptly when the illness is diagnosed as terminal (Gordon & Klass, 1979). As one hospital staff member pointed out: "When you've exhausted everything you can do for a patient medically, it becomes difficult to walk into the room every day and talk to the patient" (Barrow & Smith, 1983, p. 364). In an effort to cope with their feelings of frustration, helplessness, and embarrassment, doctors and nurses also tend to stereotype terminally ill patients as already dead or at least as different from the living. The hospital staff may become abrupt and tense with dying patients, and confess that they don't want such patients to die on their shift (Kübler-Ross, 1975).

The previous paragraph is something of a stereotype in itself. Many doctors and nurses genuinely care for their dying patients and miss them when they are gone. These medical people have learned to be comfortable with dying people; they accept death as a natural event rather than a frightening consequence of a medical error, and do their best to help patients come to terms with it. Realizing the importance of this attitude and the need for psychological as well as technical training of hospital personnel, medical educators have begun to emphasize the psychology of death and dying in their teaching. Medical and nursing students are being trained to help terminally ill patients and their families view death less fearfully and to make the passage from life to death more dignified for all concerned (Aiken, 1982). One training procedure that has been used to help medical students and hospital personnel become more sensitive to the role of psychological factors in dying is a *psychological autopsy*—an in-depth, postmortem analysis of the psychosocial aspects of the patient's death (Weisman & Kastenbaum, 1968).

Sustaining Life and Resuscitating

For understandable reasons, the quality of medical care and efforts to arrest the decline in a patient's condition often diminish when the patient is diagnosed as incurable or terminal. This is especially likely in the case of elderly patients or those who are perceived as being less valuable to society (Troll, 1982). Research findings suggest, for example, that both doctors and nurses often let terminally ill patients in nursing homes simply die, without making any special efforts to prolong their lives (Brown & Thompson, 1979).

A medical decision, or *coding,* specifying the extent to which efforts at resuscitation should be made when the heart and lungs stop functioning is frequently made beforehand and entered into the patient's chart. *Code blue* is a directive for all-out efforts, including heroic or extraordinary measures as well as cardiopulmonary resuscitation (CPR) procedure. A *no code* directive indicates that neither CPR nor medical heroics are to be applied with the patient. Finally, a *slow code* directive, which is often not even entered into the patient's chart, instructs nurses to initiate only CPR (Horowitz, 1982). Although the extent to which such a coding system is followed varies with the circumstances and the medical personnel involved, most physicians probably do as much or more than can be reasonably expected to sustain the lives of patients. Sometimes doctors do appear insensitive to dying patients and their right to live as long as possible. Perhaps more common, however, is the doctor who is unwilling to recognize when further efforts on behalf of a dying patient will not only fail but also cause even more suffering to the patient and his or her loved ones.

Much has been said and written about the right of a dying person to decide when extraordinary medical procedures should be terminated and he or she permitted to die a "natural" death (see Chapter 6). Physicians and nurses are well-acquainted, however, with the ambivalent feelings of terminally ill patients toward living and dying (see Report 6-2). A dying person should certainly be permitted a voice in deciding whether to die at home and whether to prolong life by artificial means, but other voices, including those of family members and the attending medical staff, also have a right to be heard.

In addition to ambivalence within patients, there are individual differences among patients in their expressed desires to have doctors make special efforts to keep them alive. For example, when elderly people in a veterans home were asked their preferences concerning what medical efforts should be employed to keep them alive if they were terminally ill, under great physical stress, and were bearing heavy medical expenses, the responses were mixed. Almost 50 percent of the respondents wanted the physician to try to keep them alive, but another 25 percent stated that they would wish their deaths to be speeded up under such circumstances (Preston & Williams, 1971). The remaining 25 percent wanted neither heroic medical measures nor efforts to hasten death used.

Thanatomimesis

Many writers of horror stories have capitalized on the fact that the traditional indicators of death—absence of heartbeat, pulse, breathing, and reflexes—are not always valid. The fact that these accounts are not entirely fictional is seen in cases of catalepsy and other conditions in which people (and animals) only appear to be dead—*thanatomimesis*. None of the traditional vital signs are present in these instances, but the person, who seems to have been "playing possum," recovers after a period of time. The following is a graphic description of such a case, that of an Italian carabineer (a soldier) who had presumably died from an attack of asthma.

> A doctor, glancing at the body, fancied he detected signs of life in it. A lighted taper was applied to the nose of the carabineer—a mirror was applied to his mouth; but all without success. The body was pinched and beaten, the taper was applied again, and so often and so obstinately that the nose was burned, and the patient, quivering in all his frame, drew short spasmodic breaths— sure proof, even to a non-professional witness, that the soldier was not altogether dead. The doctor applied other remedies, and in a short time the corpse was declared to be a living man.[1]

This kind of situation, which took place in the 1880s, was not especially unusual in the nineteenth century. Such reports led to distrust of the traditional vital signs of death and the practice of leaving corpses above ground for several days before they were buried.

Modern Definitions of Death

The lack of a completely objective, uniform legal definition of death, as well as ambiguities concerning the responsibilities of attending physicians toward dying patients and their families, has resulted in many malpractice suits and a number of manslaughter and murder charges against doctors in recent years. Thus far no U.S. doctor has been convicted for killing a patient in order to end that person's suffering. However, in the absence of a legal and medical consensus on what constitutes death, the threat of legal action by the families of persons who die in hospitals is a continuing possibility.

The fifth edition of *Black's Law Dictionary* defines death as "the cessation of life; permanent cessations of all vital functions and signs." It goes on to say that "numerous states have enacted statutory definitions of death which include brain-related criteria" (Black, 1979, p. 360). According to the laws of most states, a person is alive as long as a heartbeat and respiratory movements, no matter how they are maintained, can be detected. In states that have not passed legislation defining death, the definition is based on hospital policy. Because different hospitals may follow different definitions, it is conceivable that a resident of one of these states could be dead in one hospital and not in another!

Until the past 15 years or so, failure to detect a heartbeat and cessation of breathing were the definitive signs of death in most hospitals throughout the United States. Since then, the criteria recommended by an

---

1. From Robert Kastenbaum and Ruth Aisenberg, *The Psychology of Death,* pp. 138–139. Copyright © 1972 by Springer Publishing Company, Inc., New York. Used by permission.

Ad Hoc Committee of the Harvard Medical School (1968) have been widely considered and adopted by some states. These criteria of death include (1) unreceptivity and unresponsiveness to external stimuli, (2) absence of movements, especially spontaneous breathing, and (3) absence of reflexes. A flat electroencephalogram (EEG) pattern is also used as confirmatory evidence of death defined by these three criteria, but the criteria are not trustworthy in cases of severe hypothermia or barbiturate overdose. The Harvard criteria are met in cases of irreversible coma, and the Ad Hoc Committee did indeed recommend that irreversible coma patients be certified as medically dead.

Some states have adopted the concept of brain death, flat EEG for at least 10 minutes, as the legal definition of death and a condition for the removal of donated organs for transplant purposes. Most states, however, still use the traditional definition of death as the cessation of all vital functions. In an attempt to provide some legal uniformity throughout the 50 states, the President's Commission for the Study of Ethical Problems in Medicine and Biomedical and Behavioral Research recommended in 1981 that the states adopt the following legal definition of death. A person is considered dead if there is an irreversible cessation of circulation and breathing or irreversible cessation of all functions of the entire brain, including the brain stem (Rossiter, 1981). Meanwhile, the problem of how to determine exactly when a patient has died and when all heroic measures should be suspended has not been solved. To protect themselves, most physicians are advised to consult with the family of the dying person and obtain legal counsel before deciding to pull the plug on a patient. Even so, the individual physician continues to bear a heavy responsibility for the final decision.

Controlling Pain

Another responsibility of physicians is concerned with the extent to which drugs such as heroin, morphine, and marijuana should be used to make terminally ill cancer patients physically and emotionally comfortable. The need for pain control in dying patients has been demonstrated by the results of various studies (e.g., Rees, 1972; Simpson, 1976). A consensus of findings from various studies revealed that approximately one-half of the patients with terminal illnesses had unrelieved pain and another one-fourth had severe or very severe pain. It might be objected that the consequence of greater use of heroin with these patients would be more drug addicts. However, this hardly seems of foremost concern with terminally ill patients who are allergic to or have developed tolerances for high doses of morphine and other addictive drugs and may very well die in agony without heroin (Quattlebaum, 1980).

The use of heroin and other analgesics makes it possible for the majority of terminally ill patients to die without pain. A combination of drugs, the disease process itself, and psychological withdrawal usually result in the patient being drowsy rather than terrified at the moment of death. The release of beta-endorphins at the time of death is also thought to play a role in making the moment less stressful (Thomas, 1975). In any event, only about 6 percent of patients are conscious just before they die (Hinton, 1972); for the great majority, death appears to be a peaceful, painless experience.

Hospice Treatment of the Terminally Ill

As is true of almost everyone, the interest that terminally ill people take in life depends greatly on the care and human concern that other people show toward them. Dying people can be stimulated to live life more fully until the end when they feel that genuinely concerned individuals are doing everything humanly possible to help them. Allowing and encouraging the terminally ill to exercise some control over their own activities and to participate in decisions concerning their treatment leads them to take a greater interest in their surroundings and make the most of the remaining time (Rosel, 1978). Although most doctors and nurses would probably agree with this statement, the relatively impersonal, technology-based modern hospital with its busy atmosphere oriented primarily toward curing illness and prolonging life does not always permit the implementation of these humanitarian principles (Holden, 1980). Consequently, many people who die in hospitals and other health-care institutions end their days feeling abandoned, alienated, and embittered.

History of the Hospice Movement

In the late 1960s, a medical staff member in a busy London hospital developed the idea of an environment for dying people that would be psychologically superior to terminal hospital wards or nursing homes. This idea, which came to be known as the *hospice concept,* stemmed from a friendship between Cicely Saunders and a Polish refugee. The first hospice, St. Christopher's Hospice in London, was started in 1967 to provide an atmosphere that would foster positive attitudes toward death in terminally ill cancer patients by helping them die with comfort and dignity (Saunders, 1980). Following its initiation in England, the hospice movement spread to the United States in the mid-1970s and subsequently throughout the world. The first U.S. hospices, including the pioneering efforts at St. Luke's Hospice in New York and the New Haven Hospice in Connecticut, were modeled after St. Christopher's Hospice. By the early 1980s, an estimated 300 hospices were either already operating or in the process of being established (Teltsch, 1980). These hospices are designed to provide an alternative for terminally ill people and their families, not only an alternative between impersonal hospital care and personalized but exhausting home care but also an alternative to euthanasia.

Although active euthanasia has been proposed, particularly in England but also in the United States, as a means of avoiding death in a dehumanized hospital environment, Cicely Saunders has been an outspoken opponent of attempts to legalize it. To her and other hospice advocates, the pain experienced by dying people—not only physical but also psychological and spiritual pain—does not require a speeding up of death but can be controlled in a specially designed hospice environment. Thus, the goal of hospice treatment is similar to that expressed in Saunders's original concept of the term—an easy or painless death, but not one that is hastened by an external agent.

Goals and Procedures

The major features of hospice care, as enunciated by Saunders (1980) are:

1. Control of the patient's pain and discomfort.
2. Personal caring contact and discussions of death and dying between patients and medical staff.
3. Death with dignity and a sense of self-worth rather than feelings of isolation or aloneness.

As these goals imply, hospice care is centered not only on meeting the medical needs but also the socioemotional and spiritual needs of the terminally ill. The focus of this kind of treatment is on coping with pain and depression, which are frequent companions of fatal illness, without making an extraordinary effort to prolong life.

A special pain-relieving concoction known as *Brompton mix,* a mixture of morphine, cocaine, ethyl alcohol, and a sweetener, has been used in hospice treatment to provide maximum relief from pain with minimum sedative effects. Morphine by itself is also employed with similar results. Regular periodic doses of the pain killer are used initially, but by keeping a "comfort chart," patients can learn to manage their own medication.

Hospice treatment pays a great deal of attention to pain control. Patients should not be so sedated that communication is hindered, however. To do so would ignore the important goal of bringing patients and family members together. By providing a warm, homey atmosphere in which pain is controlled, patients can remain alert, active, and productive until they die. Meanwhile, death can be discussed openly, without unnecessary fear and without the feeling that death is the end of everything. In this way, dying becomes more meaningful and acceptable to the patient.

The Hospice Team

Home care of the dying is an important part of most hospice treatment programs. With good home care, patients can remain in their own homes as long as they desire—even dying there if they wish. A typical treatment program allows the patient to be cared for at home until transfer to a medical facility is deemed advisable. In both the home and medical settings, an interdisciplinary, nurse-coordinated team of health professionals and volunteers is available to provide round-the-clock medical care for the patient and counseling for both the patient and the family. The professional members of the team are physicians, nurses, a social worker, and a chaplain. In addition, a psychologist and other health professionals are on call as needed. All members of the team treat the terminally ill as valuable persons whose significance is in no way diminished because they are dying.

Hospice treatment emphasizes the significance of every moment of life and the importance of using one's remaining time wisely. In the most desirable situation, the terminally ill patient is surrounded by family and friends and, in the home, by volunteers who perform both patient- and family-support duties of various kinds. These home volunteers, whose training, after an initial orientation program, is principally on-the-job, are important members of a hospice team. They perform such activities as reading to patients, staying with patients while family members are out, making patients comfortable, providing transportation, and assisting families to understand and cope with other problems created by the dying process. The importance of these volunteer services underscores the need for carefully designed training and orientation programs that will sensitize the volunteers to the rewarding but demanding nature of hospice work (U.S. Dept. of Health, Education & Welfare, 1980).

Family members are also important, integral participants in any hospice treatment plan, not only in the home but after the patient has been moved to a medical facility as well. Provisions can be made for overnight accommodations for family members in the medical facility in order to provide every opportunity for patients and families to work through their problems and provide mutual support. The hospice team also assists the family to understand the dying person's feelings, need, and behavior, and to deal with their own problems related to the patient's death.

Patient Admission Criteria

Only patients with a diagnosis of terminal cancer or other terminal illness are accepted for hospice treatment. Other criteria for admission include a prognosis of death in weeks or months, not years, and an agreement on the part of the referring physician to continue his association with the patient and cooperate in the treatment (Charles, 1977). The patient must live within a 30-mile radius of the hospice, and a primary care giver (spouse, relative, trusted friend) must agree to assume continuing responsibility for the care of the patient. These criteria vary somewhat with the particular setting, but they have been adopted by most hospices. Once a patient has been accepted for hospice care, a treatment program centering on the features described, but also designed to meet the patient's individual needs, is put into action.

Models and Problems

As described, *hospice* is a concept rather than a place or building. One model of a hospice, however, is that of a house where people go for visits and counseling. A second model is hospice care in a segregated or separate ward of a hospital, where patients are cared for by a roving hospice team. A third model, which is more in line with the primary thrust of the hospice movement toward home care, is home-care service only. The original British model emphasizes the coordination of home care with a central hospice administration.

The existence of various models, ranging from free-standing buildings to hospitals and home care, has led to a certain amount of confusion about what hospice really means. In some instances, the term has been used so loosely that it is difficult to differentiate between what is called a hospice and a back ward or terminal-care unit of a general hospital. Such confusion has created problems of identity and quality control for the hospice movement.

To date, federal grants, charitable foundations, and private donors have provided the major financial backing for most hospices, but use of these funds and the quality of patient care have not always been carefully regulated. Profiteering, quackery, and other forms of exploitation are, as they have been in the case of nursing homes, always a possibility in the uncontrolled expansion of health-care facilities and procedures. It would indeed be tragic if, because of overzealous development, unethical practices, or gross mismanagement, hospices began to be viewed, as some nursing homes have been, as "houses of death" run by self-serving, untrained, and inefficient individuals.

Associated with the problem of quality control is the attitude of the medical and nursing professions. Doctors and nurses, who are traditionally trained in curative therapy and rehabilitation, are not always prepared to accept the hospice approach of helping patients cope with death. Many health-care professionals may view the hospice concept as an overly romantic notion of death and dying. Supporters of the hospice movement have argued, however, that health professionals have a responsibility for dealing with society's denial and fears of death and other negative attitudes that are perpetuated when death is hidden away in back wards of hospitals. To its advocates, the hospice approach provides one way of bringing death back into the community, so to speak, and getting the entire health-care system back on the right track (Kimmel, 1980).

Communicating with and Counseling the Dying

Most people can accept death in the abstract, but the actual fact of dying usually makes them somewhat anxious and uncomfortable. This is especially true when the dying person is a relative or close friend. Having had no training and usually little experience with dying people, the average individual does not know how to relate to a terminally ill person at anything other than a superficial level. After reassuring the person and trying to cheer him or her up, the conversation usually turns to more "pleasant," but psychologically less meaningful, subjects.

Even medical personnel have tended to shun discussing death with patients whenever they can, and to avoid the patients themselves when death is imminent. Believing that a terminally ill patient will be unable to cope with the knowledge that he or she is dying and that such knowledge may even accelerate the disease process, physicians have traditionally favored not sharing this knowledge with the patient (Butler, 1975; Powers, 1977).

A Conspiracy of Silence

The overall results of surveys have revealed that approximately 80 percent of patients reportedly would like to be told if they are going to die in the near future (e.g., Powers, 1977), but only about 20 percent of physicians voluntarily give this information to their patients (Butler, 1975). It is also interesting that more patients believe that they should be told than are sure that other patients should be told (Kalish & Reynolds, 1976).

Even when patients realize that they are dying and want to discuss it with someone, the physically oriented training of physicians typically fails to prepare them to handle the emotional needs of those patients. Carrying out one's medical duties in a technically proficient but fairly impersonal manner is viewed as safer than becoming emotionally involved with patients and trying to answer their questions about death.

Sometimes it seems as if family, friends, and medical personnel are participating in a *conspiracy of silence,* a conspiracy that the patient may also tacitly comprehend and agree to. Unfortunately, this conspiracy of silence, which is ostensibly for the good of the patient, often leaves him or her to face death psychologically alone—a frightened, less-than-human thing attached to a mass of sterilized tubes and machinery. A classic description of the conspiracy of silence was given in "The Death of Ivan Ilych."

> What tormented Ivan Ilych most was the deception, the lie, which for some reason they all accepted, that he was not dying but was simply ill, and that he only need keep quiet and undergo a treatment and then something very good would result. He, however, knew that do what they would nothing would come of it, only still more agonizing suffering and death. This deception tortured him—their not wishing to admit what they all knew and what he knew, but wanting to lie to him concerning his terrible condition, and wishing and forcing him to participate in that lie. Those lies—lies enacted over him on the eve of his death and destined to degrade this awful, solemn act to the level of their visitings, their curtains, their sturgeon for dinner—were a terrible agony for Ivan Ilych. And strangely enough, many times when they were going through their antics over him he had been within a hair-breadth of calling out to them: "Stop lying! You know and I know that I am dying. Then at least stop lying about it!" But he had never had the spirit to do it. The awful, terrible act of his dying was, he could see, reduced by those about him to the level of a casual, unpleasant, and almost indecorous incident (as if someone entered a drawing-room diffusing an unpleasant odor) and this was done by that very decorum which he had served all his life long. He saw that no one felt for him, because no one even wished to grasp his position. Only Gerasim recognized it and pitied him. And so Ivan Ilych felt at ease only with him. (Tolstoy, 1886, pp. 137–138)

Open Communication

It is unfortunate that relatives and medical professionals find it difficult to discuss death with dying persons, because many dying individuals are eager to share thoughts with others. Medical judgment clearly is an important factor in determining whether or not to tell a patient that death is imminent; not all patients can or want to deal with this kind of information. Such denial, however, is less likely to be true of the elderly, who see death as inevitable in any case and have already made preparations for it. Neither is it true in the case of most dying people—young or old; they are usually grateful for being told the truth and welcome an opportunity to discuss it (Puner, 1974).

In general, physicians and nurses are now more willing than they once were to tell dying patients the truth. Over 20 years ago, Feifel (1963) reported that 60–90 percent of the physicians who were interviewed did not approve of telling a patient that an illness is terminal. Today, however, a gentle but honest approach is favored by most physicians so long as it is considered in the patient's best interest (Schulz, 1978). Health-care professionals who work intensively with the dying, as in hospices, almost always advocate an honest approach to the patient (Saunders, 1980). Knowing the truth provides terminally ill patients with the time and, it is hoped, an incentive to review their lives and prepare for death. Rather than being devastated by the knowledge of a terminal diagnosis, they are more likely to be strengthened (Weisman, 1972).

Even when they are not told directly by a family member, a friend, a doctor, or a nurse, a large majority of terminally ill patients realize that they are going to die in the very near future. They sense it in the changes in their bodies and the attitudes of other people. Consequently, honesty on the part of others frequently comes as no surprise but simply confirms what the patient suspected all along (Kübler-Ross, 1969). Being told, whether outright or by intimation, however, opens the door for the ventilation of feelings and constructive discussion. Thus, a consequence of openness toward death is meaningful communication with others. It also gives patients a chance to take care of financial matters, items pertaining to bequests, and other business or family affairs.

Companionship

Communication and companionship go hand in hand. Dying people need to know, but that knowledge can be dealt with more effectively in the presence of loving care and companionship. Fears can be expressed, confessions made, and emotional support and forgiveness found only with someone who cares. The need of a dying person for a warm, supportive, caring listener, however, cannot be met by just anyone. As Kübler-Ross (1969) pointed out, to listen to a dying person in a warm and supportive manner requires acceptance of one's own mortality and a comfortableness in the presence of death. Such companionship is usually provided by a relative or perhaps a caring professional. Although it may strike some people as a kind of macabre commercialism, at least one business organization, "Threshold" of Los Angeles, provides trained companions to help ease lonely, dying people out of this world ("Death Companionship," 1975). Regardless of how it is obtained, honest communication is certainly essential in assisting dying people to cope with their physical, emotional, and spiritual suffering.

Counseling Procedures

Counseling and psychotherapy with the dying involve no fixed prescription and are not limited at this time to practitioners possessing specific professional credentials. Family members, medical staff members, clergymen, and social workers all perform counseling services at one time or another.

219

Professional counselors, such as clinical psychologists and psychiatrists, are also available to work with terminally ill persons whose dying trajectories often permit more prolonged psychological treatment efforts. Whoever the counselor may be, he or she should be a compassionate individual who shares a feeling of mutual trust with the patient and can help him or her deal with fears of the unknown.

In addition to helping dying people concentrate on taking life one day at a time and living each day as joyfully and peacefully as possible, professional counselors and psychotherapists employ a variety of techniques. These techniques include uncritical acceptance, attentive listening, reflection of feelings, life review, group-oriented therapy, and even consciousness-altering drugs (Kalish, 1977). The specific objectives of counseling with the dying vary with both the patient and the situation, but some overall goals are to help patients overcome their feelings of sadness and despair, to resolve interpersonal (especially intrafamilial) conflicts, and to obtain insight into the meaning and value of their lives. Counselors must be careful not to force their own values—religious or secular—on dying patients. Rather, counselors should attempt to understand and share the fears, hopes, and other feelings of dying persons and assist them in finding their own ways of meeting death.

One phenomenon that frequently occurs when a patient becomes aware that he or she is dying is a *life review.* According to Butler (1971), mentally reviewing one's life is a universal process ranging in duration from a split-second overview to a lengthy reminiscence. Whenever a life review occurs, in later life (which is more likely) or earlier, it provides an opportunity to relive old pleasures and sufferings and to work through persisting problems. Consequently, reviewing one's life can be a healing process, and is recommended by Butler (1971) and others as a counseling technique for use with dying patients. Butler maintains that surveying, observing, and reflecting on one's past experiences leads to insight and understanding, a sense of continuity, a strengthening of one's identity, and a feeling of inner peace.

It is a major principle of hospice care and other psychosocially oriented programs of treatment for the dying that patients (and their families) benefit from discussions with doctors and nurses. Aronson (1959) maintained that a major question in interactions between medical personnel and terminal patients is how patients can be helped to be individual human beings despite their condition and prognosis. Maintaining one's individuality and identity as a human being becomes difficult when the severe pain and feelings of despair experienced by a patient lead to regressive, childlike behavior. Aronson (1959) cautioned doctors not to tell the patient anything that might induce psychopathology, not to let hope die before the patient is dead, and not to minimize the gravity of the situation.

For those physicians and nurses who are comfortable with Kübler-Ross's five-stage theory of dying, Herr and Weakland (1979) offer a number of suggestions for counseling the dying. To begin, counselors of the dying must realize that the counseling goals are limited and that the least they can do is to refrain from making a painful and difficult situation worse. In general, it is recommended that counselors be gently available, quiet, and compassionately realistic. Being *gently available* means that the counselor does not force himself or herself on the patient or push the patient to talk. The counselor is attentive, however, and aware of subtle clues indicating that the patient may be ready to talk about death (e.g., a sudden interest on the part of the patient in disposing of his or her property, giving up valued activities, arranging for the welfare of people and pets). Being *quiet* does not imply complete silence on the part of the counselor, but rather controlling his or her own anxieties while watching and listening to the patient. *Compassionate realism* means refraining from unrealistic optimism about the patient's condition on the one hand and abject pessimism on the other.

Concerning specific aspects of counselor behavior based on Kübler-Ross's (1975) five-stage model, in responding to a patient who is *denying* the reality of the situation, the counselor should realize that confronting the patient with the truth or arguing about it is futile. Rather the counselor should be quietly available, neither confronting the patient with the terminal prognosis nor supporting unrealistic plans for the future.

Anger is one of the most difficult emotions for the counselor to contend with, because the patient's anger is often indiscriminate. Everyone, including the counselor, is subject to attack. As with denial on the part of the patient, confronting anger is useless; about all that the counselor can do is accept the patient's anger, but not necessarily agree with it in terms of particulars.

Bargaining behavior is usually easier to deal with than denial or anger, but even so, the hope experienced by the patient in bargaining should be tempered with caution on the part of the counselor. *Depression* is contagious and difficult to deal with, but when it is expressed the counselor should continue to be available and not make the patient feel abandoned. Finally, if and when the patient has come to *accept* his or her impending death, the counselor can help with any practical matters or tasks that need attending to. Family and friends can be brought in to say their last goodbyes, and, under certain circumstances, the counselor may even say the goodbyes for the patient.

Modern Funeral Practices

Historically, the purposes of funeral rites were to honor the dead, supply them with the necessities for the next world, and to gain favor with the gods. The first of these—honoring the dead—still forms a part of funeral rituals today, but the emphasis has shifted somewhat from the deceased to the survivors. Thus, a primary function of the modern funeral is to provide a mechanism for those who were close to and/or admired the deceased to work through their own feelings connected with the death. Honoring the deceased and grieving for her or him at the funeral and during the subsequent mourning period serve both to affirm the deceased's value and provide an opportunity to achieve emotional closure with respect to the life and death of the departed individual.

Funeral Rituals

The time between the death of a person and consignment of the body to its final resting place has traditionally been divided into three intervals or activities: wake, funeral service, and committal. Mourners are no longer summoned to the wake by bidders or to the funeral service by bell ringers, as they were in earlier times. Rather, a notice is usually placed in the obituary column of a newspaper, and relatives and close friends are informed by telephone, telegram, or in person.

During the wake, the groomed and often embalmed corpse is on display in a funeral home, a church, or (rarely nowadays) a private home. A variety of social activities, depending on the customs of the social group to which the deceased belonged, may take place during the wake. In general, family, friends, and others who knew or admired the deceased come to express their feelings and comfort the bereaved. The principal activity, however, is to visit the deceased and view the remains. Modern funeral directors maintain that the resulting "memory picture" of the deceased should be positive and lifelike, thus justifying the expense of embalming and cosmetically preparing the corpse. This beautification of the corpse to make it seem almost alive, however, appears to impress some groups (e.g., Protestants) more than others (e.g., Catholics) (Khleif, 1976).

A wake need not be held, of course, especially when the casket, for whatever reason, is kept closed. The holding of a wake is reportedly favored more by persons of low or middle socioeconomic status than those of high status, and by blacks more than whites (Salomone, 1968). Also of interest is Fulton's (1971) finding that widows and widowers who chose a conventional funeral, in which the body was exposed to public view, had fewer problems adjusting to the death and more positive memories of the deceased than those who opted for a closed casket or immediate disposal of the corpse.

The nature and location of the funeral service itself varies with the cultural and religious background of the participants. Catholics, for example, are more likely to hold the funeral service in a church, whereas Protestants are as likely to use a funeral home as a church (Khlief, 1976). Wherever it is held, the funeral service still provides an opportunity for a group of people to acknowledge the value of the deceased and to affirm their social and religious ties. The trend during this century, however, has been to tone down the more emotion-arousing features of the service. Another modern trend has been away from large church funerals and toward simpler funerals or memorial services.

The deemphasis on funerary rituals in recent years has been interpreted by Aries (1981) as another manifestation of the denial of death that has come to characterize Western culture during the twentieth century, a deemphasis seen more in England than in the United States and Canada. In all three countries, neither the funeral service nor the procession from the place where the service is held to the final resting place is as dramatic or flamboyant as it once was. There are exceptions, however; some individuals, like the kings of old, are still "sent off" in lavish, spectacular style (see Report 9-1).

REPORT 9-1

Much Ado About Death, or Crying in the American Bier

By Dave Larsen

Since life in Southern California is so unreal, or at least perceived to be, it follows that the one reality we have to cling to is death.

Californians we are and Californians we will be, right until the time a local member of the Flying Funeral Directors of America drops our ashes from his plane (not catching the propeller backwash, we hope) and into the Pacific, or until we rest in peace beneath the latest innovation, the talking tombstone.

O death, where is thy sting? Not here, not where funeral processions use the freeways to hasten the deceased to his destination, where a certain cemetery is one of the top tourist attractions, where a do-it-yourself coffin entrepreneur sent a set of his blueprints to one man who had been contemplating having himself strapped to a surfboard and launched at sea.

Remember that although it happened in Texas, it was one of our own, Beverly Hills millionairess Sandra Ilene West, who scribbled a handwritten will that resulted later in having herself buried in her black nightgown while at the wheel of her baby blue Ferrari, "with the seat slanted comfortably."

As is true with everything in Lotusland, don't question our life style and don't question our death style.

Even for elephants, the riddle of where they go when they die was answered two years ago when Dr. Jack Adams of Cal State Dominguez Hills buried a pachyderm on the grounds, possibly the only campus with such a distinction. Ashes to ashes, tusk to tusk.

As for us humans still here, because the colleges generally accept only the living (ostensibly), our only recourse in the long run is the numerous memorial parks, the most celebrated of which is Forest Lawn.

The late Humbert Eaton of Beverly Hills, after gaining control of the cemetery, embarked upon a series of innovations that made it a subject of worldwide comment, especially from Evelyn Waugh. Today not only are there burials at Forest Lawn's four locations, but many weddings, and even christenings. Babies, brides, corpses. Center attractions at different events.

And where else but in this area could one bid for the privilege of spending

223

eternity in the crypt next to Marilyn Monroe?

When the Hollywood woman who happened to own that empty slot at Westwood Memorial Park offered it for sale, it went quickly, although for what the seller said was less than the asking price of $25,000.

This location, of course, is where thrice weekly, six fresh red roses are placed in the holder of the beauty queen's crypt, courtesy of former husband Joe DiMaggio. A standing order for a Hollywood florist since her death in 1962.

In Delano, from 5 P.M. to 7 P.M. daily, music of the Swing Era has been played for decades over radio station KCHJ. The disc jockey, however, has been dead since 1968. His widow, Jean Johnes, has seen fit to continue broadcasting tapes of the program all these years, making only one change. He used to close each show by saying goodnight to his mother, but she also is dead, so that ending was cut.

Let us not forget that enterprising San Diegan who for a while was turning a nice profit with his company called "Play Dead." He rented coffins to the living. One customer was an 80-year-old woman who wanted to stage a funeral so she could enjoy it this time around.

An Azusa man found an old coffin in a scrap yard, added two wheels, hooked it to his motorcycle, and registered it as a trailer with the Department of Motor Vehicles.

Death in California. It becomes Can You Top This? Although, of course, it is off the coast of Oregon where a former Coast Guard lighthouse was recently bought for conversion to an oceanic mausoleum.

But that, as all Easterners will assume, may be attributed to a quirk of geography. There simply were no lighthouses in the current Southland multiple listing.

Regardless, we do our share. A firm here called Personal Words puts together eulogies for delivery at funeral services. Jules (Ghouls) Mattland not only labors over the phrases, but, if asked, will choreograph the event. For a man who loved dogs, Mattland had two of the dearly departed's Great Danes sit on either side of the casket.

At the mortuary science department of Cypress College, students are taught to make wax replica death masks, in the event a family requests it.

Then there is the brisk business in guides to the graves of movie stars, such as Michael's Memory Map, an alternative to visiting the homes of the worshiped. Or you may choose to tour Angeles Abbey Memorial Park in Compton, where the fifth row in one of the mausoleums has side-by-side crypts with the names Lucky and Strike.

And the beat goes on. Two years ago, at a motel in North Hollywood, there was an auction—of a 2,700-year-old mummy. He fetched $32,000. Which brings to mind the Long Beach amusement park, which for years had on display what they thought was a wax dummy, until his arm fell off and he was found to be a real mummy of an Oklahoma badman shot by a posse in 1911.

Earlier this year the first Reincarnation Ball was held at the Shrine Auditorium, for those who felt they had lived a previous life. The early arrivals got a free psychic reading.

Just what the effect of all this will be on the rest of the nation remains to be seen. Or rather the remains must be seen.

Or at least dealt with in a California manner.

In the majority of cases, the final resting place is in a private cemetery maintained by a religious order or other nonprofit organization, or by a commercial enterprise. When the body has been cremated, the remains, which are actually a few pounds of calcified material rather than ashes, may be sprinkled over a mountain or ocean (perhaps with an expensive bottle of wine) or saved in an urn or vault. Columbaria, which are multistoried walls divided by vaults or niches, are quite popular in certain areas of the world where land is scarce. Each niche bears a commemorative plaque containing a picture and the name of the deceased, in addition to the date of death (Weisskopf, 1982). Atheneums, which look like air conditioned houses, built near cemeteries are also becoming popular in Europe as places to house the remains of the dead (Aries, 1981).

The Funeral Business

Prior to the nineteenth century, there were no undertakers, morticians, or funeral directors as such. Families, with the assistance of friends and other members of the community and church, were responsible for disposing of their own dead. The cost of an elaborate funeral, even in the Middle Ages, could be quite high and potentially ruinous for the survivors. However, the existence of mutual-aid societies and burial groups helped keep costs under control for those who were willing to settle for less extravagant ways of disposing of their dead ("Embalming, Burial, and Cremation," 1983).

Undertaking first became a profession in the early nineteenth century; the first undertakers were craftsmen or carriage hirers who obtained transportation and coffins (Aries, 1981). The titles *mortician* and *funeral director* came into use later in the century, underscoring the growing commercialization of funerary activities. These activities are now handled quite professionally by a team of specialists, including not only funeral directors and embalmers, but also doctors, lawyers, ministers, florists, grave diggers, and many others. The problem is that all these services cost money. The average price of a funeral and burial in the United States in 1981 was almost $3,000. The total cost depended on the specific items and services requested, reaching $8,000 in some instances. A major item in the total cost was the casket, which ranged from $145 for a coffin made of particle board to $16,624 for an ornate bronze, velvet-lined container (Whitley, 1983).

Religious and cultural customs may dictate to some extent what items are included in a funeral and their costs. For example, Orthodox Jewish custom requires that hand-tooled wood and no metal be used in making the casket and that the corpse not be embalmed. Funeral cost differentials are also related to sex, age, and social status. Pine and Phillips (1970) found that, in terms of funeral expenses, women tended to spend more than men, older adults spent more than younger adults, and lower- and middle-class people spent relatively more than upper-class people. According to these findings, it would appear that, in many cases, those who are least able to afford expensive funerals are most likely to select them.

Legal Regulation of the Funeral Industry

Some 20 years ago, exposés written by Jessica Mitford (1963), Ruth Melvey Harmer (1963), and other influential individuals led to public concern about the funeral industry in the United States. Allegations of exorbitant prices and high-pressure salesmanship inflicted on confused, grief-stricken consumers by self-styled "grief-therapist" undertakers proved all too accurate in some cases. Subsequently, the U.S. Federal Trade Commission (FTC) took up the cause of bereaved consumers in a series of recommendations concerning the choices and prices offered by funeral homes. Under these regulations, funeral directors are required to provide itemized lists of goods and services and their prices rather than selling a preselected package to consumers. Prices have to be given over the telephone on request, and misrepresentation of state laws governing embalming and cremation is prohibited. These recommendations, some of which went into effect on January 1, 1984, have been objected to by the funeral industry as being biased against the traditional American funeral (Whitley, 1983). One provision of the regulations, that requiring funeral directors to provide consumers with an item-by-item list of funeral costs, went into effect on April 30, 1984. Although still maintaining that this regulation is unwarranted, the National Funeral Directors Association decided not to actively contest it ("Funeral Association Won't Appeal . . . ," 1984).

Although the FTC's "funeral rule" will help, the responsibility for policing the funeral industry continues to fall to some extent on private consumer organizations. One important service that such organizations and other interested parties perform is to make the public aware of exactly what the laws of various states require and do not require in connection with funerals. For example, *no* state requires an outer burial container, a casket for cremation, or routine embalming (except in specific circumstances such as the presence of certain diseases, a lengthy preburial interval, or transporting the corpse for a long distance). Furthermore, the funeral laws/rules in a large majority of states prohibit misrepresentation of prices and services and misrepresentation of cemetery and legal requirements connected with burial. On the other hand, very few states require funeral establishments to make available to consumers a preselection itemized price list, price information over the telephone, a separate casket price, or an outer burial container price list. Nor do most states require explicit permission to embalm, truthful disclosures of service charges for cash advances, or that a majority of the members on the state funeral board be individuals who are not connected with the funeral industry (Continental Assn. of Funeral & Memorial Societies, 1980).

Changing Attitudes and Practices

Due to a number of factors, including exposés of the funeral industry, inflation and economic hard times, and changes in public attitudes toward death, the traditional funeral business in the United States has declined during the past two decades. The decline has been especially marked in metropolitan areas of the East and West Coasts, where cremation is also more popular. For example, compared with a national figure of approximately 217,000 (11 percent), 58,000 (31 percent) of those who died in California in 1981 were cremated. The national cremation rate is expected to reach the current California rate by the year 2000, which will still place it significantly below that of England and Japan. The popularity of cremation as a means of disposal of the dead also varies with ethnicity, education, religion, and socioeconomic status. It is more common among white, college-educated Protestants with above-average incomes (McGraw, 1983).

The increasing popularity of cremation, however, is only one of the factors in the decline of the funeral business. Many authorities believe that the main reason for the decline is a change in public attitudes about death and funerals. Public discussion of death and light treatments of the topic by the media in the United States have helped people become more comfortable with death. Simultaneously, people have become more mobile and experimenting, and, as a result, traditional family and religious ties have weakened. The greater openness about death and the loosening of cultural constraints have contributed to a fundamental change in attitudes and a consequent trend toward simpler, more economical funerals (Sherwood, 1982).

Economic reasons for the simplicity movement are found in a comparison of the cost of a traditional funeral with that of a memorial service and cremation. In 1981, most members of memorial societies paid less than $1,000 for a funeral and less than $500 for cremation or immediate burial. And the cost was typically less than $100 when the body was donated to a medical school. By comparison, an average traditional funeral cost nearly $3,000 (Continental Assn. of Funeral & Memorial Societies, 1982).

In the forefront of the movement toward simpler funerals are not only intellectuals and social reformers but also religious authorities. Sharing the mistrust of superstition and irrational sentimentality that characterize lavish funerals, these individuals agree in pointing out that a memorial service is not only simpler and more economical, but also quite dignified and meaningful to the survivors.

SUMMARY

Unlike yesteryear, most of the dying today is done in health-care institutions rather than at home. The consequences of this shift in the place of death have been mixed. Hospitals are better equipped to meet medical emergencies, and the treatment of dying patients is technically proficient. Compared to the private home, however, hospitals and other health-care establishments are rather impersonal places where the psychological needs of patients are not always attended to. Medical personnel, who are trained principally to cure illness and rehabilitate, often experience difficulties in relating to dying patients.

Efforts made to sustain life and resuscitate persons who have stopped breathing tend to be less vigorous in the case of terminal patients, the elderly, and persons of lower socioeconomic status. These efforts also vary with the definition of death, both legal and medical. There is no uniform definition of death to which all states subscribe, but common definitions include cessation of circulation, breathing, and brain functions.

Effective control of pain—physical, psychological, and spiritual—in terminally ill patients is a primary goal of hospice care. Other important goals are personal, caring contact between dying patients, their families, and health personnel, and facing death with dignity. Hospice treatment, inaugurated by Cicely Saunders during the late 1960s, uses no heroic measures to keep dying patients alive, but rather concentrates on making dying as pleasant as possible. The traditional hospice model views treatment of the terminally ill as an individualized, team-oriented effort involving patient, medical staff, volunteers, and family members, in which the patient is maintained in the home environment as long as possible. However, various models of hospice care have been developed in recent years. This has led to some confusion about what hospice really is. The hospice movement also has been criticized as overly romantic in its attitude toward death and as inefficient health care. In general, however, the hospice concept has prompted a more humane approach to terminal care.

Health personnel have traditionally favored not telling patients when death was imminent, but medicine has changed in recent years and so have the attitudes of doctors and nurses toward death and dying. The conspiracy of silence, in which death was not discussed with dying patients, is now less common than it once was. Open communication between patients, medical staff members, and families is now more of the rule than the exception. Dying patients are usually strengthened rather than devastated by honesty regarding their condition; when combined with companionship and caring, open communication can be therapeutic.

Counseling terminally ill patients is an activity performed by many professionals—doctors, nurses, psychologists, psychiatrists, ministers, and social workers, as well as family members, friends, and other nonprofessionals. A variety of counseling methods may be employed, the most basic of which are attentive listening and uncritical acceptance. Herr and Weakland recommend that counselors be gently available, quiet, and compassionately realistic. Butler emphasizes the value of a life review of the patient's past. Certain counseling procedures are based on theories of personality and behavior, such as Kübler-Ross's theory of stages in the dying process.

The traditional emphasis on the funeral as a rite for honoring the dead has changed somewhat in the modern era to a concern with the feelings of the survivors. The three phases of the traditional funeral—wake, service, and committal—have been simplified and made less emotional. The elaborateness of funerals today, however, varies greatly with the sociocultural background, sex, age, and residence of the participants.

Exposés of the funeral industry, inflation and economic hard times, and changes in society's attitude toward death have led to problems in the funeral industry. Until recently, however, efforts by the Federal Trade Commission to require openness in advertising and selling on the part of the industry have not been very successful. In any event, it is hoped that the changing attitudes and funerary practices in our society, including the trend toward simpler and more economical funerals, will encourage greater sensitivity to consumer needs by the funeral industry in years to come.

SUGGESTED READINGS

Brandt, A. (1982). Last words for my father. *Psychology Today, 16*(4), 72–77.

Dickerson, R. B. (1981). *Final placement: A guide to the deaths, funerals, and burials of famous Americans.* Algonac, Mich.: Reference Publications.

Herr, J. J., & Weakland, J. H. (1979). *Counseling elders and their families* (Chap. 19). New York: Springer.

Kalish, R. (1981). *Death, grief and caring relationships.* Belmont, Calif.: Brooks/Cole.

Lack, S., & Buckingham, W., III. (1978). *First American hospice: Three years of home care.* New Haven, Conn.: Hospice, Inc.

Mitford, J. (1969). *The American way of death.* New York: Fawcett-World.

Morgan, E. (1980). *A manual of death education and simple burial.* Burnsville, N.C.: The Celo Press.

Stoddard, S. (1978). *The hospice movement: A better way of caring for the dying.* Briarcliff Manor, N.Y.: Stein & Day.

Waugh, E. (1977). *The loved one* (rev. ed.). Boston: Little, Brown.

Zorza, V., & Zorza, R. (1981). *Way to die.* New York: Knopf.

PART IV

The Survivors

10 Problems of Bereavement and Widowhood

Questions answered in this chapter:

- How are the concepts of bereavement, mourning, and grief related, and how are they different?
- What psychological and physical changes are associated with grief?
- What are the various stage theories of grief, and how accurately do they describe the grieving process?
- How do emotions and behaviors associated with grieving vary from person to person?
- Under what circumstances is grief considered to be pathological?
- What conclusions can be drawn from the results of research relating mortality to bereavement?
- What techniques or procedures are employed in counseling and psychotherapy with the bereaved?
- How are family and social relationships affected by widowhood?
- What problems are encountered by widowed persons, and how can they be solved?

*N*ot all those who survive the death of a relative or friend have been equally involved in the care of that person before and after death. The wife, husband, or daughter(s) of the deceased, in that order, typically have been most attentive at the deathbed and, presumably, suffer most from the death (Shanas, 1979). Furthermore, the greater longevity of women makes them more likely survivors than men and, therefore, the ones whom society is most likely to think of as the bereaved. The state of *bereavement,* however, applies not only to people who were very close to the deceased at the time of death, but to anyone for whom the death represents a loss or deprivation.

Grief, a mental state of sorrow and distress, is a natural reaction to bereavement, but it is not felt by every bereaved person. The term *mourning* frequently is used in the same way as *grief* to describe the feeling of sorrow resulting from bereavement. Mourning, however, is more appropriately used to designate the culturally prescribed pattern of behavior for expressing grief rather than as a synonym for grief.[1]

Bereavement has both emotional and practical repercussions. There are various problems and duties with which the bereaved individual must cope without the guidance and assistance of the deceased. In the case of a surviving spouse, for example, household and business matters need to be dealt with. In addition to taking care of one's own physical and psychological needs, there are often children and other relatives to be concerned with and financial matters that require close attention. Medical, funeral, and legal bills, as well as bills for items that the deceased apparently ordered become due rather promptly; inheritance, estate, gift, and income taxes must also be paid on time. Furthermore, the conditions of the deceased's will need to be understood and obeyed.

Other items of business that a surviving spouse or other close relative must attend to are bank accounts, insurance, and social security, all of which require specific actions on the part of the beneficiary and/or administrator of the decedent's estate. Joint bank accounts and safe deposit boxes, for example, are automatically closed at the time of a tenant's death, and the surviving tenant must be accompanied by a legal official (e.g., a clerk of court) in order for the account or box to be reopened. Survivors should also be aware of the financial benefits to which they are entitled. Under the social security law, survivors are usually eligible for a lump sum death benefit for burial expenses and a burial plot. In cases where the deceased had a service-connected disability, survivors may also be entitled to veterans benefits; other monetary benefits are paid to survivors of deceased members of certain unions and fraternal organizations. All such benefits must be applied for and require proof of death (e.g., a death certificate) and of the applicant's relationship to the deceased (e.g., a marriage or birth certificate).

In addition to financial and other practical matters associated with death and its aftermath, there are psychological and social concerns with which the survivors must contend. Whatever their relationships to the deceased may have been, the survivors now face the task of "letting go" of the dead person. It takes time, typically a year or two in the case of a

---

1. Certain religious customs prescribe not only the way in which mourners are supposed to conduct themselves, but also the duration of the mourning period. For example, the mourning rituals in Judaism, *shiva* (*shivah, shibah*), traditionally last seven days.

widow (Lopata, 1973) to let go, or get over the death, of a spouse or other loved one. This process is sometimes made easier when the survivors participate actively in the funeral—viewing the corpse and mourning. But funerals in which there is no body to mourn over, or in which the body is not displayed or viewed briefly through a "drive-in window," seem hardly designed to encourage the survivors' acceptance of the death and the importance of letting go of the dead.

The ability to let go of a deceased person and reorganize one's own life varies with a number of factors: the nature of the survivor's relationship with the deceased; the personality, age, and sex of the survivor; the manner in which death occurred and the duration of the illness or dying process; and the cultural context in which death occurred and in which the survivor must continue to live (Bornstein et al., 1973; Glick, Weiss, & Parkes, 1974). Whether the letting go, or recovery, process is rapid or slow, the death of a loved one leaves scars that, although hidden, can last for a lifetime (Shneidman, 1980b).

The Bereavement Process

Mourning and a moderate display of grief are socially accepted and expected behaviors during the wake and funeral. At this time, family members and friends usually provide both practical assistance and emotional support for the bereaved. Household chores are performed, dependents are cared for, and various business matters are attended to. The bereaved person is given a sympathetic ear, consoled, and provided with hope. Nevertheless, there comes a time—usually only a few days, and at most a few weeks after the funeral—when such assistance is, for the most part, terminated. Relatives and friends are now seen less often, and the bereaved individual is left alone for a large portion of the day. This is the quiet time, and often the time when the loss of a spouse or other loved one is felt most keenly. It is the period when real mourning begins, and therefore a time when the comfort of family and friends is needed at least as much as it was immediately after the death.

Feelings and Behavior of the Bereaved

Mourning is a normal and necessary process that does not automatically cease when the funeral is over. It not only provides a way for the social group to reaffirm the value of the deceased, but the expression of grief during the mourning period helps pave the way for the letting go process and the subsequent reaffirmation and reorganization of the survivor's own life. Friends and relatives frequently express concern that the survivor is mourning too long and would be better off to cheer up and get back into the "swing of things" as quickly as possible (see Aries, 1974, p. 99). People do, on occasion, mourn for years, and in such instances the process is rightly viewed as abnormal or pathological. But the mourning period is typically too short rather than too long; bereaved people need time to sort out their feelings and recover from their loss. In fact, a greatly shortened mourning period may be just as pathological as prolonged mourning, or at least be a forerunner of later pathology (Simpson, 1979).

Feelings of grief are a natural reaction to any loss, but the duration and intensity of those feelings vary with who is lost and when the loss occurs. Obviously, people customarily grieve more when a close relative or friend dies than when an admired movie star or public figure dies. If death is expected or seen as likely to occur, as in an elderly invalid, the intensity and duration of grief are typically not as great as when a child or young adult dies.

Grief is not the only emotion experienced by bereaved people, however. Combined with feelings of sorrow and regret are anger, anxiety, and guilt. Anger may be directed at anyone who might conceivably, by commission or omission, have played a role in the death of the deceased. Among the targets of this anger are nurses, physicians, friends, and family members whom the bereaved perceives as having been negligent in their treatment of the deceased. And for various reasons, including the failure to resolve interpersonal conflicts with the dead person and frustrations or deprivations created by the death, the bereaved may also be angry at the deceased. Such feelings of anger frequently give way to guilt, especially when the bereaved person realizes that he or she might not have done everything possible for the deceased. Many grieving persons also experience feelings of hopelessness, depersonalization, disorientation, and unreality, as well as a lack of interest in things and an inability to concentrate or remember (see Figure 10-1). Somatic and behavioral symptoms such as crying, insomnia, loss of appetite and weight, lack of energy, and reliance on tranquilizers, sleeping pills, and alcohol are also commonplace (Clayton, Halikes, & Maurice, 1971; Parkes, 1972).

Less common and seemingly pathological reactions to a severe loss, but actually fairly normal responses, are regression, hallucinations, obsessional review, overidentification with the deceased, and idealization of the deceased. In *regression,* a common reaction to extreme stress, the bereaved person behaves childishly. The regression is not total, but rather alternates with periods of maturity. *Hallucinations* occur, for example, when a widow sees her dead husband in the appearance or mannerisms of a stranger, feels the touch or presence of the deceased, or misinterprets a creak as her husband moving about the house. These hallucinations are a consequence of preoccupation with the deceased, thinking about him constantly. Not only is the deceased seen and heard, but his presence is felt, con-

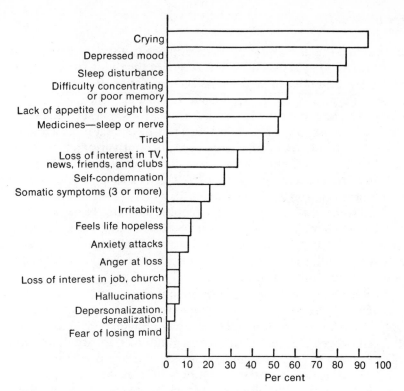

Crying
Depressed mood
Sleep disturbance
Difficulty concentrating
or poor memory
Lack of appetite or weight loss
Medicines—sleep or nerve
Tired
Loss of interest in TV,
news, friends, and clubs
Self-condemnation
Somatic symptoms (3 or more)
Irritability
Feels life hopeless
Anxiety attacks
Anger at loss
Loss of interest in job, church
Hallucinations
Depersonalization,
derealization
Fear of losing mind

0   10 20 30 40 50 60 70 80 90 100
Per cent

FIGURE 10-1
Percentages of recently widowed persons expressing various symptoms. (Adapted from Clayton, Halikes, and Maurice, 1971, Table 1. Courtesy of Physicians Postgraduate Press, Inc. In D. C. Kimmel, *Adulthood and Aging*, 2d. ed., © 1980 by John Wiley & Sons, Inc. Used by permission.)

versations are held with him, and he is dreamed about every night (Glick, Weiss, & Parkes, 1974).

Another feature of bereavement, the *obsessional review,* happens when the bereaved individual engages in frequent, periodic reviews of events leading up to and immediately following the death. *Overidentification with the deceased* is demonstrated, for example, by a widow who begins to talk and act like her dead husband—wearing his clothes, using his possessions, and so on. Finally, *idealization of the deceased* occurs when only good things about the dead person are recalled. It is as if the survivor's memories of the deceased have been purified, leaving only the positive and pleasant. This can occur even when a survivor actually hated the deceased, who is now remembered as having been an unusually good person. Idealization in this instance is an illustration of the operation of the defense mechanism of denial (Lopata, 1973).

Stages of Grief

The notion that the grieving process takes place in a series of stages, similar to Kübler-Ross's (1969) psychological stages in the dying process, has been developed by a number of writers. As seen in Table 10-1, there are three-stage, four-stage, five-stage, and even seven-stage theories of grief or mourning. The first stage in almost all formulations is described as a period of shock, numbness, or disbelief, lasting a few days or at most a few weeks. Loss of self-control, reduced energy, lack of motivation, bewilderment, disorientation, and a loss of perspective characterize this initial period in the grieving process. Following the first stage is a long period of grief and related emotions (pining, depression, guilt, anger), in which the individual tries to find some meaning in the catastrophic loss. In a large percentage of cases, the bereavement process runs its course after approximately a year following the death. By that time, the bereaved individual has given up any hope of recovering the deceased and is ready to reorganize his or her life and focus on new objects of interest.

As with any theory of developmental stages or periods, there is a danger that "stages of grief" will be interpreted as a fixed sequence through which all bereaved people must pass. Bugen (1977) has noted that the different stages of grief blend together and overlap, are not necessarily successive, vary in intensity and duration, and are not experienced by every bereaved person. Consequently, he argues against the interpretation of all stage theories of the grieving process as being anything other than descriptive accounts of various emotional stages experienced by bereaved people. In all fairness, it should be pointed out that most of the writers whose conceptualizations are summarized in Table 10-1 have recognized that a particular mourner need not go through all the stages and not necessarily in a specific order. Be that as it may, Bugen (1977) is correct in being concerned about possible misinterpretations of stage theories. Research evidence supporting the concept of stages of grief is neither extensive nor convincing.

Individual Differences

Although it is normal to grieve when a severe loss has been sustained, some people never go through the process but remain emotionally calm and efficient throughout the wake, the funeral, and the postfuneral period. At the other extreme are those who react with great emotional intensity and take years to recover, or who perhaps never recover. These individual differences in the intensity and duration of the bereavement process are a function of multiple variables, including age, sex, personality, the sociocultural context, the relationship of the mourner to the deceased, and whether or not the death was expected.

TABLE 10-1
Stages of Grief According to Five Theories

Gorer (1967)
1. Initial shock (first few days)—characterized by loss of self-control, reduced energy, lack of motivation, bewilderment, disorientation, and loss of perspective.
2. Intense grief (several months)—periodic crying, confusion, and inability to understand what has actually happened.
3. Gradual reawakening of interest—acceptance of reality of loved one's death and all it means.

Glick, Weiss, and Parkes (1974)
1. Shock and disbelief, followed by crying and weeping (first few weeks).
2. Repetitious review of events leading up to death (few weeks to one year).
3. Recovery (approximately one year after bereavement).

Parkes (1972)
1. Numbness—lack of emotionality; person in a daze.
2. Pining—preoccupation with deceased at its greatest.
3. Dejection—extent and nature of loss achieves full awareness; life devoid of meaning.
4. Recovery—unrealistic hopes of recovering loved one are relinquished.

Bowlby (1960)
1. Concentration directed toward the deceased.
2. Anger or hostility toward the deceased or others.
3. Appeals to others for support and help.
4. Despair, withdrawal, and general disorganization.
5. Reorganization and direction of the self toward a new love object.

Kavanaugh (1974)
1. Shock—physical and emotional shock; real and unreal worlds collide.
2. Disorganization—person feels totally out of touch with ordinary proceedings of life.
3. Volatile emotions—mourner unleashes volatile emotions, upsetting those around him or her.
4. Guilt—mourner feels guilt and depressed.
5. Loss and loneliness—may be the most painful stage.
6. Relief—may be difficult for mourner to acknowledge and openly adjust.
7. Reestablishment—friends become important at this stage.

With respect to the factor of age, children who have sustained the loss of a close relative or friend experience grief just as adults do. Every year, over three million U.S. children under age 19 lose one or both parents (Bernstein, 1977), and many of these children have adjustment problems. In general, children experience greater difficulty adjusting to the loss of a family member when intrafamilial relationships are strained (Hilgard & Newman, 1959). But children tend to work through their problems and get on with their lives more quickly than adults, to whom the loss of a friend or family member is usually more traumatic (Cohen, 1980).

Among adult women, it has been found that emotional reactions to the loss of a husband are usually less intense in older than in younger widows. For example, Ball (1977) found that widows in the 18–46 year age bracket grieved more intensely than widows who were over age 46. One explanation for this age difference in grief is that in the case of an older widow, the death of her (older) husband is more likely to have been anticipated, thus providing an opportunity to prepare for it. Regardless of the age of the survivor, it would seem that *anticipatory grieving*— grieving in advance of a loved one's death—might give the survivor a chance to begin working through the complex of emotions associated with the loss and therefore hasten the recovery process (Parkes, 1975). Certainly when death occurs suddenly or unexpectedly, and the survivors have no opportunity to prepare psychologically for the loss, it is especially shocking. On the other hand, a long period of anticipatory grieving (as when death occurs after a prolonged chronic illness) is often predictive of poorer recuperation by survivors than when the dying trajectory and hence the anticipatory grieving period are shorter (Gerber et al., 1975). In any event, the therapeutic effects of a preparatory period prior to the death of a loved one seem to be greater in the case of younger widows than in older widows (Ball, 1977).

The duration and intensity of grief, as well as its quality, are also associated with the personality and sex of the bereaved individual. As noted previously, bereaved persons manifest a wide range of reactions. Although there is little consistency in the grief responses among different individuals, there is a substantial degree of consistency within the individuals themselves. Thus, the frequency and intensity of emotions and other behavioral manifestations shown shortly after a loss are positively related to the symptoms present one year later (Bornstein et al., 1973). The sex of the bereaved is also a factor in the symptom picture. Men are expected to respond less emotionally than women. The death of a loved one also appears to mean different things to men and women; women tend to feel abandoned, but men feel dismembered (Glick, Weiss, & Parkes, 1974). This finding is consistent with the fact that women in our society are usually more concerned with other people, whereas men are more interested in their jobs and other life ventures.

The effects that interpersonal or social factors such as the relationship of the survivor to the deceased, the socioeconomic status of the family, and the presence of children in the home have on grieving have also been investigated (e.g., Harvey & Bahr, 1974; Hutchison, 1975; Lopata, 1979). One finding is that the strength of the relationship between a married couple has a pronounced effect on the grief shown by the surviving member. The stronger the emotional bond, the more difficult the recovery process (Lopata, 1973). Relationships characterized by extreme dependency or persisting conflict are indicative of a poor recovery prognosis. But when the relationship is built on mutual trust and fulfillment, the bereaved person can more easily get on with the process of readjustment and self-renewal.

Social class and ethnicity have also been found to be related to the intensity of grief experienced by bereaved people. The popular stereotype is that upper-class widows (e.g., Jacqueline Kennedy) show less public emotion than those of lower social class. However, the middle-class widows in Lopata's (1973) Chicago study actually experienced more difficulty than their working-class counterparts in dealing with grief. It would also seem that the presence of children in a family would tend to affect the severity and duration of the grieving process, but such does not appear to be the case (Lopata, 1973; Glick, Weiss, & Parkes, 1974).

Effects of Bereavement on Illness and Mortality

Caring for a chronically ill person is emotionally and physically taxing under the best of circumstances, but particularly so when the illness is terminal. In this case the effects of prebereavement stress can combine with the shock and grief of bereavement to produce both physical and mental disorders. Sometimes the resulting emotional and physical symptoms are so intense that the individual becomes seriously ill.

Pathological Grief

Emotions such as anxiety, fear, depression, guilt, and anger are not in themselves abnormal responses to bereavement. Whether or not they are considered pathological depends on their intensity, how long they persist, and what other behavioral and physical symptoms are present. Most normal people react to bereavement with some combination of these symptoms, and occasionally even experience hallucinations and suicidal thoughts. In pathological grief, however, the symptoms either persist in intensified form or become noteworthy by their total absence. In the great majority of cases, the grieving process is resolved by finding a new direction for one's life or engaging in some kind of creative endeavor (Pollock, 1978). But a small percentage of bereaved individuals find it impossible to accept the death of a loved one. Rarely is the shock of bereavement so great that it immediately precipitates a severe mental disorder, but it can happen (see Report 10-1). More common pathological reactions are chronic grief, delayed grief, or even a permanent inhibition of grief.

In *chronic grief,* the bereaved person yearns and sorrows for the lost loved one for years after the death. Time does not heal the grief of this person, who is deeply depressed, apathetic, has illogical fears, and even occasional hallucinatory experiences and other symptoms of fragile contact with reality. Another symptom of chronic, pathological grief is *mummification* of the deceased, in which everything that the deceased

Pathological Grief Reaction

Marilyn, a 37-year-old woman, lived with her 63-year-old invalid mother. Marilyn had always lived in her parents' home except for two brief periods when she was hospitalized for depression at ages 18 and 24. She had never married because she felt obligated to care for her mother and to help raise her two younger sisters (now ages 30 and 32, married, and living in distant cities). In her early thirties she had resigned herself to her situation: feeling duty-bound to support her mother, she gave up on the idea of having a family of her own and threw herself into her full-time secretarial work, attending to her rather overbearing mother in the evenings. She had no outside social life and no close friends.

One evening Marilyn came home from work and found her mother dead. She was stunned and became quite confused. Without calling for assistance, she simply tucked her mother in bed and went about business as usual. She went to work for the next two days but acted so

unusual that her supervisor sent her home. The next day, her worried supervisor came to her home to check on her. He found the mother dead in bed and Marilyn sitting on the floor in a stuporous condition. She was hospitalized and treated with antidepressant medication, electroconvulsive therapy, and limited psychotherapy. After six months she was discharged from the hospital. On the following day she attempted to take her own life with an overdose of sleeping medication. She was discovered in a coma by a neighbor, and was then given emergency treatment. Afterwards, she was returned to the psychiatric hospital for further treatment.

During her second hospital admission Marilyn was given further electroshock and antidepressant treatment along with psychotherapy. After two months, she was discharged and was placed in an aftercare facility, where she was supervised during reentry into her work and social world.

From ABNORMAL PSYCHOLOGY AND MODERN LIFE, 6th Edition by J. C. Coleman, J. N. Butcher, R. C. Carson. Copyright © 1980, 1976, 1972 by Scott, Foresman and Co. Reprinted by permission.

owned is kept in order, his or her clothes are laid out every day, and the bereaved individual continues the routine of living just as if the deceased were still alive. Such was reportedly the mental state and behavior of Queen Victoria for years after Prince Albert's death. Chronic, unresolved grief is also seen in *anniversary reactions,* in which the emotional response precipitated by the death of a loved one recurs on the anniversary of the death.

In other pathological cases, grief is delayed for 5, 10, or even as long as 40 years after the death (Pincus, 1976). This *delay* or *permanent inhibition* of grief is not without its costs. The blocking of feelings normally associated with death has repercussions in other areas, being expressed in physical and psychological disorders. In most instances, repressed grief leads to neurotic and even psychotic behaviors of various kinds, including regression to earlier stages of development and suicide attempts. Suicide is believed to be almost always the result of some kind of loss—if not the death of a loved one, then the loss of a job or position of status, health, youth, or a relationship. Because they are likely to have suffered several such losses, elderly people—and elderly widowers in particular—fall in the high risk group of potential suicides. The risk of suicide among the widowed is especially high during the first year of bereavement, falling off sharply but continuing to be higher than average during the second and subsequent years following the death (Miller, 1978).

Pathological grief reactions are more common in certain situations than in others, for example, in the case of a child or young adult in apparently good health whose death was unanticipated. Because of their unexpected nature, suicide, homicide, stillbirth, and death caused by accident are especially likely to produce pathological reactions in the survivors. A pathological response is also more common when the bereaved has unresolved conflicts with and ambivalent feelings toward the deceased or lacks other social and emotional supports (Hinton, 1972).

Physical Illness

In addition to psychological symptoms, grief-stricken people suffer from various physical problems. Loss of appetite, weight loss, and sleep disturbances are particularly common symptoms during the first stages of grief (see Figure 10-1). General body pains, headaches, dizziness, visual problems, and menstrual irregularities are also prevalent. These symptoms seem to occur more often in younger than in older adults, and they may be harbingers of further deterioration in health during the first year of bereavement and even afterward (Clayton, Halikes, & Maurice, 1971).

The frequency of physical symptoms associated with grief is underscored by the results of a study by Parkes (1972). He found that 75 percent of the group of widows surveyed had seen their physicians for physical and psychological problems associated with grief during the first six months after bereavement. Compared to the six months prior to bereavement, there was a 63 percent increase in visits to doctors' offices during the postbereavement period. The increase in physical disorders and visits to physicians after bereavement, of course, may have been due to some extent to the cumulative effects on survivors of prolonged illness in dying persons. Attending to a spouse during a long illness seems to have a debilitating effect on the health of the survivor. Although a long-term terminal illness would appear to provide more opportunity than a short-term illness for the reputed beneficial effects of anticipatory grief in the survivor to take place, Gerber et al. (1975) found that the medical prognosis for survivors was better when the dying period in chronic terminal illness was short.

Mortality Rate

The results of a number of studies (Parkes, Benjamin, & Fitzgerald, 1969; Clayton, Halikes, & Maurice, 1971; Helsing, Szklo, & Comstock, 1981) reveal that the bereaved have a higher death rate than other individuals of comparable age. In the Parkes et al. (1969) study of 4,500 British widowers aged 55 and over, 213 died during the first six months after bereavement. The rate of death was 40 percent higher than expected in the entire group during the first year, but it returned to normal after five years. Parkes referred to the heightened rate of death, most instances of which resulted from coronary thrombosis, arteriosclerotic heart disease, and other forms of heart disease, as the "broken heart syndrome." Although the dynamics of this syndrome are not clearly understood, the condition has been known for centuries. Parkes argued that bereavement may produce changes in blood pressure and heart rate, as well as affect the circulation and chemistry of the blood, thereby acting as a precipitating factor in clot formation in coronary arteries.

Increased mortality after bereavement is a function of several demographic variables, including age, sex, ethnicity, marital status, and living situation. The increase in mortality is greater in people in their late fifties or early sixties than in those over age 65; it is also greater in men than in women and in nonwhites than in whites (Helsing, Szklo, & Comstock, 1981; Heyman & Gianturco, 1973; Lopata, 1973). With regard to sex differences, the same factors—whatever they may be—that make women live longer than men also apparently make them more resistant to the stresses of bereavement and widowhood.

Consistent with the physiological and psychological benefits of marriage discussed earlier in the text, remarriage after the death of a spouse has been found to lower the mortality rate dramatically. The effects are particularly pronounced in men, for whom the marital state makes more of a difference in mortality than it does for women. Also associated with marriage is the living situation of the widowed person. Compared to the marital situation, in which physical care and socioemotional supports apparently reduce mortality, living alone contributes to higher mortality rates. Moving into a nursing or retirement home is also related to increased mortality, in fact, substantially so (Helsing, Szklo, & Comstock, 1981).

Earlier reports on the effects of bereavement on mortality indicated that the rate was higher, and hence the risk of death greater, during the first six months after bereavement (e.g., Clayton, Halikes, & Maurice, 1969). But a more recent investigation of 1,204 men and 2,828 women in a semirural Maryland county who were widowed between 1963 and 1974 (Helsing, Szklo, & Comstock, 1981) found no evidence that either widows or widowers were significantly more likely to die than nonbereaved persons during the early months after bereavement. However, a higher mortality rate for these widowed persons, more specifically the widowers, was noted *after* the first few months following bereavement. This finding suggests that the important factor in promoting increased mortality is the stress of widowhood rather than the stress of bereavement.

The findings of Helsing et al. (1981) are consistent with the *desolation-effects hypothesis* described by Epstein et al. (1975). This hypothesis states that both the event of widowhood and the circumstances stemming from it have deleterious effects in terms of grief, feelings of hopelessness, new worries and responsibilities, and alterations in the diet, work routine, and financial situation of the bereaved person. Epstein et al. (1975) also discuss four other hypotheses that propose to explain the increased mortality rate after bereavement. The two most plausible, but certainly not as convincing as the desolation-effects hypothesis, are the *non-grief related behavior-change hypothesis* and the *joint unfavorable environment hypothesis.* According to the former hypothesis, survivors are more likely to die because they fail to eat properly, do not take their medicines regularly, and are less likely to visit the doctor when ill without a spouse around to provide support and encouragement. The joint unfavorable environment hypothesis points out that by having shared a common unfavorable environment, widowed persons and their spouses are exposed to similar environmental risk factors. Obviously, these three hypotheses are not mutually exclusive; the factors described in any or all of them may influence mortality after bereavement.

Grief Counseling and Therapy

Time by itself does not heal all things, but it is a curative force in grief. Given enough time, most people are able to adjust to the death of a loved one and reconstruct a life independent of the presence and support of the deceased. The adjustment process is usually easier when there has been an opportunity to prepare for the loss, when the bereaved feels that there is some meaning in the death, and/or when there is something left to live for. Thus, recovery from a severe loss can be facilitated by relying on religious or philosophical beliefs that stress the future (Peterson & Briley, 1977), intensifying old social relationships or forming new ones, or becoming actively involved with children, work, and other activities (Ball, 1977). Many people, however, require special assistance in coping with bereavement and grief.

Interpersonal Relationships and Grief Groups

The support of other people is crucial after the death of a loved one. Warm, supportive family members and friends who appreciate the bereaved person's situation and feelings and continue to visit him or her in the weeks and months after the funeral can have a definite therapeutic influence. In addition to family members and friends, the physicians, funeral directors, lawyers, clergymen, and other professional persons with whom the bereaved person interacts can be helpful. Reviewing the circumstances of the death and the effects of it with any one of these professionals and, perhaps even more significant, with a trusted companion or confidant, can be of therapeutic value to the bereaved. The presence of an interested, sympathetic and understanding human being can do more than all the tranquilizers, sleeping pills, and other medicines combined to assist bereaved people in coping with loss and grief.

In many localities, social and psychological assistance for bereaved people is available from a number of public and private organizations. Churches, mental health clinics, community bereavement centers, and mutual-aid societies such as various widow-to-widow programs, Compassionate Friends, Parents Without Partners, and Big Brothers/Big Sisters of America all offer assistance to bereaved persons and their families. These organizations are staffed by professionally trained individuals who provide both individual and group counseling to help people deal with personal and family problems caused or aggravated by bereavement. Among these problems are alcoholism, sexual dysfunctions, marital discord, child behavior disorders, and other family difficulties.

Compassionate Friends, an organization that began in Britain and now has chapters in most areas of the United States, focuses on providing help for parents who have lost children. The counselors, or "befrienders" as they are called in Britain, are often mothers and fathers who themselves have lost a child and wish to help others learn to cope as they did (Cohen, 1980). Similar motivations are basic to widow-to-widow counseling programs, in which newly bereaved widows are counseled by trained individuals who themselves have lost a spouse and already completed their grief work. In addition to providing understanding and sympathy, these volunteer counselors make referrals to other sources when assistance and information beyond their training are needed.

Social support for bereaved individuals is also provided by *grief groups* that consist of a small collection of persons who share the common trauma of having lost a loved one. Under the direction of a professional counselor, the members of a grief group talk about their feelings and how to survive bereavement. The role of the counselor-director is to provide both information and a focus for group discussion. Group counseling can also be supplemented with individual counseling or psychotherapy for members who require it.

Individual Counseling and Psychotherapy

Individual, one-to-one counseling or psychotherapy with bereaved individuals is perhaps even more common than group counseling. Various techniques and methods are employed in individual psychological treatment for grief. Special techniques are available for working with the bereaved in addition to traditional counseling and psychotherapeutic methods. As in any form of psychological treatment, the specific techniques must be adapted to the personality, problems, circumstances, age, and sex of the bereaved individual (Marmar, 1981). Directive techniques such as providing advice and reassurance, and giving the counselee homework assignments or tasks to test reality and practice coping with frustration, are used by some counselors.

Recognizing that a major psychological problem associated with bereavement is an unwillingness to let go of the dead, some sort of reworking technique is fairly standard in grief therapy. Report 10-2 describes a special reworking process known as *guided imagery.* In the first therapy session, the bereaved person is instructed to recall the affection that he or she shared with the deceased spouse. This reexperiencing process is disturbing to the bereaved, but Frederick Melges, originator of the method, maintains that a sense of self-identity and worth is revived by it. During a second session, the person closes his or her eyes and mentally goes through the experiences of receiving the news of the death, viewing the body, attending the funeral, and walking away from the grave. The bereaved person is told to describe these events out loud exactly as if they were occurring at that moment. The person is also encouraged to converse with the deceased, to ask the deceased's permission to find new relationships and a new life. At the end, the bereaved is encouraged to say his or her last goodbyes to the deceased (Melges, 1982).

Counseling Bereaved Children

Adults who are preoccupied with their own grief and the life reorganization necessitated by the death of a spouse or other loved one sometimes overlook the fact that surviving children also experience grief and other emotions associated with death. The death of a parent or sibling, in particular, can be quite disturbing and confusing to a child who is unknowledgeable about death and has not been prepared by being taken into the adults' confidence. Whatever the circumstances may be, a bereaved child should be permitted to ask questions and encouraged to express his or her feelings about the death and the deceased. Adults should take the time to answer the child's questions and to acknowledge the child's feelings, including anger, guilt, anxiety, and sadness. Although negative feelings and memories should be accepted and worked through with the child, adults should also try to get the child to focus on happy moments that were shared with the deceased and to think about something that the child did to please the deceased (Schlesinger, 1977). Throughout the counseling, the child should be given frequent reassurances of love and understanding.

REPORT 10-2

"Guided Imagery": Relief for Prolonged Grieving

By Arthur Snider

Normal grief following the death of a loved one lasts about a year, during which the bereaved goes through stages of shock, anguish, mourning and, finally, recovery.

It is widely believed that "time heals" and the grieving person will overcome pain and sorrow over the passing months. But psychiatrists see thousands of people who still grieve years after the death.

They continue to have deep depression, lack of interest, insomnia and weight loss. They are often out of touch with reality, even experiencing hallucinations in which the voice of the deceased is heard or the face seen across the room. They respond to the mention of death with explosive weeping or avoidance of the subject. Time does not heal their feelings.

Dr. Frederick Towne Melges, professor of psychiatry at Duke University, lists some of the signs of unresolved grief:

- Continued yearning for the loved one. The deceased is referred to in the present tense rather than in past tense. Pictures and mementos are often touched to maintain hope for a reunion. Dreams of a reunion are common.
- Overidentification with the deceased. The bereaved has unexplainable bodily symptoms or changes in personality that are remarkably similar to those of the dead person.
- Inability to cry. The bereaved does not cry at the time of death to keep from "falling apart" and at a later time because it seems inappropriate. Weeping and anger are natural responses that bring about a realization that the loss is final.

- Unfinished business. The survivor feels he must keep the deceased "alive" in his heart so that he will have a chance to express the love he never did while the deceased was living.
- Misdirected anger. Anger intended for the deceased is misdirected at one's self. The anger results from the feeling that the deceased has deserted the bereaved. The self-reproach is for guilt over being angry at the deceased.
- Unrevealed secrets. Some patients cannot accept the death of a loved one for fear the deceased, all-knowing in a new spiritual kingdom, will have knowledge of a carefully guarded secret, such as an extramarital affair or greed for inheritance money.
- Unspoken contract. Just as contracts are made in marriage vows, the bereaved makes a silent contract that says, "I will not leave you. I will stay by your side."
- Secondary gain. Some patients remain grief-stricken because they learn from the support of others that this is a way to gain continued comfort and to escape responsibilities. (Sometimes the reverse occurs. The support is so short-lived and superficial that the patients cling to the memory of the support they had from their spouse.)

Through a process he calls "guided imagery," Melges has his patients "relive" the loss by leading them through the grieving stage with more insight into what the process involves. He finds they can give up their loved ones and cure their depression.

It begins with a session in which the bereaved is asked to recall the affection between him and his spouse before the death.

Though distressing, says the psychiatrist, reexperiencing the death helps revive the bereaved's sense of self-identity and worth.

At the second session, the patient is told to close his eyes and go through the news of the death, viewing the body, the funeral and the walk away from the grave. The patient is asked to speak out loud in the present tense as though the events were happening now.

The patient is encouraged to engage in "dialogues" with the deceased, to reveal secrets, express tears and rage, unfinished business, love and forgiveness, to get permission from the deceased to look for new relationships and options.

Finally, at some point, the bereaved is encouraged to exchange "last words" and to say "goodbye." If he cannot say goodbye at that time, he is allowed to say "goodbye for now" and to try again the next session.

"Our experience is that present-time guided imagery can quickly get to core issues needing resolution and to detach the binds to the deceased," says Melges. "It is not enough to talk about the loss in the past tense. The patient must reexperience it in the here and now through reliving and revising events of the loss."

© Chicago *Sun-Times,* 1980. Column by Arthur Snider. Reprinted with permission.

When the deceased is a parent or other adult who was very close to the child, the child will need to learn to redirect his or her love toward another adult. It is important for all the child's love not to be reinvested in a single individual, of course, such as the surviving parent; otherwise, a condition of extreme dependency may develop. The child should be encouraged to establish close relationships with several adults, especially those within the family circle (Schlesinger, 1977).

Effective counseling of bereaved children requires the cooperation of various adults, not only parents and other family members, but also teachers, doctors, and professional child therapists. Recommended counseling activities include reading and discussing fairy tales that refer to death in a nonthreatening manner, play therapy, role playing or reenacting a situation or story related to death and dying, and drawing pictures with the deceased in them (Ryerson, 1977). Fundamental to all therapeutic efforts with bereaved children, however, are patience, openness, understanding, and love.

Widowhood in the Western World

Widowhood is, by definition, a state in which a man (a widower) or woman (a widow) has lost his or her spouse by death and has not remarried. Statistics indicate that in 1981 in the United States, approximately 12.8 million people, or 7.3 percent of the noninstitutionalized U.S. population 15 years and older, fell into this category. Of the 12.8 million widowed persons, 10.8 million (85 percent) were women, 1.9 million (15 percent) were men, 11 million (86 percent) were white, and 1.6 million (13 percent) were black (U.S. Dept. of Commerce, 1982).

According to the statistics presented in Table 10-2, there were 10,796,000 widows and 1,861,000 widowers in the United States in 1982, a ratio of 5.5 to 1. The ratio of widows to widowers varied somewhat with age level, but widows outnumbered widowers at all ages. Two reasons for these sex differences in the incidence of widowhood are that men tend to die at younger ages than women, and a greater percentage of widowers than widows terminate their widowhood status by remarrying fairly soon after bereavement. Consequently, widowhood in the United States is primarily a status of women, and the problems of widowhood are, by and large, women's problems. This is a major reason why so much of the research on widowhood has focused on women rather than men.

TABLE 10-2
Number and Percentage of Widowed Persons in Nine Age Groups

	Men		*Women*	
Age	*Number*	*Percent*[a]	*Number*	*Percent*[b]
20–24	1,000	—	14,000	.1
25–29	3,000	—	50,000	.5
30–34	11,000	.1	69,000	.7
35–39	15,000	.2	114,000	1.5
40–44	29,000	.5	217,000	3.5
45–54	166,000	1.5	789,000	6.8
55–64	355,000	3.5	2,019,000	17.3
65–74	510,000	7.5	3,419,000	38.3
75 & over	770,000	21.7	4,104,000	68.5
All ages	1,861,000	2.2	10,796,000	11.7

Source: U.S. Dept. of Commerce, Bureau of the Census. (1983). *Current Population Reports.* Series P-20, No. 380. *Marital status and living arrangements: March 1982.* Washington, D.C.: Superintendent of Documents, U.S. Government Printing Office.
a. Percentage of men in the respective age group who are widowed.
b. Percentage of women in the respective age group who are widowed.

Family Relationships

Widowhood has an effect on all of an individual's family relationships. If there are children in the home, the widow or widower has to play the roles of both mother and father. Although members of the extended family (brothers, sisters, aunts, uncles, etc.) are usually in close contact with the widowed person for a while after the death of the spouse, interactions with them become less frequent as time passes.

Younger widows reportedly have more difficulty adjusting than older widows because of their lack of preparation for widowhood, the need to care for younger children, and assorted practical problems (Blau, 1961; Lopata, 1973; Glick, Weiss, & Parkes, 1974). The parents of a young widow are her most important source of social support; widowhood can be extremely trying for a young woman who has no close relatives living nearby. Unlike the awkward social status of a young widow, however, widowhood in older women is considered more "normal." Older widows tend to receive greater social support from family members and the widei community, making the transition from wife to widow less traumatic for older than for younger women (Blau, 1961).

Regardless of age, a widow who was not congenial with her in-laws while her husband was alive may now experience even greater problems with them. In any event, social support is more likely to come from the widow's own family. Older widows, for example, tend to grow closer to their own children, and their daughters in particular. Sometimes they move in with their children, but the potential for intergenerational conflict makes this situation an undesirable one for most people (Adams, 1968; Lopata, 1973):

> Never try to live with your children. It's no good. I stayed there (at her daughter's house) a couple of months and I couldn't stand it. The kids, you know, have to do what they want to do. When I was listenin' to my TV, they were playin' games on the other side. . . . My daughter has a husband you can't take to, you know what I mean? The minute he come home, I went upstairs and I stayed there (Vinick, 1977, p. 3).

Widows who live with their adult sons or daughters are expected to help with the household chores and grandchildren. Unfortunately, the widow's position in her son's or daughter's household usually carries no real status or authority, and the fear of intruding makes her feel uncomfortable.

In addition to their relationships with living family members, widows may still "consult" or interact with their dead husbands. Uncertain about what to do—where and how to live, whether to buy or invest in this or that—a widow can become so desperate for advice and guidance that she even attempts to communicate with her husband in the spirit world. Be that as it may, in most cases there are living relatives and close friends who are willing to act as confidants and counselors without pestering the dead.

Social Relations

A person who has just lost a spouse is likely to disengage somewhat from social activities. Temporary social disengagement, of course, is not pathological, but rather a normal part of psychological recovery. In cases where the widow's social entrees were provided in large measure by her husband's occupational contacts, the reduction in social activities can continue for some time (Lopata, 1979; Glick, Weiss, & Parkes, 1974).

However, it is not usually very difficult for a widow to establish friendships with other widows in similar circumstances. Most widows reach out beyond their homes to gratify their social needs. Churches, senior citizens centers, and various voluntary organizations provide opportunities to socialize. But widows are usually careful to avoid heterosexual situations in which they are apt to be perceived as "swinging singles" or "merry widows" who are making a play for someone else's date or mate.

Compared with widows, widowers frequently have more of a problem making friends with other bereaved persons. The explanation is twofold: the number of widowers is smaller than that of widows, and men tend to be less socially adept than women. Even when her husband is alive, a woman is more likely to have a confidante or other close friend of the same sex. Married men may also have close friendships with other men, but such is less often the case. And those men who failed to develop close relationships with other men while their wives were alive typically become even more socially isolated as widowers. Middle-class widowers are reportedly less socially isolated than lower-class widowers (Atchley, 1975), but both groups are not as involved as widows in religious and social organizations.

Sex Relationships and Remarriage

Widowers. There are obvious compensations in being a widower, especially when one considers the large number of "casserole-carrying" widows who vie for the attentions of a few widowers. The competition among widows for their favors can be embarrassing to some widowers, but other widowers are undoubtedly pleased by all the fuss and the many social-sexual outlets provided by it. Because men tend to be less close to others than women are, widowers are apparently lonelier than widows and seem to need marriage more. Widowed men discover that the companionship, sex, and physical and emotional support provided by a wife are things they would prefer not to do without. Furthermore, the relatively larger number of available women provides a better opportunity for men to remarry. Whatever the reason may be, the majority of widowers remarry within a year or two after their wife's death. Quite often they marry someone whom they have known for years, long before they were widowed, and usually someone quite a few years younger.

Widows. The ancient Hebrew custom of the *levirate* dictated that a widow should marry the brother of her deceased husband. This custom may have been appropriate in a culture that permitted multiple spouses, but it would not work in a monogamous society such as ours in which widows far outnumber widowers. Consequently, the U.S. widow who wants to remarry usually finds herself in competition with several other women in similar circumstances. Remarriage is not a highly probable event for most widows.

Even widows who eventually remarry tend to manifest greater loyalty to their departed spouse than widowers do, for when they do remarry it is usually several years after the death. For example, 50 percent of the widowers but only 18 percent of the widows questioned in one survey had remarried by the end of the first year of bereavement (Glick, Weiss, & Parkes, 1974). As might be expected, younger widows are more likely than older widows to remarry. An older widow is supposed to respect and preserve the memory of her dead husband and not be interested in other men. Despite the cultural bias against older widows remarrying and the lesser availability of unmarried males, however, some older widows successfully take the initiative.

> He was sitting near me at the Golden Agers, and I didn't even know him. He was looking so depressed. You could see that the man needs something. The trouble is, when I see someone lonely, I want to know what's the matter. He was sitting just like a chicken without a head [sic]. After that, he went his way, I went my way. So (the next meeting) he was sitting there again. So, my friend said, "Let's sit down with him. It will warm him up a little." It was awfully windy. We sat down, and then we started to talk. You know the way it is. . . (Vinick, 1977, p. 6).

Motives for Remarrying. Sex and romance are motives for marriage at any age, but apparently less so in later life. Newly married older people mention companionship, affection, regard, a desire to take care of someone, and intimacy more often than sex and romance as their reasons for remarrying. And when sex is mentioned, it is generally the warmth and feeling of togetherness rather than the physical pleasure that is stressed. As was true the first time around, remarriage does not guarantee happiness; however, people who remarry after the death of a spouse generally are happier than those who remain alone and unattached (Butler & Lewis, 1977).

Living Alone and Loneliness

As a result of their changed status, widowed persons are faced with many problems and choices, where to live being one of these. To a great extent, the decision about where to live depends on the economic situation of the individual. The status of widowhood is usually accompanied by reduced economic circumstances for most women, and decreased income may mean a move to smaller, less desirable living quarters. Many elderly widows in particular prefer to live alone rather than with a married child or in an institution, and a sizable percentage own their own homes (U.S. Dept. of Health & Human Services, 1981). However, the costs of maintenance and utility bills, possible health problems, the fear of crime, and loneliness force many widows to move in with a married son or daughter or into a retirement home or rental quarters. Others may solve the problem by taking in renters or, if the health or loneliness problems are more serious than the financial ones, hire a live-in companion or nurse. But for whatever reasons—habit, a desire to be free and independent, a concern with imposing on other people—a majority of widows who own their own homes remain in them as long as possible and prefer to do so by themselves.

Still, loneliness is a problem for the widowed. Older widowed people are, as a group, lonelier than older married people, and younger widows are even lonelier than older ones (Atchley, 1975; Troll, 1982). In addition, working-class widows are lonelier than middle-class widows on the whole (Atchley, 1975). These differences are associated with the number of social contacts maintained or established by the individual. Older widows, for example, have more friends than younger widows, mainly because the pool of older widows is larger and they have had more time to make friends. It is noteworthy in this connection that older widows have higher rates of social interaction than older married women (Atchley, Pignatiello, & Shaw, 1975). Similarly, middle-class widows, like middle-class women in general, have more time and a greater tendency than working-class widows to establish friendships with individuals of their same sex and age group.

Comparisons between groups of widows and widowers indicate little or no sex differences in degree of loneliness (Atchley, 1975). A majority of these comparisons, however, are not really fair, because a much larger percentage of widows than widowers live alone (Murphy & Florio, 1978). Widowers are slightly more likely than widows to live in group quarters such as hotels and rooming houses (Troll, 1982). In any event, most widows find ways of coping with loneliness. A widow is more likely than a widower to maintain close relationships with other family members and to have a same-sex confidant (Lopata, 1975). Even when she is lonely, the problem is less severe if she lives in a neighborhood with a high concentration of other widows. Loneliness also can be lessened somewhat by owning a pet that can be cared for, talked to, and loved.

Economic and Identity Problems

Widowhood is, without question, a major life crisis for most women and men. A widowed person loses more than a friend, a lover, a helpmate, and a part of his or her identity as a human being. There are also economic losses in most instances. The financial condition of a typical widow is far from good, although an exceptional few—the recipients of windfall income from insurance policies, estate settlements, and profit-sharing trusts—are even better off than they were during their married lives. The great majority of widows, however, have to get by on small savings, a modest insurance or other death benefit, and social security payments that are less than those received when the husband was alive. Younger widows tend to have even more financial woes than older widows, but both groups find that money and its management are serious problems for them (Wyly & Hulicka, 1975).

Decreased income has repercussions in many areas of living. Social and other interests and activities that cost money to pursue have to be reduced; the overall lower standard of living also has an effect on one's self-concept (Kaplan & Pokorny, 1970). Widows who depend almost completely on their husbands to keep the home, car, and other possessions in good repair, to drive the car, and to manage their finances feel insecure and inadequate when they are forced to rely on their own resources. Some widows are unable to adapt successfully to their changed circumstances and the necessity for developing a new identity and different social roles. The resulting adjustment difficulties may be expressed through alcohol and drug addiction, mental illness, and even loss of the will to live. Widowers, for whom the role of husband was a central part of the self-concept, may experience similar identity and adjustment crises when they lose their wives (Glick, Weiss, & Parkes, 1974).

Changes in Lifestyle

Despite the image of the widowed as poor, forlorn creatures in bad health whom nobody cares about, only a small proportion of widows are physically or emotionally incapacitated. Widowhood is certainly not a highly desirable state, but its features are not all negative. Widowhood appears to be kinder to women than men, but even for men the increased freedom and independence of widowhood can provide new opportunities and rewards. Understandably, most widows and widowers miss the deceased spouse's companionship. But widows now find that their housework is lightened, they have more time to travel, and more time to devote to the development of interests and abilities that lay dormant during their years of marital service. In fact, because of their greater social aptitude and the blossoming of special skills, older women are frequently better able to cope with widowhood than older men (Lopata, 1979; Seltzer, 1979). Perhaps for similar reasons, some surveys have found that older widows have even higher morale than older married women (Morgan, 1976).

Whether or not they choose to exercise them, there are a number of options open to widows. Not all widows need to or do retreat into isolation, becoming what Lopata (1973) calls "social isolates." Many elect to continue the same levels of activity in similar roles and situations that were characteristic before widowhood. Another broad option, chosen by widows whom Lopata (1973) labeled "self-initiating women," is to select new roles and develop new friends. In any event, widowhood for some women provides a long-awaited opportunity to control their own lives. These are not poor old souls relegated to the rocking chair, but women whose average age is 45 and who can look forward to living as long as another generation and getting much more joy out of life (Bucholz, 1982).

SUMMARY

Bereavement refers to the state of loss or deprivation that results from the death of another person. Grief is the feeling of sorrow and distress that results from bereavement. Mourning is the culturally prescribed behavior pattern for expressing grief.

Numerous practical, psychological, and social considerations must be dealt with by bereaved persons. An important psychological process is learning how to "let go" of the deceased, which is rarely easy to do. Letting go typically requires a year or more of recovery from the loss, and may even necessitate professional counseling.

Not only grief, but also anger, anxiety, guilt, and hopelessness are common emotional reactions to bereavement. Other responses are disorientation, an inability to concentrate or remember, crying, insomnia, losses of appetite, energy, and weight, and a reliance on tranquilizers, sleeping pills, and alcohol. Regression, hallucinations, obsessional review, overidentification with the deceased, and idealization of the deceased are less common responses to bereavement, but they are not necessarily pathological.

Various stage theories of grief have been proposed, the great majority of which conceptualize the process as beginning with a period of shock or numbness, giving way to a long period of grief and related emotions, and ending in recovery and life reorganization. Stage theories of grief are probably best viewed as descriptive accounts of emotional reactions experienced by grieving people rather than fixed sequences through which all bereaved individuals must pass on their way to recovery. Certainly there are wide individual differences in the intensity and quality of reactions to bereavement, depending on such factors as the age, sex, social class, and personality of the bereaved.

Whether or not grief is considered pathological depends on its intensity, its duration, and the presence of other symptoms. Abnormal reactions to bereavement include chronic grief, mummification, anniversary reactions, delayed grief, and suicide. Pathological grief is more likely when the death was unexpected, when the bereaved has unresolved conflicts with or ambivalent feelings toward the deceased, or when social and emotional supports are lacking.

In addition to mental disorders, physical illness and even death are contributed to by prolonged grieving. The "broken heart syndrome," in which the bereaved individual develops coronary thrombosis or another form of heart disease, is most often cited as an important cause of the increased mortality rate observed after bereavement. The stress of caring for the dying and the stress of widowhood are undoubtedly as important as the stress of bereavement itself in the increased mortality rate of survivors. The desolation-effects hypothesis, according to which both the event of widowhood and the circumstances stemming from it have deleterious effects on the body, is the most plausible and popular explanation of the high mortality rate during the first year or so after bereavement.

Positive factors in recovery from bereavement include time and the support of other people. Various organizations, such as Compassionate Friends and widow-to-widow projects in cities throughout the United States, offer assistance to bereaved people. Group-oriented bereavement counseling (grief groups) and individual counseling or psychotherapy for the bereaved employ a variety of techniques. Reworking through the events associated with the death and funeral is a common therapeutic approach. The specific therapeutic techniques vary with the age and personality of the bereaved, however.

Although substantial numbers of men and blacks are widowed, the problems associated with widowhood in the United States are primarily those of elderly white women. The ratio of 5.5 widows to every widower is a consequence of the fact that husbands tend to die before their wives, and widowers remarry more often than widows. A large percentage of widows live alone, and loneliness is a problem for many of them. Widows are more likely than widowers, however, to have a number of same-sex friends of their own age and to participate in various social organizations.

In addition to loneliness, widows list money and its management as one of their most serious worries. Problems of identity—who am I, what are my social roles, and so on—are also common in widowhood. Most widows adapt fairly well to their situation despite these problems, but others suffer serious adjustment difficulties. Drug and alcohol addiction, mental illness, and suicide are frequent results of unresolved grief and the stresses of widowhood.

In widowhood, as at other times of life, an individual usually has a number of lifestyle options—to continue doing the same things as before widowhood, to select new roles and develop new friends, to retreat into isolation, and so on. The options that are selected obviously depend to some extent on economics and social supports, but to an even greater degree they are determined by individual personality and interest in controlling one's own life and making the most of it.

SUGGESTED READINGS

Bowlby, J. (1980). *Attachment and loss: Vol. III. Loss: Sadness and depression.* New York: Basic Books.

Burgess, J., & Kohn, W. (1978). *The widower.* Boston: Beacon Press.

Doyle, P. (1980). *Grief counseling and sudden death.* Springfield, Ill.: Thomas.

Glick, I. O.; Weiss, R. S.; & Parkes, C. M. (1974). *The first year of bereavement.* New York: Wiley.

Grollman, E. A. (1977). *Living when a loved one has died.* Boston: Beacon Press.

Kalish, R. A. (1981). *Death, grief, and caring relationships.* Monterey, Calif.: Brooks/Cole.

Lopata, H. Z. (1979). *Women as widows: Support systems.* New York: Elsevier.

Parkes, C. M. (1975). *Bereavement.* Baltimore, Md.: Penguin.

Pincus, L. (1974). *Death and the family: The importance of mourning.* New York: Pantheon Books.

Ryerson, M. (1977). Death education and counseling with children. *Elementary School Guidance and Counseling, 11,* 165–174.

Silverman, P. R. (1977). Widowhood and preventive intervention. In S. H. Zarit (Ed.). *Readings in aging and death: Contemporary perspectives.* New York: Harper & Row.

A Poems of Love and Death

Thoughts of the Dying

I

There is no time now for the game
Of mutual pretense.
To act as if I'm still the same
Quite simply makes no sense.

Observe me here, the worn remains
Of what I used to be.
This weary mass of aches and pains
Is plain for all to see.

But still it loves and wants to share
Its feelings with its friends.
So listen now and show some care
Before my sweet life ends.

II

I cherish life and have such fun
That I should hate to leave.
But death must come to everyone,
And all loved ones must grieve.

So now before my time is through,
I make this last bequest.
I hope that it will comfort you
When I have gone to rest.

The total of my property
To my dear wife should go.
Whatever else belongs to me,
I will as said below.

I leave my love to all the earth,
My body to the sod,
And finally, of greatest worth,
I give my soul to God.

III

One little word that would not let me go,
One senseless hope that helped me bear the pain,
One transitory dream that let me know
My fleeting life had not been lived in vain.

259

My life was cut off from humanity,
A barren, selfish soul enclosed within.
I made my god invincibility,
And lived for nothing else except to win.

But soon a time came when my fortress broke
Like some great dam that blocked me from the Nile.
I could not see the truth that others spoke,
And I was helpless for a little while.

Then in the dusk before my light was spent,
I felt that there was someone at my side.
And so I came to know what others meant
By love, which found me just before I died.

Thoughts of the Survivors

I

Dear little child who never grew
Beyond the age of five,
I wish I could have died for you,
And you were still alive.

I loved you so and loved each day
When you and I were near.
I never thought that I would stay
And you would not be here.

But I survive and dream about
The times that used to be.
How hard it is to live without
Your sharing life with me!

II

My life has lost its meaning since the hour you went away.
Now all I do is sit and wonder how to pass the day,
Or how to spend the lonely nights without you near to me.
Why you were taken from me now is more than I can see.

For we had just begun to find the love we lost before.
We planned again to stay together now and evermore.
But suddenly misfortune struck, and our plans disappeared.
Despite our hopes, despite our prayers, it happened—what we feared.

One long embrace, a promise sweet, a lingering goodbye,
Then you were gone and all that I could do was wonder why
Your life was taken from me when we learned to love again.
And now it seems to me that I shall never lose the pain.

Lewis R. Aiken

B Organizations Concerned with Dying, Death, and Widowhood

General and Journals

Ars Moriendi
7301 Huron Lane
Philadelphia, PA 19119

Center for Death Education and
   Research
1167 Social Sciences Building
University of Minnesota
267 19th Avenue, South
Minneapolis, MN 55455

Foundation of Thanatology
630 West 168th Street
New York, NY 10032

Omega, Journal of Death and Dying
Baywood Publishing Co., Inc.
120 Marine Street
Farmingdale, NY 11735

Thanatology Today
Atcom, Inc.
Atcom Building
2315 Broadway
New York, NY 10024

Accidental Death

Metropolitan Life Insurance Co.
One Madison Avenue
New York, NY 10010
(*Statistical Bulletin*)

National Safety Council
425 North Michigan Avenue
Chicago, IL 60611
(*Accident Facts*)

The Travelers Insurance Companies
1 Tower Square
Hartford, CT 06103
(*The Travelers Book of Street and
   Highway Accident Data*)

Aging

American Geriatrics Society
Ten Columbus Circle
New York, NY 10019

National Institute on Aging
U.S. Dept. of Health and Human
   Services
9000 Rockville Pike
Bethesda, MD 20205

Capital Punishment

National Coalition Against the Death
   Penalty
132 W. 43rd Street
New York, NY 10036

U.S. Department of Justice
Bureau of Prisons
101 Indiana Avenue, NW
Washington, DC 20537

Children and Death

Big Brothers/Big Sisters of America
220 Suburban Station Building
Philadelphia, PA 19103

Candlelighters Foundation, Inc.
123 C Street, SE
Washington, DC 20003

International Council for Infant Survival
510 5th Street, NW
Washington, DC 20001

National Sudden Infant Death Syndrome
  Foundation
310 S. Michigan Avenue, Suite 1904
Chicago, IL 50504

The Compassionate Friends
P.O. Box 1347
Oak Brook, IL 60521

Counseling

Ackerman Institute for Family Therapy
149 E. 78th Street
New York, NY 10021

Forum for Death Education and
  Counseling
P.O. Box 1226
Arlington, VA 22210

Make Today Count
218 South Sixth Street
Burlington, IA 52601

National Institute for the Seriously Ill
  and Dying
Henry Avenue & Abbottsford Road
Philadelphia, PA 19129

Euthanasia

American Euthanasia Foundation
95 N. Birch Road, Suite 301
Ft. Lauderdale, FL 33304

Concern for Dying
250 W. 57th Street
New York, NY 10107

Society for the Right to Die
250 W. 57th Street
New York, NY 10107

Fatal Diseases

American Cancer Society
219 East 42nd Street
New York, NY 10017

American Heart Association
7320 Greenville Avenue
Dallas, TX 75231

American Medical Association
535 North Dearborn Street
Chicago, IL 60610

Cancer Information Clearinghouse
Suite 1320
7910 Woodmont Avenue
Bethesda, MD 20014

National Cancer Foundation
One Park Avenue
New York, NY 10016

Funerals and Corpse Disposal

Continental Association of Funeral
  and Memorial Societies
1146 19th Street, NW, 3rd floor
Washington, DC 20036

Cremation Association of America
1620 West Belmont Avenue
Fresno, CA 93701

National Funeral Directors and
  Morticians
734 West 79th Street
Chicago, IL 60620

The National Funeral Director's
  Association
135 Wells Street
Milwaukee, WI 53203

Hospices

National Hospice Organization
Suite 402
1901 N. Fort Myer Drive
Arlington, VA 22209

Legal Matters

American Bar Association
1155 E. 69th Street
Chicago, IL 60637

Near-Death Experiences

International Association for Near
  Death Studies
Box U-20
University of Connecticut
Storrs, CT 06268

Suicide and Murder

American Association of Suicidology
Department of Health
2151 Berkeley Way
Berkeley, CA 94704

Federal Bureau of Investigation
U.S. Dept. of Justice
Washington, DC 20535
(*Uniform Crime Reports*)

Internal Association for Suicide
  Prevention
2521 West Pico Boulevard
Los Angeles, CA 90006

National Save-A-Life League
20 West 43rd Street, Suite 706
New York, NY 10036

Widowhood

National Association for Widowed
  People, Inc.
P.O. Box 3564
Springfield, IL 62708

Parents Without Partners
7910 Woodmont Avenue
Washington, DC 20014

Society of Military Widows
P.O. Box 1714
La Mesa, CA 92041

The Compassionate Friends
P.O. Box 1347
Oak Brook, IL 60521

Theos Foundation, Inc.
Suite 306, Penn Hills Office Bldg.
Pittsburgh, PA 15235

Widowed Persons Service (WPS)
NRTA-AARP
1909 K Street, NW
Washington, DC 20049

C Questions and Activities

1. Describe a time when you came close to losing your life. Did your whole life flash before you? What emotions did you experience? How did you feel afterward?
2. Have you ever experienced the death of a close friend or relative? What did the person mean to you, what reactions did you have to the death, and what did you miss most about him or her?
3. Would you like to live a long life? Do you expect to do so? What exercise, diet, and/or other regimen do you follow in order to increase your chances of living a long time?
4. Suppose that you had an incurable illness and were given only six months more to live. Would you change your lifestyle? In what way? What else would you do to get ready for death?
5. Suppose that you were a member of a board whose task it was to decide which patients should be provided a new expensive medical treatment that might prolong their lives. What factors, both personal and social, would play a role in your recommendations?
6. Have you ever had an out-of-body experience in which you felt that you were in heaven or some other afterlife place? Describe your experience and evaluate it in the light of both scientific and religious knowledge and belief.
7. Suppose you were permitted to choose the manner in which you are going to die. What factors would play a role in that decision and what would the decision be?
8. Can you imagine your own death? What do you think it will be like? Imagine your own funeral. Who will be there? What will be said and done?
9. Schedule a visit to a funeral home and interview the funeral director and his or her assistants about their activities, training, and sources of job satisfaction.
10. Schedule a visit to a nursing home and/or a hospice and discuss the activities of the institutional staff and patients with the director. Talk with several of the patients about their activities, the treatments, and their feelings.
11. Visit a cemetery with a group of friends and read the writings on the tombstones or monuments. What were your emotional reactions to the experience? What did you learn from it?
12. Describe the happiest death you can imagine, and then compare it with the saddest death you can think of. What makes a death happy or sad? Is it happy or sad to the dying person, the survivors, or both?
13. Arrange to visit an estate attorney's office and discuss his or her activities and experiences. What rewards and other sources of satisfaction are to be found in this type of work?
14. Interview some terminally ill or older people about their feelings, pleasures, concerns, and philosophy of life. Do the attitudes of these individuals toward

dying and death correspond with your own private assessment of the reality of their situation? Why or why not?

15. What novels or other fictional accounts of dying, death, and bereavement have you read? Describe any common features that these works possess.

16. What can painting, sculpture, music, and other nonverbal arts communicate to us about death that are not expressible in poetry or other written works of art?

17. Have you ever known anyone who committed suicide, or at least made a bona fide attempt to do so? What do you believe were the reasons for the person's act? Was there anything unique or different about the person as far as you could tell?

18. Arrange to visit a suicide prevention center or community hot-line and interview the staff about their activities, training, goals, and the sources of gratification to be found in their kind of work.

19. To what extent do you believe that extraordinary or unusual medical measures should be taken to extend the life of a person? What circumstances or factors affect the decision to employ such superhuman techniques, and by whom should the decision be made?

20. Contact a cryonics society in your region or elsewhere (see Appendix B) and obtain as much information on the activities and procedures of the organization as you can. If you had an incurable or terminal disease, would you be willing to have your body placed in a deep freeze for a century or two, at which time you might be resuscitated, cured, and permitted to resume your life?

21. Suppose you discovered that you were going to die fairly soon. How would you break the news to your family and friends—or would you? What factors would affect if, when, and how much you told them?

22. What responsibilities does a person whose death is imminent have toward the survivors and the living in general? Describe the plans involving others that you would make if you knew that you were going to die fairly soon.

23. How would you say goodbye to a loved one who is about to die? Discuss this question with others and role play the scene.

24. Construct a questionnaire or scale to measure attitudes toward death and dying. Administer your questionnaire to several classmates and tabulate the results. Discuss your findings and conclusions.

25. How have your feelings and knowledge about dying and death changed as you have grown older? What specific experiences or events had strong influences on these feelings and knowledge?

References

A better way to care for the dying. (1978, November). *Changing Times,* pp. 21–23.

Abrahamsen, D. (1973). *The murdering mind.* New York: Harper & Row.

Ad Hoc Committee of the Harvard Medical School to Examine the Definition of Brain Death. (1968). A definition of irreversible coma. *Journal of the American Medical Association, 205,* 337–340.

Adams, B. (1968). *Kinship in an urban setting.* Chicago: Markham.

Adams, C. J. (1983). Islam. *The world book encyclopedia* (Vol. 10). Chicago: World Book.

Aiken, L. R. (1982). *Later life* (2nd ed.). New York: Holt, Rinehart & Winston.

Aitken-Swan, J., & Easson, E. C. (1959). Reactions of cancer patients on being told their diagnosis. *British Medical Journal, 1,* 779–783.

Alsop, S. (1973). *Stay of execution.* Philadelphia: Lippincott.

Altrocchi, J. (1980). *Abnormal behavior.* New York: Harcourt Brace Jovanovich.

American Heart Association. (1977). *Heart facts.* New York: Author.

Am I suicidal? A computer may know. (1978, July 24). *Time,* p. 42.

Ambron, S. R., & Brodzinsky, D. (1979). *Lifespan human development.* New York: Holt, Rinehart & Winston.

American Bar Foundation. (1976). Survey of legal needs: Selected data. *Alternatives, 3*(1), 1–23.

Anthony, S. (1972). *The discovery of death in childhood and after.* New York: Basic Books.

Arenson, J. T. (1982). Inheritance. *Encyclopedia Americana.* (Vol. 15). Danbury, Conn.: Grolier.

Arias, R. (1981, November 2). The Mexican way of death: Celebrate it, play with it, challenge it. *Los Angeles Times,* p. II-7.

Aries, P. (1962). *Centuries of childhood: A social history of family life* (R. Baldick, Trans.). New York: Vintage Books.

Aries, P. (1974). *Western attitudes toward death: From the Middle Ages to the present.* Baltimore: Johns Hopkins University Press.

Aries, P. (1981). *The hour of our death* (H. Weaver, Trans.). New York: Knopf.

Aronson, G. J. (1959). Treatment of the dying person. In H. Feifel (Ed.), *The meaning of death.* New York: McGraw-Hill.

Atchley, R. C. (1975). Dimensions of widowhood in later life. *Gerontologist, 15,* 176–178.

Atchley, R. C. (1977). *The social forces in later life* (2nd ed.) (Chap. 10). Belmont, Calif.: Wadsworth.

References

Atchley, R. C.; Pignatiello, L.; & Shaw, E. (1975). *The effect of marital status on social interaction patterns of older women.* Oxford, Oh.: Scripps Foundation.

Back, K. W. (1971). Metaphors as a test of personal philosophy of aging. *Sociological Force, 5,* 1–8.

Ball, J. F. (1977). Widow's grief: The impact of age and mode of death. *Omega, 7,* 307–333.

Bardis, P. D. (1981). *History of thanatology.* Washington, D.C.: University Press of America.

Barker, J. C. (1968). *Scared to death.* London: Frederick Muller.

Barnard, G. W.; Vera, M. I.; Vera, H.; & Newman, G. (1981, October 15–18). *Till death do us part: A study of spouse murder.* Paper presented at the annual meeting of the American Academy of Psychiatry & the Law, San Diego, California.

Barrow, G. M., & Smith, P. A. (1983). *Aging, the individual, and society* (2nd ed.). St. Paul, Minn.: West.

Barry, H. (1939). A study of bereavement: An approach to problems in mental disease. *American Journal of Orthopsychiatry, 9,* 355–359.

Beck, A. T.; Sethi, B. B.; & Tuthill, R. (1963). Childhood bereavement and adult depression. *Archives of General Psychiatry, 9,* 129–136.

Becker, E. (1973). *The denial of death.* New York: Free Press.

Bengston, V. L.; Cuellar, J. B.; & Ragan, P. K. (1977). Stratum contrasts and similarities in attitudes toward death. *Journal of Gerontology, 32*(1), 76–88.

Bennett, R. (1976). Attitudes of the young toward the old: A review of research. *Personnel & Guidance Journal, 55,* 136–139.

Berkowitz, L. (1968). Impulse, aggression and the gun. *Psychology Today, 2*(4), 18–22.

Bernstein, J. E. (1977). Helping young children cope with death. In L. G. Katz (Ed.), *Current topics in early childhood education* (Vol. 1). Norwood, N.J.: Ablex.

Best, C. H. (1983). Diabetes. *The world book encyclopedia* (Vol. 5). Chicago: World Book.

Big rise in life expectancy. (1983, May 31). *Los Angeles Times,* p. I-2.

Birren, J. E., & Renner, V. (1977). Research on the psychology of aging: Principles and experimentation. In J. E. Birren & K. W. Schaie (Eds.), *Handbook of the psychology of aging.* New York: Van Nostrand Reinhold.

Black, H. C. (1979). *Black's law dictionary* (5th ed.). St. Paul, Minn.: West.

Blau, Z. S. (1961). Structural constraints on friendship in old age. *American Sociological Review, 26,* 429–439.

Bluebond-Langner, M. (1977). Meanings of death to children. In H. Feifel (Ed.), *New meanings of death.* New York: McGraw-Hill.

Bluebond-Langner, M. (1978). *The private worlds of dying children.* Princeton: Princeton University Press.

Blum, G. S., & Rosenzweig, S. (1944). The incidence of sibling and parental deaths in the anamnesis of female schizophrenics. *Journal of General Psychology, 31,* 3–13.

Boase, T. S. R. (1972). *Death in the Middle Ages.* New York: McGraw-Hill.

Bootzin, R. R., & Acocella, J. K. (1980). *Abnormal psychology: Current perspectives.* New York: Random House.

Bornstein, P.; Clayton, P.; Halikes, J.; Maurice, W.; & Robins, E. (1973). The depression of widowhood after thirteen months. *British Journal of Psychiatry, 122,* 561–566.

Botwinick, J. (1978). *Aging and behavior* (2nd ed.). New York: Springer.

Bouquet, A. C. (1982). Transmigration of the soul. *Encyclopedia Americana* (Vol. 27). Danbury, Conn.: Grolier.

Bouvier, L.; Atlee, E.; & McVeigh, F. (1977). The elderly in America. In S. H. Zarit (Ed.), *Readings in aging and death: Contemporary perspectives.* New York: Harper & Row.

Bowlby, J. (1960). Separation anxiety. *International Journal of Psychoanalysis, 41,* 89–113.

Bowlby, J. (1974). *Attachment and loss: Vol. II. Separation: Anxiety and anger.* New York: Basic Books.

Boyar, J. I. (1964). *The construction and partial validation of a scale for the measurement of the fear of death.* Unpublished doctoral dissertation, University of Rochester.

Brody, J. (1979, June 6). Exercising to turn back the years. *New York Times,* pp. 18C–19C.

Brown, F. (1961). Depression and childhood bereavement. *Journal of Mental Science, 107,* 754–777.

Brown, N. K., & Thompson, D. J. (1979). Nontreatment of fever in extended-care facilities. *New England Journal of Medicine, 300,* 1246–1250.

Bryce, N. (1982, February 23). 30% of all fatal cancer attributed to cigarettes. *Los Angeles Times,* p. I-1.

Bucholz, B. B. (1982, October 25). Agency makes new image for widowhood. *St. Louis Post-Dispatch,* p. 3B.

Buckingham, R. W., III; Lack, S. A.; Mount, B. M.; MacLean, L. D.; & Collins, J. T. (1976). Living with the dying: Use of the technique of participant observation. *Canadian Medical Association Journal, 115,* 1211–1215.

Bugen, L. A. (1977). Human grief: A model for prediction and intervention. *American Journal of Orthopsychiatry, 47,* 196–206.

Bugen, L. A. (1979). *Death and dying.* Dubuque, Iowa,: Brown.

Busse, E. W. (1969). Theories of aging. In E. W. Busse & E. Pfeiffer (Eds.), *Behavior and adaptation in late life.* Boston: Little, Brown.

Butler, R. N. (1971). Age: The life review. *Psychology Today, 5*(7), 49–51, 89.

Butler, R. N. (1975). *Why survive? Being old in America.* New York: Harper & Row.

Butler, R. N., & Lewis, M. I. (1977). *Aging and mental health* (2nd ed.). St. Louis: Mosby.

Caldicott, H. (1982, August 8). Growing up afraid. *Family Weekly,* pp. 4–7.

Callahan, D. (1983). Abortion. *The world book encyclopedia.* (Vol. 1). Chicago: World Book.

Cartwright, A.; Hockey, L.; & Anderson, J. L. (1973). *Life before death.* London: Routledge & Kegan Paul.

Cavan, R. S. (1982). Suicide. *Encyclopedia Americana* (Vol. 25). Danbury, Conn.: Grolier.

Cavendish, R. (1970). Death. In R. Cavendish (Ed.), *Man, myth and magic* (Vol. 5). New York: Marshall Cavendish Corp.

Cavendish, R. (1977). *Visions of heaven and hell.* New York: Harmony Books.

Chalmers, S., & Reichen, M. (1954). Attitudes toward death and future life among normal and subnormal adolescent girls. *Exceptional Children, 20,* 259–262.

Charles, E. (1977, March 13). A hospice for the terminally ill. *New York Times,* p. XXIII-10.

References

Cherico, D. J., et al. (Eds.). (1976, 1978). *Thanatology course outlines.* New York: Irvington.

Childers, P., & Wimmer, M. (1971). The concept of death in early childhood. *Child Development, 42,* 1299–1301.

Children who want to die. (1978, September 25). *Time,* p. 82.

Choron, J. (1963). *Death and Western thought* (I. Barea, Trans.). New York: Macmillan.

Cimons, M. (1983, March 22). Panel would give patients death decision. *Los Angeles Times,* p. I-5.

Clarke, J. W. (1982). *American assassins: The darker side of politics.* Princeton, N.J.: Princeton University Press.

Clayton, P. J.; Halikes, J. A.; & Maurice, W. L. (1971). The bereavement of the widowed. *Diseases of the Nervous System, 32,* 597–604.

Cohen, S. (1980, November 15). She turned grief into help for others. *Los Angeles Times,* p. IA-4.

Coleman, J. C.; Butcher, J. N.; & Carson, R. C. (1980). *Abnormal psychology and modern life* (6th ed.). Glenview, Ill.: Scott, Foresman.

Comfort, A. (1964). *Ageing: The biology of senescence.* New York: Holt, Rinehart & Winston.

Continental Association of Funeral and Memorial Societies. (1980). *Funeral practices: Survey of state laws and regulations.* Washington, D.C.: Author.

Continental Association of Funeral and Memorial Societies. (1982). *Last rights.* Washington, D.C.: Author.

Crichton, M. (1975). *The great train robbery.* New York: Knopf.

Crook, T., & Eliot, J. (1980). Parental death during childhood and adult depression: A critical review of the literature. *Psychological Bulletin, 87,* 252–259.

Dead, disposal of the. (1976). *Chamber's encyclopedia* (Vol. 4). London: International Learning Systems.

Death. (1983). *Encyclopaedia Britannica* (Vol. 5). Chicago: Encyclopaedia Britannica.

Death: 2. Psychological aspects of death. (1981). *Encyclopedia Americana* (Vol. 8). Danbury, Conn.: Grolier.

Death and gift taxes. (1983). *Encyclopaedia Britannica* (Vol. 5). Chicago: Encyclopaedia Britannica.

Death companionship. (1975, February 17). *Time,* p. 68.

Death rites and customs. (1983). *Encyclopaedia Britannica* (Vol. 5). Chicago: Encyclopaedia Britannica.

DeBakey, M. E. (1983). Heart. *The world book encyclopedia* (Vol. 9). Chicago: World Book.

DeFleur, M. L., & Quinney, R. (1966). A reformulation of Sutherland's differential association theory and a strategy for empirical verification. *Journal of Research in Crime and Delinquency, 3,* 1–22.

Demography. (1983). *Encyclopaedia Britannica* (Vol. 5). Chicago: Encyclopaedia Britannica.

Denckla, W. D. (1974). Role of the pituitary and thyroid glands in the decline of minimal O_2 consumption with age. *Journal of Clinical Investigation, 53,* 572–581.

De Vries, H. A. (1977). Physiology of exercise and aging. In S. H. Zarit (Ed.). *Readings in aging and death: Contemporary perspectives.* New York: Harper & Row.

Diggory, J. C., & Rothman, D. Z. (1961). Values destroyed by death. *Journal of Abnormal and Social Psychology, 63,* 205–210.

Dingle, J. (1973). *The ills of man: Life and death and medicine.* San Francisco: Freeman.

Douglas-Hamilton, L., & Douglas-Hamilton, O. (1975). *Among the elephants.* New York: Viking Press.

Dublin, L. L. (1963). *Suicide: A sociological and statistical study* (p. 211). New York: Ronald.

Eaton, J. W. (1982). Euthanasia. *Encyclopedia Americana* (Vol. 10). Danbury, Conn.: Grolier.

Ellsworth, P. C., & Ross, L. (1980). *Public opinion and capital punishment: A close examination of the views of abolitionists and retentionists.* New Haven, Conn.: Yale University Press.

Embalming, burial, and cremation. (1983). *Encyclopaedia Britannica* (Vol. 6). Chicago: Encyclopaedia Britannica.

Engel, G. L. (1971). Sudden and rapid death during psychological stress. *Annals of Internal Medicine, 74,* 771–782.

Epstein, G.; Weitz, L.; Roback, H.; & McKee, E. (1975). Research on bereavement: A selective and critical review. *Comprehensive Psychiatry, 16,* 537–546.

Erickson, J. D., & Bjerkedel, T. (1982). Fetal and infant mortality in Norway and the United States. *Journal of the American Medical Association, 247,* 987–991.

Erikson, E. H. (1976). Reflection on Dr. Borg's life cycle. *Daedalus, 105*(2), 1–28.

Ettinghausen, R. (1983). Islamic art. *The world book encyclopedia* (Vol. 10). Chicago: World Book.

Farberow, N. L. (1974). *Suicide.* Morristown, N.J.: General Learning Press.

Farberow, N. L. (1975). Cultural history of suicide. In N. L. Farberow (Ed.), *Suicide in different cultures.* Baltimore: University Park Press.

Farberow, N. L., & Litman, R. E. (1970). *A comprehensive suicide prevention program.* Suicide Prevention Center of Los Angeles, 1958–1969. Unpublished final report DHEW NIMH Grant Nos. MH 14946 & MH 00128, Los Angeles.

Feifel, H. (1959). Attitudes toward death. In H. Feifel (Ed.), *The meaning of death.* New York: McGraw-Hill.

Feifel, H. (1963). Death. In N. L. Farberow (Ed.), *Taboo topics.* New York: Atherton Press.

Feifel, H. (Ed.). (1977). *New meanings of death.* New York: McGraw-Hill.

Feifel, H., & Jones, R. (1968). Perception of death as related to nearness of death. *Proceedings of the 76th Annual Convention of the American Psychological Association, 3,* 545–546.

Felkenes, G. T. (1983). Capital punishment. *The world book encyclopedia* (Vol. 3). Chicago: World Book.

Ferrare, N. A. (1962). *Institutionalization and attitude change in an aged population.* Unpublished doctoral dissertation, Western Reserve University.

Fischer, H. K., & Dlin, B. M. (1972). Psychogenic determination of time of illness on death by anniversary reactions and emotional deadlines. *Psychosomatics, 13,* 170–172.

Follett, C. (1980, December 19). Danes' suicide rate highest in West. *Los Angeles Times,* p. I-1.

Fraiberg, S. (1977). *Every child's birthright: In defense of mothering.* New York: Basic Books.

Franklin, J. H. (1956). *The militant South*. Cambridge, Mass.: Harvard University Press.

Freese, A. S. (1980). *The end of senility*. New York: Arbor House.

Fries, J. F., & Crapo, L. M. (1981). *Vitality and aging: Implications of the rectangular curve*. San Francisco: Freeman.

Fulton, R. (1971). The funeral and the funeral director: A contemporary analysis. In H. C. Raether (Ed.), *Successful funeral service practice*. Englewood Cliffs, N.J.: Prentice-Hall.

Fulton, R. (Comp.). (1981). *A bibliography of death, grief, and bereavement, 1975–1980*. New York: Arno.

Funeral Association won't appeal FTC price rule. (1984, March 22). *Los Angeles Times*, p. I-15.

Futterman, E. H., & Hoffman, I. (1970). Transient school phobia in a leukemic child. *Journal of the American Academy of Child Psychiatry, 9*, 477–494.

Gallup, G., & Proctor, W. (1982). *Adventures in immortality*. New York: McGraw-Hill.

Galton, L. (1979, November 4). A serious threat to the elderly. *Parade Magazine*, pp. 9–11.

Gambino, R. (1978). The murderous mind: Insanity vs. the law. *Saturday Review, 5*(12), 10–13.

Garrett, D. N. (1978). The needs of the seriously ill and their families: The haven concept. *Aging, 6*(1), 12–19.

Gatch, M. M. (1980). The Biblical tradition. In E. S. Shneidman (Ed.), *Death, Current perspectives* (2nd ed.). Palo Alto, Calif.: Mayfield.

Gerber, I.; Rusalem, R.; Hannon, N.; Battin, D.; & Arkin, A. (1975). Anticipatory grief and aged widows and widowers. *Journal of Gerontology, 30*(2), 225–229.

Glaser, B. G., & Strauss, A. L. (1968). *Time for dying*. Chicago: Aldine.

Glick, I. O.; Weiss, R. S.; & Parkes, C. M. (1974). *The first year of bereavement*. New York: Wiley.

Glueck, S., & Glueck, E. T. (1956). Physique and delinquency. New York: Harper.

Goodman, L. M. (1981). *Death and the creative life*. New York: Springer.

Gordon, A. K., & Klass, D. (1979). *They need to know: How to teach children about death*. Englewood Cliffs, N.J.: Prentice-Hall.

Gorer, G. (1967). *Death, grief, and mourning*. Garden City, N.J.: Anchor Books.

Gorer, G. (1980). The pornography of death. In E. S. Shneidman (Ed.), *Death: Current perspectives* (2nd ed.). Palo Alto, Calif.: Mayfield.

Gottlieb, C. (1959). Modern art and death. In H. Feifel (Ed.), *The meaning of death*. New York: McGraw-Hill.

Granick, S., & Patterson, R. D. (1972). *Human aging, II: An eleven year followup biomedical and behavioral study*. Washington, D.C.: U.S. Government Printing Office.

Green, M. (1966, November 17). Care of the dying child. In A. B. Bergman & C. J. A. Schultle (Eds.), *Care of the child with cancer*. Proceedings of a conference conducted by the Association for Ambulatory Pediatric Services in conjunction with the Children's Cancer Study Group A.

Green, M., & Solnit, A. J. (1964). Reactions to the threatened loss of a child. A vulnerable child syndrome. Paediatric management of the dying child. *Paediatrics, 37*, 53–66.

Grobstein, R. (1978). The effect of neonatal death on the family. In O. J. Sahler (Ed.), *The child and death*. St. Louis: Mosby.

Grof, S., & Halifax, J. (1977). *The human encounter with death.* New York: Dutton.

Guthmann, R. F., & Womack, S. K. (1978). *Death, dying and grief: A bibliography.* Lincoln, Neb.: Word Services & Pied Publishers.

Guttmacher, M. S. (1960). *The mind of the murderer.* New York: Farrar, Straus & Cudahy.

Halleck, S. L. (1971). *Psychiatry and the dilemmas of crime.* Berkeley, Calif.: University of California Press.

Hambly, W. D. (1974). Funeral customs. *The world book encyclopedia* (Vol. 9). Chicago: Field Educational Enterprises.

Hamilton, J. (1978). Grandparents as grievers. In O. J. Sahler (Ed.), *The child and death.* St. Louis, Mo.: Mosby.

Hamilton, J.; Hamilton, R.; & Mestler, G. (1969). Duration of life and causes of death in domestic cats: Influence of sex, gonadectomy, and inbreeding. *Journal of Gerontology, 24,* 427–437.

Hardt, D. V. (1979). *Death: The final frontier.* Englewood Cliffs, N.J.: Prentice-Hall.

Harman, D.; Heidrick, M. L.; & Eddy, D. E. (1976, September). *Free radical theory of aging: Effects of antioxidants on humoral and cell-mediated response as a function of age.* Paper read at the 6th annual meeting of the American Aging Association, Washington, D.C.

Harmer, R. M. (1963). *The high cost of dying.* New York: Crowell-Collier.

Harvey, C., & Bahr, H. (1974). Widowhood, morale, and affiliation. *Journal of Marriage and the Family, 36,* 97–106.

Haskins, G. (1956). The capital lawes of New-England. *Harvard Law School Bulletin, 7,* 10.

Hayflick, L. (1980). The cell biology of human aging. *Scientific American, 242,* 58–66.

Helsing, K. J.; Szklo, M.; & Comstock, G. W. (1981). Factors associated with mortality after widowhood. *American Journal of Public Health, 71,* 802–809.

Hendricks, J., & Hendricks, C. D. (1981). *Aging in mass society* (2nd ed.). Cambridge, Mass.: Winthrop.

Henry, A. F., & Short, J. F., Jr. (1954). *Suicide and homicide.* Glencoe, Ill.: Free Press.

Herr, J., & Weakland, J. H. (1979). *Counseling elders and their families* (Chap. 19). New York: Springer.

Heyman, D. K., & Gianturco, D. (1973). Long-term adaptation by the elderly to bereavement. *Journal of Gerontology, 28*(3), 359–362.

Hilgard, J. R., & Newman, M. F. (1959). Anniversaries in mental illness. *Psychiatry, 22,* 113–121.

Hines, W. (1980, April 17). Crib death study saving lives. *Los Angeles Times,* pp. V-16, 17.

Hinton, J. (1972). *Dying* (2nd ed.). Baltimore: Penguin.

Hogan, R. A. (1970). Adolescent views of death. *Adolescence, 5,* 55–56.

Holden, C. (1980). The hospice movement and its implications. *Annals of the AAPSS, 447,* 59–63.

Holmes, W. (1983). Cirrhosis. *The world book encyclopedia* (Vol. 4). Chicago: World Book.

Horowitz, J. (1982, July 23). Doctors' dilemma. *Los Angeles Times,* pp. V-1, 10, 11.

Hurlock, E. B. (1980). *Developmental psychology* (5th ed.). New York: McGraw-Hill.

Hutchison, I. (1975). The significance of marital status for morale and life satisfaction among low-income elderly. *Journal of Marriage and the Family, 37,* 287–293.

Huyck, M. H., & Hoyer, W. J. (1982). *Adult development and aging.* Belmont, Calif.: Wadsworth.

Jameson, S. (1981, March 8). Japan's parent-child suicide phenomenon blamed on social change. *Los Angeles Times,* p. IA-1.

Johnson, R. (1982, August 20). Death row is no life, it's legalized torture. *Los Angeles Times,* p. II-11.

Jonas, D. T. (1976). Life, death, awareness, and concern: A progression. In A. Toynbee et al. (Eds.), *Life after death.* New York: McGraw-Hill.

Kalish, R. A. (1976). Death and dying in a social context. In R. H. Binstock & E. Shanas (Ed.), *Handbook of aging and the social sciences.* New York: Van Nostrand.

Kalish, R. A. (1977). Dying and preparing for death: A view of families. In H. Feifel (Ed.), *New meanings of death.* New York: McGraw-Hill.

Kalish, R. A., & Reynolds, D. K. (1976). *Death and ethnicity: A psychocultural study.* Los Angeles: University of Southern California Press.

Kallmann, F. J., & Jarvik, L. F. (1959). Individual differences in constitution and genetic background. In J. E. Birren (Ed.), *Handbook of aging and the individual.* Chicago. University of Chicago Press.

Kalven, H., Jr. (1974). Death, civil. *The world book encyclopedia* (Vol. 5). Chicago: Field Educational Enterprises.

Kaplan, H. B., & Pokorny, A. P. (1970). Aging and self-attitude: A conditional relationship. *International Journal of Aging and Human Development, 1,* 241–250.

Kastenbaum, R. (1959). Time and death in adolescence. In H. Feifel (Ed.), *The meaning of death.* New York: McGraw-Hill.

Kastenbaum, R. (1969). Psychological death. In L. Pearson (Ed.), *Death and dying: Current issues in the treatment of the dying person.* Cleveland, Ohio: Case Western Reserve University.

Kastenbaum, R. (1971). Age: Getting there on time. *Psychology Today, 5*(7), 52–54, 82–84.

Kastenbaum, R. J. (1977). *Death, society, and human experience.* St. Louis: Mosby.

Kastenbaum, R., & Aisenberg, R. (1972). *The psychology of death.* New York: Springer.

Kastenbaum, R. J., & Costa, P. T. (1977). Psychological perspectives on death. *Annual Review of Psychology, 8,* 225–249.

Kavanaugh, R. E. (1974). *Facing death.* Baltimore: Penguin Books.

Keith, P. M. (1979). Life changes and perceptions of life and death among older men and women. *Journal of Gerontology, 34,* 870–878.

Kerby, P. (1982, August 19). The death penalty—as arbitrary and unjust as ever. *Los Angeles Times,* p. II-1.

Keyser, M. (1977, July). When Wendy's brother died. *Reader's Digest,* pp. 95–97.

Khleif, B. (1976). The sociology of the mortuary: Religion, sex, age and kinship variables. In V. R. Pine et al. (Eds.), *Acute grief and the funeral.* Springfield, Ill.: Thomas.

Kimmel, D. C. (1980). *Adulthood and aging* (2nd ed.). New York: Wiley.

Kimsey, L. R.; Roberts, J. L.; & Logan, D. L. (1972). Death, dying, and denial in the aged. *American Journal of Psychiatry, 129,* 161–166.

Kitagawa, E. M., & Hauser, P. M. (1973). *Differential mortality in the United States: A study of socioeconomic epidemiology.* Cambridge, Mass.: Harvard University Press.

Kobrin, F., & Hendershot, G. (1977). Do family ties reduce mortality? Evidence from the United States, 1966–68. *Journal of Marriage and the Family, 39,* 737–745.

Kohn, R. R. (1963). Human disease and aging. *Journal of Chronic Diseases, 5,* 16.

Krakoff, I. H. (1983). Cancer. *Encyclopedia Americana* (Vol. 5). Danbury, Conn.: Grolier.

Kramer, S. H. (1982). Gilgamesh epic. *Encyclopedia Americana* (Vol. 12). Danbury, Conn.: Grolier.

Kübler-Ross, E. (1969). *On death and dying.* New York: Macmillan.

Kübler-Ross, E. (1974). *Questions and answers on death and dying.* New York: Macmillan.

Kübler-Ross, E. (Ed.). (1975). *Death: The final stage of growth.* Englewood Cliffs, N.J.: Prentice-Hall.

Langer, E., & Rodin, J. (1977). The effects of choice and enhanced personal responsibility for the aged: A field experiment in an institutionalized setting. *Journal of Personality and Social Psychology, 34,* 191–198.

Lee, M.; Zimbardo, P. G.; & Bertholf, M. (1977). Shy murderers. *Psychology Today, 11*(6), 68–70.

Lefcourt, H. M. (1973). The function of illusions of control and freedom. *American Psychologist, 28,* 417–425.

Leonard, C. V. (1974). Depression and suicidality. *Journal of Consulting and Clinical Psychology, 42,* 98–104.

Lerner, M. (1980). When, why, and where people die. In E. S. Shneidman (Ed.), *Death: Current perspectives* (2nd ed.). Palo Alto, Calif.: Mayfield.

Lessa, W. A. (1976). Death customs and rites. *Chamber's Encyclopedia* (Vol. 4). London: International Learning Systems.

Lester, D. (1973). Murder: A review. *Correctional Psychiatry, 19,* 40–50.

Leviton, D. (1977). Death education. In H. Feifel (Ed.), *New meanings of death.* New York: McGraw-Hill.

Leviton, D., & Forman, E. C. (1974). Death education for children and youth. *Journal of Clinical Psychology, 3,* 8–10.

Lewis, C. E., & Lewis, M. (1977). The potential impact of sexual equality of health. *New England Journal of Medicine, 297,* 863–869.

Lewis, C. I. (1982). Philosophy. *Encyclopedia Americana* (Vol. 21). Danbury, Conn.: Grolier.

Lieberman, M. A. (1965). Psychological correlates of impending death: Some preliminary observations. *Journal of Gerontology, 20*(2), 181–190.

Lieberman, M. A., & Coplan, A. S. (1969). Distance from death as a variable in the study of aging. *Developmental Psychology, 2,* 71–84.

Lifton, R. J. (1979). *The broken connection: On death and the continuity of life.* New York: Simon & Schuster.

Lindzey, G.; Hall, C. S.; & Manosevitz, M. (1973). *Theories of personality: Primary sources and research* (2nd ed.). New York: Wiley.

Long, C. H. (1982). Mythology. *Encyclopedia Americana* (Vol. 19). Danbury, Conn.: Grolier.

Long, J. B. (1975). The death that ends death in Hinduism and Buddhism. In E.

Kübler-Ross (Ed.), *Death: The final stage of growth*. Englewood Cliffs, N.J.: Prentice-Hall.

Lopata, H. Z. (1973). *Widowhood in an American city*. Cambridge, Mass.: Schenckman.

Lopata, H. Z. (1975). On widowhood: Grief, work, and identity reconstruction. *Journal of Geriatric Psychiatry, 8*, 41–55.

Lopata, H. Z. (1979). *Women as widows: Support systems*. New York: Elsevier North-Holland.

Lord, W. (1955). *A night to remember*. New York: Holt.

Lunde, D. T. (1976). *Murder and madness*. San Francisco: San Francisco Book Co.

Lynch, J. J. (1977). *The broken heart: The medical consequences of loneliness*. New York: Basic Books.

Margolis, O. S., et al. (Eds.). (1978). *Thanatology course outlines* (Vol. 2). New York: Irvington.

Marmar, C. (1981). Age as a factor in widows' grief—and psychotherapy. *Behavior Today, 12*(42).

Mathieu, J. T. (1972). *Dying and death role-expectation: A comparative analysis*. Unpublished doctoral dissertation, University of Southern California.

Maurer, A. (1964). Adolescent attitudes toward death. *Journal of Genetic Psychology, 105*, 79–90.

Maurer, A. (1966). Maturation of concepts of death. *British Journal of Medicine and Psychology, 39*, 35–41.

McGraw, C. (1983, April 13). Cremation: Boon or controversy. *Los Angeles Times*, pp. I-1, 24–25.

McIntyre, M. S.; Angle, C. R.; & Struempler, L. J. (1972). The concept of death in midwestern children and youth. *American Journal of Diseases of Children, 123*, 527–532.

Medical Electronics and Data. (1977). *The Heart Watcher*, No. 25. Columbus, Ohio: United Color Press.

Melear, J. D. (1973). Children's conceptions of death. *Journal of Genetic Psychology, 123*, 359–360.

Melges, F. T. (1982). *Time and the inner future: A temporal approach to psychiatric disorders* (Chap. 10). New York: Wiley.

Mercer, N. A. (1982). Inheritance tax. *Encyclopedia Americana* (Vol. 15). Danbury, Conn.: Grolier.

Mertz, B. (1983). Pyramids. *The world book encyclopedia* (Vol. 15). Chicago: World Book.

Meyers, D. W. (1977). The California Natural Death Act: A critical appraisal. *California State Bar Journal, 52*(4), 326–383.

Middleton, J. (1982). Death customs and rates. *Encyclopedia Americana* (Vol. 8). Danbury, Conn.: Grolier.

Miller, G. H., & Gerstein, D. R. (1983). The life expectancy of nonsmoking men and women. *Public Health Reports, 98*, 343–349.

Miller, M. (1978). Geriatric suicide: The Arizona study. *The Gerontologist, 18*, 488–496.

Mitford, J. (1963). *The American way of death*. Greenwich, Conn.: Fawcett.

Moment, G. (1975). The Ponce de Leon trail today. *Bioscience, 25*, 623–628.

Moody, R. A. (1975). *Life after life: The investigation of a phenomenon—survival of bodily death*. Atlanta: Mockingbird Press.

Morgan, L. A. (1976). A re-examination of widowhood and morale. *Journal of Gerontology, 31,* 687–695.

Morison, R. S. (1973). Dying. *Scientific American, 229*(3), 55–62.

Morrissey, J. R. (1963). Children's adaptation to fatal illness. *Social Work, 12,* 210–214.

Muhlbock, O. (1959). Factors influencing the life span of inbred mice. *Gerontologia, 3*(3), 177–183.

Murphy, J., & Florio, C. (1978). Older Americans: Facts and potential. In R. Gross, B. Gross, & S. Seidman (Eds.), *The new old: Struggling for decent aging.* Garden City, N.Y.: Doubleday-Anchor.

Nagy, M. H. (1948). The child's theories concerning death. *Journal of Genetic Psychology, 73,* 3–27.

National Center for Health Statistics. (1982). *Monthly Vital Statistics Report, 31* (6). Washington, D.C.: U.S. Dept. of Health and Human Services.

National Center for Health Statistics. (1983). *Monthly Vital Statistics Report, 31* (13). Washington, D.C.: U.S. Dept. of Health and Human Services.

National Interreligious Task Force on Criminal Justice. (n.d.). *Capital punishment: What the religious community says.* New York: Author.

Natterson, J. M., & Knudson, A. G. (1960). Observations concerning fear of death in fatally ill children and their mothers. *Psychosomatic Medicine, 22,* 456–466.

Nelson, B. (1982, July 7). Venereal, liver diseases deaths higher in state. *Los Angeles Times,* p. I-15.

Nelson, L. P., & Nelson, V. (1973). *Religion and death anxiety.* Presentation to the annual joint meeting, Society for the Scientific Study of Religion and Religious Research Association, San Francisco.

Neustatler, P. (1982). Aluminum tie to Alzheimer's? Intake of metal now an issue. *Medical Tribune, 23*(9), 1.

Noffsinger, L. (1983, Dec. 18). Race a factor in death penalty, study claims. *Los Angeles Times,* pp. I-3, 14.

Noyes, R. (1972). The experience of dying. *Psychiatry, 35,* 174–183.

Orgel, L. E. (1973). Ageing of clones of mammalian cells. *Nature, 243,* 441–445.

Osterfeld, A. M. (1968). Frequency and nature of health problems of retired persons. In F. M. Carp (Ed.), *The retirement process* (U.S. Public Health Service Pub. No. 1778, pp. 83–96). Washington, D.C.: U.S. Dept. of Health, Education & Welfare.

Packer, L., & Smith, J. R. (1977). Extension of the lifespan of cultured normal human diploid cells by vitamin E: A reevaluation. *Proceedings of the National Academy of Sciences, 74,* 1640–1641.

Palmore, E., & Cleveland, W. (1976). Aging, terminal decline, and terminal drop. *Journal of Gerontology, 31*(1), 76–86.

Pardi, M. (1977). *Death: An anthropological perspective.* Washington, D.C.: University Press of America.

Parkes, C. (1972). *Bereavement: Studies of grief in adult life.* New York: International Universities Press.

Parkes, C. M. (1975). Determinants of outcome following bereavement. *Omega, 6,* 303–323.

Parkes, C. M.; Benjamin, B.; & Fitzgerald, R. G. (1969). Broken heart: A statistical study of increased mortality among widowers. *British Medical Journal, 1,* 740–743.

Pattison, E. M. (1977). Death throughout the life cycle. In E. M. Pattison (Ed.), *The experience of dying*. Englewood Cliffs, N.J.: Prentice-Hall.

Peck, R. C. (1968). Psychological development in the second half of life. In B. L. Neugarten (Ed.), *Middle age and aging*. Chicago: University of Chicago Press.

Peterson, J., & Briley, M. (1977). *Widows and widowhood: A creative approach to being alone*. New York: Association Press.

Phillips, D. P. (1975). Deathday and birthday: An unexpected connection. In K. W. C. Kammeyer (Ed.), *Population studies* (2nd ed.). Skokie, Ill.: Rand McNally.

Phillips, D. P. (1979). Suicide, motor vehicle fatalities, and the mass media: Evidence toward a theory of suggestion. *American Journal of Sociology, 84*, 1150–1174.

Phillips, D. P. (1983). The impact of mass media violence on U.S. homicides. *American Sociological Review, 48*.

Phillips, D. P., & Feldman, K. A. (1973). A dip in deaths before ceremonial occasions: Some new relationships between social integration and mortality. *American Sociological Review, 38*, 678–696.

Pier, D. (1982, November 15). When a parent dies, the child stands alone. *News-Chronicle* (Thousand Oaks, Calif.), p. 9.

Pincus, L. (1976). *Death and the family: The importance of mourning*. New York: Pantheon Books.

Pine, V. R., & Phillips, D. (1970). The cost of dying: A sociological analysis of funeral expenditure. *Social Problems, 17*, 405–417.

Pollock, G. (1978). On siblings, childhood sibling loss, and creativity. *Annals of Psychoanalysis, 6*, 443–481.

Pomerleau, O. F. (1979). Behavioral medicine: The contribution of the experimental analysis of behavior to medical care. *American Psychologist, 34*, 654–663.

Porterfield, A. L. (1949). Indices of suicide and homicide by states and cities: Some Southern-non-Southern contrasts with implications for research. *American Sociological Review, 14*, 481–490.

Post, A. (1944, January). Early efforts to abolish capital punishment in Pennsylvania. *Pennsylvania Magazine of History and Biography*.

Power, L. (1982, September 7). A second opinion on cancer/fat. *Los Angeles Times*, pp. V-3, 10.

Powers, T. (1977). Learning to die. In S. H. Zarit (Ed.), *Readings in aging and death: Contemporary perspectives*. New York: Harper & Row.

Preston, C. E., & Williams, R. H. (1971). Views of the aged on the timing of death. *Gerontologist, 11*, 300–304.

Puner, M. (1974). *The good long life: What we know about growing old*. New York: Universe Books.

Quattlebaum, J. H. (1980, August 1). Use of heroin to ease pain of terminally ill. *Los Angeles Times*, p. II-2.

Radzinowicz, L. (1948). *A history of English criminal law*. London: Pilgrim Trust.

Raleigh, J. W. (1982). Emphysema. *Encyclopedia Americana* (Vol. 10). Danbury, Conn.: Grolier.

Rawlings, M. (1978). *Beyond death's door*. Nashville, Tenn.: Thomas Nelson.

Rees, W. D. (1972). The distress of dying. *Nursing Times, 68*, 1479–1480.

Retherford, R. D. (1977). *The changing sex differential in mortality*. Westport, Conn.: Greenwood Press.

Riegel, K. F., & Riegel, R. M. (1972). Development, drop, and death. *Developmental Psychology, 6,* 306–319.

Rockstein, M.; Chesky, J.; & Sussman, M. (1977). Comparative biology and evolution of aging. In C. Finch & L. Hayflick (Eds.), *Handbook of the biology of aging.* New York: Van Nostrand Reinhold.

Rodin, J., & Langer, E. (1977). Long-term effects of a control-relevant intervention with institutionalized aged. *Journal of Personality & Social Psychology, 35,* 897–902.

Rosel, N. (1978). Toward a social theory of dying. *Omega, 9*(1), 49–55.

Rosenblatt, R. (1982, December 20). Do not go gentle into the good night. *Time,* p. 88.

Rosenman, R. H.; Brand, R. J.; Jenkins, C. D.; Friedman, M.; Straus, R.; & Wurm, M. (1975). Coronary heart disease in the western collaborative groups study: A final follow-up experience to eight and one-half years. *Journal of the American Medical Association, 233,* 872–877.

Rosenzweig, S., & Bray, D. (1943). Sibling death in anamnesis of schizophrenic patients. *Archives of Neurology and Psychiatry, 49*(1), 71–92.

Rossiter, A. J. (1981, September 25). Technology brings need for new definition of death. *Los Angeles Times,* p. IA-3.

Rudestam, K. E. (1971). Stockholm and Los Angeles: A cross-cultural study of the communication of suicidal intent. *Journal of Consulting and Clinical Psychology, 36,* 82–90.

Rust, M. M. (n.d.). *The growth of children's concept of time, space, and magnitude.* Unpublished. New York: Columbia University, Teachers College.

Ryerson, M. (1977). Death education and counseling for children. *Elementary School Guidance and Counseling, 11,* 165–174.

Sabom, M. (1983, January 16). "Clinically dead" patients reveal the peacefulness of dying. *Family Weekly,* pp. 11, 13.

Salomone, J. J. (1968). An empirical report on some controversial American funeral practices. *Sociological Symposium, 1,* 47–56.

Saltin, B., & Grimby, G. (1968). Physiological analysis of middle-aged and old former athletes. *Circulation, 38* (Suppl. 17), 1–78.

Saunders, C. (1980). St. Christopher's Hospice. In E. S. Shneidman (Ed.), *Death: Current perspectives* (2nd ed.). Palo Alto., Calif.: Mayfield.

Schlesinger, B. (1977). The crisis of widowhood in the family cycle. In *Issues in the study of aging, dying, and death* (Vol. 1). Atkinson College Press.

Schmale, A. H. (1971). Hopelessness as a predictor of cervical cancer. *Social Science and Medicine, 5,* 95–100.

Schroeder, O., Jr. (1982). Death: 1. Legal aspects of death. *Encyclopedia Americana* (Vol. 8). Danbury, Conn.: Grolier.

Schultz, D. P. (1982). *Psychology and industry today* (3rd ed.). New York: Macmillan.

Schulz, R. (1978). *The psychology of death, dying, and bereavement.* Reading, Mass.: Addison-Wesley.

Schulz, R., & Bazerman, M. (1980). Ceremonial occasions and mortality: A second look. *American Psychologist, 35,* 253–261.

Scott, G. R. (1950). *The history of capital punishment.* London: Torchstream Books.

Seele, K. C. (1983). Sarcophagus. *The world book encyclopedia* (Vol. 17). Chicago: World Book.

Seligman, M. E. P. (1975). *Helplessness.* San Francisco: Freeman.

Sellin, T. (1980). *The penalty of death.* Beverly Hills, Calif.: Sage Publications.

Seltzer, M. M. (1979). The older woman: Facts, fantasies and fiction. *Research on Aging, 1,*(2), 139–154.

Selye, H. (1976). *The stress of life* (rev. ed.). New York: McGraw-Hill.

Sennholz, H. F. (1976). *Death and taxes.* Washington, D.C.: The Heritage Foundation.

Shaffer, T. L., & Rodes, R. E., Jr. (1977). Law for those who are to die. In H. Feifel (Ed.). *New meanings of death.* New York: McGraw-Hill.

Shanas, E. (1979). Social myth as hypothesis: The case of the family relations of old people. *The Gerontologist, 19,* 3–9.

Shanas, E., & Maddox, G. L. (1976). Aging, health, and the organization of health resources. In R. H. Binstock & E. Shanas (Eds.), *Handbook of aging and the social sciences.* New York: Van Nostrand Reinhold.

Sherwood, B. (1982, August 9). Funeral industry mourns its slow passing. *Los Angeles Times,* p. IV-6.

Shneidman, E. (1973). *Deaths of man.* New York: Quadrangle.

Shneidman, E. S. (1976). Death work and stages of dying. In E. S. Shneidman (Ed.), *Death: Current perspectives.* Palo Alto, Calif.: Mayfield.

Shneidman, E. S. (1980a). The death certificate. In E. S. Shneidman (Ed.), *Death: Current perspectives* (2nd ed.). Palo Alto, Calif.: Mayfield.

Shneidman, E. S. (1980b). *Death: Current perspectives* (2nd ed.). Palo Alto, Calif.: Mayfield.

Shneidman, E. (1980c). *Voices of death* (Chap. 4). New York: Harper & Row.

Shneidman, E. S., & Farberow, N. L. (1970). The logic of suicide. In E. S. Shneidman, N. L. Farberow, & R. E. Litman (Eds.), *The psychology of suicide.* New York: Science House.

Siegel, R. K. (1980). The psychology of life after death. *American Psychologist, 35,* 911–931.

Siegler, I. C.; Nowlin, J. B.; & Blumenthal, J. A. (1980). Health and behavior: Methodological considerations for adult development and aging. In L. W. Poon (Ed.), *Aging in the 1980's: Psychological issues.* Washington, D.C.: American Psychological Association.

Simonton, O. C.; Matthews-Simonton, S.; & Creighton, J. (1978). *Getting well again.* Los Angeles: J. P. Tarper (dist. by St. Martin's Press, New York).

Simpson, M. A. (1976). Brought in dead. *Omega, 7,* 243–248.

Simpson, M. A. (1977). *Death and modern poetry.* In H. Feifel (Ed.). *New meanings of death.* New York: McGraw-Hill.

Simpson, M. A. (1979). *The facts of death.* Englewood Cliffs, N.J.: Prentice-Hall.

Smith, D. W.; Bierman, E. L.; & Robinson, N. M. (1978). *The biologic age of man* (2nd ed.). Philadelphia: Saunders.

Spinetta, J. J. (1974). The dying child's awareness of death: A review. *Psychological Bulletin, 81,* 256–260.

Spinetta, J. J.; Rigler, D.; & Karon, M. (1973). Anxiety in the dying child. *Pediatrics, 52,* 841–845.

Stein, S. B. (1974). *About dying, an open family book for parents and children together.* New York: Walker.

Stillion, J., & Wass, H. (1979). Children and death. In J. Stillion & H. Wass (Eds.), *Dying: Facing the facts.* New York: Hemisphere.

Sudnow, D. (1967). *Passing on: The social organization of dying.* Englewood Cliffs, N.J.: Prentice-Hall.

Suicide. (1983). *Encyclopedia Britannica* (Vol. 17). Chicago: Encyclopaedia Britannica.

Surge in murders, search for solutions. (1980, December 22). *US News,* pp. 22–24.

Tallmer, M.; Formaneck, R.; & Tallmer, J. (1974). Factors influencing children's concepts of death. *Journal of Clinical Child Psychology, 3*(2), 17–19.

Teltsch, K. (1980, April 10). Young terminal patients to get a loving hospice. *New York Times,* p. II-14.

Templer, D. I. (1972). Death anxiety in religiously very involved persons. *Psychological Reports, 31,* 361–362.

Templer, D. I.; Ruff, C. F.; & Franks, C. M. (1971). Death anxiety: Age, sex, and parental resemblance in diverse populations. *Developmental Psychology, 4,* 108.

Terry, R. D., & Wisniewski, H. (1975). Structural and chemical changes of the aged human brain. In S. Gershon & A. Raskin (Eds.), *Aging, Vol. 2: Genesis and treatment of psychological disorders in the elderly.* New York: Raven Press.

The suicide factor. (1982, March). *Health,* p. 33.

Thomas, L. (1975). *Lives of a cell: Notes of a biology watcher.* New York: Bantam.

Timiras, P. S. (1972). *Developmental physiology and aging.* New York: Macmillan.

Tolstoy, L. (1960). The death of Ivan Ilych. In L. Tolstoy, *Death of Ivan Ilych and other stories.* New York: New American Library. (Originally published in 1886.)

Toynbee, A. (1980). Various ways in which human beings have sought to reconcile themselves to the fact of death. In E. S. Shneidman (Ed.), *Death: Current perspectives* (2nd ed.). Palo Alto, Calif.: Mayfield.

Trelease, M. L. (1975). Dying among Alaskan Indians: A matter of choice. In E. Kübler-Ross (Ed.), *Death: The final stage of growth.* Englewood Cliffs, N.J.: Prentice-Hall.

Troll, L. E. (1982). *Continuations: Adult development and aging.* Monterey, Calif.: Brooks/Cole.

Tuchman, B. W. (1978). *A distant mirror.* New York: Knopf.

U.S. Bureau of the Census. (1981). *1980 Census of Population, Supplementary Reports* (PC80-S1-1). Washington, D.C.: U.S. Government Printing Office.

U.S. Dept. of Commerce, Bureau of the Census. (1982). *Current Population Reports* (Series P-20, No. 372). *Marital status and living arrangements: March 1981.* Washington, D.C.: U.S. Government Printing Office.

U.S. Dept. of Health and Human Services. (1981). *Facts about older Americans, 1980–81* (HHS Pub. No. 81-20006). Washington, D.C.: U.S. Government Printing Office.

U.S. Dept. of Health, Education, and Welfare. (1980). *Special report on aging: 1979* (NIH Pub. No. 80-1907). Washington, D.C.: Author.

U.S. Dept. of Justice, Bureau of Justice Statistics. (1982). *Capital punishment, 1981* (NCJ-86484). Washington, D.C.: U.S. Government Printing Office.

U.S. Dept. of Justice, Bureau of Justice Statistics. (1983). Capital punishment, 1982. *Bureau of Justice Statistics Bulletin* (NCJ-89395). Washington, D.C.: U.S. Government Printing Office.

U.S. Dept. of Justice, Federal Bureau of Investigation. (1983). *Uniform Crime Reports. Crime in the United States, 1982.* Washington, D.C.: U.S. Government Printing Office.

Veatch, R. M., & Tai, E. (1980). Talking about death: Patterns of lay and professional change. *Annals of the AAPSS, 447,* 29–45.

Vermeule, E. (1979). *Aspects of death in early Greek art and poetry.* Berkeley: University of California Press.

Vinick, B. (1977, September). *Remarriage in old age.* Paper presented at the annual meeting of the American Sociological Association.

Vital statistics. (1981). *Encyclopedia Americana* (Vol. 28). Danbury, Conn.: Grolier.

Von Hug, H. H. (1965). The child's concept of death. *Psychoanalytic Quarterly, 34,* 499–516.

Waechter, E. H. (1971). Children's awareness of fatal illness. *American Journal of Nursing, 71,* 1168–1172.

Wass, H. (1979). Death and the elderly. In H. Wass (Ed.), *Dying: Facing the facts.* Washington, D.C.: Hemisphere.

Wass, H., & Scott, M. (1978). Middle school students death concepts and concerns. *Middle School Journal, 9*(1), 10–12.

Weir, R. F. (Ed.). (1980). *Death in literature.* New York: Columbia University Press.

Weisman, A. D. (1972). *On dying and denying: A psychiatric study of terminality.* New York: Behavioral Publications.

Weisman, A. D., & Kastenbaum, R. (1968). The psychological autopsy: A study of the terminal phase of life. *Community Mental Health Journal,* Monograph No. 4.

Weisman, A. D., & Worden, J. W. (1975). Psychosocial analysis of cancer deaths. *Omega, 6,* 61–75.

Weisskopf, M. (1982, September 3). The dead go begging in Hong Kong. *Los Angeles Times,* pp. IA-5, 6.

Wessel, J. A., & Van Huss, W. D. (1969). The influence of physical activity and age on exercise adaptation of women, 20–69 years. *Journal of Sports Medicine, 9,* 173–183.

WGBH Educational Foundation (Copyright). (1981). Transcript of NOVA (#805), *The science of murder.* Boston: Author.

What does cancer do to brothers, sisters? (1982, September 15). *News-Chronicle* (Thousand Oaks, Calif.), p. 20.

White, E.; Elson, B.; & Prawat, R. (1978). Children's conceptions of death. *Child Development, 49,* 307–310.

Whitley, G. (1983, September 15). Death: A $6-billion industry in U.S. *Los Angeles Times,* p. V-14.

Wilcox, S., & Sutton, M. (1982). *Understanding death and dying* (2nd ed.). Sherman Oaks, Calif.: Alfred.

Williams, G. L. (1982). Abortion. *Encyclopedia Americana* (Vol. 1). Danbury, Conn.: Grolier.

Williamson, J. B.; Evans, L.; & Munley, A. (1980). *Aging and society.* New York: Holt, Rinehart & Winston.

Wolfgang, M. E. (1969). Who kills whom. *Psychology Today, 3*(5), 54–56, 72–75.

Women are still the stronger sex. (1982, January 21). *Los Angeles Times,* p. V-3.

Woodford, J. N. (1965, October). Why Negro suicides are increasing. *Pageant,* p.13.

Woolley, C. L. (1965). *Ur of the Chaldees.* New York: Norton.

Wyly, M., & Hulicka, I. (1975, August). *Problems and compensations of widowhood: A comparison of age groups.* Paper presented at the meeting of the American Psychological Association, Chicago.

Yochelson, S., & Samenow, S. E. (1976). *The criminal personality* (Vol. 1). New York: Aronson.

Yudkin, S. (1967). Children and death. *The Lancet, 1*(7480), 37–41.

Author Index

Subject Index